GENE SHARP

HOW TO START

A REVOLUTION

BY RUARIDH ARROW

Gene Sharp
How To Start A Revolution

Ruaridh Arrow

The Big Indy Books

First Published in the United Kingdom by The Big Indy Books.
Published by Big Indy Books in 2020

Copyright © Ruaridh Arrow, 2020

www.howtostartarevolution.org

A CIP catalogue record for this book is available from the British Library

ISBN 979-8-68658-8257
ISBN 978-1-5272-7161-6   Hardback

Cover design by Selman Design

Contents

Foreword

Gene Sharp's work on how to bring down dictatorships and fight oppression has been translated into more than 40 languages, his books slipped across borders and hidden from secret policemen all over the world. For more than 30 years, if you wanted to start a revolution, you went to see Gene Sharp for help.

In 2009, I began filming the documentary, *How to Start a Revolution*, following the impact of Sharp's work from his home at Cottage Street, East Boston, across four continents, interviewing the participants of almost every uprising of the past 30 years. In 2011, the trail of Gene Sharp led me to Tahrir Square where I slept on the streets alongside protesters during the Egyptian revolution. This book is the full story of that journey to understand the spread and influence of his work.

Although written in an academic environment, this is a journalistic treatment – part biography of Gene Sharp, part adventure story of his books and the brave individuals who have used them in some of the world's most dangerous places.

In the past 20 years, the international system has been shaped by political uprisings and whether they remain nonviolent or descend into violence is having a far reaching impact on millions of people.

In 2019, assaults upon free and fair elections, the rights of minorities, freedom of the press and the rule of law were at their worst level for decades. Sixty four countries suffered a reduction in their political rights and civil liberties, with only 37 reporting gains. 2019 was the 14th year of consecutive decline in global freedom.

The question posed for hundreds of years by people facing this kind of oppression is what to do about it – how can they resist? Is violence an effective response or is nonviolent action the most effective means of achieving freedom? Should democratic countries assist democracy movements in less free states, or refrain from potentially destabilising interventions? How we answer these questions will have a profound impact on future conflicts.

This subject is impossible to navigate without understanding the impact of Gene Sharp who not only laid down the foundations for this academic field, but whose work is shaping many of the uprisings that we are watching unfold on our screens day after day.

This book should not be read as claiming credit for Gene Sharp in any of the revolutions discussed. Gene resisted taking credit for anything, and was embarrassed when the media sometimes did this on his behalf. He insisted the attention should be focused on the brave men and women fighting for freedom in their own countries, not outsiders. The objective here is to shed a light on the strategic planning that has gone into many of the political uprisings of the modern age and the contribution of Gene's work to that process.

I have not attempted to write a complete history of each revolution discussed – many factors influence the outcome of an uprising, so this book aims only to restore this missing element of nonviolent strategy to those existing narratives. There are notable omissions that you might expect to appear here, including Venezuela, Hong Kong and Belarus, but I have decided not to discuss the inner workings of movements which are still ongoing. Hopefully, in time, they can be added in subsequent additions.

For years Gene Sharp's writings have threatened dictatorships who have responded by denouncing him, banning his books and arresting his readers. Today these governments are becoming more sophisticated in their attempts to undermine the credibility of his work. Academics, bloggers and fake social media accounts have been used to misrepresent his theories, argue that his ideas undermine rather than strengthen social movements and claim he was working for the CIA. I knew Gene and studied his work for just over a decade and have found no basis for any of those accusations. To those who might reasonably question whether any claim found on the internet might be true I would simply ask that you study his work in its original form, read this book and judge for yourself.

The Square

It was a long and lonely walk from my hotel on the tip of Gezira Island to the newly installed tank barrier at the Southern end of Tahrir bridge. My progress was monitored all the way by young soldiers who watched me from high on the walls of an army barracks which lined the route. I smiled and waved up at them as I passed. Some raised a hand from their rifles in acknowledgment, others just stared anxiously into the distance. Across the River Nile, red tracer fire from an assault rifle arced into the sky and a low roar carried across the water – the sound of the revolution.

Somewhere ahead of me supporters of President Hosni Mubarak were hunting and beating journalists. The Egyptian president's 30 year grip on power, once thought unassailable, was being shaken by days of resistance across the country. Now his police force were shedding their uniforms and re-forming into a militia intent on spreading fear among the protesters and the reporters arriving to tell their story. I had already spent many hours in the custody of the secret police at Cairo airport. They had confiscated most of my camera equipment, but eventually let me go after paying them a small 'taxi fare'.

Over breakfast, a Polish cameraman had told me how he had been caught by a mob who held a knife to his throat. They chanted, 'kill him, kill him!' until some unknown faction had intervened and spirited him away. He sat, still trembling, cradling a strong cup of coffee while he told the story. I shut out the thought and kept walking, hoping my brief contact with the soldiers on the wall might convince them to help out if I got into trouble.

The bridge onto the east bank of the Nile was flanked by two enormous bronze lions and beneath them was stationed a small unit of tanks commanded by a young major who looked like he hadn't slept in days. He stepped into my path, thrust his hands into my pockets and pulled out my passport. I had no media visa or accreditation, which meant he could easily have turned me back. Instead he flicked wearily through the dog-eared pages and waved me on.

The new entrance to Tahrir Square lay directly ahead – a barricade composed of tanks, barbed wire and burned out cars. A queue snaked back from the entrance and as I joined its tail, two thick set men in civilian clothes approached me from behind. 'Who are you? Where are you from?' they demanded. 'I'm a journalist', I told them in my poor Arabic. 'If you go in there, tonight we'll come and find you and we'll kill you. You understand?' one of them replied in English. I shrugged, said nothing and shuffled forward with the crowd looking straight ahead. 'Are you stupid?' the other man asked, prodding his temple with a fat nicotine-stained finger. They snarled, spat at my feet and walked away.

At the makeshift gate to Tahrir Square, soldiers and protesters were working together, each checking for identification documents and concealed weapons in turn. First a soldier inspected my passport and pushed me through to a protester, his face blackened by tire smoke, a makeshift gas mask on elastic bouncing around his neck. He patted me down and emptied my pockets looking for weapons until I was passed on to another soldier who checked me again.

The queue zigzagged through this strange alliance until I finally burst through the last line into the square – an amphitheatre roaring with music and chanting. A man was being held above the crowd weeping and shouting in rage at the sky – his brother had been killed by security forces the previous day. Another procession crossed the square, this time with children being carried aloft by their fathers and uncles. 'Down with Mubarak!' the young boys chanted until their unbroken voices were husky and strained.

One of their fathers grabbed me by the arm and stood screaming into the lens of my camera. He'd been shot through the arm by men in civilian clothes in a volley that had killed his friend. He spun a bullet casing in his fingers and wiped away the muck to reveal the country of origin etched into the base, 'Egypt' he yelled in a rage, boiling over, 'Egypt', *Egypt!*' He couldn't comprehend that ammunition made by Egyptians was killing Egyptian people on their own streets.

In the centre of the square hung a 30 foot wide banner, spray-painted in English, which declared, 'The People Demand the Removal of the Regime'. It was perfectly positioned as the backdrop for the dozens of international television news crews whose live broadcasting positions looked down into the square. Along the soft grass verges, below the banner, were people sleeping in the morning sunshine after taking night watches to defend against attacks by the pro-Mubarak police and militia. They lay with the masks that protected them against the teargas still around their necks, most wearing bloodstained bandages. There had been a fierce battle the previous day when the police had attacked the protesters, thrashing their batons wildly at the heads of those who stood in their path. People had died but nobody was clear how many. The attempt to dislodge the protesters had been repelled and now the morning papers told their story, the pages filleted and spread out on the sidewalks, held down by stones to stop them blowing away. Men and women stood squinting down at them to make out the latest government propaganda.

Unlike most journalists, I hadn't come just to report on the events in Tahrir Square, I was searching for a book – a guidebook on how to start a revolution. For two years I'd been following the work of American academic Gene Sharp, the author of 'From Dictatorship to Democracy', used in many of the most influential political uprisings of modern history. Written for the democratic opposition in Burma who had fled into the jungle after the imprisonment of Aung San Suu Kyi, it quickly spread between revolutionary groups from Serbia to Georgia, Ukraine, Venezuela and Iran. The people who used it often called it their 'bible', but just possessing it in a place like Burma could earn activists seven years in jail. To find the book in Egypt in the midst of the Arab Spring was a clue that this might not be the spontaneous uprising now being reported, that there was pre-planning, a leadership group and international connections.

Somewhere in the crush I came face to face with Ahmed who smiled and asked where I was from. 'Iskutlanda' I told him. He raised both his thumbs, grinning, 'Scotland! Braveheart, like Egyptians!' I asked if he could translate for me and he agreed to help enthusiastically. We set about identifying and interviewing the leaders in the square while trying to find any evidence that Gene Sharp's work was informing their strategy. In the evening we stopped for prayers and Ahmed joined the thousands who fell silent, aligning themselves with Mecca. Nobody who watched the thousands of bodies sweeping in waves of prayer from one end of the square to the other could fail to be moved by the spectacle. Lining the boundary of the prayers were Christian Egyptians keeping watch over their Muslim brothers and sisters. That action was practical, but deeply symbolic. They were showing Mubarak and the institutions that supported him that the people were united.

After searching for almost two days I was taken to one of the people rumoured to be an important leader of the uprising. I asked some broad questions about the strategy of the movement before probing whether he had seen the book I was looking for. While he had been happy to answer all of my other questions in detail, he paused, gently placed his hand on top of my camera and lowered it towards the ground. 'Yes, we have seen this work. These books have been printed here and we have used some of it in our own guides', he explained, 'but we cannot talk about it because it is the Egyptian people who are doing this, not America'.

Out of his shoulder bag he pulled a pamphlet printed out on A4 paper and stapled together. The writing was in Arabic, but what was clear was the unmistakeable annexe at the back – Sharp's famous list of 198 methods of nonviolent action compiled in the 1960s. This was a guide for the revolution which had extracted certain sections of his work. After I'd been shown the document I began to notice it being read around the square. In one corner a small group were being introduced to the rules of the uprising sitting in a circle in the shadow of a tank's caterpillar tracks.

'One of the main points which we used was the idea of identifying a regime's pillars of support', he told me. 'Every dictator is only kept in power by these pillars, the police, the army the judges. Without the cooperation of these pillars he is nothing'. 'We knew if we could build a relationship with the army, Mubarak's biggest pillar of support, to get them on our side, then we knew he would quickly be finished.'

Another protester, Mahmoud, had been given photocopies of a handout containing the list of 198 methods of nonviolent action. He proudly pointed out how many of the methods had been used in Egypt, but had never heard of its author. On my last night in Tahrir I was settling down to sleep on the sidewalk, exhausted after a basic meal of dates and flatbread when some of the protesters came to show me text messages from the soldiers in the square. The soldiers promised they would ignore orders to shoot if they received them. 'We know them and we know they are on our side now!' the protesters told me triumphantly.

As I drifted off to sleep on the sidewalk, the temperature dropped and I felt the people around me cover me in extra blankets. Throughout the night there were frequent alarms warning of attacks at the barricades. I blinked hard to clear the sleep from my eyes as groups of marshals rose from the sleeping mass that covered the square and headed off to investigate, only to return to stoke the fires and fall back to sleep. When I woke at first light, I felt something strange lying inside my blanket – a stack of flexible plastic. Holding them up to the amber street light I saw the outlines of shattered bones – X-rays of the injured, perhaps the dead. While I'd slept, someone had smuggled the films out of a hospital and obviously found me easier to reach than the reporters staying in government surveilled hotels.

Unofficial sources were already quoting several hundred people had been killed – by the time the revolution was over, the official toll would be closer to a thousand. I stuffed the X-rays inside my jacket and got to my feet. Most of the square was still asleep – a vast field of jostling bodies with wood smoke drifting gently across them. I looked at Ahmed, gently shook him awake and squeezed his hand to say goodbye. Mubarak's fall seemed tantalisingly close, but I had to get back to my day job in London.

Wrapping my head in a shemagh, I made for the western Exit, tiptoeing between makeshift beds, weaving my way back through the tank barrier, past the barbed wire coils and back onto the bridge through the drifting smoke.

Ahead, mysterious figures moved under street lamps in a smoky, orange gloom. Were they Mubarak loyalists? The same men who had threatened to kill me on the way in? I continued towards the second tank barrier on the far side of the bridge where a different soldier stopped me, patted me down and felt the X-rays which made me bulge awkwardly in the chest. Pulling them from my coat he motioned with his head for me to move on. I looked at him disappointed. 'I'm sorry', he said in English, looking at the ground. I passed the shadowy figures, straining my peripheral vision for any sign of movement towards me – none came. I took one last look back towards the square, now eerily silent and disappeared into the dark.

On the 11th February 2011, just days after I flew out of Cairo, President Mubarak stepped down as President of Egypt. The New York Times went to press with a front page story – 'Shy US Intellectual Created Playbook Used in Revolution', describing Gene Sharp as the strategic mastermind behind the Arab Spring. At the US State Department, Secretary of State Hillary Clinton read the Times report, describing the training activists had received in nonviolent strategy, and asked to know more. Her Middle East specialist, Peter Mandaville, was called in to be issued with an additional tasking for his upcoming fact finding trip to Egypt – who was the mysterious 84-year-old, Gene Sharp and what part, if any, did he play in the toppling of Mubarak?

That report has never been officially released, but this is the story of the journey to discover what really happened in the run up to the Arab Spring and beyond. It's an unlikely story which takes us from a humble upbringing in rural Ohio to the brink of a Nobel Peace Prize with the help of Albert Einstein, a Vietnam war hero, a chess grand master and the world's most prolific collector of Gandhi memorabilia .

Eastie

East Boston was once a rough neighbourhood. Built on landfill poured into the gaps between a small clutch of islands in Boston's harbour, its cheap housing had offered a stepping stone into the country for the Irish, Italian and, most recently, Latino immigrants starting out on their American dream. Gangs had once fought openly for control of the neighbourhood, but these days Harvard grads were moving in amongst the old timers, who still sat in the street on plastic chairs looking up at the looming underbellies of jets landing at Logan Airport.

There weren't many landmarks to celebrate in 'Eastie', as the locals called it, but one anonymous red brick townhouse on Cottage Street had become something of a curiosity. At four stories tall, it jutted above its rickety wooden-clad neighbours on either side, its windows shielded by dusty venetian blinds squeezed tightly shut, even on the brightest days. Neighbours often noticed groups of serious looking foreigners coming and going as if on some sort of pilgrimage. Occasionally, people stopped outside to point at the building and whisper the story to a friend, 'What? There?' They looked disbelieving and walked on. Some would snatch a photo quickly, as if someone was watching.

Only a handful of locals really knew what went on in this house. The owner of a coffee shop around the corner had snatched enough fragments of conversation from her customers to piece it all together. 'Yeah I know what goes on up there, the old man and the girl, they help people start revolutions don't they?'

I was an undergraduate at the Department of War Studies, Kings College London, when I first heard his name. A classmate went home to Belgrade in the summer of 1999 to join the super cool revolutionary group 'Otpor' which was campaigning to end the dictatorship of President Slobodan Milosevic in Serbia. A year later Otpor finally achieved their objective in a brilliantly organised nonviolent campaign. On 5th October 2000, the news was filled with footage of young Serbs storming the parliament building in Belgrade and throwing fraudulent ballot papers, pre-marked for Milsosevic, out of the windows. My friend returned with exciting stories of their exploits and a small guidebook on overthrowing dictatorships by an author called Gene Sharp.

The revolution in Serbia appeared to kickstart a wave of copycat 'colour revolutions' in the former Soviet states of Georgia, Kyrgyzstan and Ukraine, still run by authoritarian governments loyal to Moscow. The 'colour revolution' moniker came from the choice of a unifying colour worn by demonstrators which filled the drab streets of their respective cities with vibrant swathes of orange, green or purple.

There were other similarities too – slick branding messages and professionally designed symbols – often a stencil of a menacing clenched black fist, first used by Otpor in Serbia. All of the movements carried signs in English to communicate their messages effectively to the international community. But most importantly, their strategy was nonviolent and took influence from the same small guidebook by Gene Sharp.

As a trainee journalist I covered these colour revolutions for a national paper, checking in, morning and night, down crackly phone lines with the press officers of the revolutionary groups. They read out the tallies of injured and arrested activists and told tales of the latest blockades, boycotts and funny stunts, designed to make their governments look ridiculous.

As they talked about their plans it became clear to me, and many other journalists, that these uprisings were all being organised in the same way – almost to the same blueprint. It wasn't just Eastern Europe either. One lunchtime I was walking through a shopping centre when I came across an Iranian human rights group handing out flyers about the crimes their regime was carrying out against their people.

When I stopped to talk, they told me how their colleagues would soon start a revolution in Iran. Workers in the power grid were going to symbolically turn off the electricity to Tehran for a minute to protest against the government that weekend. Their ideas, they told me, came from an American academic called Gene Sharp.

The leading theory among many journalists was that America's Central Intelligence Agency was at work behind the scenes, steering uprisings to depose governments unfriendly to the US and installing new leaders supportive of free markets and closer ties with NATO. Then there were whispers about the mysterious American academic who wrote the book that they used, but who seemed to shy away from any media. Who was Gene Sharp? A front? An agent? Perhaps he didn't even really exist.

Uprisings seem to come and go in waves, and so it was with the colour revolutions. The change in governments they produced did not bring the promise expected and the news cycle moved on. That final step to understand the academic influence of those tumultuous events was never properly made.

Almost four years later I'd started working as a documentary producer, when by chance, I saw a YouTube clip of Venezuela's President Chávez, standing at a whiteboard on his regular Sunday TV show, Aló Presidente (Hello, Mr. President). Surrounded by his senior officials he launched into a tirade about how he had personally taken command of a counter revolutionary operation to stop a 'revolutionary explosion' caused by Gene Sharp's books in Venezuela. When I looked a little further, I found more videos – one by the Iranian Intelligence Service who had also released a warning about Gene Sharp in an animated film.

The cartoon, broadcast on national television, portrayed him sitting at a table in the White House, plotting the overthrow of the Iranian government with a CIA chief and billionaire George Soros. 'Gene Sharp – the theoretician of civil disobedience and velvet revolutions', droned a forbidding voiceover, 'he is one of the CIA agents in charge of America's infiltration into other countries.' Another shaky video from Burma showed a senior military officer giving a press conference revealing an alleged plot to overthrow the military government planned by Gene Sharp, and others, with the collusion of Aung San Suu Kyi.

From Sharp himself, there was almost no response – just a few polite denials of any part in a global conspiracy. A few newspaper reports described him as a lonely, grandfatherly figure, who lived a modest life tending orchids in a rooftop garden. Life in East Boston appeared to go on as normal. One photo showed him sitting at a desk petting an enormous Great Dane at his knee. Standing awkwardly in the background looking into the camera was his only member of staff, Jamila Raqib, the Executive Director of Sharp's Albert Einstein Institution.

So what was the truth about Gene Sharp? By 2009 I was producing news and current affairs films for the BBC and was convinced that Gene's story might make an interesting documentary. I found an email address to send a request for an interview and was surprised to receive a reply from Jamila asking for more information.

The response was cautious, but over time we talked more about what I wanted to do – a simple interview overlaid with archive footage of the revolutions in which his work had been used. She promised to recommend the project and one sunny afternoon a few weeks later I received the email I'd been hoping for. 'I recognize that films can convey ideas powerfully', Gene wrote, 'and continue to do so long after I am not here to write or speak.'

A few months later, in May 2009, I scraped together the money for the flight and found my way to 36 Cottage Street. Jamila opened the pastel green door which swung outwards awkwardly over the sidewalk towards me. She was cooler than her formal emails had suggested, part academic, part hipster, in her late twenties with big glasses and a rainbow tattoo stuck to her wrist. 'Well this is it', she laughed, 'Welcome!'

As the door closed, plunging us from spring sunshine into near darkness, we made our way past Gene's desk, a modest work-station with an anglepoise lamp drawn close to illuminate a few papers. Sagging shelves of foxed old books clung to the cracked plaster walls and pushed into the corners were towers of unpacked cardboard boxes which looked like they had washed up from a shipwreck long ago. An iMac computer hummed, gently waiting, festooned with instructions on how to send emails. Looking down on all of this with a kindly, benevolent smile, was a large yellowing portrait of Gandhi.

In the back room, Jamila's office, the light had found its way in, illuminating bare redbrick walls which held new books with shiny covers in different languages, from Burmese to Russian, Arabic and German.

A black and white cardboard sign stuck to the bricks by her desk read 'Gotov Je!' 'He's Finished' in Serbian, with the infamous black clenched fist from the Serbian revolution.

Jamila turned to me, smiled and shrugged her shoulders, 'Most people are pretty shocked when they arrive and see us here. It doesn't seem to compute, just two people in this small office, doing this work. We've been waiting for a sort of breakthrough…. I think you coming might be part of that'.

In 2005 a loss of funding had left them unable to pay the bills. The staff had all found new jobs but Jamila refused to leave Gene and his work, which she knew was only growing in importance. Together they hatched a plan to keep the organisation going by moving to the ground floor of Gene's home. For almost five years they had worked like this, clinging on, half unpacked, hoping that a windfall of some kind might win them their offices and staff back. Yet in this difficult time, Jamila had overseen the translation of Gene's work into more than 40 languages, putting it into the hands of hundreds of democracy activists working against some of the world's most repressive regimes. That spread had turned this slightly battered townhouse into a mecca for those activists, who regularly arrived here looking for help.

'I've ordered him some more clothes, 3 identical shirts and pants for filming continuity like you asked.' Jamila told me, 'He'll get tired after a couple of hours, so make sure he gets breaks or you won't get the best out of him.'

There was a commotion above us as Gene's dog Caesar, a Great Dane, sensed a visitor and galloped down the bare wooden stairs bursting into the room ahead of his master. Gene appeared through the passageway and we stood almost to attention in the back room. He was dressed in a light green shirt, open at the neck with the sleeves rolled up and a clutch of biros weighing down his top pocket. His hair was combed neatly straight back across his head. As he made his way across the office he hovered his walking stick tentatively just above the floor. 'Look Caesar, we've got visitors!' He smiled, swinging the stick up towards me with a wink. 'It's so good to see you'.

When we were ready, the camera was in position and the lights adjusted, Gene took his seat by his desk and squinted slightly into the lens. 'Anything I mess up you fix right!?' he joked. Caesar was locked in the apartment upstairs and barked furiously in protest. Phil Bloom, my friend and director of photography started the camera and Gene began to talk. 'I'm sorry for the mess.' he told me, surveying the crumbling cornicing, 'I've never been very good at raising money. I thought it was better to just keep working instead of spending all my time writing to donors and getting no luck'. Through the passageway I could just see Jamila's shadow listening as he began to tell the story.

'I didn't set out to do this... I had a religious background that led me to want leave the world in a bit of a better condition than when I came here, and how to do that was always a bit of a problem. I knew I wanted to do something to find an alternative to violent conflict and war. I was trying to build a better mousetrap, you know?'

He noticed I didn't understand the reference.

'It's a fable,' he continued, 'there's a man who lives in a wood up a hill far, far away from anyone else and he builds a better mousetrap. Well it takes a lot of time, but gradually people get to hear about the mousetrap and eventually, when enough people hear about it, word gets back to the cities and everybody is beating a path to the house in the woods to find it. That's what I've been trying to do. Build a better mousetrap.'

Letters from Einstein

On the morning of 30th January 1948, Mohandas Gandhi was running late. After finishing a simple breakfast, his grandniece, Abha, raised a pocket watch anxiously to show him the time. He was now 78 years old and moved only slowly, but he hated keeping people waiting. Abha and another grand niece, Manu, supported his fragile frame on either side as they walked him out towards the prayer ground of Birla House, where hundreds of people were gathering to see him.

Gandhi was at the height of his fame. Stories of his 250 mile protest march across India, rallying the nation to defy the British salt tax, had been heard around the world and the country's independence from colonial rule had just been achieved. As he approached the people, they wept, cried and threw themselves to his feet. But that day, as he pressed his palms together in the traditional Hindu greeting, an assassin appeared from the crowd and fired three pistol shots into his body.

As the shots rang out, Gandhi crumpled, his stopwatch and spectacles fell to the dust beneath him, blood soaking through his white robes. His entourage hauled him back into the house, where vain attempts were made to save his life, but his heart had probably given its last beat before Abha had swept up his glasses and sandals from the ground.

Half the world away in the basement library of Ohio State University, a 20-year-old undergraduate student called Gene Sharp read the news of Gandhi's death in desperate sorrow. After the horrors of the Second World War and the devastating nuclear attacks against Japan, the nonviolent movement against the British in India had given a whole generation of idealistic young men and women hope of a credible alternative to violent conflict. Gene had followed Gandhi's campaigns through his childhood and adopted him as a hero to be studied and emulated in his own life. It

13

was in that moment of loss that Gene began to imagine how he might in some way continue Gandhi's work.

It had been clear to everyone in the railway town of Fostoria, Ohio, that Gene Sharp was slightly different from all of the other children. Every Sunday the 8-year-old Gene would sit alone on the front pew looking up at his father, Reverend Paul Sharp, delivering his sermon. Nobody ever sat beside him and it became a lonely ritual which nobody ever fully understood.

Paul and his wife Eva had celebrated Gene's birth in the flat railway junction town of Baltimore, Ohio, on the 21st January 1928. They were both farm kids from the North West corner of the State. Eva had been one of just a handful of women at the time to attend college and qualify as a school teacher. Paul, from the town of Bryan, was working his way up in the church as an itinerant minister, visiting homes across the state. Calvin Coolidge, 'the forgotten President' was in the White House and the first ever transatlantic flight had yet to be made. Many Ohio men had not returned to their farms after the bloodbath of the First World War in Europe and among them was Eva's first love, the man she thought she would marry. Paul sometimes joked that he had just been her rebound.

The Sharp household was not poor, but money was tight. As a young married couple their income and parsonage was dependent on the church and Paul's slim $18 a week income. Sometimes an unexpected bill meant evening meals might just consist of fried cornbread. Paul was frequently absent, travelling the flat agricultural plains of the state and Gene remembered missing him terribly. A younger sister and brother followed and Eva stayed at home to look after her growing family. Her professional training, frustrated by the expectations of marriage at the time, was channeled into teaching each of her children to read as early as possible. When the time came for school, that meant the Sharps were always a little ahead of the others.

Gene was 6 years old when the family left for a bigger parish, the railway town of Fostoria. It was a promotion for Paul. He'd earned a larger church, less travelling and a substantial parsonage. The Bishop even welcomed the family with a pet puppy. It was here that Gene began to listen intently for the first time to his father's sermons. One of the first images he was captivated by in the church was a painting of Jesus surrounded with children of all nations and colours.

Even at a very young age Gene was struck by the picture because it was quite obvious that this vision was not practised by many in the church at all. Despite being kind and committed public servants to all members of the community, even Paul and Eva casually referred to the black families in town by the standard derogatory terms of the day.

Being brought up in the church also exposed Gene to people who were struggling for the very basics of life and often required the support of charity from the church. A couple of blocks from the Sharp's house were a group of families left destitute by the great depression, living above a row of grocery stores. Gene was running some errands for his mother when he noticed some of the children, malnourished and dressed in rags. They were playing with the head of a china doll stuck on the end of a two foot stick which they made dance in the air. He stopped to look at them and they stopped and stared back at him, their faces filled with deep suspicion.

Gene thought that there must be a better way to have fun with the doll's head and, trying to be helpful, asked them if he could play. They recoiled, terrified that he might break their only toy, but after he promised he would be careful, they let him have it. His idea was to swing the stick and let the head roll on the grass, but he mistimed the swing and the doll's head hit the pavement, shattering into pieces. The girls burst into tears, distraught and Gene ran home, hating himself. Eighty years later he still remembered that searing guilt as the moment he wanted to make amends by doing work for people who had nothing.

The Second World War broke out in Europe in 1939 and the picture house newsreels in Ohio were showing German troops pouring into Poland. Just over a month before Gene's 13th birthday, the Japanese attacked Pearl Harbour drawing the United States into the war. Gene sat in the cinema horrified as the audience around him cheered pictures of American troops burning Japanese soldiers alive with flamethrowers. While some writers would credit Gene's first interest in nonviolence to the horrors committed by the Germans in Europe, it was those images of Americans killing Japanese soldiers which seem to have had the first impact.

Moving every two to three years was emotionally disruptive; North Baltimore, Toledo, Fostoria, Van Wert, Bowling Green, Wharton-Willard, Westerville, Columbus, came and went. Constantly leaving friends would deeply affect Gene making him feel isolated, rootless and cautious of forming close relationships. While he excelled academically, Gene's first memories of school were of being bullied remorselessly for having a 'girls name'.

Perhaps as a riposte to this and the horrors unfolding in Europe and South East Asia, he began organising mixed reading groups of black, Japanese and Jewish children who hung out at each other's houses to discuss books and newspapers. They talked for hours about the social and political problems of the world and although they never achieved anything of note, just their meeting was a small act of resistance against the status quo. Gene gained solace in his solidarity with the outsiders, but racial segregation in Ohio was still firmly entrenched and by making friends with the 'coloured' kids he was ostracised too as the weird white kid who made friends with them.

Estranged from the normal social circle he might have inhabited, he threw himself into his books and graduated high school with some of the top grades in his final exams. Gene was accepted to study political science at Ohio State University which meant a fresh start from the social awkwardness that had marred his high school years.

At 18 years old, Gene was not tall, but he was strikingly handsome. With his neatly brylcreemed hair in a side parting and Hollywood smile, he wouldn't have looked out of place propping up a bar with Gene Kelly or Dirk Bogarde. Despite this, he fretted constantly about his reputation as a 'sad apple' and poor performance at sports. He embarked upon what he called, 'attempts to consciously improve my personality', putting hours of extra training into golf and fencing, with little return on the investment.

For the first six semesters at university he was also required to join the ROTC, the university's army cadet force, which he enjoyed at first, writing that he found it quite a thrill to wear a uniform and march. But as the military indoctrination began to intensify, he rebelled, refusing to study for assignments on military affairs and proudly getting some of the lowest grades in his troop until his time was done.

In 1948 Arthur H. Compton, a Nobel Prize winning physicist and a leading scientist in the development of America's atom bomb, came to speak at Ohio State University. Compton was no pacifist, he supported conscription and strong conventional military forces, but in the question and answer session he told the audience, 'if we knew that Russia was going to attack us tomorrow morning, I would say, surrender immediately before the fighting starts and let them come into the country.' He said he would let them come in without a fight because if there was a war with atomic weapons it would take 1000 years to recover, but if the Russians invaded it would take at most 50 years to recover self rule. Most importantly, humanity would not have been destroyed.

Many of the audience were horrified by the prospect of submitting to a Soviet invasion, but Gene was struck by Compton's lecture and spent days thinking about it. The question he pondered was how Compton's 'recovery of self-rule' could be achieved. The obvious answer was a campaign similar to the one that Gandhi had used to drive the British out of India.

Gene found some more answers in a book by Richard Gregg. Gregg, like Gene, was the son of a Christian minister and had set out by boat to India in 1925 to find Gandhi and study his methods. On his return to the United States in 1930, he published the first edition of his book, *The Power of Nonviolence,* containing 8 cases in world history where nonviolent action had been used. Most importantly, he introduced the concept of 'moral jujitsu' which argued that the use of unnecessary violent force against nonviolent people could be used against the attacker, in the same way as the Japanese martial art, to unbalance the opponent. Gregg explained that moral jujitsu worked because:

'When the public sees the gentle person's courage and fortitude, notes his generosity and good will toward the attacker, and hears his repeated offers to settle the matter fairly, peaceably and openly, they are filled with surprise, curiosity and wonder. If they have been hostile to the victim before, they at least pause to think. His good humour, fairness and kindness arouse confidence. Sooner or later his conduct wins public sympathy, admiration and support, and also the respect of the violent opponent himself.'

Gregg also argued that proper training was the key to keeping a movement from descending into violence. Why, he asked, when men are knocked down to the ground in a football game are they not inclined to hit out at their assailant as they would if the same thing happened in the street? He called for an equivalent of a soldier's field manual that could be issued to all nonviolent activists. 'If constructive pacifists are to be engaged in action that is a substitute for war, and that must be made just as effective as war, let us try to learn from military men. They know so well how to prepare for vigorous, effective, prolonged action.'

Gene's four year undergraduate course was completed in three years by working through the summer holidays and, inspired by Gregg's book, he moved directly on to a masters degree on war and sociological studies. Good looks and his kind, but serious, manner made him a poster boy for the Ohio Council of Churches, which elected him as their youth president, sending him to speak on religious, economic and social issues all over Ohio and beyond. The handsome Gene Sharp from Colombus became a kind of young preacher and was even given a monthly column in *The Ohio Christian News*.

At this point many in the Church might have assumed that Gene was on a trajectory to follow in his father's footsteps into the church – but then he shocked everyone. He went to his father to admit that he was having doubts about Christianity and that he needed to explore other belief systems. At first he would join the Quakers, which meant resigning from his family church.

Paul took the news calmly – there was no challenge or scolding, and he even came along to a Quaker meeting to try and understand his son's decision. Though this was Gene's choice, the resignation from the church was yet another emotional shift and separation.

These issues were soon eclipsed by a brewing storm in South East Asia which would test the whole family's faith. Gene had been too young for conscription for the Second World War, but now news reached Ohio that US forces were engaged in military action to defend South Korea. It was June 1950 and Communist North Korean forces had invaded the US-backed South. More than 300,000 US soldiers were poured into the Korean peninsula, requiring a general call up of young American men of fighting age.

Just as Gene's studies were concentrating on the potential of nonviolent action, a conscription card arrived in the post from the local recruitment office. Gene decided that he could never take any part in the war effort and decided to take a civil resistance position to conscription which was advocated by the most extreme of the pacifist groups, 'The Peacemakers'. The Peacemakers had been founded by a group which included one of America's most famous pacifists, A.J. Muste who advocated an approach of total non-cooperation with the conscription system.

So while it would have been possible to gain exemption by declaring officially that he was a conscientious objector, Gene did not issue this defence. He refused to report for medicals and other administrative meetings and returned his draft cards with carefully worded letters to the draft board explaining his position.

'I can no longer cooperate with the machinery of military conscription. I am aware that this is a violation of established law. I ask no special privileges. I am willing to accept the consequences. Wars will never cease until men realise that we get peace by being peaceful, until they refuse to participate in war. When people are running headlong toward a high cliff's edge they will perish unless they stop and turn around. We and our world seem to be running headlong toward the edge of a very high cliff. Unless we stop, we shall destroy ourselves. I am stopping now and urge all others to do the same. Our world needs a committed dynamic minority that shall be able to change the course of history because they know what they believe and are willing to practice it. I am willing to try to become one who can help. What about you? Yours for tomorrow.'

For weeks there was no response from the authorities, but eventually news arrived that he had been granted exemption. The rumour was that one of the administrators in the draft office had been reading Gene's column in the *Higher Christian News* and was impressed by the reasoning in his letters. His focus on finding pragmatic alternatives to preventing war may have struck a chord with those who had lost friends and loved ones just years earlier.

Whether the official on the draft board had orchestrated a back room stay of execution for Gene wasn't clear, but it would not last for long. As those around him were called away to fight, he continued his studies, graduating with his masters degree in the summer of 1952. There was no such thing as academic work on nonviolent action so he thought it best to become an activist for the poor and other social causes. He set off from the wide empty plains of Ohio to a place he knew was brimming with social issues, a thriving academic community and some of the best public libraries in the country – New York City.

Gene's new home was a shared apartment with fellow pacifists in a red brick block in the downmarket Gowanus Basin neighbourhood of Brooklyn. The rooms were damp and cold and for some time he slept curled up inside a dirty old carpet he had found discarded on the street. Despite the discomfort, the company was good and he began work immediately, holding meetings with people in the civil rights movement and activists doing good works in the slums. It was the perfect starting place.

The housing conditions were so bad in Harlem at the time that mothers claimed rats were creeping into their apartments at night and biting their babies. Gene heard this news and organised a group to renovate their rooms and fill up the holes where the rats were getting in. Their plastering work was shoddy at best and probably didn't keep the intruders out for long, but it brought them into contact with the community and through this they heard of new problems that needed to be addressed. Later a workshop for East Harlem kids was set up to promote nonviolent means to escape from a cycle of violence which was blighting the neighbourhood.

To earn money for food and rent, Gene worked by day as a messenger boy and a hospital lift operator before moving on to a more suitable job escorting a blind social worker around the streets of New York. Mr Venturi could get around fine on his own, but it was slow and inefficient and Gene acted as his 'seeing eye dog', speeding up his rounds.

The real work though was happening after hours. In the evenings Gene took a desk in the New York Public Library to research and write his first book, *Gandhi Wields the Weapon of Moral Power*. Written in around six months, it provides a starting point to understand the development of his ideas. As the title suggests, he argued that the power of Gandhi's nonviolent strategy came from an intrinsic moral and ethical core belief. This was derived from Gandhi's own notion of the *Satyagrahi* – an individual who believes that the practice of love and self-suffering will bring about a change in the heart of his opponent.

'We must become integrated loving individuals', Gene wrote in the introduction. 'Unless people can sense in our lives that of which we speak, it is useless for us to talk of a new life'. What's more he continued, Gandhi had condemned those whose following of nonviolence was temporary, limited and not rooted in 'goodness' as the, 'nonviolence of the weak'. Later in his career Gene would spend considerable effort debunking these beliefs. The point of departure from Gandhi's thinking did not happen overnight, but he had already noticed the first evidence that things might not be the way Gandhi described.

Back when he was studying at Ohio State, Gene had been looking through old Indian newspapers on Gandhi's 1930 campaign for his masters thesis when he realised that what he had assumed about Gandhi's moral nonviolence was completely wrong. Many of Gandhi's followers and supporters had not believed in nonviolence or pacifism in purely moral terms. They had started to support it, not because it was 'good', but because it was proving effective. 'The evidence was there! These people did not believe in nonviolence as an ethic!' He remembered, 'That was a shock. I thought: Oh dear! We didn't have copy machines then. I had to

21

copy the whole thing by hand and I thought, "Should I copy that down? It's not supposed to be that way", but my focus on reality won out, fortunately, and I copied it down.'

Perhaps he lacked the confidence and more importantly the evidence, at this stage, to challenge the accepted wisdom that 'goodness' and morality were the major sources of power for nonviolent action, but he did not reveal his doubts. The introduction to the book provides two clear insights about the path on which he was embarking. The first echoed Richard Gregg's call for people to study, analyse and evaluate nonviolent campaigns in the same way that military strategists treated military campaigns. The second was a succinct, poetic statement of the futility of armed struggle. Those who would use violence to further their aims, he wrote, 'become the destroyers of their own dreams'.

The Gandhi manuscript was typed out, bound into neat brown paper packages and mailed out to publishers with polite covering letters. Every morning he would wait anxiously for the postman to deliver a positive reply, but as the weeks passed by only rejections arrived in the mailbox. As a young, first time writer, he didn't have the name to attract a publishing deal and soon became downcast by the lack of positive responses. Worse still, by March 1953 it was becoming clear that a change in the draft law for Korea meant he was going to be sent to prison.

Possibly concerned by her son's financial struggles and hints about his living conditions, Eva Sharp arrived in New York after a 500 mile train journey from Ohio. The Brooklyn apartment was a shock for his visiting mother, even by 1950s standards, but to make things even worse, the FBI chose this moment to come looking for her son. Eva may have been trying to make Gene's apartment a little more habitable when there was a knock on the door and she was confronted by two grave looking FBI officers who showed her the arrest warrant. Gene was at work guiding Mr Venturi on his rounds and Eva had little choice but to tell the feds where he was likely to be. Gene was arrested and taken downtown to face the charges, before being released on $5000 bail. This sum, around $50,000 in today's money, must have been a stretch to find, even for his mother and father. He returned home to his apartment that evening and scribbled a note to himself.

'What is it I have done for which I may be sentenced up to five years plus fine? How is it that I am such a dangerous man that $5000 is demanded for me. My crime is that I think for myself. My crime is that I follow that which is right. My crime is that I plan to spend my life working to build a better world. My crime is that I cannot kill. My crime is that when the government tells me to do that which I know to be wrong, I refuse to do it. My crime is that I take seriously the values which our civilisation pays lip service to.'

Paul and Eva were distraught. For Paul, there was the inevitable embarrassment of having to provide spiritual guidance for a congregation who were waving their sons off to war while his own son refused to go. It was also possible that he would soon have to conduct funerals for those who didn't make it back. He wrote to Gene begging him to change his position, but the reply was resolute.

'An important part of my conviction is that of vigorous action against the evil of war and totalitarianism. But this is simply an expression of a broader positive way of looking at life, in which truth, love and right actions are so important. It means that I must spend my life for these and implementing them in the building of a new society and the creation of new men, starting with myself'.

For politicians in Washington, the growing threat of communism extended beyond the war in Korea or even mutual nuclear annihilation. The real menace, many believed, would come from communist sympathisers and agents within the United States itself. This hysteria was driven by Senator Joseph McCarthy of Wisconsin, who established investigations to root out potential traitors serving inside the government, industry and academia. The unlikely lightning conductor for the fears of the academic community during this time was the physicist, Albert Einstein, who decided to speak out publicly against the McCarthy investigations. His interventions made him a hero for embattled academics and government workers, who wrote to him in their hundreds for support.

Gene read Einstein's comments in the papers and with just weeks until his trial and still no sign of a publisher for his manuscript, he decided to take a long shot. On 30th March 1953 he drafted a letter to Einstein describing the book he had written on Gandhi and that he was about to be sent to prison for noncooperation with the draft. In 1953 Einstein was 74 years old and living in a modest timber house with a white picket fence at 112 Mercer St, Princeton, New Jersey. Helen Dukas, his personal secretary of 25 years, vetted letters and house callers to filter out time wasters, but occasionally she advocated for particularly strong requests. History does not record Dukas's contribution very well, but it is likely that she had more to do with what happened next than she is credited with.

Dear Dr. Einstein,

In about three weeks, I shall be sent to prison because of my refusal to be inducted into the army. This I accept because according to my philosophy I must try to live and work for the ideals in which I believe and their application in building a better world. We have nearly forgotten that it is the power of truth and love which gives meaning and worth to individual lives and is capable of meeting the crisis of our time. Gandhi's philosophy, life and program, have had an important influence on me. I might say that I am a member of the Society of Friends and Peacemakers and the Fellowship of Reconciliation. As an expression on my outlook on life, I have been writing some books and articles on Gandhi's message, non-violence and some things that are needed if we are to be able to begin to build a better world.

At the time of Gandhi's death, you said in your statement: '...in our time of moral decadence, he was the only statesman to stand for a higher level of human relationship in the political sphere. This level we must with all our force, attempt to reach.'

Accompanying the letter is the manuscript of a book I have recently finished. It contains three historically moving accounts of Gandhi's application of this method in the political sphere. The study, analysis and evaluation of past non-violent campaigns, I believe to be an important step in the preparation for the future applications of this method. Unfortunately, not enough positive steps in this direction have been taken. Consequently, I have done some research on these campaigns, with the hope that it will offer the public some evidence that there is another way of opposing injustice rather than through the holocaust of atomic war and that it will be a basis for some to begin serious study and practice of this application of moral power.

In light of your personal concern with the war-totalitarian condition of our time and your feelings about Gandhi, I felt that perhaps you would be willing to write an introduction to this book. Would you?

I trust that the details of returning my manuscript by express collect will not be too much of an inconvenience.

Thanks for your consideration. I realize that you are an extremely busy man, and so I hesitated writing you about this. However, I also knew of your concern and interest in such matters, and so I felt that I might not be too forward in asking you to do this.

Many thanks.
Sincerely,
Gene Sharp

The letter arrived on 2nd April and would have been vetted by Dukas and placed on the desk in Einstein's study, where he read his morning mail. To Gene's astonishment, Einstein replied within days.

Dear Mr Sharp,

I earnestly admire you for your moral strength and can only hope, although I really do not know, that I would have acted as you did had I found myself in the same situation. Your manuscript arrived today. I shall read it carefully and prepare some introductory remarks if I sufficiently agree with its contents.

There is a sphere of conflict between the written laws of one's country and the unwritten laws, the existence of which becomes manifest in what we call our conscience. In the event of conflict the state adheres to the written law; only with great reluctance does it take into account the unwritten law of conscience. But even the state has recognized the duty of the individual to act according to the unwritten law when commands based on national laws are in striking conflict with the laws of his conscience. This principle was unmistakably established in the Nuremberg trials. Such a precedent is a precious tool in the fight against slavery resulting from the civic duty to kill.

Sincerely yours,
Albert Einstein.

Dear Dr Einstein,

Thanks very much for saying what you did in your letter. It means very much to me. It may also make things somewhat easier on my parents in Ohio who have found it difficult to understand my position. I shall be sentenced on April 23rd here in Brooklyn. I have pleaded guilty to both counts (refusal to report for the physical examination and for induction). The sentence will probably be 3 years, though maybe less. Enclosed are copies of my letters to the draft board.

If there is any question about the book that you might want to discuss I can come down to Princeton. If after looking at it you feel that this is not the book for which you like to write some introductory remarks I shall understand. In any case I am very grateful for your kindness.

Sincerely yours,
Gene Sharp

Einstein must have sat down to read Gene's book almost immediately because he replied barely a week later, not only having read the book, but with the foreword written too. 'I have read your book with sincere admiration and I have written a short introduction for it,' He wrote. 'Have you already found a publisher for it? If not I am ready to help you find one.' Gene replied, 'there are times when a simple "thanks" seems hardly enough.'

The Einstein letters arrived just in time for Gene's trial. Eva Sharp travelled down from Ohio to be there and maintained her bravest face as she watched Gene enter the courtroom. She must have wondered how her gentle son, who had done nothing but dream about making the world a better place, had come to face 3 years being stolen from his life. What kind of man would emerge on the other side when his time was done? Eva Sharp wrote about that day, 'I found it to be the most difficult situation I ever was in'.

In court, Gene took the stand and argued his position to the judge. Einstein had telegrammed his consent for the contents of his letters to be read out in court and the judge listened with some curiosity. Gene concluded his defence and stepped calmly back to his seat to await his fate, looking confident in his action. Watching from the public gallery was his friend, the writer, John Clellon Holmes whose first novel, *Go,* was considered the first novel about the post-war bohemian 'beat generation' and the lives of his friends, Jack Kerouac, Neal Cassady and Allen Ginsberg.

'I thought you conducted yourself magnificently', wrote Holmes. 'From where I sat it appeared that the judge was more impressed by Einstein than by Christ, which is something of a comment on our world. That Einstein who is a scientist and is thus in touch with certain immutable laws himself, should recognise the validity of your action and indeed, make so succinctly clear the relation of the written law to the higher law, gave the judge pause for thought.'

Despite the strength of his argument Gene was found guilty and the judge returned a sentence of two years. His mother wrote, 'It took all the courage I had to come out with a smile for Gene and to hold onto that courage when I was permitted to go into Manhattan in the afternoon where he was to be held until they moved him'. She took with her a letter from his father who was unable to travel due to work commitments.

'We will be remembering you daily and hourly. Never doubt the love of your parents for you and their sincere concern for your welfare. You will be looking beyond this experience … for even when you are free,

27

you will be young with a lot of life before you. What your plans and activities may be then none of us can prophesy now. Do guard your health so that you will have a strong body to go on with your work. Lovingly, Dad'

After returning to Ohio, Eva wrote to Einstein to thank him for his support. She described how the Assistant District Attorney, Mr Morracco of Brooklyn, had gone so far as to state that Gene, and conscientious objectors in general, should not have to serve a sentence for their beliefs. The lawyer stated that the Draft Board, understanding Gene's sincerity, had dealt compassionately with his position until the draft law changed in November and compelled his arrest.

'It was one of his last wishes before his sentence that I try to express again his thanks. Your letters, telegram and introduction were like a ray of sunshine to him when he most needed it. He has an utter faith that somehow that book will be published. Briefly I want to say that your statements concerning him could not have been more true had you known him. His entire life (25 years old) has been one of purity and goodness – sacrificing and sharing his bit with others regardless of race or color ... Not because I am his mother but I have never known Gene to do or say a wrong – his life example to others has been without reproach.'

Einstein wrote back to Eva straight away. 'I thank you for your kind and interesting letters. In reading I see that he has not stolen his extraordinary qualities! He is irresistible in his noble sincerity. Be Confident!'

Prison

Danbury Federal Correctional Institute was a modern prison by American standards of the time. No bars were visible from the outside and its green concrete walls and glass bricks made it look more like a modern factory than a prison. The building enclosed a yard containing a baseball diamond, bleachers and a grass football field. Prisoners were sent to work on farmland, producing a diet of fresh tomatoes, potatoes, cucumbers, and squash – though any temporary sensation of freedom was broken by the sound of the guards practicing to shoot escaping prisoners from their watchtowers.

Most of Gene's cellmates were minor offenders doing time for marijuana, check forgery, auto theft and desertion, but among them were other conscientious objectors and a sprinkling of alleged Communists. Their day started at 6:30am, when the prisoners were woken either courteously or with casual violence depending on the guard on duty. A count would commence to check for anyone missing and this would be repeated throughout the day and night. The food was better than expected and Gene reported in letters that his cell was warm, clean and painted. Each prisoner was restricted to just a few named correspondents with whom they could send and receive mail and these letters were closely monitored. All the guards knew that on Gene's list were his parents and Albert Einstein. On 14th June 1953, Gene wrote his first letter to Einstein from prison.

'As you know I was sentenced to two years and am serving that time at the Federal Correctional Institution at Danbury Connecticut. The prison facilities and treatment have been far better than I expected. I am working on the farm almost 35 hours a week. Mostly doing gardening type of work. I enjoy this very much; the fresh air sun and exercise are good for me. Among other things I read, study, do some writing and talk with friends. This experience is one from which I can learn very much.'

There were few physical discomforts at Danbury, but his fellow inmates were plagued with tragedy which filled the pages of Gene's prison diary. Gene was disappointed to find that resistance against racial segregation at Danbury by World War Two conscientious objectors (COs as they were known) had been rolled back. Now the segregation was not enforced by the prison system, but voluntarily continued by the inmates themselves. He wrote letters to the authorities, tried to get moved into an African American block and sat with the black men in the dining hall. 'The men are lonely men, frantic men, lost men and do not know it. They are little men who want to be big men. They are fearful men who want to show their courage. They are selfish men, emotionally sick men.' Perhaps what frustrated Gene most about his time was watching the corrupting influence of prison take hold of ordinary men and boys.

'Take away his escapes, his freedom, his chance for initiative and decisions. Fill his emptiness with more emptiness, with vulgarity, frenzy and void; take his rebellion against authority and pour into it complete regimentation and stifling of initiative; Take his twisted mind and drain from it the last desire for knowledge and pour in conniving and treachery; Take his wicked soul and fill it with the devil himself; Warp and twist the human being, grind his humanity under your foot haughtily, sneer at gentleness and love; twist justice into tyranny; take a confused boy and ruin his life, take a lost man and lead him to his worst. This is what prison does to men. And there are so many men in prison. It hurts to think of it.'

As Gene was settling into his first months of prison life, William Frauenglass, a high school English teacher working in Brooklyn, had come to the attention of a McCarthy investigations committee. Six years earlier he had given a talk to colleagues on 'techniques of intercultural teaching' which was deemed so suspicious by the authorities that it triggered a subpoena. Frauenglass refused to be a co-operative witness, ensuring almost guaranteed dismissal by the New York City School board and he, like Gene, wrote to Einstein for help. Perhaps inspired, in part, by Gene's book on Gandhi that he had read only weeks earlier, Einstein replied to Frauenglass:

'What should intellectuals do against this evil? Frankly I can only see the revolutionary way of non-co-operation in Gandhi's sense. Every intellectual who is called before one of the committees ought to refuse to testify. If enough people are ready to take this grave step they will be successful. If not, then the intellectuals of this country deserve nothing better than the slavery which is intended for them.'

At a time when US citizens were being asked to name names and testify against their colleagues, Einstein took a simple but radical approach. He urged the use of Gandhi's methods in America – to break the law if necessary. Einstein must have known that his letter would be explosive if it was made public, but attached a note that it was not to be considered confidential. Frauenglass duly sent it to *The New York Times* where it was published on 12th June 1953.

News of the letter hit the front pages of newspapers around the world and American commentators flew into rages of vitriol on their leader pages.

'He has put himself in the extremist category by his irresponsible suggestion. He has proved once more that genius in science is no guarantee of sagacity in political affairs.' *The Washington Post*

'It is always astonishing to find that a man of great intellectual power in some directions is a simpleton or even a jackass in others.' *The Chicago Daily Tribune*

'It is particularly regrettable when a scholar of his attainments, full of honors, should permit himself to be used as an instrument of propaganda by the enemies of the country which has given him such secure refuge.' *The Philadelphia Enquirer*

Now embroiled in the midst of a hate campaign by some of America's most famous newspapers over the Frauenglass letter, Einstein still took time to write to Gene at Danbury, apologising that his friend Mr Commins, who he had asked to help with the publication of Gene's book on Gandhi, had not yet had any luck.

Decades later, Gerald Holtom, an Einstein historian and Professor of The History of Science at Harvard University, came across the correspondence with Gene and was astonished by it. 'It was almost as if he [Einstein] was adopting him as a favoured son, because he immediately replies and he does whatever is asked of him and more.' 'I believe he saw in this man, Gene Sharp, the very model of what Gandhi was able to achieve ... a person who was not just fighting to keep his position against McCarthy as most people did who approached him. This man said, I am ready for my resistance ... by taking the consequences, hoping that many of us will do it, so the state will have to give in. That's a theory that finds it's exemplar in Gene Sharp.'

On 5th September 1953, Gene wrote home to his parents telling them how desperate he was to get his book published, but that he knew his approach was unconventional and the road ahead laden with challenges. 'I shall have difficulty in getting my things published even among pacifists, Peacemakers and Quakers. Few people have the humility to even think for a moment that there is the possibility they may be wrong,' he wrote. Gene also penned a personal note to his father. 'I know this has been especially hard on you, yet in many ways we've come together through it. You've been a very good friend throughout and a great help to us all. I don't say this very well, but thanks.' Perhaps to soften the blow he reported that he had not given up on the bible, reading half an hour each night from the Old Testament.

After three months working on the farm, forking hay for silage and harvesting cucumbers and tomatoes, Gene was assigned to train as an assistant to the prison dentist. He was given a couple of books on anatomy and a real human skull to study, which he kept under his bed. Very quickly he was allowed to perform injections and take X-rays, establishing a prodigious work rate. He wrote to his parents in late August, 'Yesterday I took 77 X-rays of teeth and developed them. I mix the mercury and cement for the fillings and he is going to have me giving the novocaine shots pretty soon too. Hold on to your teeth when I get out!'

As the first frost of fall descended upon Danbury, the prisoners huddled together in the yard in their thick navy blue pea coats. Gene had enough money sent from his parents to buy a new book, 'Social Philosophies in an Age of Crisis' by Pitirim A. Sorokin, but despite the fact he could still order books, his academic work had all but ground to a halt. There would be no major insights to come from his incarceration, a fact he attributed to prison's, 'stultifying effect on the mind, which impacts decision making and independent thinking'.

Occasionally he would undertake long periods of fasting in an attempt to improve his concentration. 'I felt it gave me self confidence and clarity', he wrote. 'After about 2 weeks your thinking becomes better and things you didn't understand before become clear. You might call it spiritual if you stretch the term but it was about exerting some measure of control over my own body.' The fasts never required him to receive medical treatment and it was a process he would continue throughout his life when he encountered problems with his work.

Fellow inmates often saw Gene walking alone around the baseball oval deep in thought, looking directly upwards. By staring up at the great piles of clouds tumbling across a vast sky he saw no walls or watchtowers and could feel, for a moment, as if he was strolling in an open park like a free man.

That Christmas, his parents drove the 600 miles from Ohio to visit Danbury. They were calm, despite the circumstances, and brought a modest hamper with fruit cake and other small luxuries that weren't available in prison. 'Even the eating of a single pecan took on a new intensity ... a great delicacy, long to be remembered' Gene wrote of its arrival.

While his parents remained supportive in person, back in Ohio they were attempting to conceal the family's shame from their community and

Paul's congregation. One of Gene's friends received a severe scolding in a letter from Eva Sharp after writing to her about Gene's imprisonment on the back of a postcard which could easily have been read by the postman or workers at the local sorting office.

Gene was friendly with many of his fellow inmates at Danbury, but remembered only one clearly. William 'Bill' Remington was an Ivy League educated federal economist whose promising government career had been destroyed by allegations that he was a Soviet spy. The evidence had come from Elizabeth Bentley, a former Soviet agent, turned by the FBI and set to work entrapping suspected American communists.

Bentley alleged that Remington had passed her the details of a top secret synthetic rubber manufacturing process used in the US nuclear programme, telling her, 'The Russians will need something very much like this'. The case had dragged on for years, receiving regular coverage in the New York Times, but the authorities only managed to achieve a conviction on a minor perjury charge.

Gene first noticed Remington in the library where he was seeking some mental stimulation rearranging the books with a more sophisticated cataloguing system. In their free time they wandered the prison yard together for hours debating politics, war and Gandhi's teachings. Although he tried, Gene never detected any traces of communist ideology in his thinking and became convinced he was innocent.

Bill's biggest concern was his pregnant wife Jane and their unborn baby who he desperately wanted to be able to see when the time came. The prison governors assured him he would be allowed to remain at Danbury to make visits easier for his family, but they would renege on their promise with tragic consequences.

Shortly before Gene's release, the internal tannoy barked into life with an announcement calling out names of men who were to report to the main desk for transfer – Bill Remington was among them. Gene rushed to Bill's bunk where he found him distressed, but there was little he could say to help. The prison authorities were sending him to Lewisburg, a much tougher prison than Danbury. They said goodbye, not knowing when they would meet again, and parted telling each other they would look each other up when they were free.

After nine months and six days of detention, Gene was granted parole. On the day of his release, his friend, Rossalyn, from New York, drove to Danbury to pick him up. As they turned out of the prison and onto Route 6, north, for New York, Gene looked with wonder at the miles of open road stretching out in front of them. For the best part of a year he hadn't been able to walk much more than 100 yards before turning around again. Now this road was a symbol of his restored freedom, the longest highway in the United States. If they'd wanted, they could have driven all the way to California.

Months later, Gene was sitting on a plane on his way home for Thanksgiving when his eye caught a headline in the *New York Times* that turned his blood cold. 'Remington Dies In Prison; 2 Inmates Named as Killers'. Bill had been murdered. Two fellow inmates at Lewisburg had brutally attacked him, smashing his skull with a brick in a sock. When they admitted the crime, they told the FBI it was because they hated communists. It was recorded as one of the few murders attributable to McCarthyism.

The prison parole board required that an inmate be released into a supervised place of work and Gene had spent many evenings in his cell at Danbury writing to potential sponsors. Bizarrely, the authorities had eventually agreed to release him into the supervision of A.J. Muste, the chief architect of the civil resistance position which had resulted in his imprisonment.

A.J. was almost 70 years old when Gene joined him at his offices in New York where he was trying to unite social radicals and pacifists in opposition to defence policy. One of A.J's previous aides, Bayard Rustin, was brilliant, black and openly gay – a powerful orator and campaigner who would later become a key adviser to Martin Luther King. But, after an FBI surveillance operation had caught him having sex in a car with two men, just months before Gene's release from prison, A.J. had forced him out, telling him his homosexuality was an illness which had to be hidden and 'treated psychiatrically'.

Gene had the uncomfortable realisation, days into his new employment that he had taken over Bayard's old job – a position from which he'd been fired, solely for being gay. If the prison board had not compelled him to take the job, it is unlikely he would have been able to live with hypocrisy. Gene never campaigned openly on gay rights, but he did not make it a secret that his sympathies on this issue lay firmly with Bayard.

The work was basic and not highly paid, but it exposed him to a great network of thinkers and activists. He respected A.J. as a brilliant mind, but despite being a leading activist for peace, he was a conservative Christian when it came to the rights of other minority groups. After just months working with him, Gene became increasingly disillusioned. A.J. was a true believer in pacifism and Gene was coming to the conclusion that it wasn't pacifists who were going to change the world. Human conflict was inevitable he thought – the real challenge was to replace the violence in traditional conflicts by developing an alternative form of fighting.

It was a chance meeting with an Australian Quaker called Tom Wardle which now pointed Gene in a new direction. Wardle had worked as a journalist in England and was on a lecture tour of the US when Gene offered to let him stay in his Brooklyn apartment. They talked about Gene's frustrations in his current position and his desire to do something new. Wardle continued on his tour, but some months later a letter from London arrived at Gene's Brooklyn apartment which would signal a radical new start.

On the March

It was a freezing December night in 1955 as the bright white, double-funnelled steam ship, *Italia,* slipped her moorings and headed out into Hudson Bay, bound for England. The United States was changing. Just a few days earlier Rosa Parks had refused to give up her seat on the bus to a white passenger and move to the back. A bus boycott was now in action across the state of Alabama and would soon inspire a civil resistance movement across America.

On the other side of the Atlantic, the Soviet Union had just conducted the largest atomic bomb test ever recorded. Although he would write about the civil rights movement from London, it would be the threat of nuclear war that would concentrate Gene's attention most in the coming decade. As he watched Manhattan's skyscrapers slowly disappearing in the ship's wake, he thought to himself, 'It's more than an ocean I cross tonight'.

The *Italia* sailed east up the English Channel and into Plymouth harbour on the 18th December. A weatherbeaten sign on the docks welcomed Gene cheerfully to the 'Gateway to England', but he was immediately shocked by the sight of bombed out buildings – the scars of years of Luftwaffe bombing which had killed hundreds of people in the city. He collected a ticket and boarded the special 'boat train' – a steam locomotive heading for London.

His new job was Assistant Editor of *Peace News*, a pacifist newspaper which had built a readership of more than 40,000 people in the run up to the Second World War. Advertising billboards of the time declared, 'If YOU believe in freedom, justice AND peace you should regularly read this stimulating paper!' Its editor was Hugh Brock, a conscientious objector who had helped evade a wartime parliamentary banning order on the paper in 1940 by setting up a covert distribution chain with peace groups across Britain.

Tall, handsome, with gentle manners and a long stride, Brock had helped form an organisation called 'Operation Gandhi', which had carried out its first nonviolent direct actions in 1952. Now the aim of the paper and its affiliated organisations was to write about and organise nonviolent actions which would force the withdrawal of US weapons from Britain and end the embryonic British nuclear bomb programme. With his background as a conscientious objector, a completed book on Gandhi and a foreword by Einstein, Gene was just the kind of person Hugh Brock wanted at his newspaper.

If you take a right out of Finsbury Park underground station in North London today and walk down Blackstock Road, you will see a quite unique sight. Sitting among the plasticised, modern frontages of estate agents and chain restaurants which now monopolise London's streets, is a window into the past. The frontage of Fish & Cook stationers stands exactly as it did in 1955, when Gene first arrived. Two single windows above the shop mark the former home of *Peace News*.

The landlord of the building, Mr Fish, was extremely supportive of the activities above his shop, in part because he had been a conscientious objector during the First World War, but even more so due to the paper's incessant demand for his stationery. The rooms were crammed with people marshalled by Hugh Brock's formidable secretary, Constance Willis, who barked ferociously at anyone who blocked up the single phone line in the building for too long.

The paper was a ready made social life of activists, academics and campaigners. There were frequent parties and speaking events set against the background of the increasingly vibrant London night life. Gene threw himself into the London activist scene, but aware that he was an American in a foreign country was careful to give lectures rather than political speeches.

Peace activist, April Carter, met him for the first time at a meeting in the House of Commons, 'He was a very good lecturer dynamic, authoritative and physically striking but he was in a minority' she remembered, 'The left at the time were lionising violent guerrilla struggles, Marxists had always been contemptuous of bourgeois capitalists and nonviolent action just didn't seem challenging enough to many of the radicals of the time.'

Despite theoretical divisions within the peace movement there were plenty who did believe in the power of nonviolent action. One of the regular visitors to *Peace News* was Michael Randle, who was working on his parents' farm in the south of England. Despite an intelligence that was apparent to everyone, Michael had left school at 16 without the qualifications necessary for university. Young, passionate and with a taste for adventure, he was 23 years old when he first encountered Gene at a pacifist youth group. Gene was explaining the importance of American trade unions and delighted the small crowd by giving a rousing rendition of one of the traditional union songs. This scene seems out of character for someone who continued to struggle with his, 'less than life of the party' personality in his diary, but he was also very fond of whisky and it's quite possible that on this occasion he had had far too much to drink.

On 4th November 1956, Russian forces invaded Hungary and were soon occupying its towns and cities. The invasion gave Michael his first shot at some real action. He proposed at a *Peace News* meeting that a party of activists should enter Hungary, illegally if necessary, across the Austrian border and stage an action to encourage Hungarian citizens to carry out nonviolent resistance against the Russians. The plan was enthusiastically approved, but one by one the volunteers found their excuses until the party dwindled to just Michael.

Now planning a, one man, nonviolent invasion of a country currently occupied by the Soviet Union, Michael enlisted Gene's help. They set to work writing the materials that would be distributed, producing leaflets and posters expressing support of strictly nonviolent resistance and calling upon Russian troops not to fire on unarmed protesters.

Michael set off from London, crossing the English Channel by ferry before reaching the Austrian capital Vienna without event. But when he finally made contact with his pacifist and Quaker contacts there, he was told in no uncertain terms that he was quite mad and should turn back immediately. Undeterred, he found a friendly print shop owner willing to translate his materials into Hungarian and German.

The following day he set off on a 50 mile walk towards the Hungarian border, trudging through deep December snow with his haul of leaflets and posters in a large rucksack. Sadly this audacious display of verve and bravery ended ingloriously when the Austrian border guards stopped him crossing and called the police in Vienna to come and pick him up. A man from the British Embassy arrived, obviously incandescent with being deprived of his afternoon sherry, and looked Michael up and down angrily. 'So you're the one who's been causing all the trouble are you?'

On his return from Vienna, Michael sat with Gene telling him the stories about his adventure. The mission had not gone as planned, but the exercise of producing the materials had been a useful one and there was now an appetite for carrying out similar actions.

The British government was planning its first test of thermonuclear weapons in the South Pacific Islands and preparations for the tests under the codename 'Operation Grapple' had been in process for some time. The selection of the islands, based on geographic studies, had been made in Spring 1956 and there were soon more than 1000 military and scientific personnel stationed at an outpost on Kiritimati island, preparing for the first test.

Brock and the staff of *Peace News* were horrified by the prospect. A plan was agreed to send protesters into the testing area by boat to disrupt the detonation. However, much like Randle's mission to Hungary, a group of initially enthusiastic volunteers gradually dropped out and the job was left to a white-haired, former chicken farmer called Harold Steele. Harold got as far as Japan, alerting the interest of British intelligence on his way, but was unable to commandeer an adequate boat to reach the testing area.

Nevertheless, his ambitious, perhaps hair-brained, plan was interesting enough to receive widespread press attention in Japan, where he conducted dozens of newspaper, TV and radio interviews before returning to London. His plan to disrupt the British government plans created almost as much publicity as if he'd actually achieved his aim, but the tests would go on undisrupted.

On 15th May 1957, a Victor Valiant Bomber flown by RAF pilot, Group Captain Kenneth Hubbard, dropped the first bomb, which detonated in the atmosphere above Malden Island with a power of 300 kilotons – more than 15 times as powerful as those dropped on Hiroshima and Nagasaki. Downing Street announced proudly to the world that Great Britain had officially become a thermonuclear power.

The announcement sent a shockwave through the peace community. Back in London, Brock formed a new organisation he called the Direct Action Committee. He was determined to mount a major demonstration to grip the attention of the nation and shake the establishment – a national march against atomic weapons.

Gene was immediately attached as an advisor, a position he would adopt for the rest of his career, never becoming directly involved in a struggle only cautiously contributing academic support to it. Whatever his official position though, Randle described Gene as, 'The power behind the throne'. He was about to shape one of the most defining moments in the history of the peace movement – the 1958 anti-nuclear march from London to the atomic bomb factory at Aldermaston.

Gene's role was to keep the Aldermaston march entirely nonviolent in line with Gandhi's teachings, but that would not prove as easy as it might have seemed. The need for a code of discipline was reinforced by one Campaign for Nuclear Disarmament (CND) meeting shortly before the march that got quickly out of control. As the meeting broke up, the chairman of CND, an Anglican priest called Canon John Collins, announced that a few people were going down to Downing Street for an impromptu protest. There were no gates at the entrance to Downing Street in the 1950s – the level of threat to the British Prime Minister was considered so remote that passers by could walk right up to the front door if they wanted to.

After an otherwise quiet day, the police were taken by surprise by a rabble of activists in a state of some animation coming out of nowhere and getting right up to the Prime Minister's windows. The policemen began frantically driving back the crowd and Michael Randle looked down the street to see his friend Ernest being pummelled on the ground by several officers. One of the group took out his camera and photographed the scene only to be pursued at full sprint up Whitehall by a policeman who rugby tackled him to the tarmac and ripped the film clean out of his camera. Michael confronted the offending police officer and in his most upper crust English accent protested, 'I do think that was rather unreasonable!' The police officer snarled back angrily, 'Shurrup, or I'll smash yer face!'

Back at *Peace News*, Gene had been hard at work drafting a code of nonviolent discipline leaflet for the Aldermaston marchers and took the news of the disturbance at Downing Street quite badly. With the march fast approaching, the early breakdown in discipline by one of the core organisations was deeply worrying. If it happened with just dozens of people, the potential damage that could be done with thousands was unthinkable. 'We have to make sure this kind of thing doesn't happen again', he told Michael anxiously.

Another concern was that government or pro-nuclear supporters might provoke the marchers into lashing out or committing an act of violence which would portray them as reckless vandals and trouble makers.

Gene made sure his leaflets were absolutely clear on how to behave if an agent provocateur tried to cause a violent confrontation and how to stop it spreading. If violence broke out, he initially argued that people should place themselves between the fighters, but changed his mind later, arguing they should, 'immediately withdraw, leave an empty space and sit down. Isolate the violence.' He also insisted that the police would always be informed of planned actions as Gandhi had done. The police at Downing Street had been surprised and lashed out. A similar event on a larger scale at the march would cause chaos.

Six key points were highlighted and he told readers of the flyer, 'If you believe in the objectives of this demonstration we ask you to abide by the following discipline. If you cannot comply we ask that you do not take part in this demonstration and withdraw quietly.'

1. Do not use any language or take any action which is likely to provoke violence by others. A dignified bearing and courteous determination will greatly contribute to victory for this cause.

2. If you are jeered at or called names do not shout back or jeer those who differ from our views. Silence and a friendly smile are the best reply to hostility.

3. If anyone attempts to pull down your banner, seize your sign, remove an armband or destroy leaflets, let go at once. Do not struggle with the attacker. This prevents opponents from provoking a fight which can be widely used to discredit this demonstration. Stand silently with your hands at your sides looking straight ahead or continue marching as before with hands at sides.

4. Do not under any conditions use any violence regardless of provocation. If you are struck keep hands at side and do not strike back. Do not allow opponents to make you stoop to using violence which will degrade a noble campaign. Dignity, restraint, courage and a friendly smile are the best answer in such demonstrations to violence and attack. This may mean you will be injured, but such suffering bravely borne without retaliation advances our cause.

5. If anyone else is attacked do not use any violence against the attacker. Each demonstrator must himself or herself be responsible for standing up to such violence and suffering for achieving our objective.

6. If a fight or struggle does begin near you and there are no police to deal with it, you must be prepared to separate fighters by standing between them, even if you are thereby injured. By isolating the violence and those whose behaviour would discredit our objective, by being willing to take blows without retaliation or fear, you will be doing a great service to our cause.

As news of the march spread, a designer called Gerald Holtom, who lived in the London suburb of Twickenham, wrote to *Peace News*. Holtom believed that it was the responsibility of all individuals to work towards the eradication of nuclear weapons and he was convinced there needed to be a strong visual image signifying nuclear disarmament.

Holtom had designed a symbol combining the semaphore signals for the letters N and D standing for Nuclear Disarmament. A semaphore letter N is signalled by a person holding two flags in an upside down V and the letter D by holding one flag directly up and the other directly down. Superimposing these signals formed the now universally recognised peace symbol. He described the emotions behind his design in a letter to Hugh Brock. 'I was in despair. Deep despair. I drew myself: the representative of an individual in despair with hands palm outstretched outwards and downwards in the manner of Goya's peasant before the firing squad. I formalised the drawing into a line and put a circle round it.'

The leadership of the Campaign for Nuclear Disarmament initially rejected the design as their logo and Holtom now offered it to the Aldermaston marchers instead. Brock recognised the power of the symbol and asked Holtom to come up with more designs and visual material, including placards and banners, to be displayed on the march.

On completion of this work, Holtom took the train from Twickenham into central London where he was greeted warmly by the team at the offices of *Peace News*. 'So, Gerry, let's see what you have for us,' they said, excited for the first reveal. Holtom untied the string on his portfolio and unfurled some large sheets of paper. Hugh Brock and the others on the committee gathered round eagerly to see what he had come up with. 'I've tried a simple approach' he told them.

Not only had he designed the symbol itself, but he had also sketched how they would look on a march, how they should be displayed (on lollipop sticks and banners) and the way they should be grouped to maximise the visual impact in the street. In effect he was stage managing how photographs of the march would look when they were printed in the newspapers. The group were delighted and quickly gave the go ahead to print the symbol on all of the materials. Holtom was to print the symbol onto hundreds of banners, lollipop placards and Gene's instruction leaflets immediately.

The staff of *Peace News* may have been slightly more progressive than most of their readers. The newly born peace symbol was met with sheer horror in some quarters when the first prints were released. There were no broken rifles, doves or olive branches, it was so completely stark and abstract that many people found it quite shocking. Examples of the symbol were sent out to peace groups across the country so that they could be replicated by local organisations, but some sent it straight back. One member of the Quaker Church, Barbara Webb, refused to use it at all. 'We have decided to provide our own posters', she wrote, 'It conveys no meaning at all and we fear people seeing it may think us members of the Klu Klux Klan!'

Harry Mister, the boss of Housmans bookshop which sold radical peace literature was mystified by the leadership's choice. He collared Michael at the office. 'What on earth were you thinking about when you adopted this symbol?' he scolded them, 'It doesn't mean a thing and what's more it'll never catch on!'

Holtom himself later regretted the image of despair and wanted the symbol to be turned upside down to give the impression of a hopeful human form throwing the arms into the air instead of to the floor, but by then it was too late. The design stood and, despite his concerns, the Aldermaston march would become the debut of one of the most iconic images of the 20th century.

On the 4th April 1958, with the planning complete and the marchers issued with their leaflets, lollipop placards and banners, more than 2000 people assembled in London's Trafalgar Square. Bayard Rustin, A.J. Musté's former assistant, was now a key advisor to Martin Luther King Jr. and travelled from the US to deliver what many remembered as the most powerful speech that afternoon.

'We are nonviolent because injury to one is injury to all!' he told the crowd from the base of Nelson's column, before comparing the struggle against nuclear weapons with the struggle for civil rights in America. Bayard was so taken with the new peace symbol he saw all around him that day that he took it home to America and began its spread as an international icon.

The march set off for the Atomic Weapons Establishment at Aldermaston, 52 miles away, on one of the wettest Easter weekends on record. Jazz bands and singing ushered the march into each new town and village while a catering van followed the peaceful army with hot tea and biscuits.

Organisers in a 'command vehicle' found accommodation for the marchers in tents and guest houses. Frequently soaked through and walking 3 abreast, the procession tailed back for miles along country roads. A sea of Holtom's lollipop signs bobbed along with them looking just as they had in his sketches and in their hands they carried Gene Sharp's leaflet on nonviolent discipline.

What is striking looking at the footage from that time is just how well dressed the marchers all looked. The anti-nuclear protesters of 1958 were keen to wear their best suits, sensible hats and coats so as not to be thought of as yobs or anarchists. They were also drawn from across the spectrum of Britain's distinct social classes.

The spectacle was unusual for Britain in the 1950s and attracted considerable attention from the press. *The Daily Telegraph*, *The Times* and the BBC all sent reporters and they got drenched alongside everyone else. On the Saturday morning the marchers awoke in Hounslow for the longest leg of the walk to find the weather had become even worse. Snow was now falling hard, which at Easter in the south east of England was almost unheard of.

At night, they lay like tinned fish on the hard floors of Quaker halls and boy scout huts along the route and then limbered up again in the morning to head back out into the relentless weather. That resilience, reported by the embedded media pack, swelled their numbers even further in the next two days.

The press coverage however was not uniformly positive. From the moment the march set off from Trafalgar Square the organisers received word that a pro-nuclear counter-demonstration had been set up at Hyde Park Corner with the intention of baiting the nonviolent marchers into a violent confrontation. From Hyde Park the march was shadowed by a small group of men led by a pair of brothers called the Macwhirters. They would be the first example of 'agent provocateurs' that Gene would witness.

On approaching the Aldermaston site, the marchers had been asked to walk in silence before observing a vigil in Falcon Field near the Aldermaston buildings. But as the front of the march neared the finishing point the Macwhirters made their move, driving a van with loudspeakers across their path and bawling amplified abuse down the road at them. Sympathisers who had gathered to greet the march flew at the van in a rage, ripping the loudspeaker off the roof and a melé ensued. Veteran campaigner, Pat Arrowsmith, ran across the field and threw herself in front of the driver shouting, 'this is a nonviolent demonstration, we will have no violence here'.

But it was too late – despite hours of peaceful disciplined marching, a photographer had captured the moment and the negatives reached London in time for the late edition of the *Evening Standard*. 'Aldermaston March Ends in Riot' was the headline on every street corner in the city that evening.

The national papers picked up the story the next day. One of the Macwhirters admitted to the BBC that it had been their intention to provoke a scene to discredit the march, but few would hear that side of the story. *The Times* also caused fury among the organising committee by publishing an aerial photograph of the march as the crowd was dispersing, thereby making it look far smaller than it had been upon its arrival.

A vigorous letter of complaint was dispatched to the editor requesting a reason for the choice of this picture, but they received no satisfactory reply. Despite this, the media coverage was judged to be, on balance, positive. Features ran on the BBC news, the front pages of many national newspapers and the march even became the subject of an early black and white documentary narrated by the Oscar-nominated actor Richard Burton.

The Aldermaston march had been a success, but a split was developing in the Direct Action Committee led by those who felt that more radical actions were required to make the government take notice. In 1960 Michael Randle was appointed Secretary of a new organisation called the Committee of 100 (C100). Pat Arrowsmith was a rising star in the new organisation and rode around with Michael Randle on a motorbike organising demonstrations. Arrowsmith had suffered forced feeding via nasal tube while in prison for her protests and was particularly disdainful of Gene's stand of not becoming directly involved. 'I couldn't understand his position and I was quite contemptuous of him because of it. I never understood how he could write about these things but never put himself on the line.'

She was not the only one to hold this view, but Gene had already decided that co-opting the system was the only way that change could be made. If nonviolent struggle was going to take the place of nuclear weapons, it would be governments that would have to be convinced.

In contrast the, more militant, Committee of 100, decided to challenge the government and military head on, raising concerns in the heart of the British establishment. In the iciest moments of the Cold War, left-wing activists were often considered potential spies or agitators and the security service, MI5, were kept busy with plots and intrigues – most of them fictional, but some of them a real. Was it possible that the Committee of 100 was being infiltrated or influenced by Soviet agents to stir up trouble and interfere with British defences? It was a C100 action at the American nuclear bomber airbase at Wethersfield that gave the security services a genuine threat to worry about, and it would curtail Michael Randle's activities for some time.

The Committee came up with a plan to enter Wethersfield airfield, occupy the runway and stop the nuclear bombers getting airborne. Despite what they thought was meticulous planning they must have been under surveillance, or someone snitched, because the day before the action the police swooped and arrested the organising committee. In trying to interfere with the nuclear deterrent the members of C100 had crossed the line and they were about to receive everything the Official Secrets Act and the English legal system could throw at them.

The judge in the case, Mr Justice Havers was notable for being the last judge in Britain to sentence a woman to death, and appeared to have little time for anti-nuclear campaigners. The trial of five organising members of C100, including Michael Randle, took place in the Old Bailey, Britain's most famous courthouse, where everyone from mass murderers, spies and bank robbers were sent down in front of the baying mob of Fleet Street.

Gene was called as a witness for the defence by Pat Pottle, one of the five accused, to explain the importance of nonviolent resistance to a democracy. The court records found buried in the British National Archive read like a farcical play. Judge Havers looked on with some exasperation as Pottle chose to question the witnesses himself.

The Prisoner Pottle: What I have been trying to get to is that I would like Mr Sharp to explain to the members of the jury what is meant by non-violence.

Mr Justice Havers: I am afraid you cannot turn this court into a Ruskin College group to be lectured by this witness upon the principles of non-violence.

The Prisoner Pottle: Could I ask Mr Sharp his definition of nonviolence?

Mr Justice Havers: No.

The Prisoner Pottle: Then I have no further questions.

Mr Justice Havers: Thank you Mr Sharp.

Gene was dismissed and the proceedings continued to amuse the press gallery when the famous philosopher, Earl Bertrand Russell, who had written some of the leaflets calling for the invasion of the airfield, was called to the witness box. Justice Havers, employing all of his powers of persuasion to prevent a member of the aristocracy incriminating himself, failed catastrophically.

The Prisoner Pottle: Have you thought it funny ….

Mr Justice Havers: Funny?

The Prisoner Pottle: Yes my Lord, that the six people in the dock gave out the leaflet and they are in the dock for doing so, and yet the gentlemen who wrote the leaflet are not accused?

Mr Justice Havers (to Lord Russell): Don't answer!

The Prisoner Pottle: Lord Russell, did you conspire and incite persons to incite people to go to Wethersfield Base?

Mr Justice Havers: Remember my warning Lord Russell. You are not bound to answer unless you wish to do so.

The Prisoner Pottle: My Lord the judge is saying you have no need to answer this question, because if you do answer it it would incriminate you.

Mr Justice Havers: If he *thinks* it would incriminate him. I did not say more than that.

Earl Russell: Have I not a *right* to incriminate myself if I wish to?

Mr Justice Havers: Of course you are perfectly entitled to. It is my duty to warn you that you need not. I have a duty to protect a witness who may not know that. You are perfectly entitled to incriminate yourself if you wish to do so.

Earl Russell: Well, I do.

Mr Justice Havers: Now you can repeat your question.

The Prisoner Pottle: Thank you; Earl Russell did you conspire and incite people to block Wethersfield Base on December 9

Earl Russell: Yes!

The Prisoner Pottle: Do you feel you are just as responsible for the preparation of that demonstration as the six people in the dock.

Earl Russell: I do most emphatically!

In his summing up, Pottle gave a theatrical performance for the jury. 'I would like you to ask yourselves a question. Have the authorities applied the law fairly? Then another question – why is it that they chose to prosecute only six members of the Committee of 100 when the Attorney General himself has said that the other 94 are just as guilty? I ask you again. Have they applied the law fairly? Or is it that they are trying to intimidate the movement by victimising individuals?

Let us now look at some of the Committee of 100, or to put it in the words of the Attorney General 'The irresponsible people who think they can flout the law at any time." Pottle listed Bertrand Russell, the actress Vanessa Redgrave, the scientist Lord Boyd Orr and Martin Hyman the Olympic 10,000m runner, but his argument did not find a receptive audience. After a short deliberation the foreman of the jury announced the verdict that they were, 'guilty as charged', but added an unusual plea that the court consider leniency.

The court officers took the six down to the cells below the court and Pottle, who had been suffering from a cold for some days, began coughing. One of the guards feigned sympathy, 'Oh dear. Have you got a cold?'. 'Yes', Pottle replied, unaware of the guard's sarcasm. 'Well you've got 18 fucking months to get over it' he laughed, slamming on the handcuffs.

However much he liked and valued the company of this band of rogues in the Committee of 100, Gene felt he had made the correct decision not to get involved in the more radical actions. After more than two years as a journalist at *Peace News* he knew a return to academia was essential if he was going to be taken seriously by the political establishment.

He wrote, 'I do not call myself a pacifist as although I do not now support military polices I have come increasingly to the conviction that it will only be possible to remove reliance on military polices when more effective nonviolent means have been found.'

Gene was beginning to believe that a population trained in nonviolent resistance might have the potential to deter or frustrate an invasion of Europe by the Soviets and therefore replace the requirement for nuclear weapons. At first glance this might seem hopelessly naive, but there was at least one serious case study of this kind of resistance in Norway during its occupation by Nazi Germany.

In the summer of 1958, Gene accepted an invitation to further his theoretical work with a research position at the Institute of Philosophy and History of Ideas in Oslo. It was here that he would meet and study the civilians who had defied Hitler and his puppet regime led by Vidkun Quisling.

Norway

Gene had never been interested in developing a mere theory of nonviolent action. What he really wanted was for his work to find a way of replacing military conflict. To do this he had to prove to the political elite, and ordinary citizens, that nonviolent action was a realistic alternative to violence. The Norwegian's had one of the most powerful examples of civilian nonviolent resistance against occupation by the Nazis – but very few people outside Norway knew anything about it. It was a case study that would lay the groundwork for all of his future work on dictatorships.

Gene's academic supervisor in Oslo was Arna Naess, a philosopher and mountaineer who had been the youngest professor ever appointed to Oslo University. Arna introduced Gene to a nonviolent resistance operation run by a group of Norwegian teachers against the Nazi Quisling regime. It was still less than 15 years since Hitler's Germany had been defeated and many of the leaders of the teachers resistance were still alive to tell their story – one of them was Hakon Holmboe.

Holmboe was no soldier or pacifist, yet he had been instrumental in one of the most unreported nonviolent resistance campaigns in history. In the post-war hubris the young men who had waged armed resistance from the mountains had received most of the glory and the teachers were quickly being forgotten, but their actions had perhaps the most impact of any campaign, military or civilian, in Norway's war.

On April 9th 1940, Hitler's troops had rolled easily across Norway's borders, but the German naval force sent to capture Oslo was beaten back by Norwegian forces operating a coastal fortress at Oscarsborg. The delay allowed the King and his cabinet to escape by Royal Navy warship to London to form a government in exile. After the Norwegian military resistance finally collapsed, the Germans consolidated their hold on the towns and cities of the country and demanded that all government employees sign an oath of loyalty to the Nazi Quisling regime.

The first signs of civilian resistance came quickly, but they were only symbolic. People began wearing a single paperclip on their lapel to signify 'keeping together'. These protests grew wider and more threatening to the regime. On the King's 70th birthday, the people went out wearing a flower in their button hole to affirm their loyalty to the royal family and government in exile in London. Gene classified this activity as, 'overcoming atomisation' – atomisation being the process by which a dictator makes each and every citizen feel afraid of his or her neighbour or even a family member informing on them to the regime.

The small symbolic actions of wearing paperclips or flowers were a way of overcoming atomisation with a very low risk activity which demonstrated unity of resistance against the regime. Once this fear barrier was broken, the population was more likely to attempt higher risk activities.

On the royal birthday, several hundred people were arrested for simply wearing a flower, but as the Nazi occupation inflicted more severe punishments, the Norwegians' will to resist only became stronger. Actors refused to act in radio plays or perform in theatres attended by Germans. When Quisling tried to get the churches to preach the 'Nazi word', bishops and priests resigned their positions and delivered covert sermons in secret makeshift churches.

The puppet government even attempted to make athletes join a Nazi sports club. This too was resisted – the sports clubs went on strike and sporting events were carried out in secret away from German eyes. The resistance in each of these important pillars of society, the church, the cultural sector, sports and soon education, denied the Quisling regime the legitimacy it craved and exposed its weakness.

As plans for a more organised resistance campaign took shape in the autumn of 1941, Hakon Holmboe was asked to lead the resistance in a large district of Eastern Norway. His task was to recruit reliable people in each professional or occupational group, but none of them were to know who each other were. This 'cell' structure, today more associated with terrorist organisations, would ensure that if a member of the group were captured, interrogated or 'turned', they would be unable to betray the others. In February 1942, Quisling issued a decree declaring that all teachers were automatically members of a new teachers organisation headed by the Nazis. A youth organisation mirroring the Hitler Youth in Germany, was also established and membership was made compulsory for all 10–18 year olds. The new organisations were a step too far for ordinary Norwegians and they began a more sophisticated campaign of resistance.

A secret meeting was held in Oslo between the 11th and 12th of February 1942 where it was decided that all teachers should refuse to become members of the new organisation and were to write to Quisling's education department formally resisting with a common statement. One afternoon, Holmboe received a telephone call from a friend who asked to meet him urgently at the railway station. When he arrived his friend told him about the Oslo meeting and that Holmboe was to spread a statement of refusal. He was handed a mysterious matchbox and the friend departed.

'Inside the box of matches contained the plan for the resistance. My job was to circulate it secretly among the teachers in my district,' he told Gene. 'That was all I knew. I didn't know who the leaders were who met in Oslo.' The instructions in the matchbox soon spread every bit as effectively as a Tweet or a Facebook post would in today's social media age. Between 8000 and 10,000 teachers – nearly two thirds of the entire profession in Norway, sent their letters to the education department. It was a huge success which contributed to a significant loss of fear among the population.

'When the demonstration succeeded it gave us a pleasant feeling that so many people had the courage to stand up. It gave us a feeling of not being alone, a feeling of strength.' Holmboe remembered.

The nonviolent resisters continued to plan ahead, correctly anticipating the actions the Nazis were likely to take. When Quisling closed the schools with the excuse that there was a fuel shortage and threatened to fire the teachers and wipe out their pensions, the resistance was ready. Preparations had been made for financial hardship with a strikers fund. Most of the teachers had been contributing two percent of their incomes to the resistance and this money now began to flow back to those who needed it. Holmboe received 20,000 Kroner from a resistance contact to distribute among those teachers who needed it. Many of them continued to teach in private homes and farm buildings to demonstrate their will to work.

The Education Department then faced a torrent of letters of complaint from parents, creating an additional headache for Quisling. On 20th March, five days after the deadline for compliance had passed, around 1000 teachers were arrested. The Nazis couldn't possibly arrest all of the teachers so they aimed instead at widespread intimidation while leaving most of the schools able to function. In some areas the police were asked to arrest a defined number of teachers, but were not given specific names. Meetings at the schools were held to decide who to put forward for arrest.

Holmboe was one of those who volunteered with eight others from his school, including the headteacher, but their planning was paying off. Families were receiving the equivalent of their husband's salary from the fund that had been prepared. Around 650 teachers, including Holmboe, were then transferred from local prisons to the Grini concentration camp, just outside Oslo. The SS Commander of the camp was a sadist by the name of Koch who carried a whip and was always followed closely by a large Alsation. On one occasion he was haranguing the imprisoned teachers. 'You must not think you will be martyrs or that a few dirty teachers will be able to stop the New Order for Europe!' he bellowed at them. But his dog was not impressed and at the conclusion of this lecture promptly vomited onto the ground.

The treatment at Grini was a brutal mix of severe physical exercise including running in snow, 'torture gymnastics' and starvation designed to wear down their morale. At regular intervals the men were marched into the administration block and asked to retract their protests, but only 32 of the 867 gave in.

On the outside, the remaining teachers faced a difficult problem. There were persistent rumours that if the free teachers did not comply, some of the prisoners would be shot. How could they continue to resist if their actions caused the execution of husbands and fathers? At this, Hakon Holmboe's wife made a brave decision. She went to those who were considering giving up and told them, 'The wives don't want you to give in. We will take the chance'. On 12th April 1942 the prisoners were transported by rail in cattle trucks and transferred to a ship which sailed north for the port of Kirkenes, well inside the Arctic Circle. Here, the men were forced into labor at the docks in freezing conditions, unloading and loading ships for the German war effort. Their well publicised exile in the Arctic Circle only made their fate more prominent in Norway. Quisling knew that any further action against the teachers at Kirkenes would create a backlash even more difficult to deal with.

On 22nd May, Quisling arrived by car at the local high school in the village of Stabekk with his Minister for Education. The teachers were gathered together in the gymnasium and Quisling proceeded to rant and yell at them. He ended with words which became folklore in Norway, 'You teachers have destroyed everything for me'. 'That sentence was a triumph for us' said Holmboe, 'The teachers had blocked Quisling's whole plan of organising the new corporate state'. Gradually the teachers were shipped back from Kirkenes – most of them had never signed the agreement to join the Nazi teachers organisation. They returned as heroes, met at train stations across the country with flowers and food and offered rooms at the best hotels. Holmboe himself reached home on 20th November after exactly eight months in captivity.

Gene's time in Norway had been happy and productive. He loved the wild open spaces and the spectacular views down the fjords and had even learned to speak pretty good Norwegian. Crucially, in his study of different struggles around the world, he had begun to collect references to individual nonviolent methods of action, listing and categorising them like a taxonomist. By the spring of 1960, he had compiled a paper listing 65 distinct methods of nonviolent action and took a number of copies to 'The Positive Action Conference on Peace and Security' in Accra, Ghana.

In a continent where many countries were still under European colonial rule, the list of nonviolent methods was a revelation among the African delegates. Copying machines at the conference ran hot as hundreds of facsimiles of the list were spat out. Many just wrote the list down with paper and pen. 'I was amazed at the intense interest shown by delegates from Somalia and South Africa, both still under European rule', Gene wrote, 'This was an indication that descriptive studies could be seen to be relevant in real-world conflicts.'

There was still substantial cynicism about the effectiveness of nonviolent action among some of the delegates including Frantz Fanon, a West Indian political philosopher from the French colony of Martinique. Fanon had written a book, 'Wretched of the Earth', which advocated violence by colonised people against their colonisers. He remonstrated with Gene about the use of nonviolent strategy. 'In Algeria we tried nonviolence. We had a labour strike and school boycott and the French came down and arrested so many people we had to give it up', he told him. Gene bristled at this, now well-worn criticism. 'When they went over to guerrilla warfare and suffered the first casualties they didn't give up guerrilla warfare.'

Gene argued it was a myth that nonviolent struggle produced greater numbers of casualties than armed insurrection. In Algeria the estimates of Algerian dead during the War of National Liberation eventually reached one million out of a population of nine million. It had left more than 10% of their population dead.

In a later lecture Gene told an audience, 'There is this romantic belief that violence is the most powerful thing. You can hold it in reserve. When other means give you grounds for discouragement you fall back on it without any careful calculation or strategic analysis of why you're going to succeed more easily, more quickly, with fewer casualties or with better results as far as the kind of society and political system that results.' In case after case where Gene talked to people who had shifted from nonviolence to violence, no one could give him a satisfactory answer as to why resistance groups could gain greater success by shifting to violence. Gene returned from Accra enthused by the reception to his work and the challenge laid down by its critics, but he was about to clash with a man who would become a titan of peace research in Europe – Johan Galtung.

Galtung was a Norwegian child prodigy whose teacher had allowed him to teach his own classmates in elementary school. His parents were influential physicians and he was known to have a very high opinion of himself, with some justification. By the age of 27, Galtung had already earned two PhDs, one in mathematics and the other in sociology. He had been appointed as an assistant professor at Columbia University for five semesters, but at the end of 1959 he returned home to Oslo and suggested that Gene should become his assistant. This went down very badly indeed, and to make matters worse, the funds that Gene needed for his work on 'nonviolent struggle' were now diverted into Galtung's very different field of 'peace research'. Gene had long since concluded that 'peace studies' were not going to make the necessary impact.

George Lakey a young American academic at the university heard the discontent from both sides. 'To Galtung, Gene wasn't a social scientist, he was a journalist who was fascinated with stories of people's struggles. He writes them down and makes lists of things that might or might not be variables, or conditions, or something. Gene to him was list maker.' In seeking an escape from Galtung, Gene set off for his next position at Oxford University on a mission to prove Galtung wrong.

The lessons he would take back from Norway were quite clear – an organised nonviolent defence of a country could be a significant form of combat against an occupying force attempting to gain administrative control. If advanced correctly, a civilian based, nonviolent defence, might just replace the requirement for military conflict or, act as a deterrent to an invasion. If a population could be trained to use nonviolent resistance effectively against an invading force by refusing to operate the factories, mine the natural resources or co-operate with new laws – if they could blockade the communications systems and cause enemy soldiers to refuse to carry out orders and even defect, perhaps they could make a country so ungovernable that they could actually repel or deter an invasion without the need for weapons. The theory would be called 'civilian based defence'.

Gene published a pamphlet about the Norwegian teachers called, 'Tyranny Could Not Quell Them'. At the end of the book he included a list of 14 actions inspired by the struggle to be taken in a nonviolent defence of a country. These ranged from 'decentralisation of power and decision making' to 'creation of a nonviolent defence academy' and preparation of 'an elaborate contact system of persons thoroughly versed in unarmed defence'.

In his conclusion he wrote, 'The deterrent effect of a nation prepared for nonviolent resistance to any oppression might well be far greater than that produced by military means today – and without the threat of universal destruction. In this search for freedom there is a special place of honour for the heroes of the Kirkenes Journey'.

For the rest of his career Gene would be confronted by a common refrain – nonviolent action could never work against a dictatorship as brutal as Hitler's Germany, but the story of Holmboe and the Norwegian teachers proved that it *was* possible.

Eureka

Gene's Oxford was not the one of dreaming spires and May balls. He rented a semi-detached house in the suburb of Headington which was unheated and kept barely above freezing in winter with some unattractive plastic insulation on the windows. A family of white mice served as a distraction from study.

One afternoon, in a moment of inspiration, or perhaps frustration, he pushed the cheap furniture to the sides of the sitting room and collapsed to his knees, scattering the carpet around him with hundreds of pieces of paper, scrawled with faded writing. For years he had been collecting every historical reference to a nonviolent action he could find, writing them down on index cards and tying them together into small bundles. It was here, not at the desk of an ancient Oxford college library, that he would have his eureka moment.

Since he had begun seriously studying his subject, he found that historical examples where nonviolent struggle had won victories against tyranny had been almost entirely written out of the history books. But when he looked more closely he began to find small references and mentions of nonviolent resistance activity going back hundreds of years.

In around 26 AD, Jews protesting the raising of idolatrous images in Jerusalem were surrounded by the soldiers of Pontius Pilate who threatened them with death. The Jews responded that they would rather die than allow the Torah to be violated. In 5th century Greece, the playwright Aristphophanes wrote an anti-war drama called Lysistrata where Athenian women banded together and refused sexual favours to their husbands until they agreed to stop fighting.

There had also been nonviolent resistance by the people of the Netherlands to Spanish rule in the 16th century, but all of these accounts were fragments and footnotes and never taken seriously by classic or contemporary historians. This contrasted with the most detailed records of military warfare kept through the centuries and carefully studied at defence academies.

It is perhaps not surprising that rulers through the ages have wanted to keep the full potential of civil resistance a secret from their citizens and to starve this idea of attention or study. Governments have always sought to hold the monopoly on military force, but dictators and even democratic leaders have also feared the power their own people could develop, if they learned to organise properly.

Gene's mission in Norway and now at Oxford University was to put that right – to uncover the lost history of nonviolent struggle and piece together a coherent analysis of how it worked in theory and practice. In the process, he hoped, he might be able to produce a good enough thesis to win his doctorate.

His supervisor on arrival at St Catherine's College was John Plamenatz, a 48-year-old political philosopher who had been a member of his native Yugoslav government in exile during the Second World War. Thoughtful and patient, Plamenatz knew that despite the absence of rich narrative historical records, clues on the power of nonviolent struggle survived in the writings of the most revered political theorists. Hobbes, Locke, Rousseau and Etienne De La Boetie all had something important to say about the 'dangers' of nonviolent resistance to a ruler.

Born in 1530, the French philosopher Etienne de La Boetie published his discourse 'On Voluntary Servitude', also known as 'The Anti-Dictator' at just 18 years old. 'Why in the world do people agree to be looted and otherwise oppressed by government overlords?' he asked. 'It is not just fear, for our consent is required and that consent can be nonviolently withdrawn'.

In his guidebook for heads of state, 'The Prince' (1532), Niccolò Machiavelli said of the potential power of citizens. 'Who has the public as a whole for his enemy can never make himself secure; and the greater his cruelty, the weaker does his regime become.' English philosopher, Thomas Hobbes, In his classic work, 'Leviathan' (1651), feared society falling into a 'nasty brutish and short' 'state of nature' so much that he implored obedience to an authoritarian ruler. But in acknowledging the potential chaos if the people did not obey, he revealed an understanding of the power of ordinary citizens over their rulers if they chose to withdraw that obedience.

As Gene studied the political theorists and their ideas of political power, he continued to unearth previously forgotten examples of nonviolent struggles which had taken place all over the world and recorded them in ever-growing stacks of index cards.

What he realised when spreading all of these out on his living room floor in Oxford was that all of the dictators he had studied relied on the support of the people they ruled for their maintenance of power. A ruler was just a man or woman born like any other, they had no special qualities other than their ability to maintain the consent of those they ruled. 'I realised if you can identify the sources of a government's power, such as legitimacy, popular support, institutional support – then you know on what that dictatorship depends for its existence.' These sources of political power, he wrote, included:

Authority, the belief among the people that the regime is legitimate, and that they have a moral duty to obey it.

Human resources, the number and importance of the persons and groups which are obeying, cooperating, or providing assistance to the rulers.

Skills and knowledge, needed by the regime to perform specific actions and supplied by the cooperating persons and groups, including scientists, engineers and key workers in industry.

Intangible factors, psychological and ideological factors that may induce people to obey and assist the rulers, including religion, tribal loyalty and social class.

Material resources, the degree to which the rulers control or have access to property, natural resources, financial resources, the economic system, and means of communication and transportation; and

Sanctions, punishments, threatened or applied, against the disobedient and noncooperative to ensure the submission and cooperation that are needed for the regime to exist and carry out its policies.

These sources of power were contained in institutions like the police, the army, religious organisations, the judiciary, corporations, media and civil society that would later be called the 'pillars of support' – a helpful image in describing the function they played in 'holding up' a government.

'Since all those sources of power are dependent upon the good will, cooperation, and obedience of people and institutions, then your job becomes fairly simple'. Gene explained. 'All you have to do is shrink that support and that legitimacy, that co-operation and the regime will be weakened, and if you can take those sources away, the regime will fall.'

This idea that power wasn't monolithic, but instead came from many sources within society was totally at odds with fashionable thinking in the 1960s. Power was traditionally understood to come from the top down to the people and thus revolution was seen as a violent action designed to decapitate the ruler from the body, instead of removing the sources of power from their grasp.

Violence had been the traditional option with little track record of success. Historical examples showed that activists who violently attacked the sources of a ruler's power, generally fared much worse than those who concentrated on co-opting them.

If the police, army and those supporting the government were attacked with violence, their people killed and injured, they would rally around a dictator more strongly, giving them legitimacy in suppressing the resistance. Fighting the armed forces of a dictatorship meant fighting against their best weapons, often against an expertly trained military, in a type of conflict where they had overwhelming force.

However, if these institutions could be infiltrated and convinced of the legitimacy of the democratic cause, so that they refused to shoot, stopped following orders and joined the resistance, the dictator would be left unable to carry out his will. This was the means by which an unarmed democratic movement could win.

A nonviolent campaign allowed all citizens to take part in the struggle – men, women, the very young and the very old, shopkeepers, farmers and administrators. They would almost certainly face severe repression, casualties and even considerable loss of life, but this form of action had distinct advantages.

Physical destruction of the state could be avoided by maintaining a nonviolent campaign, its resources and infrastructure could be preserved and the path to stable democracy far more easily navigated if the society had not been torn apart by its citizens killing one another. At the very least the number of deaths might be vastly reduced.

The evidence that nonviolent campaigns could be more successful than violent campaigns was anecdotal at this time and it would take another 50 years before this theory was proved by a major quantitative data study by Erica Chenoweth and Maria Stephan in 2011 – but the theory *was* eventually proved.

The identification of the sources of power was a breakthrough in Gene's thinking – people didn't have to have a religious or moral belief in nonviolence like Gandhi or Martin Luther King in order for them to act nonviolently. Nonviolent action was the most effective way of shifting the sources of a dictator's power to the democratic side and winning freedom. 'That was a sort of eureka moment', Gene remembered, 'this was not just a theory, it was something that had actually been applied in many different historical cases. That was very, very important. I felt greatly relieved because that's what made it all reality'.

Despite the feeling of enormous breakthrough, Gene told nobody of his eureka moment. With practically no contemporaries in his academic field, he was still pretty much working alone, 'I just didn't know anyone who was interested in that kind of thing'. That loneliness and stress of his workload frequently threatened to overcome him. The academic hothouse of Oxford University was far harder than anything he had experienced. In addition to work on his thesis, he was expected to write book reviews and complete endless reading lists. 'I was sometimes overwhelmed and I got a little depressed because I was trying to do so many things… It seemed like too much.'

Sometimes in order to regain some clarity he undertook some minor actions of his own. In December 1962, Gene suggested the idea of a public hunger strike to protest against the disproportionate amount of money the British government was spending on weapons. He wanted to carry it out from the 23rd December through Christmas Day and Boxing Day, which he felt would be the most disturbing to the citizens of Oxford. The location was the corner of All Saints Church on the High Street. Not only were there plenty of passing Christmas shoppers, but All Saints was the official city church of Oxford where the Mayor and the city's business leaders were expected to worship.

Four pacifist undergraduate students were recruited, including Hugh Brody, who would go on to become a famous anthropologist. The five men sat shivering by some railings in near freezing temperatures, wearing nothing but their normal jeans and coats, holding placards telling the public what they were doing. One read, 'Britain spends £53 a second on weapons!'

Gene looked after the four younger men, making sure they were drinking hot drinks and even supplied Hugh Brody with some battery powered, heated socks, when his toes began to suffer badly from the cold.

When Christmas Day came, the dignitaries of Oxford filed past their protest, perched just adjacent to the main doors of the church. 'The impact was astonishing', Brody remembered, 'Gene's instincts were so good. The idea that we would fast over Christmas was close to unbearable for people. It was a drop in the ocean in history, but at that moment, at that time, for the citizens we talked to and for us it was very, very powerful.' The day after Boxing Day, Gene broke the fast with a home made nut loaf at home in Headington. It was the combination of the intellectual and his care for the younger students that Hugh Brody remembered most.

Hunger strike was just one of many nonviolent methods stored away in Gene's card indexes, collected over the course of years of research. He had now identified 198 methods of nonviolent action and subdivided these into three categories. The first was, 'Methods of Nonviolent Protest and Persuasion', which included symbolic acts like No.2 Letters of opposition or support, No.18 Display of flags and symbolic colours, No.38 Marches, No.44 Mock funerals, No.51 Walkouts and No.35 Humorous skits and pranks.

Then there were the stronger 'Methods of Social Noncooperation' – No.57. Lysistratic nonaction (sex strike), No.69 Collective disappearance, No.71 Consumers boycott and No.117 General Strike. The final category was 'Methods of Nonviolent Intervention', which included some of the most serious methods available, No.59 Hunger strike, No.183 Nonviolent land seizure and No.192 Alternative economic institutions, among many more.

He would later describe all of these methods as 'nonviolent weapons', 'the direct equivalent of military weapons'. An army might use guns and bombs, but a nonviolent movement would use strikes, boycotts and blockades, social and economic weapons. After a decade of work he stopped the list at 198. There was no point in continuing beyond that number – every campaign and every movement would originate its own methods and though he could quite easily have rounded up to 200, 198 was a number that suggested incompleteness and invited addition.

None of the 198 methods were new inventions, but once classified, the list showed for the first time how many nonviolent weapons were available for fighting repression and demonstrated how few of the available methods were routinely used.

Often groups would stage a significant protest march like the one to Aldermaston and when there was no change in the government's policies they would become despondent and give up. The list showed that marching was just one of the least powerful of 198 methods available. Lamenting the small promotion of the available methods of nonviolent action in regular use, Gene told George Lakey, 'We are simply at the bow and arrow stage of the development of nonviolent struggle'.

Gene now decided to pursue an avenue first suggested in Richard Gregg's (1934) book *The Power of Nonviolence*. A nonviolent movement had to develop strategic planning, and the best place to learn about strategy was from the military. No military commander would ever dream of putting 1000 soldiers on a battlefield without a strategy for how to use them and so it was of nonviolent action. Just as the uncoordinated use of military weapons like bows and arrows or tanks and guns without any strategy for their use would ultimately lead to failure, nonviolent weapons would need the same kind of strategic vision to be successful. By applying military-style discipline and training to nonviolent campaigns, Gene believed it was possible to turn nonviolent action into a credible national 'defence system' against invasion or for bringing down a dictatorship.

Emboldened by his successful experience with Einstein, Gene sought out one of the most eminent and influential military strategists in Britain to help him. Sir Basil Liddell Hart had seen the slaughter of the First World War first hand. Injured on the Western Front by a shell burst in 1915, he returned to the trenches in time to take part in the Battle of the Somme. On 18th July 1916, he was hit and injured three times, but continued advancing toward the enemy until he was overcome by poison gas and evacuated by medics.

His injury would save his life. Sixty thousand men lost their lives that day and his own battalion was all but wiped out. The experience of this abject slaughter affected him profoundly for the rest of his life. He went on to write the biographies of several major military figures and became a military advisor to British Prime Minister, Neville Chamberlain. He won similar acclaim on the other side of the Atlantic, John F. Kennedy writing shortly before becoming US President, 'No expert on military affairs has better earned the right to respectful attention than B.H. Liddell Hart'.

An unconventional visionary, Sir Basil thought about all of the factors which could throw an enemy off balance, not just the military components. Many experienced military figures would have dismissed a young researcher on nonviolent action, but not Liddell Hart. He was a radical inside the establishment, challenging the military thinking which had orchestrated the slaughter of the First World War. He knew that his theories, if applied to nonviolent action, could be as innovative as they had been with military warfare.

In the summer of 1958, just after moving to Oslo, Gene wrote to Liddell Hart explaining that he was undertaking a major piece of writing comparing the methods of analysis of military struggle with those of nonviolent struggles and asking for some advice on readings. 'I wonder if you could suggest two or three of the best sources for the objectives and method of analysis applied to military campaigns?.... I thought you would be the best person to advise me.' On the question of the best books on the subject, Liddell Hart was less than modest. He wrote back, 'I do not know of any modern book which really provides an epitome of the principles of military strategy – apart from my own book, *Strategy: The Indirect Approach*.

Shortly after his return from Norway to England, Liddell Hart noticed Gene's reappearance in the country and wrote to him at Oxford to invite him for tea.

'Dear Mr Sharp, I was very interested to see in the Sunday Telegraph yesterday that you are now at Oxford … If you see a chance of coming this way any time, I should much enjoy having a talk. You could also see my files which might be of possible help to you.'

Gene set off in his car a few weeks later, tearing through the country lanes and villages of Oxfordshire until he reached the Dog and Badger Inn, the sign to turn off and climb the hill to the Liddell Hart manor. Gene was ushered into an armchair in the study where Lawrence of Arabia had once sat when Liddell Hart had been writing his biography. Tall, stooping, with a wisp of hair whipped across his head and a thick moustache, Liddell Hart stood at his mantlepiece chewing his trademark pipe, a Duncan De Luxe No. 34.

Over tea and cake, he told Gene that work on nonviolent resistance was extremely valuable and suggested he investigate nonviolent resistance in Denmark during the Nazi occupation which, 'had the least mixture of violence, while in many ways proving to be the most effective and most baffling to the occupiers.'

Liddell Hart's most celebrated theory was 'The Indirect Approach', derived from his experience of trench warfare which had seen thousands of young men advance directly into devastating machine gun fire. He suggested that the key components of 'The Indirect Approach', despite being conceived with military means in mind, might be consistent with well planned and co-ordinated nonviolent action.

1. Direct attacks against an enemy firmly in position almost never work and should never be attempted.
2. To defeat the enemy one must first upset his equilibrium which is not accomplished by the main attack, but must be done before the main attack can succeed.

Later, in *The Politics of Nonviolent Action*, Gene wrote, 'The technique of nonviolent action can be regarded as an extreme development of 'the indirect approach to military strategy as formulated by Liddell Hart'. The 'general principles are all applicable to the use of nonviolent action against an opponent using military means, so that the opponent's means of action are always confronted indirectly and his power of repression made to rebound against him in a kind of political jujitsu. Finally, the very sources of his power are reduced or removed without having been confronted by the same means of action.'

Gene set off back to Oxford energised by his encounter. For some time he had recognised the potential for nonviolent resistance to become a realistic deterrent to a Soviet invasion of western Europe. Gandhi's resistance to the British and the Norwegian teachers' non-cooperation with the Nazis proved that there was potential in nonviolent action. If the technique could be further refined he was confident that a belligerent population trained in its use, could be a difficult enough prospect to deter invasion.

This was a new form of warfare, but it had no agreed name. Journalists, politicians and even participants themselves used the terms 'peaceful protest', 'civil resistance', 'passive resistance', 'non-violent resistance' and 'nonviolence' interchangeably. Gene began efforts to define the vocabulary and sort out the linguistic chaos that hundreds of years of academic neglect had waged on the words used to describe the phenomenon.

Gene hated the terms 'non-violence' and 'passive resistance', which seemed to mean 'no violence' but the presence of nothing else to replace it. 'Passive resistance' meant not doing anything but refusing – 'civil resistance' was the resistance of civilians but didn't necessarily mean the absence of violence. To some of the most devout Christians and purist

Gandhians, even name calling was 'psychological violence' which had to be avoided. According to some of them, an opponent must be loved until their heart melted. Gene regularly told them in no uncertain terms that he thought this approach was 'mushy'.

To bring some order, the term he decided upon was 'nonviolent struggle'. He struck the hyphen from 'non-violent' making it for the first time a fully fledged word, not a conjunction, and teamed it with 'struggle' or occasionally 'action' to make it clear that this was an activity, not simply the absence of violent behaviour. 'Nonviolent struggle' and 'nonviolent action' – these were the foundations of an academic field – the opening shots in a battle for terminology that he would wage for the next 50 years.

Basil Liddell Hart's encouragement was a major victory and there were others in the establishment who thought the same way too. Stephen King-Hall was a retired naval commander, Minister of Parliament and aristocrat who carried the title of 'Baron'. In 1958 he published a book, *Defence in the Nuclear Age*, which advocated a policy of nuclear disarmament and a defence policy based upon a mixture of conventional military forces and nonviolent resistance. He called for a Royal Commission to study the potential of this form of defence for Britain and its allies, which might render nuclear weapons redundant. His arguments received positive reviews, but King-Hall was frustrated by his failure to breach what he called the 'thought barrier' among his peers in the establishment.

Nevertheless, there were enough credible thinkers in the west to bring together a meeting on the topic. Gene set about organising a conference in Oxford which would gather the biggest names in the field to discuss the potential of what he now called 'Civilian Based Defence'. The speakers would present papers on a variety of subjects, including: 'Forms of Military Attack' by Alun Gwynne Jones, then military correspondent of the *London Times*, later Minister of State for Foreign Affairs; 'The Coup d'Etat' by Lieutenant-Colonel D.J. Goodspeed, military historian; and 'Aspects of Totalitarian Systems' by Professor Ernest Bramsted, a noted researcher on dictatorships. The conference led to the publication of a book of these contributions titled, *The Strategy of Civilian Defence,* in 1967. Together, the conference and the book that followed established civil resistance as a serious subject, not just empty optimism, and considerably raised the profile of the subject among the academic and political elite.

The term 'Civilian Defence' began to be deliberately employed by the few academics operating in the field. 'Trans-armament' was substituted for 'disarmament' to indicate that the idea was not to leave a country defenceless, but to change from one type of defence system to another.

Gene had now established a modus operandi. He was concerned with peace, but while the bulk of the peace community stood outside of the establishment, he saw the cooperation and collaboration of establishment figures like Liddell Hart and Stephen King Hall as essential to his success. For civilian based defence to work, it had to win the approval of the most senior figures in western governments.

However naive anyone believed this mission to be, they could not fault its audacity. Thousands of troops stared each other down across the iron curtain in Eastern Europe and hundreds of nuclear warheads with many times the explosive power of those that destroyed Hiroshima and Nagasaki were targeted at cities in Europe, the United States and the Soviet Union.

Most political leaders, academics and military officers accepted this as an irrevocable status quo, but Gene was working towards another way, by actually turning the populations of countries threatened with Soviet invasion into a weapon system.

Cold War

Few people understood as well as Thomas Schelling how nuclear war and the end of the known world would play out if it came. The Harvard professor was the US government's umpire in some of the most high level nuclear war games ever conducted. He presided over the reactions of the key decision makers from the White House to the State Department, the Department of Defense and the CIA, and then analysed them so the game could be played better.

It was this experience which made Schelling push for the installation of the first presidential hotline or 'red telephone' to Moscow, to prevent an escalating conflict turning nuclear. He also provided director, Stanley Kubrick, with much of the nightmarish reality for his apocalyptic film, *Dr Strangelove*. Perhaps it was no surprise then that when he noticed someone trying to provide an alternative to mutually assured destruction, he would try and help.

In 1963, Schelling was based at Harvard University's Center for International Affairs, a revolving door of elder foreign statesman and a think tank for the up and coming US foreign policy elite. It was here that he first came across Gene's work – two articles in the Journal of Conflict Resolution – one on Gandhi's strategy and another on nonviolent resistance.

He found the ideas so intriguing that he assigned them to a class he was teaching and included questions on Gene's theories in end of year exams. 'Two things impressed me', Schelling told me. 'This was the first time I had ever heard of the subject of nonviolence [as an academic discipline] and secondly I was astonished that he had so much to say about it.'

Just a few months later he was travelling to Norway for a conference at the Nobel Peace Centre in Oslo when a colleague told him Gene Sharp was in town. They arranged to meet up over dinner and Gene made his pitch – mass training of European citizens in nonviolent resistance might make Western Europe so difficult to occupy successfully that the Soviet Union could be deterred from mounting an invasion. Schelling was intrigued, if not entirely convinced. Gene handed over an 800 page draft of his doctoral thesis which he said he wanted to turn into a book, *The Politics of Nonviolent Action*, and asked whether there might be a place at Harvard for him finish it.

Handing over such a weighty manuscript could have backfired, but Schelling found time in his packed schedule to read it, and found it fascinating. 'I couldn't believe that you could fill a whole book with nonviolent resistance. He not only had an argument but a lot of historical examples.' he remembered. A month later, he wrote to tell Gene that he had found some funds to offer him a place at Harvard and provide a modest salary. This was partly, Schelling joked, so that he could shorten the manuscript. In the end Gene would make it even longer.

Just before his move back to the United States, Gene was one of the guests invited to watch Martin Luther King Jr. receive the Nobel Peace Prize for his work leading the civil rights movement in the United States. In the echoing marble clad walls of Oslo City Hall, King told the packed assembly of invited guests;

'this award which I receive on behalf of that movement is a profound recognition that nonviolence is the answer to the crucial political and moral question of our time – the need for man to overcome oppression and violence without resorting to violence and oppression. Civilization and violence are antithetical concepts.'

In King's speech Gene heard the unmistakable influence of his friend Bayard Rustin whose job he had taken in the office of A.J. Muste and with whom he had marched to Aldermaston. Bayard was one of the key advisors to King on nonviolent struggle and credited with much of the civil rights movement strategy. King's Nobel speech re-energised Gene and reassured him that his work was only growing in importance.

In 1965 he arrived in Cambridge, Massachusetts for his appointment at Harvard and began work in a cube office just down the hall from

Schelling. Although they rarely met up, Schelling was immediately struck by his dedication, 'He did nothing but work – not very outgoing, almost religiously committed to working on nonviolence. He was relieved at my support because I don't know that he really had any other prospect.'

The support Schelling offered was primarily financial, not academic. He began looking for funding for Gene's work from the Ford Foundation, set up by Henry Ford's family to spread democratic values, but it was the US Department for Defense 'Advanced Research Projects Agency' (ARPA) which would stump up the first serious cash. Although he was not aware of it at the time, the ARPA money was a component of a classified US government effort to develop weapons and strategies for fighting counter-insurgencies and curtail communist advances in remote parts of the world. The scope ranged from the design of flamethrowers to development and testing of the defoliant Agent Orange which would cause lasting birth defects and misery in Vietnam. At the more mundane end of the spectrum were academic studies of revolution, insurgency and counter-insurgency run by academics at universities throughout the country.

When challenged on this later by members of pacifist organisations, Gene was unapologetic about receiving the Department of Defense money. He'd been arguing since his time at Oxford that governments should finance research into nonviolent resistance as a substitute for war and that this should be fully integrated into national defense strategy.

Gene's ambition was not to do away with human conflict but to provide a realistic alternative – for people to fight wars without violence. His vision was always that it would be used by civilians either dominated by a dictatorship or occupied by an outside force – empowering people to take control over their own struggles and to liberate themselves. When asked this question in public events he would often answer simply by asking, 'would you rather the money be used for waging war?'

Far from being embraced by the foreign policy elite at Harvard, he often spent months battling to stop the authorities kicking him out. Strict rules governed how long a visiting academic could stay as a lecturer in the department and he had to use every possible bureaucratic manoeuvre to overstay. His magnus opus and the reason he had been given a desk, *The Politics of Nonviolent Action,* had still not been completed and worse still, the ARPA funding had run out. 'I would much prefer to stay around here, I am tired of moving all around the world', he wrote to Schelling, begging for another extension.

The man deciding Gene's fate was the director of the Centre for International Affairs, Joe Nye, a former Rhodes Scholar at Oxford and Harvard PhD. Nye would go on to develop the influential theory of 'soft power' and chair the National Intelligence Council for President Bill Clinton. When the administrators began their attempt to eject Gene from the Center for International Affairs, Joe Nye stepped in. 'There were questions as to whether he had been there too long and I said, "no, we're going to keep him". I always admired Gene as original, thoughtful and committed. He's always marched to his own drum and that's a good thing. He had a particular area he wanted to cultivate and he wanted to relate it to policy. He wasn't going to play the academic game of publishing articles and refereeing journals.'

Saved from expulsion, Gene continued his research at Harvard with an additional stipend from teaching 'revolution, guerrilla warfare and nonviolent action' at the Southeastern Massachusetts University. In July 1969, the Oxford examinations board wrote, earlier than expected, to arrange his 'viva', the oral defence of his thesis, and the final hurdle to win his doctorate. After a short trip back to England for the exam, he returned to the United States as Dr. Gene Sharp.

With his doctorate from one of the most famous universities in the world and a secure job, he was at last able to buy his own home. No.36 Cottage Street was a handsome four-story townhouse just a few minutes walk from East Boston's harbour, but the building was in a desperate state of repair. The real estate agent admitted that the former owner had been killed in some kind of dispute and a sale was needed urgently. It wasn't a great sum of money, but Gene had to borrow almost all of it and there were few modern conveniences, not even a working toilet.

The sale went through in the Fall and he improvised a bed on the fourth floor of his new home, slinging a door across some bricks and laying a mattress on top. It wasn't much better than the living conditions he had endured 20 years previously in New York, but at 40 years old, he at last owned his own home.

After almost ten years of writing and research, *The Politics of Nonviolent Action* was finally completed in 1973. First published in a single hardback volume, it quickly gained the highest praise from across the political, military and peace community. Among those who published reviews were Martin Luther King's wife, Coretta Scott King and economist Kenneth Boulding who wrote, 'this volume... reminds one of (Adam Smith's) *The Wealth of Nations.*' Others described Gene as the 'Clausewitz of nonviolent warfare' and 'the Machiavelli of nonviolence'. Senior army officers said it should be required reading at military schools. The publication of *The Politics*, as he would call it, at last cemented Gene's position in the academic community, but it was never likely to be a commercial success and his money was soon running out again.

In 1975, Gene was searching for another two-year funding grant and Schelling recommended him back to the Department of Defense. It was clear Schelling had potential funding contacts in the CIA, but Gene was adamant that he would refuse to take their money. This seems like a slightly nebulous position given that the State Department and the CIA were both tasked by the same political masters in the White House, but at the time there were increasing press reports which indicated that the intelligence agency was out of control.

Several exposés of CIA election manipulation in foreign states were so serious that 'The Church Committee' was set up in 1975 to publicly investigate the role of the agency in overseas elections. This dark art had been christened by those who developed it as 'political warfare'.

The CIA involvement in election manipulation dated back to the end of the Second World War when communism was on the rise in Europe and it was feared that a Soviet takeover might not happen by conventional war, but by covert influence upon elections. The first ever CIA operation began with a growing horror that the communists were likely to win the Italian election due to be held in 1948.

Italy was a key strategic ally of the United States with vital ports on the Mediterranean that the Americans believed were too important to lose. If the Soviet Union gained control of Italy they believed it, 'could dominate the Western Mediterranean and apply substantial military power against the Balkans and Western Europe'. *Time* magazine published a near hysterical article declaring that a communist victory in Italy would bring the west to 'the brink of catastrophe'.

The Soviets were equally aware that Italy was almost within their grasp and redoubled their efforts to secure an election victory, funding the local communist party in an operation run out of their headquarters in Villa Abomelek, a palatial 17th century residence on the outskirts of Rome.

The Italian Communist Party was the biggest outside the Soviet Union and its membership was rising sharply among the disaffected workers in the country's famous industrial plants and car factories. The Soviets aimed to stir up that dissatisfaction further with propaganda. They published newspapers, leaflets and posters with disinformation about the serving government and funded student organisations, womens groups and labour unions. At its peak, US intelligence estimated that the Soviets were spending between $8–10 million a month on their Italian operation.

The mastermind of the US counter-attack was General George Marshall who, after an illustrious military career had just been appointed US Secretary of State by President Truman. It was his eponymous 'Marshall Plan' that made his name, releasing millions of dollars to rehabilitate the war ruined economies of Europe. But while the economic assistance package was celebrated publicly as an example of American economic might and beneficence, Marshall believed that in order to fight Soviet propaganda and keep the communists out of Italy, they needed a separate, secret programme. This policy was driven by a man who was perhaps the most powerful Sovietologist in Washington.

In July 1947, *Foreign Affairs* magazine published an alarming despatch by a Moscow based, US diplomat. The author who wrote under the pen name, Mr X, argued that Stalin's aggressive foreign policy had to be urgently contained. 'The main element of any United States policy toward the Soviet Union must be that of a long-term, patient … and vigilant containment of Russian expansive tendencies.' He continued, 'my conviction is that the problem is within our power to solve, and that without recourse to any general military conflict'. The notoriety of the article won much admiration from the anti-Soviet hawks in Washington and was credited with birthing the US policy of 'containment' towards the Soviet Union.

The mystery author was George Kennan, the US Deputy Chief of Mission to the USSR. On his return to the United States, George Marshall appointed Kennan as the first Director of Policy and Planning at the State Department (the Secretary of State's internal think tank). Here he would become Marshall's right hand man and have enormous influence over Cold War policy. Kennan wanted to protect US interests by influencing the way people voted – even in democratic countries like Italy.

Italian democrats urgently needed assistance to stop the Communists gaining control, but at first no-one in the US establishment wanted to take responsibility for doing this work. Marshall didn't want a covert programme run out of the State Department because the mission was too sensitive and the department was leaky – it had to be a secret operation. But the director of the newly created CIA, Admiral Roscoe H. Hillenkoetter, didn't want it either, arguing that it was too far from the traditional intelligence gathering mission. In the end Hillenkoetter relented and took on the mission, but only on the assurance from Kennan that he would be held equally politically responsible if anything went wrong.

National Security Council Directive NSC 4-A, 'Report to the National Security Council by the Executive Secretary on Psychological Operations', was approved on the 22nd December 1947, ordering a range of covert activities to prevent the communists winning the imminent Italian election. It established that while the State Department would oversee 'informational activities', the CIA would be charged with executing 'covert psychological operations'. The directive was considered so secret that only three copies were produced – the first kept in Hillenkoetter's safe at the CIA, another at the State Department with George Kennan, and the third at the White House.

One of the men charged with the execution of NSC 4/a was Felton Mark Wyatt, a 27-year-old CIA officer and Second World War navy veteran. Wyatt pulled together a team of influential US political consultants, some of whom had Italian heritage or could speak Italian and were willing to be flown into the country to give advice to Italian political parties on how to win elections.

The mission was to support the existing centrist coalition government led by Prime Minister Alcide De Gasperi and his Christian Democrat Party. The CIA money was poured into anti-communist newspapers, publishing houses and radio stations. Cartoonists were employed to ridicule communists and the Soviet Union and portray Stalin as a buffoon. The plan was not sophisticated – it often involved simply depositing black bags of cash at dead drops and handing suitcases through car windows in lay-bys across Italy. The new CIA was making it up as it went along.

They quickly developed more devious methods of subversion, including the leaking of forged letters to discredit the leadership of the Italian communist party, spreading fabricated sex scandals and rumours of repressive measures the communists would take against the Catholic Church if they won. The financial assistance and training by election specialists and branding experts involved everyone from local civic committees to Pope Paul VI while he was still serving as the Archbishop of Milan.

There was delight in Washington and particularly at CIA headquarters when the news came through of the Christian Democrat's victory in the election. Gasperi had won with 48% of the vote, with the communists polling just 7% – a result which must have prompted questions about whether there had been any real threat at all. Nevertheless, the CIA's first covert political action was hailed as a stunning success by those who were permitted to know. It served as a model for their political operations all over the world for at least the next 35 years. George Kennan was so enthused by the prospect of non-military means of containing the Soviets he wrote a short treatise, titled, 'The Inauguration of Organized Political Warfare'. He described this new phenomenon as:

'the employment of all the means at a nation's command, short of war, to achieve its national objectives. Such operations are both overt and covert. They range from such overt actions as political alliances, economic measures … and "white" propaganda to such covert operations as clandestine support of "friendly" foreign elements, "black" psychological warfare and even encouragement of underground resistance in hostile states.'

The Soviets were engaged in election manipulations with equal fervour. A study by political scientist Dov Levin has calculated that between them, the two super-powers 'intervened in 117 elections around the world from 1946 to 2000 – an average of once in every nine competitive elections.' Many of these interventions would later be seen as unethical and even potentially criminal. In 1953 the US orchestrated the removal of Iranian Prime Minister Mohammed Mossadegh and replaced his government with an authoritarian monarchy favourable to US and UK oil interests.

Just a year later Guatemala's left-wing president, Jacobo Arbenz was deposed after he passed legislation to protect Guatamalan farmers from the unfair practices of the American owned United Fruit Company. In Chile, the US attempted to stop Salvador Allende from winning the national election in 1964. In an operation that was virtually a clone of the Italian plan, the CIA spent nearly four million dollars supporting political parties, publishing and broadcasting propaganda and radicalising slum dwellers.

Almost a decade later, in 1973, they backed a military coup which brought to power General Augusto Pinochet, who went on to perpetrate some of the worst human rights abuses ever recorded.

There can be little doubt that by 1975 Gene must have come to understand both the scope and the scale of the US security establishment's interventions into the electoral systems of foreign states. Despite this, in April 1975, he despatched a new funding proposal to Schelling's Department of Defense contact – the head of the newly created office of 'Net Assessment' – a discreet unit of Pentagon futurologists whose job was to plan for strategic problems 30 years ahead.

The Director was Andrew Marshall, a statistician, strategist and infamous polymath, recently appointed by President Nixon. He would serve as the head of Net Assessment for more than 40 years, only retiring in 2015 at the age of 93. Convincing Marshall that Western Europe could be made ungovernable by training in nonviolent techniques could have been a game changer for the funding of Gene's work – Marshall would survive 10 presidential elections in the job and report directly to the next 13 Secretaries for Defense.

However, recently declassified CIA documents show Marshall made it clear that his unit wasn't the right place for Gene's proposal. The documents show that he forwarded it on to the Deputy Director for Intelligence at the CIA, Ed Proctor, who was one of the officials still under investigation by the Church Committee. Marshall wrote in his referral letter:

'I thought CIA might be interested in this work. Dr Sharp opens up an avenue of thought about a different type of conflict which could occur in the future to which analysts should probably be exposed. However, while the work looks interesting I am not in a position to judge its utility.'

The last sentence here is a euphemism. Marshall knew that Gene's proposal was none of his business, it fell firmly under the covert action umbrella. Democracy promotion and support was the CIA's patch. No record has yet been released on Proctor's response to this letter, but Gene remembered a tentative offer of funding which he refused. He explained that he had intended the proposal to stay within the Department of Defense and had not wanted Marshall to forward it on to external agencies. While he was happy to take Defense Department money, he drew a line at the CIA. He feared from the stories in the press that the intelligence agency had gone rogue and would hijack the work for what he described as 'bad dealings'.

When the Church Committee reported, it called for improved political oversight of CIA operations and its findings created a temporary chilling effect on political warfare activity. After a significant hiatus during which the Soviet propaganda programs continued unabated, newly elected President Carter's National Security Advisor, Zbigniew Brzezinski, urged the re-establishment of political warfare activity. US agents and front organisations renewed their secret funding of human rights and democracy promotion organisations and began a covert propaganda campaign consisting of dissident literature known as 'Samizdat', to spread disinformation. Despite the investigations and adverse publicity, by the early 1980s the CIA had funded, owned or gained influence over more than 50 foreign newspapers, magazines, radio stations and news wires. Its publishing efforts were prolific too – more than 1000 books or pamphlets were 'sponsored, subsidised or produced' by the intelligence agency.

In 1981 President Ronald Reagan inherited this political warfare campaign and built upon it with a new National Security Strategy designed to destabilise 'the evil empire'. Its aim was to use propaganda to make populations more favourable to the United States, encourage discontent with communism, sponsor social movements and back that up with economic and diplomatic pressure. But Reagan would take a distinctive new approach. Instead of continuing these programs in secret under the CIA, he opted to take democracy promotion out of the shadows. In effect, he privatised it.

On 8th June 1982, the President flew to London to make a landmark speech in the British Houses of Parliament. Flanked on either side by crimson-clad beefeaters in starched white ruffles carrying spears and watched by Prime Minister Margaret Thatcher, he delivered a speech which signalled the beginning of a new era in democracy promotion abroad. He opened with a quote from Thomas Jefferson, 'A little rebellion now and then is a very good thing.'

'The objective I propose is quite simple to state: to foster the infrastructure of democracy, the system of a free press, unions, political parties, universities, which allows a people to choose their own way to develop their own culture, to reconcile their own differences through peaceful means. It is time that we committed ourselves as a nation – in both the public and private sectors – to assisting democratic development. Let us ask ourselves, "What kind of people do we think we are?" and let us answer, "Free people, worthy of freedom and determined not only to remain so but to help others gain their freedom as well.'"

The Reagan speech laid the foundation for what would become the National Endowment for Democracy (NED), the umbrella organisation through which, initially four affiliate institutions would receive congressional funding to carry out democracy promotion throughout the world.

The US press were sceptical and pointed out, correctly, that this was work previously conducted by the CIA, now being repackaged and brought out into the open. *The Wall Street Journal* quoted one official as saying, 'we used to do some of this covertly … but when we stopped being able to keep our secrets in these matters, people became unwilling to accept our money'. The main concern in Washington was whether the CIA would still be involved in the programme.

Lawrence Eagleburger, Under-Secretary of State, called a news conference to put it on record that it most certainly would not. Eagleburger explained that CIA involvement would kill the new NED organisations because it would serve as a 'pretext to discredit the entire project'. As one of its first actions the board of the NED voted to forbid any employment of CIA personnel or allow the CIA to influence its programs.

Democrat Senator William Proxmire from Wisconsin, a regular thorn in the side of the establishment, went further and called for a ban on the NED employing anyone who had been a CIA employee for the past 20 years. Director of the CIA William J. Casey moved to kill off any more discussion of the subject by releasing a rare official statement which read, 'On behalf of the intelligence community I have agreed with senator Proxmire that the National Endowment for Democracy will not be used to conduct intelligence activities.'

Nineteen eighty three was the single most important year for the advancement of democracy promotion institutions in the United States. The House Foreign Affairs Committee proposed legislation to provide initial funding of $31.3 million for the NED's four constituent organisations – The National Democratic Institute for International Affairs

(NDI), The International Republican Institute (IRI), the Free Trade Union Institute (FTUI) and The Center for International Private Enterprise (CIPE). If that sounds like a forgettable cluster of confusingly named bureaucracies, it was almost certainly intended that way. Democracy promotion by the United States was being privatised, but with a massive public financing package.

There was one outlier to this group. Freedom House, founded in 1941, was already a US government-funded organisation dedicated to promoting democracy abroad, especially in communist states, and carried out training for activists and civil society organisations. Freedom House was not made subject to any of the controls on former intelligence personnel which bound the NED organisations – in fact, former CIA director, James Woolsey, would later became chairman of the Freedom House board of trustees.

By chance or design, 1983 would also be the year that Gene Sharp would found two new organisations, both funded not from the burgeoning Cold War budget, the CIA or the Department of Defense, but by a returning protégé who would become infamous on Wall Street.

Peter Ackerman was a bright, fiercely ambitious New Yorker and Colgate University graduate who was just beginning his PhD at Tufts University in the fall of 1969. The war in Vietnam was the focus of world attention and Ackerman had become interested in the factors other than the military balance that might determine the outcomes of conflict.

A meeting with Tom Schelling after attending one of his Harvard classes opened up an unexpected path. 'If you're interested in that subject, why don't you look at why people win conflicts where people have absolutely no military capability at all?,' Schelling had told him. He walked Ackerman down the corridor to introduce him to Gene and they hit it off immediately. Ackerman realised that Gene was an intellectual pioneer and was delighted when he agreed to supervise his PhD thesis.

The two men spent increasing amounts of time together in the course of that thesis and after a couple of years work Ackerman handed Gene 350 pages of what he thought was close to a finished draft. Gene scoffed at this, '350 pages is only a quarter of the way through!' he told him. He would never respect the merits of concise writing, his own PhD had reached 1600 pages and he'd resisted all efforts to cut it down.

Ackerman eventually made it to 1100 pages which was still the second longest PhD thesis the Fletcher School had ever received. By the time he left graduate school he was broke from, among other things, the enormous typing costs associated with duplicating such a long thesis. He decided he needed a job where he could make some serious money.

Drex, as its employees called it, was not a flashy or prestigious bank in 1976, but its boss Michael Milken would pioneer a trillion dollar market for 'high yield bonds' or 'junk bonds' as their critics would call them. These were bonds that, when issued, had been good investments, but for a range of reasons had become more risky and their credit rating had dropped. Milken realised that these bonds were regularly undervalued and began aggressively buying them up. This practice would make his employees richer than they can possibly have imagined.

Ackerman rose quickly through the ranks to become Director of International Capital Markets, a position from which he would earn millions of dollars in the coming years. While some bankers might have been content with buying a property portfolio and a yacht, Ackerman was slightly different. He was an academic and a practicing Christian who believed in Gene's mission, the concept of strategic nonviolent struggle and its ability to free people from oppressive regimes.

In 1982 Gene had finally run out of road at Harvard and had reluctantly accepted a full time job at Southeastern Massachusetts University (now University of Massachusetts Dartmouth) to teach Sociology. Ackerman stepped in to stop it happening. He told Gene he wanted to form an institution which would formalise the study of Gene's work and the field itself. In fact, they started two new organisations, one an academic program at Harvard called 'The Program on Nonviolent Sanctions' at the university's Center for International Affairs, keeping the prestigious Harvard brand officially behind Gene's work.

A separate new institution was set up to carry out work independently which couldn't be done in a university environment. Several names for this organisation were mooted, but Gene was set on just one. He wanted his new organisation to be called the Albert Einstein Institution after the man who had given him so much hope during his time in prison. It made little sense from a branding and public relations point of view and meant the institution, for the rest of its existence, would have to field mis-directed enquiries about physics.

Gene was stubborn as ever in his choice and the name won out. He contacted Otto Nathan, Einstein's friend and executor of the Einstein estate to describe the mission of the institution and formally request permission to use the name. To Gene's delight formal approval was granted.

The first member of staff was Bob Irwin, a gently spoken, bearded peace activist who became Gene's assistant. Irwin was a strange choice for Gene who was now becoming rather notorious for being rude to members of the peace community. Irwin was happy to have the job, but was immediately uncomfortable with his new surroundings at the Centre for International Affairs where Kissinger and some of the foreign policy advisors most reviled by anti-war activists came to teach.

'When I first met Samuel Huntington I wanted to go and wash the blood off my hand.' Irwin remembered, physically shuddering at the memory. 'That hall filled with the pictures of people like Kissinger being applauded by his last class …. It was quite clear we were in the corridors of the foreign policy elite. That's exactly where Gene wanted to be. Gene was seen as the guy who was always trying to engage military people. The peace people would come and see him and he would make it very clear that what he was doing was very different.' Schelling also noted the dismissive approach to the peace community. 'He had a kind of contempt for pacifists, he had a different way of combat, nonviolent, and this was totally different from pacifism.'

While the Program on Nonviolent Sanctions was established in perhaps the most famous seat of learning in America, the Albert Einstein Institution was spluttering into life in East Boston. For its first months it was housed on the ground floor of 36 Cottage Street Gene had bought two thoroughbred Great Danes which were not well suited to the proportions of a tall brick townhouse with a postage stamp back yard. Every morning Bob Irwin arrived to a commotion behind the door as Gene tried to restrain two enormous dogs, both taller than him on their hind legs. He set to work in the basement on a small desk beside the washer and dryer.

The first major publication launched under the auspices of the Albert Einstein Institution was *Making Europe Unconquerable* in 1985 – a discussion of how a well-trained and prepared population could make an invading force withdraw using planned nonviolent resistance. Gene wrote in the introduction:

'This book is mostly about... "civilian-based defence"... In this policy, the whole population and the society's institutions become the fighting forces. Their weaponry consists of a vast variety of forms of psychological, economic, social, and political resistance and counter-attack... to deny the attackers their objectives and to make consolidation of political control impossible. These aims would be achieved by applying massive and selective noncooperation and defiance [and seeking] to create maximum international problems for the attackers and to subvert the reliability of their troops and functionaries.'

Making Europe Unconquerable was Gene's answer to a strategic problem which the Department of Defense was already attempting to address with a covert operation. Operation Gladio was the codename for a collection of NATO allies' plan for 'stay behind operations' in the event of a Soviet invasion of Western Europe.

This was envisaged as a military plan first – small groups of special forces, men and women blowing up vital supply lines and assassinating important military leaders – but in the margins were also ideas about encouraging factory strikes, civilian protests and blockades.

As yet, no evidence has emerged that the CIA ever incorporated Gene's work on civilian based defense into the plans for Operation Gladio. If they had asked him about doing so, it's likely he would have pointed out that violence would have acted as a powerful contaminant to any nonviolent resistance movement. Nevertheless, the ideas in *Making Europe Unconquerable* were taken seriously by senior military and diplomatic figures.

The reception was best illustrated by the comments of George Kennan in his review for the New York Review of Books.

By this time Kennan was 82 years old and had retired into academia. Despite stepping back from the front line of international diplomacy his mind was as sharp as ever and he remained a respected voice among the new young Turks in the modern State Department.

'the view in this book deserves consideration, if only because of the bankruptcy of all the visible alternatives to it. It might just be that in a world where the devices of long-range military destruction have prolif-erated beyond all reasons, the greatest security any country can hope to have, imperfect as it is, will be found to lie primarily in its confidence in itself, in its readiness to leave other people alone and go its own way, in its willingness to accept the sort of social discipline that a civilian-based defense implies'.

The review is notable for perhaps the best explanation of the difference between Kennan's 'political warfare' strategy, which would be contin-ued by the United States in the model he created, and Gene's concept of civilian based defense. 'I would have placed more weight on highly cen-tralized clandestine direction, less on spontaneous mass action. I am not sure that the nature of civilian defense planning should be so widely pub-licized', he wrote.

So while Kennan sought to secretly influence the elites, politicians, newspaper editors, senior church figures, Gene wanted to train whole populations at the grass roots level and do it in a public and transparent manner. In fact, the use of civilian based defence as a deterrent required that the training and preparations be communicated to any potential enemy.

Nevertheless, Gene was delighted by Kennan's comments – they had never met, but as the man credited with the containment strategy of the Cold War, his positive comments were enormously valuable. A second edition of the book was quickly printed, with Kennan's review in full as a foreword.

The origin of Gene's work in the belly of an establishment which was deploying political warfare would later lead to the often repeated theory that he was a CIA asset and the Albert Einstein Institution a front for the US destabilisation of governments not aligned with US political and economic interests.

Those who believe this version of events can easily be forgiven because the weight of circumstantial evidence is convincing. The type of activities pioneered in Italy in the late 1940s would be easily recognisable in the funding priorities of the National Endowment Democracy 50 years later. There is no doubt that the US, first under the CIA and later through the arms of the NED sought to influence and build democracies favourable to US policy interests.

How then can Gene Sharp's work be credibly seen as distinct from Kennan's political warfare movement? Not only did he come to know some of the key players, he actively lobbied for his work to be used as an instrument of foreign policy. His most notable work was financed with Department of Defense money from a fund intended to contain and defeat communism and protect US interests. His work would appear in most of the key strategic battles which involved nonviolent struggle for the next 40 years – where the interests of Russia collided with those of the US, Europe and NATO. The DNA of his work would soon form a literal paper trail across the globe.

Although it is difficult to prove a negative, I could find absolutely no evidence that he worked for or with the CIA or in pursuit of its objectives. In later years I watched him actively lobby democracy groups against taking any money from foreign intelligence agencies. However, as we will see, a convincing case can be made that his body of work, always in the public domain, was effectively co-opted by the US political warfare project with little consultation from the man who developed it.

Two quite distinct efforts were developing. One was a multi-million dollar state enterprise to destabilise Soviet hegemony in the East using political warfare, and the second, Gene's work on nonviolent resistance, intended for use by ordinary people, run from his home at 36 Cottage Street. The first real world test of Gene's work was in a place that certainly wasn't aligned with US interests and was actively discouraged by US officials.

Intifada

It was 4am when the phone rang in the second floor bedroom at 36 Cottage Street. Gene rolled over and picked up the handset, shaking himself from sleep. There was only one person who would call at this antisocial hour, but the annoyance at these late night intrusions had abated as their gravity became clearer. On the other end of the line, five thousand miles away, was a young activist called Mubarak Awad who was planning a nonviolent campaign in the Palestinian territories. In time he would be called the 'Palestinian Gandhi'.

At five years old, Mubarak had been forced from his home with his mother and six siblings after their father had fallen to a sniper's bullet in Jerusalem. His mother wasn't able to look after all of her children and placed them in orphanages and foster families around the city. Despite the killing of her husband which had torn their family apart, Huda Kuttab Awad taught them that they must not fight their injustice with more killing. 'She told us never to seek revenge, but to work so that other mothers don't suffer', Mubarak remembered.

After high school he moved to the United States to study at Bluffton University, followed by a masters and PhD in Psychology from Saint Louis. After years of academic study he was granted his US citizenship in 1978. Although he dreamed of a future as an academic at a prestigious university, he became increasingly determined to travel back to Palestine to help solve the conflict with Israel.

After reading about Gandhi and the US civil rights movement, Mubarak became convinced that the best way to obtain freedom from the Israeli occupation was not through violence, but by waging a nonviolent campaign. In 1983 he returned to Jerusalem to establish a new organization to carry out research and teach nonviolence and peace building in Palestinian communities.

Word of Mubarak's activities spread quickly, reaching the head of the Mennonite church in Jerusalem who travelled to attend one of the initial meetings. 'I think you will find these useful' he said as he handed over a small bundle of books and pamphlets by Gene Sharp. Mubarak began leafing through the first pages and immediately realised their importance. There was substantial oral history of Arabs using nonviolent resistance, but in Gene's work he saw for the first time a coherent strategy for a nonviolent campaign. It was an exciting moment – so much of the information that he'd been looking for was all there in black and white already. He quickly set about translating part of the book into Arabic, but it was only after the first translation was complete that Mubarak made contact with Gene in Boston. To his surprise this first encounter was 'quite unpleasant' for both of them.

Gene was upset that he hadn't asked permission for the translation and even more upset that he'd only picked the bits he liked and left out the things he didn't think were important. 'You can't do that when you don't understand the full concepts', Gene scolded him down the phone line, 'I wrote the whole thing together and if you pick and choose you miss the whole essence'.

Mubarak was crestfallen, but thanked him for writing something that was proving so useful and told him he wanted to work with him on a nonviolent strategy for the Occupied Territories. He went on to translate Gene's pamphlet, 'Power, Struggle and Defense' with the list of 198 nonviolent methods, making sure the translations were so simple they could be read by children in the fourth or fifth grade.

One of the early problems Mubarak faced was the translation of the word 'nonviolent'. The only equivalent term in Arabic was the, somewhat simplified, 'la-unf' meaning 'no violence', which didn't fully convey the correct meaning and emphasized the negative. Gene insisted that the translation of nonviolent struggle had to impart wording that showed these were powerful actions, not merely the absence of violence. They eventually decided on the title, *al-Muqawama bila unf* (Resistance with No Violence), the closest they could get to 'nonviolent resistance'.

From 1983 to 1984, between 4000 and 7000 copies of this new nonviolent resistance guide for the Occupied Territories were distributed to Palestinians. Some were deliberately left on Israeli owned buses and passed between families and youth groups. 'Once I was on a bus from Jerusalem to Ramallah and I noticed a young woman sitting in front of me reading it' Mubarak remembered. 'She didn't know who I was and she was trying to hide what she was reading. When I left I said, "It's good that you are reading that" and she said, "My whole class is supposed to read it." Her teacher had made copies and told them to study it, even though it was illegal.'

The historian, Mary King, wrote later that, 'Awad and Sharp's works were comparable to the manifestos and charters of movements seeking relief from Soviet hegemony that appeared in Eastern Europe in the same period.'

For the first few years, Mubarak worked alone, travelling from village to village, handing out books and talking to the people about nonviolence. He organised a mobile library filled with Gandhi, Martin Luther King and Gene Sharp's books. Everywhere he went he pointed to a photograph of Gandhi and said to the boys in the villages, 'You see this skinny person? He liberated India with nonviolent means and we can do it here too!'

Some local leaders were openly hostile and ran him out of their towns and villages, but he refused to become dispirited and returned again and again. Mubarak continued to phone Gene in Boston for advice, usually forgetting the time difference and Gene always did his best to sound awake answering his questions. He was beginning to take the upstart who had pirated the translation of his books far more seriously.

In March 1984, some of the most influential figures pushing for a nonviolent campaign by Palestinians met at a conference convened by the Palestinian-American historian Hisham Shirabi. Mubarak, Gene and Jonathan Kuttab, a human rights lawyer, attended with members of the Quakers and the American Friends Services Committee to discuss the deteriorating situation of Palestinians living under the Israeli occupation. The conclusion of the meeting was that a centre for nonviolent action should be established for the Occupied Territories. This centre would conduct studies rather than promote any specific actions so as not to fall foul of the Israeli government. Shirabi very quickly raised $30,000 from the Jerusalem Fund, a Washington based charity, and delivered the cheque to Mubarak to begin setting up the organisation.

The Palestinian Center for the Study of Nonviolence was officially founded in May 1985, consisting of three small rooms in a rough looking building in East Jerusalem. The first few months of the organisation were spent translating and printing a set of key texts on nonviolent action including Gene's work on civilian based defence. This body of work, intended for resisting a possible occupation of Europe by the Soviet Union, would now be applied by Palestinians against their occupation by the Israelis.

Gene made his first visit to the Occupied Territories in November 1986. Mubarak wanted him to understand the difficulties he was having on the ground in persuading young Palestinians to take nonviolent action seriously. They travelled to one of the most challenging areas, Qalandia refugee camp, which was run by tough young men who carried guns and knew how to make bombs. Gene and Mubarak joined a group who were constructing a new community centre. The young men arrived with automatic rifles and Mubarak had to ask them to set them down on a wall while they talked. As they hammered nails into the building, Gene sat and chatted with them about the potential power each of them had to resist. Every one of these people had experienced tragedy in their family – some wanted to destroy Israel and martyr themselves. They felt they had nothing to live for. Mubarak asked Gene, 'What can we tell people like these who are willing to kill? How can we change them into a nonviolent group?'

Gene gave examples of other leaders who had been in the same situation, like Martin Luther King and Gandhi. 'Change is possible by means of nonviolent action', he said, 'and it's a much better way of fighting'.

'You haven't had our experience, your mother wasn't killed, you can come and go as you like while we cannot travel and our businesses cannot function and you're coming to tell us to be nice?' one young man replied.

'No I'm telling you how people can use the methods of nonviolent action. You are willing to die for a cause, well at least martyr yourself doing something that will make a change.' Gene argued back.

There were no raised voices, the discussions were impassioned and respectful, but it was one of Gene's most difficult times. It was the first real test of selling nonviolent struggle to a community that he knew would benefit from its use. 'I had to indicate this is not pacifism, this is not submission, this is not surrender, this is not holding hands, it's a means of fighting. These are the weapons, these are the ways it works.'

Gene often found it difficult to remain emotionally detached. In his notes of the trip he wrote, 'We were in the home one time, with Mubarak, of the relatives of a Palestinian boy who had just been killed the previous day. I was deeply moved in those situations like I have never been in any other situation. So when I talked with Israelis about what was going on I would break down crying because lots of Jews were people who had helped me in my life. For other Jews to be doing these kinds of things to people who were oppressed really moved me deeply.'

Big breakthroughs were rare, but a week after their visit one of the young men Gene had talked to in the Qalandia camp walked into the Centre for Nonviolence and told Mubarak that he wanted to work on nonviolent struggle and he was giving up his gun. He went on to become one of the center's best trainers in nonviolent action.

At the end of his trip, Gene approached Mubarak about the task which lay ahead of him and suggested he travel to India to meet with some of Gandhi's people. Mubarak agreed and arranged a trip with his new wife, Nancy. They spent six weeks touring the country and meeting Indians who had worked with Gandhi on the struggle for independence from the British. His trip there also introduced him to the story of Abdul Ghaffar Khan who founded the Khudai Khidmatgar (servants of God) movement, commonly known as the Red Shirts. Khan was called the 'frontier Gandhi' and led resistance against the British in the North West region which would later become Pakistan. At the peak of their movement, the Red Shirts comprised a 100,000 strong trained and uniformed nonviolent army, with platoons and commanding officers enforcing strict discipline.

They carried their own flag, practised drill and even had their own corps of musicians playing Scottish bagpipes. 'I am going to give you such a weapon that the police and the army will not be able to stand against it.' Ghaffar Khan told his followers, 'It is the weapon of the prophet, but you are not aware of it. That weapon is patience and righteousness. No power on earth can stand against it'.

Ghaffar Khan was important because, like the majority of Palestinians, he was a Muslim. Gene's writing provided texts which were politically and religiously neutral, but to have a strong Muslim champion of nonviolence was extremely significant. Mubarak returned to Jerusalem with a greater understanding of Gandhi's strategy and new stories to tell of Abdul Ghaffar Khan.

The new nonviolent movement had not escaped the notice of the established Palestinian leadership, the Palestinian Liberation Organisation (PLO), led by Yasser Arafat who were working in exile from Tunisia. Among the Abus or fathers of the PLO was Khalil Ibrahim al-Wazir, or Abu Jihad as he was commonly known. Abu Jihad was the commander of the military wing of the Palestinian nationalist party, Fatah, and the most senior military advisor to the PLO.

Considered a high profile terrorist by the Israelis, Abu Jihad had become interested in nonviolence and was reported to have begun reading Gene's *Politics of Nonviolent Action*. After a number of attempts, Mubarak secured a meeting with Abu Jihad at a rendezvous in Cairo where Jihad told him that he believed in what he was doing with the nonviolent strategy and asked if they could work together. Mubarak said it would be impossible unless he renounced violence publicly. This would have meant political suicide for Jihad among the fathers of the PLO, but quietly, in the course of the next few years, he would support and enable the flourishing of the most sophisticated campaign of nonviolent resistance the Palestinians had ever undertaken.

Although they could never be seen to be officially working together, as Mubarak built the nonviolent movement, Abu Jihad was secretly arranging the protection he needed to work from the Fatah political leadership who controlled the territories. 'When we started the Centre for Nonviolence even a lot of Palestinians wanted to attack and harass me, and try to discourage the organisation, and try to say that I am with the CIA or an Israeli agent – Abu Jihad was the one that told some of the Fatah groups to leave me alone.' Mubarak told me.

The first intifada, as it would become known, began in the Jabalia refugee camp in Gaza on the 9th December 1987 when an Israeli Army truck hit a civilian car, killing four Palestinians. A rumour quickly spread through the Occupied Territories that the incident was deliberate and the West Bank erupted into undirected anger, stone-throwing and protests.

After weeks of rage on the streets, a clandestine co-ordination group of the leading Palestinian organisations was established in an attempt to coordinate the spontaneous mobilisation in a more productive way. The result was 'The Unified National Leadership Command of the Uprising', quickly shortened to 'The Command' which was made up of members of the main political organisations in the territories – Fatah, The Popular Front for the Liberation of Palestine and the Palestine Communist party. These organisations had always met to discuss particular crises but now that relationship was formalised.

Split into three distinct components, The Command was composed of lower ranking delegates seconded from its constituent organisations. Just like the mythical hydra water monster, if there was an arrest of a delegate to The Command, then the constituent organisation could simply supply a new delegate, making it almost impossible for the Israelis to destroy. The second component were the individuals in charge of directing the course of the nonviolent strategy and actions and the third component was a 'think tank' of around 20 senior academics who were officially independent, but performed an important role in research, policy and direction of the intifada on the ground. The first significant recommendation the think tank made was to give the uprising the name 'intifada'. Translated into English, 'intifada' means simply a 'shaking off' and was intended to carry no violent connotations.

In the mid 1980s, most of Palestine was yet to have any native media or radio station that covered the West Bank and Gaza. Only the rich had telephones and so the most effective independent media service to communicate with Palestinians took the form of a distribution of thousands of leaflets across the area. This was the means that The Command used to publicise their existence and shape the direction of the resistance.

On the 4th January 1988, the first leaflets appeared in Qalandia, the refugee camp that Gene had visited with Mubarak in the West Bank. These were produced before The Command was formalised and proper security measures put in place. This resulted in many of the authors being quickly rounded up by the Israelis and jailed.

At a meeting in Jordan, one of The Command's academics, Samir Shelandeh, and Abu Jihad agreed that the leaflets should be standardised, so as not to be contradict each other. Each leaflet ended with a list of specific tasks that people were asked to perform, like lighting candles or raising flags, beginning a boycott or staging a particular kind of strike.

When a leaflet was agreed, each of the delegates to The Command would return to their group with the page proofs and each organisation would arrange a print run. This meant that even if several page proofs were captured by the Israelis, at least one would always make it through to a printing press.

The arrival of the third leaflet, which some regard as the first true leaflet of the intifada, saw professional branding and a consistent editorial line. The masthead proclaimed, 'No Voice Rises above the Uprising'. Its distribution was a logistical tour de force – more than 100,000 copies appeared across the territories in under three hours.

The appearance of the leaflets and the efficiency of their distribution sent the Israeli army into a frenzy searching for the printing shops which had produced them. After three months, the Israelis had arrested several members of The Command and closed down 21 printing presses, yet the leaflets still appeared without fail on the 9th of each month. The Command, due to its hydra like structure, was still operating.

Analysis of the first 18 months of the leaflets show marked similarities in content and use of language from the Awad/Sharp nonviolent action texts in the Occupied Territories with inclusion in the Arabic translation of 121 of Gene's 198 methods. Mubarak insists he was never involved in drafting any of the intifada leaflets, but he was one of the contributors to the think tank who supplied materials to the writers.

Sari Nusseibeh was a respected academic, a member of Fatah and one of the most influential leaders of the movement. At various points he operated in all three components of The Command. A friend of Mubarak Awad from school in Jerusalem where they had joined the boy scouts together, his fingerprints and guidance were firmly imprinted on the strategy behind the Iintifada leaflets from the beginning.

Sari would fax a draft leaflet to an intermediary in Paris before it was forwarded on to Abu Jihad in Tunis who would then show it to Arafat. The PLO were reluctant to make changes and most were signed off without argument.

Although the leaflets suggested actions, they were never seen as strict orders and different communities interpreted them differently or varied their approach. Couriers, some of them children, went from village to village carrying the leaflets in school bags or back packs. Key points were reinforced with graffiti issuing instructions or spreading news. The rote learning the Palestinians had been exposed to under the Jordanian and Egyptian education systems became an asset – long passages were committed to memory and sometimes young people memorised large tracts to transmit the instructions from the leaflets without the fear of being intercepted carrying the physical product itself.

The people beat pots and pans, read poems together, sang songs and staged sit ins and boycotts. Mubarak came up with an idea to symbolically set Palestinian clocks to a different time zone from Israel. In April 1989, daylight saving time was adopted by Palestinians two weeks in advance of Israel. The Israeli army tried to crush this with determined brutality – people found to be doing it had their wrists broken and watches smashed.

Although Gene assessed that between 80% and 95% of the intifada was nonviolent, the Palestinians had tolerated and to some extent embraced stone-throwing, which had deep cultural significance. They argued that it was so low level as to be practically nonviolent. Many argued that the imagery of young men throwing stones against impregnable Israeli tanks created romantic comparisons with David and Goliath for the international media to capture. Gene disagreed with this analysis. 'Although stone-throwing is very limited violence in comparison with other options and expresses Palestinian rage and pain, it is almost guaranteed to produce – as it has done – high Palestinian casualties and to alienate Israeli public opinion among the population and soldiers … I have found it extremely difficult to find a Palestinian justification for this heavy price in terms of instrumental effectiveness of that type of action'. He added, 'if you want to alienate Israelis and have them not listen to your demands, then all you have to do is threaten them. Even if it is with stones, because stones hurt badly.'

Gene wrote in a trip report, 'There was no one that I met or remember among the Palestinians who said that the stone-throwing should stop. In fact, in their poetry they idolized these people'. The stone-throwing had also captured the international news media in a way that shop strikes and time changes could not. While the majority of the intifada was nonviolent, the pictures presented to the world on the TV news were of angry stone-throwing young men.

The media dilemma was a challenge that would face almost all nonviolent struggles. Violence and destruction almost always guarantees media attention – often resulting in pressure within a movement for violence to ensure an appearance on the evening news. But, while some activists might believe that media exposure is a victory in itself, if that exposure results in a decrease in domestic and international support for the cause, the overall result of the violence is a loss and needs to be avoided.

The Israelis used the Palestinian's rock-throwing to great effect in their propaganda war. To some, it gave the impression that, if the Palestinians did gain access to weapons, they would use them. The Israelis argued that the reason the intifada experienced so little serious violence was only due to the success of their security forces intercepting the majority of weapons that the Palestinians were trying to acquire.

The issue of whether the intifada should be purely a nonviolent struggle created the greatest tensions between the PLO leadership in Tunis and The Command. The leaflets are often equivocal on the issue – some suggested using 'all means of struggle', others just nonviolent methods. The Command wanted to brand the intifada as the 'White Revolution', reinforcing the image of a nonviolent campaign, but although the PLO in Tunis didn't object to the term in the leaflets, they struck it from any reprints outside of Palestine.

This became a problem for the think tank of 20 or so Palestinian intellectuals who were advising The Command, supplying experts to speak at international seminars and meeting with diplomats and journalists. The disagreement meant that a consistent message couldn't be delivered to the international community.

The argument for nonviolent action was also being seriously challenged by those who admired the victory of the Algerians in their violent struggle against their occupation by the French. Sari Nusseibeh argued back that it was futile for the Palestinians to try and model themselves on the Algerians because the Israelis had no homes to return to, they could not go back to Europe like the French had. Many of them were born in Israel and so ultimately the Palestinians had to find a way to share the land.

The Palestinians had been historically saturated with the ideology of armed struggle. After 1948, the Syrian government was encouraging military action and the Soviets were peddling what they called 'eternal revolution'. In refugee camps in Syria and Jordan the dominant thinking was to convince the Palestinians that only violence against Israel was going to work. Despite these powerful influences, virtually the entire Palestinian population during the first intifada had managed to mobilise nonviolently and resist these overtures to fight a violent campaign.

In an attempt to stamp out the uprising, the Israelis put in place a curfew and closed schools and universities that were considered a hotbed of resistance. Eventually more than 300,000 students and faculty were sent home. Mary King described this as one of the unrecognised engines of the intifada. 'As the doors of the universities shut, theoreticians joined with the families, popular committees, youths and children of the uprising. The physics professor worked with the baker to plan food distribution.'

The resistance by the students was a classic example of what Gene classified as a 'dilemma action' – an action undertaken by a movement that causes the opposition damage whatever they do to combat it. Reopening schools could cause a resurgence in the protest by bringing thousands of young people together in classrooms and lecture halls to organise, but instead these same students and teachers were sent home where they energised the organisation in their home towns and villages, further spreading the message and the techniques of the resistance.

An alternative education system was quickly engineered, but the Israelis banned it, imposing 10 year jail terms and steep fines for any teacher involved. A follow-up distance learning programme by mail order study packs was also outlawed. This attack on the education system drew enormous fire both from inside Israel and the international community. The imprisonment of teachers intent only on the education of Palestinian children made Israel look barbaric and was a perfect example of political jujitsu in action.

The success of The Command and the leaflets was a thorny challenge for the PLO and Yasser Arafat in exile in Tunis. Traditionally the Palestinians had taken their instructions from them, but now they became concerned that an effective decentralised leadership structure was developing without them.

The Command had no intention of cutting out the PLO and still saw it as the most important political power in negotiating with the Israelis and the international community. Instead, they saw the intifada as providing the leadership in Tunis with additional leverage to take to the negotiating table.

Mary King met Abu Jihad a number of times and followed his gradual adoption of the nonviolent movement with great interest. In a discussion with Mubarak Awad years later, she described that conversion. 'He had become a much greater threat to Israel once he came to understand the power of nonviolent struggle. He had even begun moving money into the popular committees, just as he had traditionally done with the military cadres'. Both Gene and Mary King believed that it was Abu Jihad's new support of the nonviolent struggle, rather than his decades in charge of the paramilitary forces that eventually led Israel to seek his assassination.

On the evening of April 15th 1988, 26 Israeli special forces soldiers arrived on the beach in Tunis and separated into two groups. They were transported by car to a spot less than 500 metres from Abu Jihad's house and two of the commandos approached the property disguised as a courting couple out for an evening stroll.

They found Abu Jihad's first bodyguard dozing outside in a car and shot him in the head with a silenced pistol hidden in a large box of chocolates. When they received the signal that the first bodyguard was down, a second group approached with equipment to break open the villa's door. They moved quickly inside and after climbing the stairs found Abu Jihad on the landing holding what looked like a gun. He was met with a long burst of automatic fire from the commandos and fell to the floor. The team confirmed they had hit the correct target and fled the scene.

People in Fatah saw Abu Jihad as a proven warrior who had earned the respect of the military cadres. He was the most likely of anyone to convince supporters of the violent struggle to consider the merits of a nonviolent approach. Faisal Husseini, the head of Fatah in the West Bank, and Palestinian Authority Minister without Portfolio told Gene that Abu Jihad had admitted to him that the Palestinian struggle could not succeed militarily and it had to shift to nonviolent struggle.

Jihad's assistance to the growing, independent Palestinian organisations was evidence for his support of this new type of resistance. Sari Nusseibeh also discussed the possibility that Israel had killed Abu Jihad because he was ready to guide Palestinians away from armed struggle towards nonviolent strategies which would be harder for Israel to deal with.

'When I raised this with one Israeli, they thought I was trying to make Abu Jihad into a saint or something' said Nusseibeh, 'They said that he was the one that organized the Munich Massacre of the Olympic athletes. It may be true. I don't know. But the killing did not occur at that time, it occurred after he decided nonviolent struggle is the way to go.' Mubarak was convinced that this was the true reason behind the killing, 'His assassination is because of the nonviolent activities that we were doing. They didn't hit the others who were so active in bringing in bombs and arms.'

The attack on the architects of the intifada continued just three weeks later. On 5th May, Mubarak was arrested by eighteen Israeli police officers and placed in solitary confinement at Muscobiyya prison in West Jerusalem. The day after his arrest, the Prime Minister, Yitzak Shamir, ordered his deportation to the United States. As the news of Mubarak's arrest spread, both Palestinians and Israelis appeared outside the prison to stand in protest. Mubarak began a hunger strike which was joined in solidarity by his friends and colleagues outside.

His impending deportation went straight to the top of the US government. US Secretary of State George P. Shultz sent a personal letter to the Israeli Prime Minister, Yitzak Shamir, to convince him to change his mind, ordering Ambassador Tom Pickering to apply further pressure. 'You need more Awads not fewer', Pickering pleaded.

Avi Pazner, an Israeli government spokesman dismissed the American pleas and branded Mubarak, 'the main brains of the intifada'. The Israelis told the press that Mubarak had authored the leaflets, the 'instructions' for the uprising that was supporting a wider, violent, PLO strategy.

In the court documents, the Israelis revealed the existence of an agent, codenamed 'Yossi', who had monitored Mubarak's activities. Yossi may have been an Israeli, a Palestinian spy or simply an invention designed to hide a more secret method of surveillance. 'Yossi' stated that 'From the outset of the uprising in the territories in December 1987, his [Mubarak's] ideas began to find actual expression in the leaflets that were issued by the command of the uprising, resulting in actions taken by the inhabitants of the territories'.

After a month of diplomatic and legal argument, Mubarak's appeals failed and on 13th June he boarded an airliner that would deport him to the United States. As he climbed the aircraft steps he paused, turned back to the assembled crowd and thrust two fingers into the air in a triumphant V that symbolised both 'peace' and 'victory'.

Press coverage of his deportation had made him and his ideas a household name across the region and demonstrated how afraid the Israelis were of nonviolent struggle. As Gene had told him repeatedly throughout their correspondence, 'If your opponent is afraid of this, this is exactly what you should be doing!'

Now expelled from Israel and the Occupied Territories, Mubarak began to work with the Palestinian exile community and international NGOs in Washington to support the uprising. In studying the strengths and weaknesses of the intifada he identified that a key problem in the movement was the unwillingness of Yasser Arafat and the PLO to commit to exclusively nonviolent resistance. 'The power in Palestine is with Arafat' he told Gene, 'I want to bring a delegation to talk to him about nonviolent action.'

The plan was to cultivate the grass roots activists in the villages but also influence the leadership. The people in the refugee camps adored Arafat, he was their leader, a true revolutionary. If he started changing some of his words and talked about giving up violence then it would be easier to convince the people.

The Albert Einstein Institution was now housed in an attic suite of offices on Church Street in Harvard Square. Old wooden beams cut through the 6 room office which was bright and airy, with skylights puncturing the pitched roof. The staff were equipped with some of the latest IBM computers paid for with Peter Ackerman's money and Gene had a large private office with space for a meeting table.

With the expansion came a requirement for new staff and an assistant for Gene. Bruce Jenkins was a 25-year-old masters student in political science at the Free University of Berlin when he first came across Gene's work in his reading list. Bruce returned to the US in 1988 and while looking for a new job he saw an advert in a local paper for a position at the Albert Einstein Institution.

Then, as always, Gene's office was bursting with piles of papers threatening to topple over at any moment. After welcoming Bruce into the office for his interview Gene flung an arm out over the papers, 'How would you help me deal with this!?' That wouldn't have been a promising start for many masters graduates, but Bruce was unfazed. 'The office was pretty cool, it was cluttered, but Gene's kind of like an archaeologist. He knows where everything is in the piles. I asked him how important the papers were and he seemed offended by the question, 'They're all very important!' The final test for Bruce was one Gene subjected many of his recruits to – the eating of some extremely hot food at either an Indian restaurant or his favourite Chinese.

Bruce passed the tests and in March 1989 he set off with Gene to Tunisia on his first assignment – to try to convert Yasser Arafat and the PLO to adopt a purely nonviolent campaign. They were joined in the delegation by Mubarak, an Iraqi academic called Khalid Kishtainy and Professor Abd al-Aziz Said from the American University Centre for Global Peace in Washington.

The delegation was collected by Arafat's people in a fleet of smart cars and driven to a five-star hotel in Tunis, famous for its lavish hospitality. In the morning they were taken to Arafat's compound which was moved regularly for security. Despite the obvious concerns, none of the delegation were searched before they were led into a room with a very long table. Arafat was sitting in the centre and greeted everyone warmly. His delegation included Salah Khalaf, second in command of the PLO, Mahmoud Abbas who would later become President and Abu Jihad's widow Intissar al-Wazir.

In Gene's first encounter with Arafat he asked if there was an example of when the Americans had listened to the Arabs. Arafat replied, 'during the oil embargo of 1973'. Gene asked if that had anything in common with the campaign he was advocating – Arafat nodded, 'It was a nonviolent method'. Gene then suggested to Arafat that the Palestinians could pursue six strategic objectives in the intifada.

1. Continue development of parallel institutions (work for de facto independence)
2. Continue the nonviolent action steps of protests, noncooperation and nonviolent intervention so that the people become unrulable by the occupying forces
3. Split Israeli public opinion on issues such as the military occupation, continuance of repression and recognition of an independent

Palestinian state including finding ways of dealing with the extremist Israeli settlers

4. Contribute to divisions in the Israeli establishment so as to undermine the reliability of the army's repression

5 Contribute to a split between the United States and Israel on the so called 'problem' of the Palestinians

6. Encourage world opinion and diplomacy to settle the conflict and assist in de jure recognition of Palestinian independence

Gene and Arafat debated whether nonviolent sanctions could be effective against Israeli settlers. Arafat told Gene he had neglected to consider the extreme violence perpetrated by Israeli settlers on the Palestinians.

The encounter in Tunis was marked as a draw. Bruce wrote in his notes, 'There is much skepticism it appears in the PLO ranks about the utility of nonviolent methods. Arafat stated that his military staff was encouraging military actions. Several leaders spoke of the necessity of continuing the struggle "at all levels". Another top official declared that armed struggle could not be dropped until material gains were achieved through the intifada.'

The US ambassador in Tunis, Robert Pelletreau, heard about the delegation and requested a briefing for the US embassy staff on what the team had been up to. Some of the US diplomats told Mubarak he was crazy, 'you'll never change these people', they said. Mubarak dismissed their doubts, 'I'm a psychologist by profession. Anyone can change', he told them.

In May 1989, the Israeli intelligence agency Shin Bet followed up their removal of Mubarak by naming Sari Nusseibeh in court documents as the man running the uprising, acting as paymaster and authoring the intifada leaflets. But as the struggle entered its third year, the rumblings of discontent from within the movement became louder. Sari was clear that the movement had a time limit, 'You're asking people to go through a lot. You have to be able to bring them to the shore earlier than when they begin to feel like they're sinking.'

Some of the actions, particularly a shopkeeper strike, had been running for years and appeared only to be hurting the shopkeepers and their employees who could only work a couple of hours a day. It had done little or nothing to harm the Israeli economy or change Israeli policies. Gradually the hours that their back doors were open for trade became longer.

Gene had warned that this type of fatigue would come to pass unless a fully worked out strategic assessment was conducted. Again he suggested, as he had in the meeting with Arafat, that a second intifada should be initiated by a symbolic hunger strike ushering in a new, entirely nonviolent phase, devoid of stone-throwing and killing. This renewal would lift the burden that the first intifada had placed upon specific parts of society like the shopkeepers.

Gene wrote in his trip notes, 'This second phase of resistance, introduced by an extended fast, would bring the Palestinian cause back to the front pages of the world's newspapers and the television news programmes in many countries. The shift to a fully nonviolent struggle would make possible more active support for Palestinian independence and criticism and resistance against Israeli repression and policies in Western Europe in the United States'.

On 20th May 1990 there was an explosion of violence from which the intifada would never fully recover. Seven Palestinian labourers waiting for a bus were gunned down by a lone Israeli attacker near Tel Aviv. The massacre sparked protests in which 15 more Palestinians were killed by Israeli security forces. In order to head off a return to violence, the leaders of the intifada broke cover and took up Gene's idea of a public hunger strike.

From a tent at the International Red Cross compound in Jerusalem they called for UN observers to be posted to the Occupied Territories while a Palestinian outreach team requested an emergency session of the UN General Assembly. James Baker the US Secretary of State suggested that he would discuss the strikers proposals, but just as the momentum was with the Palestinians, a bomb was detonated in Jerusalem killing one Israeli and injuring 9 others. If that had not been enough to wreck the process, a group of Palestinians attempted a commando style raid against civilians on an Israeli beach.

The US immediately suspended talks with the PLO and vetoed the UN observers. The overwhelming negative international press meant there was no hope for the hunger strikers and they gave up just 13 days into their action.

After the death of Abu Jihad, the PLO tried to actively take control of the intifada from Tunis. While Abu Jihad had understood the importance of a local distributed command responding to local conditions, some within the PLO wanted to take firmer control. The result was organisational disaster and alienation of those on the ground. Although pockets of resistance continued, by the end of 1990 the first intifada was all but snuffed out.

Tiananmen

On the 27th April 1989, more than 100,000 students along with 400,000 other citizens marched in protest into Tiananmen Square. For centuries the square had been the entrance to the imperial city, the centre of power in a nation which now numbered almost 1.2 billion souls. Tiananmen was built on a scale to intimidate ordinary citizens and inspire awe of their rulers, but for a brief moment in 1989, the Chinese people shook off their fear.

The students demanded democratic reforms and talks with the Chinese Premier, Li Peng. Word of the protests in Beijing quickly spread across the country and although they were virtually invisible to the international media, nearly 300 towns and cities in China were soon witnessing their own street protests. On the 17th and 18th May, nearly a million citizens from all over the country came to show solidarity in Tiananmen, but it would end in bloodshed and tragedy.

The Chinese community at Harvard had begun documenting and tracking events leading up to the 1989 uprising in Tiananmen Square for weeks before the unrest hit the international TV networks. One of those Chinese students was Huang Jing, a Harvard PhD candidate and president of the Boston Chinese Student Association. From the first stirrings of the protests, Huang had established a hotline from his home in Cambridge, Massachusetts to his friends in the student leadership in Beijing.

Over the course of the uprising he recorded hours of conversations on cassette tapes loaded into an old style answering machine, spending most of his meagre scholarship funds on international phone calls. Jing's tapes would become a veritable 'black box' of the protest movement from its birth to its brutal end.

Boston's academic community was buzzing with speculation about the outcome of the Chinese uprising and it was clear that the Albert Einstein Institution should be present at what was becoming an unprecedented nonviolent action. So many political uprisings had not been properly recorded and their lessons lost to history. Gene was determined that this shouldn't happen again – this was exactly what the Institution had been set up for.

Gene talked with Peter Ackerman and Bruce Jenkins about a research trip to Beijing and they agreed on a mission to find out how the students were organising their struggle and where their ideas were coming from. A Canadian diplomat visiting the Albert Einstein Institution had mentioned that some unidentified books on nonviolent resistance, brought from the US were, circulating around Beijing University. This produced a hair-raising moment in the office – was it possible that Gene's books might already have been smuggled into China?

Gene and Bruce heard about Huang Jing's work on the phones to Beijing and asked him to join the team as their translator and fixer. Huang was delighted to be asked. Finally he'd be able to witness the protests from closer than the end of his apartment's phone line, and get paid for it.

His wife knew the dangers and begged him not to leave her and their 5-year-old son, but the chance to see the first glimpses of a democratic China were too much. He resisted her pleas and began packing for the trip.

The team flew into Beijing on a Pan Am flight arriving at midnight on 28th May. As they shuffled through security they braced themselves for the Chinese security agents to pull them aside for questioning, but nothing happened. Waved through with just a cursory passport check and no abnormal surveillance, they hailed a taxi and made directly for their hotel just a few blocks away from Tiananmen Square.

Huang set to work on his contacts almost as soon as they reached the hotel, scheduling meetings with the students involved and tracking down their leaders. It was a short trip so there was no time to waste.

The team started their interviews with members of the 'Student Dialogue Delegation' which had been set up initially to liaise between the government and the student organisations. This made its members some of the most well placed to tell the story of the competing views of the student groups and the Communist Party negotiators.

Most of the interviews were conducted in the nondescript Hu Fan Chao Hotel, which locals believed had escaped the notice of state surveillance. When they came to the hotel room, many of the students hadn't slept or eaten properly for days. Sometimes Gene would offer them food and a bed to have a sleep before they started the interviews.

The groups numbered between three and twelve people and on at least one occasion a seminar was held in a university classroom. Huang packed the schedule so tightly that the team conducted interviews late into the night.

One of the first interviewees to arrive was Li Lu, an influential student leader in his early 20s from Wuhan province. Li Lu was considered a radical, mature beyond his years and already thinking long term about the future of the movement. He began by describing how the protests had begun spontaneously in mid-April after the unexpected death of the respected liberal politician Hu Yaobang.

Hu Yaobang had been born into a peasant family, but with natural ability had taught himself to read. He left his family to join the Communist Party at just 14 and became one of the youngest veterans of the 'Long March', the Communist Red Army's retreat from nationalist forces at the end of 1934. He rose up through the ranks with the future leader, Deng Xiaoping, before the Communist Party declared the establishment of The Peoples Republic of China in 1949.

As a senior party official Hu exonerated three million people who had been persecuted during the Cultural Revolution. He also discreetly supported a protest in 1978, when a wall to the west of Tiananmen Square was plastered with posters and slogans urging democracy. Hu even invited two of the activists into his home for a discussion of their grievances.

In 1980 he was appointed Party Secretary General and elected to the Politburo Standing Committee, making him the second most powerful official in the country after the 'Paramount Leader', Deng. He was a vigorous reforming force, pushing for candidates to be directly elected to the Politburo, advocating for more multi-candidate elections and increasing public consultations on government policy.

As time went on, his support for the autonomy of Tibet, encouragement of Western style cutlery to reduce disease, his adoption of suits instead of traditional dress and suggestions that Communist Party influence over the government be limited, began to attract deep suspicion inside the Party.

In December 1986, a pro-democracy protest began at the University of Science and Technology in Hefei. Deng Xiao Ping ordered Hu to dismiss the leaders from the Communist Party and silence them, but Hu refused. The students celebrated the news that Hu was on their side, but the continuation of their protest would seal his fate. Senior Party and military officials forced Hu to resign for being too lenient. He was made to issue a public self-criticism of his mistakes which included violating the Chinese principle of collective leadership.

His open dismissal earned Hu hero status among the fledgling democracy movement. A senior official in the Party refusing to deny his beliefs was a significant sign that there must be other sympathetic figures in the Party and that democratic reform was no longer impossible. Hu's martyrdom was assured when he died of a heart attack shortly after his forced retirement on the 15th April 1989. He was 74.

Students from universities across Beijing flocked to Tiananmen Square to place wreaths at the Monument to the Martyrs of the People. Although Hu had not held an official position at the time of his death, public opinion forced the government to hold an elaborate state funeral. The success of the students in winning this concession for Hu, emboldened them further in grief and defiance.

The week between his death and burial saw more demonstrations and poster campaigns calling for democracy and an end to corruption. On 22nd April, 50,000 people marched to Tiananmen Square to pay their respects. Hu's memorial service became a public conduit for anger about his dismissal and a celebration of his promotion of freedom of speech and the press.

The political space opened up by his death caused a serious dilemma for the government. The Party leadership refused the right of any organisation to lead political activities and branded the demonstrations a foreign conspiracy.

By early May, organising structures were growing up around the spontaneous uprising. The Beijing Universities United Autonomous Student Union was formed. Referred to simply as 'The Union', it was composed of representatives from the various pro-democracy groups at the city's universities. The Union then elected a smaller delegation of experienced student leaders, 'The Dialogue Delegation' with the intention of holding talks with the government.

When Li Peng refused to meet the students to discuss their demands, the movement called a hunger strike. Though nobody could pinpoint precisely who had suggested it, the hunger strikers who were prepared to die were deemed the most qualified to lead the new movement. After just a few days there were almost 6,000 people fasting, but the action had been so spontaneous and the students so inexperienced that nobody had researched how a hunger strike actually worked.

Instead of drinking water and sustaining themselves with small amounts of lemon juice and salts to extend the period of action, they refused all liquids meaning they were close to death within days and the strike had to be abandoned.

As new student groups from around the country began to arrive in Tiananmen, the growth in numbers required a new leadership structure to maintain order. The hunger strike committee formed the nucleus of a new authority, the 'Headquarters of Tiananmen Square'. The Headquarters brought together elected representatives from each of the student groups. Despite the new Headquarters, the Union continued to operate and the proliferation of organisations began to make it increasingly difficult to understand who was in charge.

On the 21st May, the students heard rumours that the government were ordering troops into Tiananmen to clear the square. 'I wanted to get married', Li Lu told Gene, 'That night we had the wedding on the Square and after that I thought, ok, now I can die'. The movement, however, had become more powerful than even they realised. As the revered Chinese 38th Army began rolling through the suburbs of the city with tanks and armoured personnel carriers, its passage was blocked by the spontaneous actions of civilians and workers who spilled out of their homes and factories to protect the protesters.

On hearing the news, the Tiananmen Headquarters used its communications network to mobilise thousands more people in the area to support them. The demonstrators formed barricades around the military convoys preventing their advance or retreat. As the soldiers sat motionless awaiting orders, the students took them food and water, sang and talked to them about the justness of the democratic cause. Realising the army could move no further without fighting their way out, the government ordered a temporary retreat to the outskirts of the city where they sat awaiting further orders.

As Gene and Bruce took an afternoon stroll, Tiananmen Square appeared like a vast street fair decorated with flags and banners, the smell of cooking and woodsmoke filling the air. An elderly man on a large tricycle pedalled slowly around with his wife on the back and people held up their babies to have their photo taken with the Goddess of Freedom, a 30 foot high replica of the Statue of Liberty.

Despite the atmosphere of celebration, these thousands of students knew they were beginning a dangerous stand off with the government. The students told Gene that they didn't expect to live very long, but realised that a violent uprising would be a disaster with little chance of success. Many were putting their affairs in order, hastily writing out their wills and distributing money to relatives.

Gene was initially concerned about talking to the students in public at Tiananmen, 'Do we bring people danger on the square when we talk to them?' he asked. 'Don't worry', Li Lu replied, 'old Chinese saying, "dead pigs are never afraid of hot water"'.

Millions of dollars were raised by activists in Hong Kong who staged a concert to support the protest. A shipment of camping and sanitary equipment soon appeared in the square producing bright clean lines of orange and blue tents. The students camped together, grouped by university and college. Many were from Beijing, but others had journeyed for days from as far as Inner Mongolia, Hunan and Szechuan. One student spotted Gene from his tent and came out to talk to him, 'Please tell the world why we are here and what we are doing and what we stand for. That we want freedom and democracy'.

The students had established a telephone information network operating out of the university which would make and receive calls to keep remote groups of students informed of army movements. The Headquarters in the square was equipped with a phone connected by a long cable to the Museum of the Chinese Revolution. More rudimentary means of communication included loudspeakers and even drums to pass messages and signal people to come out onto the streets. Students with megaphones were sent into the suburbs shouting their demands and encouraging ordinary citizens to support them in their pursuit of political freedom and an end to corruption.

Around the square were a phalanx of hundreds of unarmed soldiers keeping watch. The students had organised marshals to keep order and maintain nonviolent discipline. In face to face encounters with the army, Gene and Bruce watched the student marshals enforcing a three foot space in front of the lines of soldiers, walking up and down to prevent physical contact, while lobbying the soldiers to defect and support the students. Around 700 soldiers behind the Great Hall of the People had their path to the square blocked and the students brought food and water to this barricade. When tempers became frayed the marshals would protect the soldiers with their bodies.

A structure of three functional groups had been created by the Headquarters – a propaganda group told the people what they wanted to do, a finance group organised the collection of funds and the coordinating group organised the actions and marches before communicating the plans by telephone and any other means available. A tight security system with specially made ID cards prevented extremists or government spies entering the square and restricted access to the areas of command and control.

Although these innovations appeared sophisticated, Gene soon realised from his interviews that the students were improvising all the time without any apparent long term strategy. Gandhi's nonviolent struggle in India against the British had been included in Chinese school text books and the 1986 people power movement which had ousted President Marcos in the Philippines had been covered by state television, but this appeared to be the limit of the students' knowledge of nonviolent case studies. They found no evidence of the report that Gene's books had reached the students in Tiananmen.

Li Lu described how before the beginning of the uprising the key intellectual leaders of the movement had talked at length about the state of the country and dismissed, very early on, any ideas about a violent uprising. 'We were aware of improper ideas and suggestions and we refused. We insisted on a nonviolent struggle.' When Hu died, the students rose up spontaneously, but there were enough intellectuals among them who had done the thinking and could enforce nonviolent discipline quickly enough to avert an outbreak of violence.

The leadership issue was the biggest weakness of the movement. Different groups were refusing to take orders and infighting was causing a huge turnover of leaders. Envoys from other cities had visited Tiananmen and sympathetic protests were taking place all over China, but they were not coordinated and their demands were often radically different. The leadership issue was not just a problem for the student movement, it also made it difficult for the government to understand who to communicate with or even how to attempt to satisfy their demands.

For days, Gene had been testing and questioning the tactic of occupying the geographic space of Tiananmen Square, trying to spur the students into diversifying tactics and engaging Chinese citizens beyond the core student group. No issue would be more divisive or more crucial to the outcome of the movement than the decision to remain in the square.

As the interviews continued, it's clear from the transcripts that Gene was struggling with his own rule about not giving advice. The tape recordings of the sessions are peppered with leading questions and prompts. 'It's important to spread support to as many parts of society as possible. It's like pillars supporting a house, there are several supporting the government. If you only pull out one pillar then the building stands strong. Other sections are very important', he warned. Then he tested them. 'Are you thinking of a future coup and possibly worse dictator?' 'If they come tonight and arrest all the leaders are there substitutes?'

'If they arrest people, yes, we have substitutes, but if they come with machine guns and kill many people there are no plans for that,' one of the leaders responded, 'If this happened some people would consider armed struggle'.

'But the government want this!' Gene countered, 'Sometimes the government will kill many people to get you to move to armed struggle'.

The question of government agents provocateurs had been animating Gene greatly. On one of his walks through the square he had noticed two or three tents erected by a group who called themselves the 'Autonomous Workers Union'. A woman there was giving an emotional speech calling for violence against the soldiers and urged the students to 'not let even one escape'.

Something about this group was suspicious and he became convinced that they were a government plant to get the students to turn violent in order that the army would be justified in turning their tanks loose to crush the uprising. But what most concerned Gene was the Chinese students' over emphasis on a single method – the occupation of the square.

One of the most prominent leaders was Chai Ling, a 23-year-old student whose parents were both army doctors. She was given the title, 'Commander in Chief of the Defend Tiananmen Head Quarters' and often stood in the centre of the square giving rousing speeches.

'We will mobilise the people around the world to protest martial law', she yelled through her megaphone, 'Martial law won't succeed in ten days, in a year in a hundred years!'

On 30th May, a proposal was put forward to leave the square, but Chai Ling fought the move. 'I want to say to the people that the square is our only stronghold, if we lose it the conservatives will overrun China.' Many people argued that the longer the students held out in the square, the more ordinary Chinese people would have time to join the movement. Other student leaders like Liang Xiaogan vehemently disagreed. 'Holding onto the square was absolutely meaningless and harming the students cause' he told her.

At almost every nightly meeting the issue was brought up and every night the vote was defeated by around 80% who wanted to to stay. Those who believed the occupation should have been stopped just drifted away and were being replaced by increasing numbers of inexperienced new faces from the regions who, having travelled for days to get there, didn't want to miss their part in the action.

In the early hours of 3rd June, army units mounted a second attempt to reach the square. Many of the troops were disguised as students and travelled in civilian coaches just like genuine protesters arriving from the countryside.

The student wardens soon detected the Trojan vehicles, searched them and found concealed caches of automatic weapons, knives and cattle prods. They turned the seized weapons over to the city police immediately. To be found with a cache of guns would hand a propaganda victory to the government who would use it as proof the students had violent intentions.

When troops from the Great Hall of The People responded to help their undercover colleagues in the besieged coaches, they too were surrounded by throngs of protesters who blocked their path. The soldiers, unable to reach their colleagues, but reassured that they were coming to no harm sat down on the pavement and started to sing. The protesters sat opposite them and sang too. At the end of the day these troops were ordered back into the Great Hall. As they beat their retreat the students sang 'Long Live the People's Liberation Army!'

Frustrated yet again, the Communist Party signalled their move to finally end the occupation. That evening, the state TV newsreaders announced solemnly that 'martial law units will take all necessary measures. Those who incite opposition must take the consequences'.

At the end of the day, troops and armoured personnel carriers began to converge on central Beijing again, and this time they did not stop at the human barricades. As the troops forced their way through to Tiananmen, the students screamed at them, 'whose army are you!?' Even after it was clear that live rounds were being fired at the crowds, the people couldn't believe it.

Gene, Bruce and Huang had been having dinner before making their regular walk back to their hotel through the square when an armoured personnel carrier burst out of a side street and roared past at high speed. A group of students lunged towards it dragging concrete and steel fencing into the road to block its path.

Huang grabbed a metal fence and began to drag it into the path of the tank, but Gene forcibly pulled him back. 'You can't do that! That's not why we're here', he yelled over the roar of the engines and the metal tracks. As Huang looked back he saw another protester drop something in the road, a camera or a wallet. The man ran back, hoping to reach it before it was crushed under the vehicle, but just as he lifted it from the road the tracks hit him and dragged him under, killing him almost instantly.

The team picked up their pace as they passed the Great Hall of the People. At the end of the square, flashes of light streamed across the sky with a loud popping noise. Bruce thought the military might be setting off fireworks to intimidate the people, but it quickly became clear that the army were now firing live rounds.

As the team left the square, columns of troops were coming in from every direction. There was a sound like pottery breaking and people started running. Gene, Bruce and Huang ran in the direction of their hotel, but stopped for breath, huddled with others in the foyer of a Kentucky Fried Chicken restaurant, watching as more troops spilled in. As they looked back, a protester drove a double length bus across the line of advance of the soldiers, hoping to cut them off.

Some students approached Huang and told him to get Gene and Bruce out of the square quickly or the army would think they were CIA officers instructing the students. The soldiers they had seen were unarmed, but by the time they picked their way back to the hotel, the drone of helicopters hung overhead and the night was punctuated by the sound of gunfire and screaming.

The student loudspeakers began broadcasting that there was a state of emergency in Tiananmen and called on the people to come out onto the streets and show their support. The students and workers in the command tents began desperately to burn their membership books. The chants of the crowd turned to, 'animals, animals!'

In the chaos, one of the students had managed to acquire a semi-automatic rifle from a soldier. Student leader, Liu Xiaobo, wrestled the gun from him before attempting to smash it on the guardrail of the Monument to the People's Heroes. 'I was terrified if any gunshots were fired from the monument, the troops would have an excuse to gun everybody down'.

Chai Ling's voice came over the loudspeaker again. She announced that those who wanted to leave should leave, but those who wanted to stay should stay. Xiaobao thought this approach was a disaster waiting to happen, it was too dangerous to leave and those who were left behind would be put in danger.

In a last ditch attempt at saving the remaining protesters, Xiaobao came up with a plan to send representatives to the army lines to negotiate time to organise free passage from the square. 'We know you're not afraid of dying', he told the students, 'but leaving now doesn't mean you're cowards'.

Chai Ling retorted that she had heard that reformers inside the government needed the students to hold out until morning. Xiaobao shot back angrily, 'I don't care if it's true or not, no leader has the right to gamble with thousands of peoples lives at the square!'

Xiaobao and his friend Hou Dejian commandeered a van and drove cautiously to the army line. The troops nervously held their rifles to their shoulders aiming at the approaching vehicle as it slowed to a halt. They delivered the proposal to an officer who disappeared to consult his senior commanders and returned swiftly with the answer they were hoping for, 'I hope you can convince them to leave the square', he told them.

Dejian and Xiaobo raced back to the monument to tell the students about the deal, but they still couldn't agree. Dejian decided that a vote should be held and told the assembly that on the count of three, those who wanted to stay should shout 'stay' and those who want to go should shout 'go'. It was a terrible method of voting – he knew that those who wanted to stay would shout bravely, while those who wanted to go would be ashamed to have their voices heard. The vote sounded the same, so Dejian decided to fudge the result and declare that the 'Go' vote had won.

At daybreak on 4th June the remaining protesters filed wearily out of Tiananmen Square from the south east corner.

Chai Ling's reasoning for vehemently arguing to stay in the square came under severe criticism after the release of one of the most notable documentaries made about the massacre, *The Gate of Heavenly Peace*. In an interview recorded on the 28th May she is seen to tell the reporter, Philip Cunningham, 'What we actually are hoping for is bloodshed, the moment when the government is ready to brazenly butcher the people. Only when the square is awash with blood will the people of China open their eyes. Only then will they really be united. But how can I explain any of this to my fellow students?'

The footage appears to suggest that Chai Ling understood the power that the democracy movement would gain if there was a massacre of unarmed protesters. Was she really inviting a massacre in the square as an extreme political jujitsu action? She strongly denied this, claiming she was misquoted and the footage used an 'interpretative and erroneous' translation.

In the morning, Gene woke from just a few hours of fitful sleep and pulled back his curtains to see large helicopters still flying back and forth over the centre of the city. Rumours were circulating, later reported by the *New York Times*, that a line of students who had stood linking arms were all shot down, another line got up and suffered the same fate. A third line rose but the soldiers only shot at their feet and they fled hobbling from the square.

Chinese state television was reporting that the protesters had wounded and killed soldiers. Footage of destroyed army vehicles gave credence to these reports. The pro-democracy demonstrators were described as ruffians, bandits and worst of all, 'counter-revolutionaries'.

It was now clear to Gene that the team needed to get out of China. The aim of talking to the Chinese students involved was no longer possible and they weren't in a position to do any more research. All of the roads in the area were closed or blocked to cars so Bruce borrowed a bicycle from a hotel porter and rode across town to the airline office to bring their flights forward.

Everywhere lay the mayhem of the night before – burned out buses, crushed cars, rubble strewn across the roads. The shells of army vehicles testified to reports that, in the last moments, as the army overran the square, nonviolent discipline had broken down. The soldiers now positioned around the square barely looked twice at him and he soon reached the Pan Am office, changing the tickets to fly out the following day.

The final hurdle before getting out would be to ensure the safety of the 12 cassette tapes of interviews. There had been no time to transcribe or duplicate them so if they were to be confiscated by customs or the secret police the trip would have been a total failure. One option was to hide them in Beijing and collect them later when the situation had calmed down, but Bruce came up with an ingenious idea, disguising them by writing the names of Led Zeppelin albums on the cassette covers.

Once again Gene, Bruce and Huang braced themselves through passport control, expecting to be hauled aside and have the contents of their luggage tossed out and searched, but again they were waved through without suspicion. The team sighed temporary relief before the agonising realisation that some, perhaps many, of the young people they had been with were now arrested or killed. A massive manhunt and clampdown was now in full force across the country.

As the team was leaving China, one of the most famous scenes of the uprising was playing out in the city. As a convoy of tanks were making their way along Chang'an Avenue on the northern side of Tiananmen Square, a man carrying a bag of shopping walked into the road in front of them.

This moment, frozen in time by a small number of journalists, often leads to the conclusion that the tank didn't stop, that the man was crushed. But that wasn't what happened. The tank stopped and then it swerved, and swerved again. Even after the blood that had been shed the previous day, the incident proved that one single nonviolent action had the power to stop a convoy of tanks if the commanders were unwilling to kill.

In the coming weeks and months, many of the protesters were tracked down, tried and summarily executed. The pictures of the 21 most wanted were repeatedly shown on TV with mini features on their 'crimes' against the state. The introduction to one of these reports began, 'Let's see how this evil mastermind conspired with reactionary forces at home and abroad to manipulate the students and instigate dongluan (turmoil).'

A rescue operation for Tiananmen Square student leaders began just days after the tanks rolled in and the government published its most wanted list of 'counter-revolutionaries'. It was called 'Operation Yellow Bird' after a Chinese proverb, 'The mantis stalks the cicada, unaware of the yellow bird behind.' Its goal was to smuggle prominent members of the movement to safety in the West. The operation brought together an unlikely mix of ordinary Chinese citizens, sympathetic Communist officials, British intelligence, the CIA and Hong Kong triad gangsters. The extraction missions, according to a number of accounts, employed scrambler devices, infrared signallers and night-vision goggles.

Of the 21 leaders on the most-wanted list, 15, including Li Lu, Chai Ling and her husband Feng Congde, were spirited out of China to Hong Kong, given false identities, passports and disguises and sent abroad. In total, 800 escaped. Sympathisers helped student leaders travel more than 2,000km from Beijing to the Hong Kong border by bus, boat, train, car, donkey cart and in storage tanks. Many were sheltered for months before handsomely paid smugglers took them to Hong Kong.

After nearly 10 months on the run, Chai Ling arrived in Hong Kong in a cargo box full of rotting fish. The British government continued to help with extractions of dissidents until the handover in 1997, when Hong Kong returned to Chinese rule and all records of the operation were removed from the territory. Many went first to France and others travelled on to the US for scholarships at Ivy League universities.

When Gene came to analyse the research from the trip he identified five key points in the movement.

1. The students' motivations for pursuing nonviolent means of protest and resistance were purely practical.
2. The students had no detailed knowledge of the history or dynamics of nonviolent struggle.

3. The organization in the movement was weak and divisive.
4. There was very little, if any, strategic planning.
5. There was substantial evidence that the regime had used agents pro-vocateurs to instigate violence and weaken the movement.

He told me, 'They were not planned they were not prepared. There was no strategic decision on how long you stay in the square and when you leave. What became very clear to me in retrospect was that the students in the square were operating with great commitment and bravery but they really didn't know what the hell they were doing'.

Gene believed the students would have done better to have shifted their tactics from the occupation of the square to a major campaign of communication with the population. The best moment for them to have left would have been after the people of Beijing had successfully halted and turned around the 38th army. The students could then have claimed victory, and then developed a plan to spread the movement throughout the country. The pro-democracy movement needed to move from symbolic actions and nonviolent occupation of the square to encouraging large-scale defection of military units. But as Gene warned:

'The students had no plan. They were improvising all the way through. The attitude that you simply improvise and that improvisation brings you greater success is nonsense. If you don't know what you're doing you're likely to get into big trouble', Gene warned.

In frustration at the deaths in Tiananmen, he wrote in his trip report, 'It is well past time for a major expansion of our knowledge of struggle by people power and the wide dissemination of existing know-how into many languages. Why should every people seeking greater freedom and justice without using violence have to start by reinventing the wheel?'

The Barricades

On the 9th of November 1989, the Iron Curtain was being torn down. Young men and women ripped chunks of concrete from the Berlin Wall and embraced those on the other side. President Mikhael Gorbachev's reforms were ending the Cold War and he was becoming the most popular Russian in post-war history – at least to those in the West. A few weeks after the wall came down, Gene and Bruce Jenkins landed at an icy Moscow airport for a conference on the ethics of nonviolence, held just a brisk walk from the Kremlin. The fact that they were granted visas to enter the country at all is surprising, given that at least one of Gene's books already sat in the KGB library with an annotation describing him as a CIA asset.

The conference on the ethics of nonviolence might have been just another forgettable meeting in a charmless hotel with stale sandwiches, but among the audience were a handful of academics from some of the former Soviet satellite states who were searching for ways of breaking free from Moscow's control.

One of those delegates was Grazina Miniotaite who had travelled from the Lithuanian capital, Vilnius. An associate professor at the Lithuanian Academy of Philosophy, she had earned her doctorate at the elite Moscow State University and was already familiar with Gene's work. After the talk, she set aside any fear of the spies who must have been watching and sought Gene out to ask for his help.

Despite Gorbachev's opening up to the West, the Baltic states of Lithuania, Latvia, and Estonia were still being kept firmly under Moscow's control. All three had enjoyed periods of independence in their history that were later rolled back by their powerful neighbour. Most recently, the Soviet Union had regained control of them during the Second World War and the occupation saw a systematic destruction of their culture, attacks on their religion and an attempt to impose the teaching of Russian language in schools.

Thousands of people who took part in violent and nonviolent resistance against the occupations were sent to Siberia by the Soviets where many perished in prison camps from cold and malnourishment.

Until the late 1980s, the resistance of the population was spontaneous and uncoordinated. There was friction between different groups and Grazina was convinced that the disparate strands of the resistance had to be gathered together, in Lithuania and across the Baltic states, to make any real impact. 'The need for a coordinating centre of the reformist activities was acutely felt', she wrote.

In June 1988, at a meeting at the Lithuanian Academy of Sciences, a delegation of more than 500 people voted to elect leaders of what would become a powerful new organisation known as 'Sajudis'. Composed of 36 academics, journalists, writers and musicians, the group excluded career politicians and high profile activists to avoid existing political conflicts and partisan issues that might divide them. Grazina was among the first elected members.

Vytautus Landsbergis, a professor with a distinctive drooping moustache, was elected as Sajudis chairman. He had earned the trust of the people by leading many of the protests against the Soviets throughout the 1970s and '80s. The new leaders went to work planning their liberation campaign for Lithuania in a small stuffy room, gathering useful examples of nonviolent campaigns from around the world.

Sajudis started with small campaigns launched on social and economic issues – a boycott of low quality dairy products produced by state monopoly, Agropromas, and, six months later, a refusal to pay increased tax on private cars were both successful. These small actions were designed to demonstrate to the population that properly co-ordinated nonviolent resistance could win significant victories.

One of the most memorable symbolic protests for Baltic independence at this time was the 'Baltic Chain', staged on 23rd August 1989. Sajudis coordinated with pro-independence movements in Latvia and Estonia to form the longest uninterrupted human chain in history, linking the

Baltic capitals of Vilnius, Tallinn and Riga to demonstrate their unity and common opposition to Soviet rule. It was a stunning spectacle, consisting of two million people holding hands for almost 420 miles.

Later that evening, 5,000 people gathered in Vilnius's Cathedral Square, for a candlelit, protest where they sang important national songs. The churches across the Baltic states rang their bells in unison and leaders of the pro-independence movements conducted a symbolic funeral, where they burned a giant black cross in memory of those who had died under Soviet oppression.

Grazina had read extracts from Gene's work in the Lithuanian press before the conference in Moscow, but when she saw a draft of his new book, *Civilian Based Defense: A Post Military Weapon System,* which discussed how to oppose an occupation by a foreign power, she realised it was exactly what Sajudis and the Baltic states needed. Gene agreed to hand over all of the page proofs he had brought with him and Grazina stuffed her suitcase with as much reading material as it would carry. On her return to Vilnius she set to work at her desk preparing a ten page summary of the book in Lithuanian for distribution to the Sajudis leadership committee.

When the Lithuanian general election came in February 1990, Sajudis decided to run parliamentary candidates against the communists and won by a landslide – ninety nine seats to 25 for the Communist Party and 7 to the pro-Moscow CPL/CPSU party. In defiance of Moscow, Landsbergis quickly passed the 'Act on the re-establishment of the State of Lithuania' – the first declaration of independence by any Soviet republic. For the first time since the Second World War, Lithuania had declared its government was independent, but nobody knew how long the Kremlin would tolerate it.

The Sajudis parliamentary victory catapulted a young army doctor by the name of Algirdas Butkevičius to prominence as the first defence minister of the newly independent Lithuanian government. Slightly built, with a thin boyish face and a dark wispy moustache, Butkevičius was not a typical army officer, but his special interest in psychological operations would prepare him brilliantly for his new role. He had caught the attention of the country's media while still in his 20s by conducting a number of dramatic expeditions into Siberia to bring home the bodies of Lithuanians who had died in Soviet prison camps.

At just 30 years old, Audrius was now struggling with the gargantuan problem of how to resist the Soviet attempts to regain control of Lithuania while Gorbachev was seen as a hero in the West. 'I asked myself, are we really going to copy the tactics of a big state? Can we really be the bombers of Gorbachev?'

Audrius had come across Gene's work in 1984 while studying psychological operations at officer school. A Russian military texbook locked in the KGB library described Gene Sharp as a CIA officer who had written about possible ways to use civilians against an invader or coup d'état. But it wasn't until Grazina called on him in early 1990 that Butkevicius realised the potential of the work. They met in the restaurant of the parliament building – a 1970s monolith that looked like a space ship on concrete legs. They had known each other, in passing, for years and she came with her husband, the famous liberal writer Algirdas Degutis. 'Audrius, we have something for you', she leant down and reached into her case for a small red and brown booklet of basic instructions taken from some of Gene's work.

Butkevičius was not yet practiced enough to read such specialist English so he handed it to his military assistant, a young Lieutenant called Almantas Leika. Leika would one day become the General in command of the entire Lithuanian army, but the first major task of his military career would be to translate Gene's work on civilian based defense.

Leika completed the translation within a matter of weeks and Butkevicius immediately recognized the importance of the book. 'I thought to myself, there is a system to this!' He photocopied the manuscript and had his staff send out fifty copies to political and resistance leaders across the Soviet Union, making special representations to his Baltic neighbours in Latvia and Estonia.

The newly independent Lithuanian government now began to assert itself, putting up border controls, bypassing the Soviet passport control system and ending conscription of Lithuanian men into the Soviet army.

The measures were a step too far for Moscow and on 25th April 1990, the Soviets began a blockade of Lithuania, cutting off 90% of their oil and gas supplies along with other essentials.

Similar events were unfolding in Latvia, which declared its independence less than a month later on 14th May. Gorbachev announced the independence of the Baltic states was null and void. Ethnic Russians loyal to Moscow staged a protest rally and called a strike the following day. The Soviet army attempted to push their way into the Latvian parliament building, but it was quickly thronged by civilians blocking their way and the troops were withdrawn.

Latvia's pro-independence Popular Front issued a document called the 'Announcement of the Board of the Popular Front of Latvia to All the Supporters of Latvia's Independence'. Known as the, 'Appeal for X Hour' it set up the instructions on how the civilian population should act if a coup détat or re-imposition of Soviet rule was attempted. The Popular Front called upon the people to use nonviolent resistance in the face of an attack.

This was the first ever plan for national defence by nonviolent civilians. It advised people to comply only with the laws of the new independent government and to ignore the orders of the Soviet military and any imposed governors. The people were told to refuse to participate in any elections or referenda and to document all the crimes of the occupiers. Plans were also drawn up on how to protect independent government buildings by nonviolent means.

Audrius Butkevicius established a similar X Hour document in Lithuania based on the page proofs of Gene's *Civilian Based Defence*. One of his first tasks was to ensure a secure communication system for the country that would survive an assault. A Soviet force could quickly disable the phone lines which would instantly take the phones, faxes and telexes off line. Foreign journalists might be expelled and the TV and radio stations seized.

Part of the answer was a well known amateur radio enthusiast called Tadas Vysniauskas. Tadas was drafted in to set up a communications centre in the heart of the parliament building and he began installing radio equipment and an antenna needed to communicate over extremely long distances.

Given the right atmospheric conditions, Tadas would be able to communicate as far afield as the US and India. Although the radio setup was temperamental and in need of a skilled operator, it could not easily be cut off by the Soviets. Unlike a satellite dish, a radio antennae is difficult to shoot at and awkward to jam. The team would be able to broadcast until the radio room was seized by the Russians.

Tadas and his team began building a network with fellow radio operators all over the world who would be able to pass on messages to foreign media in the event of a Soviet attack on the parliament. When a good contact was made, a pin was placed on a huge world map which covered one wall of the room.

Russian TV consistently referred to the 'hostile radio station' working under cover from the parliament building which, 'transmits misinformation and lies in all the languages of the world' about events in Lithuania.

The chief broadcaster at the breakaway Lithuanian parliament was Rita Dapkute, a young English-speaking staffer from the Bureau of Information. If the parliament came under threat of takeover, she would rush to the radio room to maintain contact with the outside world. Rita was particularly useful not only for her language skills but because many of the international journalists knew her personally and recognised her distinctive voice on the air. This meant that the Soviets would never be able to fake broadcasts from the building to give the impression that all was well. If Rita went off air, the world would know that the worst had happened at the parliament.

The radio room quickly became the nerve centre of the building and therefore the most heavily protected. The doors to the room were completely blocked and the few authorised staff had to crawl through specially constructed tunnels to reach it. The elaborate disguise would give the team the maximum amount of time to keep broadcasting in the event of the building being stormed. Soon, the team began to think about how they could transmit not just radio but television. Television pictures would record the abuses of a Soviet attack much more powerfully than a radio report, but TV transmission was a far more complicated prospect. The equipment needed was sophisticated and additional power was needed to transmit the signal.

With the help of employees of a local TV station, they brought a Hungarian-manufactured 100watt transmitter to the parliament, but the signal was deemed too weak. Only a handful of people were receiving the pictures. Butkevicius was told it was impossible to produce an amplifier to boost the signal. 'How can we produce such a thing in a parliament building where there is hardly a spare nail to be had?' the technicians had asked him. Nonetheless, a plan was soon cobbled together. Boffins from the nearby Institute of Physics were drafted in to solve the problem and together they came up with a plan on a scrap of paper. Step by step, components for a home made amplifier were pilfered from all over Vilnius. Some of the parts were more than 30 years old, but they were soon being soldered together on the roof of the parliament.

The technicians worked for hours in temperatures of 25 degrees below zero before being sent into Vilnius to test the signal. With some minor modifications the amplifier began working, beaming out a signal of 10kw – more than ten times the power they had previously been operating with. In the worst case scenario the team would now be able to broadcast live video of the parliament building being attacked. A video statement by Landsbergis was pre-recorded to broadcast final instructions for the population in the event of a takeover.

The Soviets now began taking steps to counter the preparations of the Baltic states by using a sophisticated programme to incite divisions in society. Each of the Baltic countries had a sizeable ethnic Russian and Polish population. With a mixture of propaganda and secret funding, they encouraged them to stir up trouble, claim their rights were being infringed, and demand secession and a Soviet intervention to help them.

In Latvia the Soviets formed an organisation called the 'Public Salvation Committee'. This was a traditional Marxist Leninist scheme for defusing a brewing revolution, first fomenting popular discontent among the working people and then encouraging a revolutionary provisional government to ask the Soviet authorities for a military intervention on humanitarian grounds. This plan had been used by Moscow many times, in Finland in 1939, Czechoslovakia in 1968 and most recently in Afghanistan in 1979.

Audrius saw this threat developing in Lithuania and organised for Russian democracy advocates and activists from the Polish Solidarity Movement to talk to the Russian minorities. 'We told them that it is not "us" against Russia or Polish people, we are fighting communism', he said. The Lithuanian military also formed a special forces unit which was employed to counter violent protests encouraged by Moscow. In some cases the unit expressly threatened these pro-Moscow activists with death. That bit certainly wasn't in Gene's guidebook.

At the Lithuanian parliament, preparations were made to defend against the Soviet attack that everyone believed was imminent. Volunteers congregated at the building and fires were lit just inside the perimeter wall, filling the air with woodsmoke as the temperatures plunged below freezing. The people slept in shifts, sometimes only two hours a night, often in the chairs of the debating chamber. Makeshift beds were made up on every floor, in offices and corridors.

Those who had taken the night watch lay on blankets, curled up still clutching their hunting rifles. Spiked metal fencing was positioned behind the windows and sandbag positions built up along the corridors. Electrified barbed wire was strung across the roof and the stairs were wired with explosives, ready to blow up if needed. Landsbergis slept with a gas mask, a bullet proof vest and a gun under his bed. The concept of a purely nonviolent defence was clearly not winning universal acceptance.

On the night of January 2nd 1991, a Soviet paramilitary group, the 'Black Berets', launched their first attack in Latvia, capturing the press building in Riga where the principal newspapers and magazines of the country were printed. The Black Berets beat the journalists inside and this triggered a mass protest outside the Communist Party building. Moscow announced an additional division of paratroopers would be moved to the Baltics to manage the unrest.

Just over a week later on 11th January, a shadowy organisation calling itself the 'National Salvation Committee' announced its formation in

Lithuania. In reality, the Salvation Committee was comprised of the Soviet military and some Lithuanian political groups loyal to Moscow. In the early hours of the morning, Soviet troops launched an operation to invade the offices of the Lithuanian Department of Defense, followed by an attack on the parliament.

As ordinary Lithuanians phoned around and knocked on doors to spread the news, the citizens of Vilnius followed Butkevicius's X hour plan and headed out to defend government buildings and the communications network. Almost 9000 people gathered around the TV transmission tower alone, but within hours Soviet soldiers fired into the crowd, wounding four. Intelligence soon reached Butkevicius that the KGB special forces unit, Alpha, had arrived in Vilnius. At midnight on the 12th January, the Soviets demanded the independent government resign and announced the re-introduction of direct Soviet presidential rule.

The phones in the parliament building rang out as ordinary Lithuanians across the country phoned in to report that the Russian army was on the move. Paratroopers in armoured vehicles were fanning out across Vilnius and major columns were heading towards the TV studios and transmission tower. Grazina and her husband abandoned a dinner party they were hosting when they saw the coverage being broadcast live from the parliament's TV station. They left home immediately, grabbing their warmest clothes and set off at a brisk walk to join the defenders at the TV tower, three miles away.

Gunshots rang out across the city and a terrifying roar of tanks could be heard approaching through the darkness. People locked arms forming a tight human barrier, but as the metalled monsters came into view they used noise as their first weapon. They fired deafening blank rounds which caused total hearing loss for some of the people trying to obstruct their progress.

The soldiers turned around their weapons, swinging their rifle butts wildly at the heads of even elderly women in the crowd. The tanks kept coming, crushing cars, buses and trucks. A man and woman stood bravely in front of one, like the man they must have seen in Tiananmen Square photographs – but these tanks did not stop, they just rolled straight over them. The soldiers began shooting into the crowd and soon 12 civilians were dead and nearly 700 lay injured. The night was filled with sound of engines, gunfire and screaming.

Landsbergis grabbed his white formica telephone at the parliament and barked down the line, 'We have many injured, some dead, they have taken the TV tower and moved towards the central telegraph!' He demanded to be put through to Moscow, imploring President Gorbachev to call off the attack, to stop more blood being spilled, but Gorbachev did not respond.

Deep in the hiss and funk of the little radio room at the parliament, Rita Dapkute was making contact with amateur radio operators across Lithuania and the rest of the world. Her first broadcast relayed that there was shooting and many casualties. Additional transmissions were made listing medical supplies that were needed from the Red Cross. Rita kept up a broadcast every five minutes throughout the night, relaying either new information or rebroadcasting the previous status.

At one point she was surprised when she heard a high powered US State Department transmitter also begin broadcasting calls to action by native Lithuanians. After exchanging good wishes with the operator she continued her business. The international media had been relaying pictures of the TV tower attack which had already reached the newsrooms of the BBC and CNN. Clever planning and camera placement meant that almost every angle of the confrontation had been filmed to show the world what Moscow was doing.

The parliament building was the obvious next target for Soviet forces. Thousands more people held onto each other around the building as last minute tank traps were dragged into place from nearby construction sites. A Catholic priest, Robertas Grigas, led the masses in prayer and conferred absolution on the defenders. Those inside the parliament braced themselves for the thunder of tank shells hitting the building. The growl of tanks, radio chatter and Russian commands, shouted in the dark, were soon echoing in the streets nearby.

When the Latvians and Estonians saw the move on the Lithuanian parliament they assumed a coordinated Soviet operation to recapture all three Baltic States was underway. Dainis Ivans, the deputy chairman of

Latvia's Supreme Council, began broadcasts at 4am, urging their civilian population to rush to their parliament building, television tower and international phone exchange, as the Lithuanians had done. The bulletin was repeated every half an hour until the message had been heard throughout the city. When Latvians switched on their televisions they were greeted by the sight of their neighbours in Lithuania standing bravely in the way of Russian tanks.

A Latvian defence committee had drawn up a detailed plan of barricades to defend the Riga city centre from Soviet attack. At 2pm the next day, more than half a million people began a mass rally there to protest against the assault on Vilnius and assist in building the complex web of barricades that would block off all streets leading into their city. Buses and cars were thrown across the roads with coils of barbed wire until they were reinforced by larger trucks, concrete blocks and World War Two style tank traps.

Vital roads had a complex system of defences which included flammable barricades which could be set alight if they were threatened with being overrun. They were manned, not by soldiers, but by ordinary volunteer civilians. Commanders were appointed for each barricade and watches allocated to maintain a round the clock vigil of the defences. In the face of a co-ordinated assault by trained Soviet troops these barricades could not hold out long, but they hoped that the psychological barrier of having to kill civilians, might act as a deterrent to Russian commanders.

Just as Landsbergis thought that the Russians were about to make their final strike on the parliament and take the city completely, jubilant reports began to filter in that the tanks were retreating. The news was astounding. An anonymous phone call from a man who claimed to be a Russian officer told the defenders that the attack had been called off because, 'there was too much meat at the parliament.' The thousands who had gathered there and refused to move had won.

In Latvia too, the expected Soviet attack never came. The deterrence of the barricades had been enough to make Moscow think twice. 'The plan was destroyed by the courage of the people', said Landsbergis, 'Those who did not withdraw when they were threatened, shot at and saw the dead and injured falling at their feet. They did not run away and this was broadcast over satellite to the world.'

Despite this victory, the defenders knew that this might only be a temporary reprieve and the Soviets could soon try again. On 28th February, Lithuania's Supreme Council issued a press release declaring that nonviolent direct action by civilians was to be the country's primary means of defence in the event of an occupation by forces of the Soviet Union. The success of the strategy from Gene's *Civilian Based Defense* book, prompted the creation of a Commission on Psychological Defence and Civilian Resistance. Nonviolent action would now be an integral component of the national defences with an office at the Ministry of Defence itself. The unassuming academic, Grazina Miniotaite, was to be its leader and the bulk of the training material would be extracted from the works of Gene Sharp.

Grazina's first task was to prepare a set of instructions on nonviolent resistance for the Defense Department and organise the training of volunteers in the techniques of nonviolent resistance. The Supreme Council of the Republic of Lithuania went on to detail a sophisticated full-scale civilian based defense operation. The policy recognised that there was no realistic hope of successful military opposition to the Soviet Union, but that in the event of the elected Supreme Council being 'forcibly constrained from acting as the highest governing body of the state', all actions, laws, orders and decisions of the occupying force were to be considered illegal and confronted with civil disobedience and non-cooperation. The decree was signed off by Landsbergis, Chairman of the Supreme Council.

With the Baltics still under threat of a renewed attack, Audrius Butkevi-cius requested that Gene and a team from the Albert Einstein Institution travel to Vilnius as soon as possible to give the Lithuanian government advice on improving their resistance plans.

On the 24th April 1991, Gene, Bruce and Peter Ackerman arrived by train from Berlin. The visitors were driven by car to meet Landsbergis at the still heavily barricaded parliament building. As they were led through the security at the gates, the ramshackle defences were both imposing and comical in places. The approaches to the building were surrounded by concrete blocks and welded metal tank traps. The parliament itself had been surrounded by a concrete wall dropped into place by crane and topped with barbed wire. The walls had been daubed with writings, many of them in English, which read RED ARMY GO HOME and FREEDOM FOR BALTICS. Inside the grounds, the fires still burned to keep the parliament's civilian defenders warm.

While the outside defences were purely nonviolent, the defenders inside the building had maintained their small collection of near obsolete guns. As Gene and the team turned down a corridor they saw a fit young man in a green uniform carrying a single shot hunting rifle. Between them, hanging from the ceiling was a fishing net covered in two inch long barbed fish hooks. On command the net could be dropped onto the invading Soviets, snaring and cutting them.

It was a scene which struck everyone in the group. This man would be quickly torn to pieces by Soviet automatic weapons and grenades if any attempt was made to take the parliament by force, yet still he clung to his rifle and his comic book net.

Landsbergis told Gene he appreciated him coming, explaining that he had some serious concerns about the next Soviet moves. His biggest worry was that they would orchestrate violence through collaborators. How was a nonviolent approach to work against a domestic terrorist organisation? If he couldn't respond to protect the people he would lose credibility and be seen as a weak leader.

To highlight the brutality of the Soviets, a television and video player was produced and footage was shown of a young man bleeding profusely from a hole in his cheek. He had sprayed water through a high pressured hose at a young Russian officer who, in a rage, had shot him in the face with his pistol. Gene argued that it would be far better not to give invading soldiers an excuse to retaliate. As long as they were facing nonviolent opposition, any orders to use deadly force would become more difficult for the Soviets to carry out.

In a series of two-hour meetings, Gene presented an introduction to his work followed by a discussion. The meetings would follow a predictable pattern with participants often asserting that there were certain situations where the use of violence was necessary. When Gene enquired why they felt this way, their response was often that there was a dignity in violent resistance whereas nonviolence was seen as shameful and weak.

The view from the leadership was unequivocal though. 'The government viewed civilian defence as a matter of calculated organization not merely a spontaneous outburst of people power' Grazina explained. 'This was due both to practical experience and to theoretical insights provided by Gene Sharp in his book'. At a meeting of the defence principals, Audrius welcomed the visitors and described the importance of Gene's work to the Baltic struggle for independence against the Soviet Union. Holding up a copy of *Civilian Based Defence* he said, 'I would rather have Dr Sharp's book than the nuclear bomb'.

The Soviet Union was in economic free-fall and Gorbachev's policies of Perestroika and Glasnost were opening the door for more declarations of independence across the bloc. It was only a matter of time before a group of hardline officials came together in a conspiracy to try and save the Soviet Union from total dissolution. Just months after the Soviet takeover of the Baltics had failed, the lessons learned by the people of Latvia, Lithuania and Estonia were put to use on the streets of the Russian capital itself.

President Gorbachev departed from Moscow on the 4th August 1991 for a holiday at his dacha in Foros on the Crimean peninsula. It was at that moment the coup plotters chose to strike. Eight officers including Soviet Vice-President Gennady Yanayev, the Defence Minister and Chairman of the KGB, flew to Foros to force Gorbachev to resign in order to 'restore order' in the country. When Gorbachev refused, he was placed under house arrest and all communications from his dacha to the outside world were cut. KGB officers stood guard, preventing his escape.

The gang of eight flew back to Moscow where they drafted a 'Declaration of the Soviet Leadership', which declared a state of emergency across the USSR and introduced the 'State Committee of the State of Emergency', which had been created to run the country during the crisis. Vice-President Yanayev announced himself as acting President on account of

Gorbachev having an unspecified 'illness' preventing him carrying out his duties. The committee immediately banned opposition newspapers and radio, demonstrations were forbidden and a decree was issued proclaiming that the Soviet constitution was the sovereign authority over the Soviet republics.

Tanks and units of paratroopers rolled into Moscow. At the same time simultaneous moves of Soviet forces were underway in the Baltics, seizing communications facilities, ports and airports as they went.

The army moved into position around the Russian parliament building, 'The White House', poised to strike. But at 9am on the morning of the 19th August, Russian Federation President, Boris Yeltsin, arrived to announce that an un-constitutional coup had taken place. Somehow the plotters had failed to detain Yeltsin, one of their most serious mistakes. It left him free to set about touring the tanks, talking to the army officers and asking them to reject the coup.

A flyer calling for the country to initiate a universal unlimited strike against the coup was produced and circulated widely. As Muscovites heard the news, tens of thousands of people spontaneously gathered at the parliament building to join Yeltsin and protest against the coup.

In one of the earliest uses of email in a nonviolent struggle, Igor Ovchinnikov, a 28-year-old Muscovite began writing one of the first ever 'blogs' on the events unfolding inside the country. As a leader of the nonviolence group, 'Golubka', Igor had been teaching Gene's work to Russians for months. When news of the coup broke across Moscow, he was one of the first to respond. Gene was kept updated with events through one of the first email message groups. Igor described email at the time to people who had not heard of the technology as, 'computer assisted communication over phone lines'.

August 19 (am)

I hope this is not my last message but it could be if the phone lines are shut down. We don't know what's going on. We just heard the official announcement a few minutes ago. So stupid! Things are turning sour. It looks like a coup d'etat. The KGB, the Minister for Internal Affairs and the Defence Minister seem to be the rulers from now on. We hope it's not over yet. It's a miracle that email still seems to be working. But of you suddenly lose sight of us at least don't be surprised. Let's believe it's not the end of everything.

Lots of Love, Igor the Worried.

The people at the parliament began to build barricades around the building to protect it from an assault, just as the Latvians, Lithuanians and Estonians had done months before. After his first despatch, Igor and his Golubka colleagues pressed their lone laser printer into action printing hundreds of copies of Gene's 198 methods of nonviolent action and extracts from *Civilian Based Defence* in Russian. When the printer cartridge ran out, the first print run was rushed to the barricades where, according to Igor, it 'went like hot cakes'.

August 19 (pm)
This is just a few lines before we Golubka people meet and go to the rally in front of the White House (HQ of the Russian Federation) to distribute our leaflets with 198 ways of nonviolent struggle... We've survived for one day and we know time is on our side. So keep praying for us and we will keep praying for you. Igor the Direct Actor.

Huge crowds of people gathered around them every time they appeared at the barricades with a new print run. 'It's been the main thing that prevented us from falling into despair' Igor wrote in his diary. Igor's friend, Yuri, was sent out into the chaotic streets of Moscow to find replacement printer cartridges to keep the production line going.

The photocopiers at one of the activists' father's business was used to increase the output. The list of 198 methods had spread across Moscow, fly-posted to the walls of the subway and to the lamp posts lining the main streets.

The surge in popular opposition to the coup placed the military in a terrible position. Major Evdokimov, the commander of the tank battalion sent to surround the White House was torn on whether to follow the orders of the coup leaders or Yeltsin.

After discussions with his officers he became convinced by Yeltsin's speech and switched sides. In the most symbolic moment of the coup attempt, he ordered his tank barrels to swing away from the parliament. It was a turning point for the plotters. A split in the army could mean civil war inside the capital. Yeltsin climbed onto one of the tanks to speak once again to the cheering crowd.

The plotters knew that the success of the coup was now in the balance and decisive action had to be taken. General Kalnin, appointed as the military commander of Moscow by the coup committee, declared a curfew beginning at 11pm. The defenders of the barricades knew that this was a precursor to an attack on the parliament and began making their final preparations to block the path of an assault.

'Operation Thunder' was a complex operation planned by Kalnin and his deputies involving the special forces units, Alpha and Vympel, three tank units and a squadron of helicopters. Even the possibility of a parachute assault was suggested.

In preparation for the assault, the commanders of the Alpha special forces and the paratroopers removed their uniforms and slipped into the crowd around the parliament to conduct a personal reconnaissance for the attack. The commanders, General Lebed and General Karpukin, returned from their mission in a grave mood. They had walked through the peaceful crowd knowing the operation that had been devised would cause bloodshed among their own people. On their return they immediately tried to convince the coup leaders to abort the attack. Their pleas were rebuffed and the order was given for the assault to commence at 2am. But when the signal to begin the operation was received, the key special forces didn't move – they simply disobeyed, and hours later began leaving Moscow.

When the commanders of Operation Thunder refused to obey orders, the coup plotters knew they were defeated and flew to Crimea to meet Gorbachev. The KGB restored communications to the dacha and Gorbachev immediately issued a statement declaring all orders of the coup leaders invalid. At the end, Igor wrote that Golubka's actions had been a 'raindrop in the ocean', but that their main achievement had been distributing the nonviolent leaflets on civilian defence, methods of nonviolent action and historical examples of nonviolent struggle. They estimated that they had distributed between 1500 and 2000 copies.

'Without the support of the people, Muscovites in the first place, all Russians and people from other republics and all over the world, it wouldn't have been possible.' Igor wrote after their victory, 'Although Yeltsin was the right person in the right place presumably it could have been somebody else. Nobody could substitute for the people who were literally in the front line and whose blood was spilt in the streets of Moscow and whose courage obviously sobered the attackers.'

In November 1991, Gene and Bruce returned to Eastern Europe to discuss the campaigns with those who had fought them. In Moscow, the 'living ring', a citizens organisation born out of the August 1991 anti-coup actions, invited him to present his work on anti-coup defence. Finally, Gene and Bruce had the more sober duty of giving evidence to members of the Russian Parliamentary Commission investigating the 1991 coup.

In the aftermath of the resistance, the Latvian government minted a commemorative medal for the people who had manned the barricades around Riga. A shield-shaped medal on a red and white striped ribbon depicts a lion holding a smaller shield with two small keys. Par Latviju (For Latvia) is engraved on the reverse. It was the first medal ever awarded for participants in a nonviolent campaign. Audrius Butkevicius still keeps a memento of Gene's involvement on the shelf of his study, the little red and brown pamphlet on civilian based defence he was given by Grazina in the parliament restaurant that afternoon. For his part in the defence of the Baltics, Gene received an honorary degree from the Latvian Academy of Sciences. Back in the United States the award and his role in one of the most decisive engagements in the fall of the Soviet Union went almost completely unnoticed.

Colonel Bob

Bob Helvey was a fair haired, 25-year-old, captain when he was first sent to Vietnam as a platoon commander of the 5th Battalion, 7th United States Cavalry – the regiment famously commanded by General Custer at the Battle of the Little Bighorn. Bob was a deep thinker with a quick wit who cared deeply for his soldiers. After experiencing the death of his men at close quarters during one battle in Vietnam, he asked if there were any sole surviving sons in his company, so that he could excuse them from the most dangerous missions. There were, but nobody volunteered – everyone wanted to fight alongside Helvey.

In January 1968, US troops were just days away from one of the most infamous engagements of the war. Unbeknown to General William Westmoreland, Commander of US forces in Vietnam, the North Vietnamese forces were massing for coordinated attacks on US and South Vietnamese positions. It was a feat of military planning that the Americans had naively thought beyond the capacity of the communist forces.

The intelligence failure in spotting battalion strength units massing for attacks meant that small, lightly armed US patrols were still being sent into the jungle on search and destroy missions. Normally the Americans could easily outgun any opposition they met, but on the morning of 7th January they were about to meet their match. As Bob moved his men into the Que Son Valley, they stumbled into an ambush by a battalion of North Vietnamese troops. Machine gun fire cracked above their heads and mortar bombs began to fall amongst his soldiers.

Bob ran into the open to direct artillery and helicopter gunship fire onto the massing communist forces. Ambushed and surrounded, the odds were made even worse by bad weather and low cloud which meant that the normal US air support couldn't be brought in to the battle.

One helicopter that did make it to the area was shot down and lost with the battalion commander and its crew. With senior officers dead, his troops surrounded and the enemy closing in, Bob took command of the escape.

As he exposed himself again to the enemy, to find a way out, he drew increasingly accurate machine gun fire. Finally, he saw an escape route and led the charge through an enemy trench line where his platoon fought the enemy at a distance of just three feet. Bob's men survived the engagement and reached the US base at Landing Zone Ross. It had been a tour de force by the young commander.

Bob's actions that day would win him the Distinguished Service Cross, the United States' second highest award for gallantry, but the accolades from his men were the ultimate prize. They called him 'a God on the battlefield'.

The battles which became known as the 'Tet Offensive' resulted in the deaths of around 14,000 civilians and 24,000 injured who were caught in the crossfire. Bob returned to the US with one stand out conclusion – modern warfare was becoming increasingly lethal to ordinary people. He had seen too many men, women and children killed in collateral damage. A new way of fighting had to be found.

Bob proceeded through the ranks, delighting those who he served with. Anecdotes about him were legion. He famously threw a canister of CS gas into an officer professional development class as payback for some long forgotten misdemeanour. One soldier remembered him insisting on his men singing hopelessly out of tune at the front of a church service, only for them to break down, giggling like school children in front of the congregation.

He got married after officer school and had three sons, but his wife died tragically early from cancer. As a Major working at the Pentagon in Washington DC, he had to hold down a high pressured job and cope as a single father of three children while grieving the loss of his wife. A colleague suggested he find a good nanny to look after the kids and recommended an English girl called Maureen who was new in town and looking for work. Maureen came to look after the boys and after a while she began looking after Bob too. They were married a few years later. The family lived on a wooded hillside in West Virginia in an English style stone cottage.

In 1983 Bob was assigned as the Defence Attaché to Burma. Based in the capital, Rangoon, his job was to collect military intelligence – information on the weapons, capabilities and personalities within the Burmese military and security apparatus.

A fledgling democracy in Burma had been snuffed out on 2nd March 1962, by a military coup led by a general called Ne Win. The students in Rangoon University rioted against the takeover, but Ne Win ordered his troops to crush the uprising and destroy their headquarters at the student union building. Martial law was enforced and would remain in place for the next 12 years. Opponents of the regime, many of them composed of Burma's patchwork of ethnic minorities, fled into the jungle to wage a guerrilla campaign against the military dictatorship.

Burma was not a major focus for the US government, though a number of American companies previously operating in the country had been expelled and had their assets nationalised under the regime. The Cold War remained a top priority and Bob was ordered to keep a watchful eye on the communist influence in the country, along with tracking narcotics and arms smuggling through the jungle.

To prepare them for their posting, defence attachés were taught counter-surveillance, covert photography, weapon recognition and how to take notes of a conversation unobtrusively in one's pocket at a cocktail party. They were also introduced to friendly nationals of their new country, to brief them on the cultural norms and political situation into which they would soon be immersed. Bob's briefer was no neutral observer. Tin Maung Win hated the Burmese military regime. He'd been one of the students at Rangoon University who had gone onto the streets in an attempt to block General Ne Win's coup in 1962.

Win's father was the first Burmese ambassador to India and he'd spent hours as a child playing at the home of Indian Prime Minister Jawaharlal Nehru, listening to his stories about working with Gandhi. When the military coup was launched in Burma, Win knew that a Gandhi-style resistance campaign was the best hope of regaining democracy in Burma.

Win began to organise a new resistance movement against the regime, but before he could mobilise enough support, the regime's secret police arrested him and sent him to the infamous Insein prison in Rangoon. He spent three years in captivity at Insein, half of that in solitary confinement. Just months after his release Win received word that the government was planning another roundup of activists and that his name and his father, were on the list.

Facing the terrible prospect of more years spent in solitary confinement, Win and his wife gathered up some small personal possessions and fled with his father in the middle of the night. As they trekked towards the Thai border, they were sometimes just a few hours ahead of the pursuing security forces.

Soon the stress and sheer physical exertion was too much for Win's father – he slowed, clutching his chest and eventually collapsed, dying in his son's arms, just hours from safety. Win buried him as respectfully as he could by the side of the road and continued his desperate journey.

After crossing into Thailand, Win became a resistance organiser before claiming asylum in the US, where he began lobbying political contacts in Washington to assist the oppressed Burmese minorities. That was how he was eventually recruited by the Defence Intelligence School and wound up sitting in front of Bob Helvey for the first time.

The two men sat for hours drinking whiskey, Bob listening to Win's jungle war stories, tales of government brutality and the 'sons of bitches' he would soon encounter in the Burmese government. While, on the face of it, Win had been asked to help Bob navigate his new posting, it was quite clear that he was trying to recruit this new US defence attaché to the side of the resistance.

Bob and Maureen moved to Burma in the summer of 1983 and had to adjust quickly to the invasive control of the government and the overpowering humidity of Rangoon. Their stay coincided with the North Korean assassination attempt of the South Korean President who was visiting the city in October that year. That morning Maureen had answered the phone at their home to an embassy staffer relaying the news that a massive explosion had ripped through the Martyrs Mausoleum and there were many dead and injured. Bob was out playing golf and at the time and with no mobile phones, Maureen had to run to their car and drive at top speed through the city and right onto the golf course to pick him up.

Bob's two years in Burma were considered a success by senior commanders, but the horrors being inflicted on the population by the regime and the futility of the ragtag military resistance, left a lasting impression.

On his return to the United States, Bob was marked out for higher command and given one of the most prestigious prizes the military could bestow – a year as a senior fellow at Harvard University. Life at Harvard was a handbrake turn from the disciplined military life that he had known for more than two decades, but Bob loved mixing with the liberal arts students and academics. While walking across Harvard Yard one morning he noticed a flyer pinned to a board advertising a lecture on 'nonviolent sanctions'.

'I thought I'd just go up there and see who these peaceniks were, to confirm my pre-conceived notion that they probably had rings in their noses and ears and they'd just be all dirty' he remembered. But when he arrived in the lecture theatre he was surprised to be surrounded by a normal looking cohort of students and faculty. 'Then this little short gentleman walks in and he says, "My name is Gene Sharp and we're here today to discuss how to seize political power and deny it to others"'.

Gene had developed a theatrical presence in lectures at Harvard. He'd frequently open with this bold statement of intent which laid down the difference between his thinking and that of traditional pacifists for anyone who had wandered in expecting a lecture on love and tolerance.

'I say nonviolent struggle is armed struggle! And we have to take back that term from those advocates of violence who try to justify with pretty words that kind of combat. With this type of struggle one fights with psychological weapons, social weapons, economic weapons and political weapons. This is ultimately more powerful against oppression, injustice and tyranny than is violence.'

By the end of the lecture Bob was blown away by the ideas he'd just heard and waited his turn to talk to Gene at the end of the lecture. It was clear from the start that the two men would get along. If Gene had once fretted about his less than 'life of the party personality' Bob brought the party. Brash, straight talking with enough anecdotes to see out an Antarctic winter, people instantly warmed to him. His soldiers had looked up to him as a father figure and in the future he would be variously described as 'Moses', and 'coach' by the revolutionaries he would teach. All of them described wanting to please him.

Just like Gene, Bob was a straight talking pragmatist focused not on academic theory and jargon, but on practical methods that actually worked. Gene was keen to engage the military at any opportunity and Bob had a particular problem that he wanted to see if Gene could help with. He saw immediately that Gene's approach fused with military style strategic planning might be able to bring down the military dictatorship in Burma.

'I think Vietnam influenced my view about the importance of nonviolent struggle and particularly the importance of getting Gene Sharp's work out to the rest of the world because we must have an alternative. Vietnam convinced me we need to have an alternative to killing people.'

Back in Burma, dissatisfaction with the military regime was growing. In 1987, Tin Maung Win formed the 'Committee for the Restoration of Democracy in Burma' (CRDB), with another dissident, Ye Kyaw Thu, to co-ordinate student and ethnic opposition groups. In March 1988 a student was killed by riot police and security forces killed hundreds more young people who poured out onto the streets to protest against the killing.

Thousands of arrests were made and universities were closed to prevent further gatherings. A resurgence of protests a month later saw demands for wider political and economic freedoms in addition to bringing to justice those who had ordered the killings of unarmed student demonstrators. Clashes on the 21st June saw a breakdown in nonviolent discipline. The students began inflicting revenge upon the government security forces killing 20 riot police and losing 80 of their own.

The government responded with a curfew and draconian new measures to stop gatherings of more than a couple of people in public, but the news of more deaths of unarmed students in the capital caused angry protests to break out all over the country.

Realising the situation was quickly growing beyond their control, the military junta lifted the curfew and reopened universities. General Ne Win who had ruled Burma for almost 30 years resigned as party chairman and called for a referendum on multi-party democracy.

A general strike was called for 8th August 1988 which saw hundreds of thousands of Burmese and ethnic minorities calling for the resignation of the military regime and multi-party elections. Unarmed protesters marched towards Rangoon City Hall, but possibly anticipating the crowd would turn violent, as they had before, the troops opened fire, killing hundreds of people within a few minutes. The country went to war on the streets. Demonstrators fought with improvised weapons, often inflicting horrible deaths on soldiers. Within three days, more than 1,000 people on both sides were dead.

The 1988 uprising had resulted in a bloodbath for the opposition and emboldened the military dictatorship. Their intelligence had accurately discovered that much of their leadership and training in resistance techniques was coming from within Thailand. Tin Maung Win and Ye Kyaw Thu were identified as high profile targets and the regime dispatched a team of assassins to hunt them down in Bangkok. The Thai intelligence service, which was sympathetic to the movement, warned Ye Kyaw Thu and others to leave Bangkok and head north to set up a base in the city of Chiang Mai, where their security services were better able to protect them.

Bob was now a full colonel and dean of the United States Defense Intelligence School. One of his first changes was putting Gene's *Politics of Nonviolent Action* on the curriculum, ordering 240 copies for the trainee defence attachés who would soon be serving in sensitive posts at US embassies all over the world.

In January 1989, Bob suggested that Win and Ye Kyaw Thu travel to Boston to see Gene and discuss potential uses of nonviolent struggle in the face of the increased political and economic repression. Win and Gene agreed that the 1988 uprising had failed due to two fundamental reasons.

Firstly there was no organised leadership which could unite opposition political parties and secondly there was no nonviolent discipline to prevent the commission of barbaric acts, including beheading soldiers, that had been used to justify the police firing into the crowds.

Win confided that he and Ye Kyaw Thu had passed Gene's books to resistance leaders in Burma and that training using his work was already in progress in Thailand. A month after his visit to Boston, on the 6th February 1989, Ye Kyaw Thu dispatched a letter to Gene in Boston informing him that the newly-trained students were being sent back across the border as sleeper agents to organise and guide nonviolent resistance from within the cities.

'You will be pleased, I hope, to know that ...I was able to dispatch two groups of student leaders total 80 in number back inside Burma mainly to Rangoon, Moulmein, Monywa and Mandalay. Four student leaders were reported so far as being arrested; the rest are with the mass now.'

As the country prepared for the 1990 election, Gene and Bob became increasingly concerned that the poll could spark another spontaneous uprising. They agreed that it was critical the Burmese people had a clear idea of what was being sought and why. Bob called this a 'vision of tomorrow' – A statement of what the people wanted their future society to look like so that steps could be taken to achieve that vision. Bob and Win began to write up a 'Declaration of the Committee for the Restoration of Democracy in Burma', a manifesto which was based on the US Declaration of Independence and drew from Burmese history books for format and content. They agreed that an expanded mission to train a cohort of students in Gene's work might help organise the opposition more strategically, prevent a descent into the violence like 1988 and hopefully foment a nonviolent overthrow of the military government.

A Thai bookshop owner by the name of Sulak Sivaraska, who ran an organisation called the 'Santi Prachma Dhamma Institute', volunteered to fund an initial training camp using Gene's books. Bob was still employed by the army and Gene wasn't fit enough for an uncharted trip into the jungle, so another team had to be found.

Gene decided the best person to do the training was George Lakey, whom he had known since his time in Oslo. Lakey was now an established academic and writer on nonviolent movements and although his ideas often differed considerably from Gene's, the two men respected each other greatly. Lakey agreed to do the trip and requested that his close friend and colleague Michael Beer came with him. Lakey and Beer were to take copies of the Burmese translation of Gene's *Role of Power* essay into Burma and scope out the ground for more involvement by the Albert Einstein Institution. The trip was potentially dangerous and on 23rd April 1990, Bob faxed Gene from the Defence Intelligence School with his concerns.

'Given the magnitude of the physical threat against them by the Burmese armed forces, including military intelligence units operating inside Thailand, some basic survival skills about how to live and work in a high threat environment should be addressed. Counter-surveillance and other security measures could be practiced daily to become second nature'.

The team met the following day at the Westpark Hotel in Arlington, Virgina. Khin, a Burmese student, who had escaped after the 1988 crack-down, talked about the structure and culture of the student movement. Bob briefed on the strengths and weakness of the Burma military appa-ratus and Mubarak Awad came along to offer some examples of how Palestinians had addressed similar problems in the first intifada.

Bob spelled out the dangers of the trip to Lakey and Beer, but they decided to press ahead. They returned a month later with vital information about the conditions and characters along the border. The materials had been well received and they reported a growing demand for education on nonviolent struggle.

In May 1990, the pro-democracy candidate, Aung San Suu Kyi, won the Burmese general election, but the Generals stepped in, refused to respect the result and annulled her victory. Suu Kyi was the daughter of Aung San, the man considered the father of the nation after his contribution to winning independence from the British in 1948. It was her call for nonviolence after the bloody 1988 uprising that made her a figurehead for finding a peaceful route to democracy in Burma and would eventually win her the Nobel Peace Prize in 1991.

Suu Kyi was placed under house arrest for her political activity, and although she was free to leave Burma at any time, her refusal to abandon her country and incarceration in the house by the lake, made her a figurehead for the democratic cause. Her plight might have remained in the headlines for longer had Burma not been blown off the news agenda by the Iraqi invasion of Kuwait in August 1990.

As US forces began their buildup to retake the tiny Gulf state, Bob wrote a letter to Gene, outraged by Secretary of Defense, Dick Cheney, who testified that there was no constitutional requirement for a US president to consult Congress on the decision to go to war. Bob loved the army, but it was also clear that he was getting itchy feet. The plight of the Burmese people and the potential of nonviolent action to assist their struggle, or at least prevent the country from descending into a bloody civil war, increasingly occupied his thoughts.

Just a few days before Christmas 1990, Gene travelled to Arlington, Virginia to talk to Bob about a permanent job at the Albert Einstein Institution. He was already making major contributions to the work and Gene saw the potential for a well respected military officer to lend credibility to the concept of nonviolent struggle in government.

There was just one issue Gene felt he needed to be clear about. While he had always sought the inclusion of the Department of Defense and the State Department, he had grown increasingly wary about the activities of the CIA. The agency had been involved in a lot of what he called 'bad dealings' and the Albert Einstein Institution could not be allowed to be a tool of political manipulation.

Gene asked him frankly whether he had ever worked for the CIA. Bob understood the concern and assured Gene that as a brigade intelligence officer in Vietnam his duties had been exclusively tactical military intelligence, not political intelligence. As defense attaché in Rangoon, his role had also been exclusively military intelligence and he had not been involved in political intelligence or what he termed 'manipulations' on behalf of the CIA. Bob also assured Gene that his work with Tin Maung Win and Ye Kyaw Thu and the democratic opposition in Burma had been strictly personal and not part of any military assignment or responsibility.

He told Gene he would need to seek official release from the military but would be able to start work at the Albert Einstein Institution no more than 60 days after giving his notice. The deal was agreed soon afterwards. Bob was to be the newest staff member of the Albert Einstein Institution and their first mission would be to assist the Burmese in bringing down their dictatorship.

Gene Sharp 1953

The Sharp family

DEMONSTRATORS —
Please read this at once.

YOU CAN MAKE THIS DEMONSTRATION A SUCCESS. WILL YOU HELP ?

TO KEEP OUR ISSUE ABSOLUTELY CLEAR and to reduce the chances for opponents to distort our purpose, it is important that we behave with dignity and self-discipline in this demonstration.

Experience—under Gandhi in the Indian campaigns for freedom, in the non-whites' struggle in South Africa against apartheid, in the Negroes' bus boycott in Montgomery, Alabama, and many other cases—clearly shows that demonstrations such as this must be conducted with dignity and absolutely without violence if they are to be successful.

The incident with the car at Aldermaston—even though marchers were not involved—shows that even from the standpoint of publicity it is imperative for demonstrators to be strictly peaceful. There must be no violence whatsoever, regardless of provocation, even if violence is used against us.

If you believe in the objectives of this demonstration, we ask you to abide by the following discipline. If you cannot comply with it, we ask you do not take part in this demonstration and withdraw quietly.

1. Do not use any language or take any action which is likely to provoke violence by others. A dignified bearing and courteous determination will greatly contribute to victory for this cause.

2. If you are jeered or called names, do not shout back or jeer those who differ from our views. Silence and a friendly smile are the best reply to hostility, as you continue as before the interruption.

3. If anyone attempts to pull down your banner, seize your sign, remove an armband, or destroy leaflets, let go at once. Do not struggle with the attacker. This prevents opponents from provoking a fight which can be widely used to discredit this demonstration. Stand silently with your hands at your sides, looking straight ahead, or, if marching, continue as before with hands at sides. This cause is great enough: demonstrations for it are not dependent for success upon signs or leaflets.

4. Do not under any conditions use any violence, regardless of provocation. If you are struck keep hands at sides and do not strike back. Do not allow opponents to make you stoop to using violence which will degrade a noble campaign. Dignity, restraint, courage and a friendly smile are the best answer in such demonstrations to violence and attack. This may mean you will be injured, but such suffering bravely borne without retaliation advances our cause.

5. If anyone else is attacked, do not use any violence against the attacker. Each demonstrator must himself or herself be responsible for standing up to such violence and suffering for achieving our objective.

6. If a fight or struggle does begin near you and there are no police to deal with it, you must be prepared to separate the fighters by standing between them, even if you are thereby injured. By isolating the violence and those whose behaviour would discredit our objective, by being willing to take blows without retaliation or fear, you will be doing a great service to our cause.

Gene's nonviolent discipline leaflet for the Aldermaston March, the first document to be published with the peace symbol

The Center for International Affairs, Harvard University.
Gene Sharp is on the far left second row from the back. On the front
row are Henry Kissinger, Tom Schelling and Samuel Huntington

Gene at the Program on Nonviolent Sanctions, Harvard, 1983

Gene Sharp, Ye Kyaw Thu, Bob Helvey, Tin Maung Win and Michael Beer

General Bo Mya, after visiting Boston

Gene Sharp teaching in the bamboo classroom at Manerplaw, 1993

Peter Ackerman, Gene Sharp, and Audrius Butkevicius in Lithuania, 1991

Jamila Raqib and Gene Sharp discussing a consultation, May 2009

Ausama Monajed in consultation with Gene Sharp during the Syrian uprising,
April 2011

Srdja Popovic outside the Serbian Parliament building

Bob Helvey explains the 'pillars of support'

Bob Helvey, Gene Sharp, Ruaridh Arrow and Jamila Raqib at the
How to Start a Revolution premiere, Boston, 2011

Gene Sharp and Jamila Raqib in London, 2012

Credit: Emma Hardy

Jungle Fortress

Deep in the jungle, the Burmese democratic resistance established their headquarters and training camp on the banks of the Moei River. The camp was home to a mixture of refugees and resistance fighters from all over Burma who had fled there, out of reach of the military dictatorship in Rangoon. On its perimeter, a ramshackle line of defences and watchtowers looked out for the government forces who they knew would one day be sent to wipe out this last beacon of democracy. They called it Manerplaw.

To have any realistic chance of selling nonviolent revolution to the Burmese resistance, Bob needed the support of the infamous commander of Manerplaw. General Bo Mya had fought with the British against the Japanese during World War Two and was soon at war again, leading the rebels of the Karen ethnic minority when they declared independence from the rest of Burma in 1949. His credentials on the battlefield were not in question, but he was not a natural democratic leader. A beast of a man, infamous for his size and wild temper, there were rumours that he had beheaded at least seven men for betraying him. Nevertheless, any substantial training of the Burmese and ethnic minority groups in nonviolent struggle would first have to get authorisation from the general.

By chance, the person who would make that introduction was sitting in a meeting of Burmese activists in Washington DC where Bob was giving a presentation on Gene's work. Louisa Benson Craig was one of the most active Burmese democracy campaigners in the US. She had also been a famous actress, a former Miss Burma beauty queen and most recently a guerrilla commander. Her first husband, Lin Htin, had led the 5th Battalion of Burmese Karen fighters. Louisa met Htin when he visited the home of her parents in Rangoon. He was a notorious womaniser, 16 years her senior, but there was an instant attraction and they quickly eloped. The marriage did not last long.

One day in 1965, Lin Htin was summoned for peace negotiations with the government and never returned. The rumour was that he had been beheaded by a chief henchman of Ne Win, the notorious Sein Win, who would go on to earn the nickname 'the Butcher of Rangoon'. When her husband disappeared, Louisa took the unusual step of taking on his position as commander of the 5th Battalion, where she earned an awesome reputation as a fighter and one of the best shots among her soldiers.

After working with General Bo Mya for a short time in the jungle, Louisa contracted malaria and travelled to the US for medical treatment where she reunited with a former university friend and US Navy veteran, Glen Craig. Glen became Louisa's second husband and together they worked to raise the plight of the Burmese minorities with US lawmakers.

As they listened to Bob's lecture in the Spring of 1991, Louisa was totally in agreement with Gene's philosophy and the argument for a nonviolent strategy in Burma. Glen however was completely unconvinced. In the aftermath of the Soviet Union's withdrawal from Afghanistan, the US officials who had masterminded the smuggling of weapons to the Mujahadeen were being lauded and decorated in Washington. The White House wasn't very interested in Burma, but Glen still believed that if he could channel enough arms and expertise to the resistance, they could win like the Mujahadeen had done. The couple waited for Bob at the end of his talk and explained their connection to Manerplaw and General Bo Mya.

Louisa worried that time was running out for Burmese democrats. A new oil pipeline was being built by the multinational oil company UNOCAL and the deal with the Burmese government who now called themselves SLORC (State Law and Order Restoration Council) meant oil money would soon be pouring into government coffers for military training and new Chinese weapons. Something had to be done quickly before the government could strengthen their army and wipe out the ethnic minority controlled areas and the headquarters at Manerplaw. Louisa knew Bo Mya and had earned his respect. She offered to accompany Bob on a visit into Burma and ease his introduction to the general. Bob made it clear to Glen that he would only be advocating nonviolent methods.

A few months later, Louisa, Glen and Bob flew from Washington into Bangkok and took a bus to Mae Sot before enduring a bone jarring truck ride to a rendezvous point where a number of narrow motor boats were waiting to take the team up the Moei River into Manerplaw. Bob Helvey, was back in the jungle, but this time he had some new weapons.

The morning after Bob's arrival Bo Mya was slumped, exhausted, in his quarters having just returned from a major firefight with the Burmese army to the West of the camp. At 300lbs he could no longer bend over far enough to untie his own boots, but got around this problem by employing a number of young boys to do it for him. They were also given the bizarre task of painting his toe nails with bright red nail polish.

Bob appeared before the general and began a carefully prepared briefing on nonviolent resistance which he'd been preparing for weeks. He had already been innovating with some of Gene's concepts and perhaps the most powerful of these contributions was the visual metaphor of 'pillars of support'. The climax of his presentation was the moment he held up a book supported with his outstretched fingers to illustrate the pillars of support of the regime. One by one, he took each of his fingers away, symbolising the police, the army and the judiciary, until the book fell to the floor. Bob looked at Bo Mya expecting a eureka moment, but the moment of theatre fell flat. Bo Mya looked up at him unimpressed.

'He never said a fucking word, and then he just got up and walked out of the room', Bob remembered. Crestfallen, he went to one of Bo Mya's political officers to tell him the story. The official thought for a moment and said he would request another meeting with the general, 'but this time', he said 'Don't use the term, nonviolent!'

The next morning Bob was ushered back into Bo Mya's quarters and repeated the briefing, but this time he replaced the word nonviolent with a term he had invented overnight, 'political defiance'. Bo Mya sat up and listened – there was grunting and an occasional nod of approval, but he left again without saying anything. Bob was disappointed again. 'I thought, Jesus! That's that then'. But later that day, he received a note – 'Bo Mya wants you to give this course as a pilot project. But just don't ever use the term nonviolent again'.

Bob flew back to the US to report the good news to Gene. An application for funding was granted by the National Endowment for Democracy and in the weeks that followed, Bob set a date for a trip back into Burma. Michael Beer who had previously visited the area on the trip with George Lakey was hired to accompany him and act as an assistant.

Bo Mya didn't want the word to get out that he was training soldiers in nonviolent strategy, so upon their return, he hid Bob and Michael away in a remote special forces camp a kilometre north west of Manerplaw. They began training between 15 and 20 student soldiers at a time in a new bamboo classroom under the watchful eye of Bo Mya's personal secretary Mahn Shah.

After two weeks the instructors were ordered to cease the training and return to Manerplaw immediately. The recall seemed like extremely bad news, but Mahn Shah had been excited by what he had seen and sent excellent reviews back to Bo Mya. The general now ordered the training be condensed into a 5-day course and that all organisations in Manerplaw attend.

Training in 'political defiance' was now given alongside basic military instruction to new recruits of the Karen National Liberation Army. Other students included the politicians of the National Coalition of the Union of Burma, former political prisoners, representatives of all of the ethnic minorities and a group of Buddhist monks.

Bob's classes soon won respect from the fighters. One afternoon, a rebel commander who was known for being ruthless in battle, was passing by the classroom where Bob's energetic teaching style caught his attention. He ended up staying for the whole class and afterwards he approached Bob in awe of what he had just heard. 'Where in the hell has this information been! We've been fighting and killing people for 20 years! How come we didn't know this?'

The classes in Manerplaw increased in size and popularity, and with the increasing scale of the task, Bob wanted Gene to be there to assess what was being taught. The time had come for Gene's presence in the jungle, and he cautiously agreed. He was now 64 years old, and while most academics might be considering retirement, Gene was entering his most productive period.

The trip would not be easy. He would have to make the illegal entry into Burma over the border from Thailand through an area of shelling and frequent attacks by government troops. Although Gene loved the outdoors, he was not particularly well equipped for it. At his home on Cottage Street, he folded some light coloured slacks and shirts into a suitcase so huge that it would be difficult to cross a road with it – let alone run from Burmese government assassins on the Thai border.

Gene landed at Don Muang airport, Bangkok, on the 21st October 1992 and exited the terminal to a blast of sticky heat. Waiting anxiously at arrivals was Tin Maung Win who was in charge of smuggling him across the border into Burma. Forty eight hours later they took a small propellor plane North to Mae Sot and at dusk on the morning of the 24th, clambered into an unstable wooden powerboat, propelled by a truck engine. Bob was sitting in his hut reading when a young lookout ran to tell him that there was an urgent message on the radio – a white man had been spotted heading up river – and he was travelling with a very big suitcase.

A Burmese army outpost high up on a mountain had been set up to spy on the rebels at Manerplaw and looked down at the site where the boats landed, reporting back arrivals and departures to the government in Rangoon. The rebels had instigated a low tech but effective method of counter surveillance – anyone approaching the riverbank had to go down to the beach under an umbrella so the spies couldn't see who was arriving and departing.

As Gene stepped off the boat onto the sandy river beach at Manerplaw for the first time, Bob bounded down the embankment towards him grinning with his umbrella waving above his head. He grabbed Gene by the hand as he stepped out of the boat, 'Dr Sharp I presume!?' he roared with laughter.

Bob was accompanied down to the beach by one of the camp's academics who stepped forward and clasped Gene's hands eagerly in his. 'Dr Sharp I have read all of your books and I am so pleased to meet you,' he told him. Bob watched as the two men walked off toward the camp hand in hand down the jungle path. A sign above the gate to Manerplaw read, 'Give us Liberty or Death'.

The guest quarters at the camp consisted of a series of wooden huts, each with three or four rooms, centrally located in easy reach of the headquarters. The accommodation was comfortable, but full of dust during the dry season and when it rained its tin roof created a deafening racket and barely kept the occupants dry. The visitors paid a small stipend for their meals, which included rice at breakfast and an egg or chicken noodle broth for dinner. Occasionally there was a catch of fish from the river, but meat was a luxury in short supply.

After settling into the camp, Gene's first hurdle was his meeting with General Bo Mya. Gene was not prone to temper, but he could be dogmatic and Bob was worried about how he might react to the general's dismissive style. After polite introductions, Gene told Bo Mya that they were looking forward to delivering a new nonviolent strategy curriculum that he had devised for the students at Manerplaw and explained some of the contents. Despite the cordial meeting, the general didn't hide the fact that he still held nonviolent action in contempt. After dinner one evening he declared that he had very much enjoyed spending time with Gene and Bob and appreciated the help, even though they were, 'obviously cowards'.

The classes of around 20 students sat to attention, smartly dressed in their camouflage fatigues on rows of wooden benches, facing the front. Gene stood at a wooden framed blackboard teaching alongside a translator, sketching out occasional diagrams in chalk to explain a point. One of the first stories he told them was the Monkey Master Fable, a simple tale by a 14th century writer called Liu-Ji that illustrated the power of basic non-cooperation against oppression. Gene had first seen a reference to the fable in the late 1960s, but had only recently managed to track down the text and find someone skilled enough to translate it from the 14th century Chinese script.

In the feudal state of Chu, an old man survived by keeping monkeys as slaves. The people of Chu called him 'Ju Gong' (the Monkey Master). Each morning the old man would assemble the monkeys in his courtyard and order the eldest one to lead the others to the mountains to gather fruits from bushes and trees. It was the rule that each monkey had to give one tenth of his collection to the old man. Those who failed to do so would be ruthlessly flogged. All the monkeys suffered bitterly, but didn't dare complain.

One day a small monkey asked the other monkeys: 'Did the old man plant all the fruit trees and the bushes?' The others said: 'No they grew naturally.' The small monkey asked further, 'Can't we take the fruits without the old man's permission?' The others replied, 'Yes we all can.' The small monkey continued, 'Then, why should we depend on the old man, why must we all serve him?' Before the small monkey was able to finish his statement all the monkeys suddenly became enlightened and awakened. On the same night, watching that the old man had fallen asleep, the monkeys tore down the stockade in which they were confined and destroyed it entirely. They took the fruits the old man had in storage into the woods and never returned.

Gene suggested that spreading the simple Monkey Master Fable would lay the basic idea for a campaign of massive non-cooperation across Burma. He told his new students, 'Some men in the world rule their people by tricks and not by righteous principles. Aren't they just like the monkey master? They are not aware of their muddle-headedness. As soon as their people become enlightened, their tricks no longer work!'

In the evenings Gene spoke informally about his work to groups of students and fighters sitting cross-legged in candlelight. Among the group were a number of escaped Burmese army porters. The government soldiers had kidnapped hundreds of men and women to carry their weapons and ammunition through the jungle. Some escaped to Manerplaw and brought with them harrowing stories of their treatment.

When the Burmese army troops feared they were about to be attacked they would make the porters walk out in front so they would be the first to be shot, or walk into minefields. They were fed just a few spoonfuls of rice, twice a day, to keep them alive and often fell exhausted under the weight of the ammunition they were forced to carry. When their bodies were too tired and broken to be of use, the soldiers used the butts of their rifles to smash in their heads where they fell. One escapee reported seeing around thirty porters die in this way on a single march.

Even in the short time of Gene's first visit, he watched the simple cemetery at Manerplaw grow larger with the bodies of men and women who had died too young. On one occasion a young man spoke up to tell the story of how his family had been killed and his hazardous journey to the liberated area. As he talked he began to weep and Gene beckoned the young man into his arms and began to cry too.

Life at Manerplaw was precarious. There was a constant threat of surprise attack from the jungle by the Burmese Army. Bob knew from his military training that the headquarters was badly positioned on low ground and the defences were not up to scratch. The fortifications had been built backing onto the river which marked the border between Burma and Thailand. The assumption had been that the Burmese army would never try to outflank them by making an incursion into Thailand and attacking them from the rear. This would soon turn out to be a grave mistake.

Bob made some limited suggestions for the defences of the camp in order to improve their own security while teaching there, but there was no question of moving and a chemical gas attack, which some feared, would be utterly catastrophic. Gene often found himself scanning the sky looking for the government aircraft which often appeared menacingly on the horizon. At night he tossed and turned uncomfortably in his bunk dreaming about bombs falling on the camp.

The more time Gene spent at Manerplaw the more he realised the need for an organisation to be set up which would plan and direct all nonviolent action in the country and lead the revolution if it came. By his next visit, in early 1993, the organisation which he had envisaged had been brought to life. The 'Political Defiance Committee' or 'PDC' as it became known was established with the purpose of using Gene's work to bring about the, 'downfall of dictatorship'. The plan developed by Bob and Gene with the PDC was a grand strategy to start a nonviolent revolution in Burma and bring down the military regime. For years Gene had been advocating the possibility of replacing violent conflict with nonviolent warfare. Now Burma became the first experiment to see if this was possible.

Bob's involvement marked the first real fusion of military-style strategic planning with nonviolent struggle. He started with a strategic estimate which involved gathering data on the opponents' strengths and weaknesses, their sources of power and pillars of support. This data gathering exercise was a fundamental part of military planning. It included details like the weather at various times of year – is it wise to start a movement on the streets in monsoon season or wait for the dry season? If there is going to be a general strike, when do the workers get paid so that they have the most money to sustain themselves for the longest possible time? When is food in greatest supply? What are the national holidays? How will the pro-democracy forces communicate? Which journalists are friendly? Who are the government, military or intelligence personnel who might defect early or leak secret intelligence to help out? All of these questions which military commanders knew had the potential to tip the balance between defeat and victory were now applied to a nonviolent campaign.

The PDC planned three phases of action in their strategy document.

Phase 1
- Human rights violations, corruption and ecological abuse contained in regular reports
- Negative consequences of Chinese involvement in Burma reported
- Political defiance successes reported
- Anti-coup information disseminated using Gene Sharp's materials as a basic reference
- Courses in political defiance for co-ordinators
- Advanced 6 week course for the core of the strategists
- Strategic estimates prepared by the Political Defiance Committee including addresses, demographic, military, economic, political, climate, weather, transportation, communications and security

- Each regional political defiance coordination office prepares an estimate for its own region with copies supplied to central office
- The planning and coordination centres will be bi-lingual in Burmese and English to facilitate communications between groups
- The national command is responsible for developing contingency plans for the release of Aung San Suu Kyi, her death at the hands of SLORC, the death of Ne Win or a spontaneous uprising
- Primary and alternate communications systems designed and emplaced

Phase 2
- Aggressive protests, non-cooperation and intervention including boycott, shunning and infrastructure outages
- Developing a credible parallel government which actually governs the liberated area
- National elections conducted in the liberated area replete with campaigns and debates on selected issues
- Destruction of the Burma army as a tool of oppression
- Defectors are praised, protected and given safe passage to their homes
- Families of children joining the Burma army are visited by friends or relatives citing disease, likelihood of wounds, dying alone in the jungle and shunning by the community (to cut off source of recruits)
- Leaflets placed where enlisted troops frequent, calling on them not to murder their own people
- Provide religious last rites to soldiers departing for the front line (demoralise force)
- Funerals and memorial services are attended and used as a forum for discreet political defiance activities to argue that SLORC is causing unnecessary death
- Cite 'unnamed sources within the Burma army' for information about atrocities and corruption and consider issuing indictments for criminal acts

Phase 3

- Aggressive interventionist acts precipitated by assessment that critical pillars of support are collapsing or would collapse with such actions. Care is taken not to cross thresholds of violence but those thresholds are approached aggressively
- Transportation sector immobilised by obstructing movement of military units
- Offers of amnesty announced to encourage defection of police and military officials
- Nationwide 'Freedom Now' demonstrations occur
- A General Strike is the culmination of individual sector slow downs and strikes (civil service, students, railways, lawyers and merchants)
- Plans for the installation of Aung San Suu Kyi are implemented
- Diplomatic recognition pre-arranged
- UN recognition immediate
- SLORC financial assets immediately frozen
- Burma embassies seized
- No retribution
- Call for return to work and respect for democratic government
- Aung San Su Kyi to be escorted to a public ceremony and receive mantle. CNN/International media coverage. Coordination with governments announcing diplomatic recognition
- Military groups march in front to recognise legitimacy

Communications

- Must be able to get news out, satellite communications are preferred and hand held radios with perhaps scramblers

With the plan ready to be put into action, Bo Mya flew to Boston with his foreign affairs adviser Dr Em Marta, for a major strategy meeting with Gene, Bob and Bruce Jenkins. The general arrived on the last day of May 1993 and checked into the Sheraton Commander, an imposing hotel that overlooks Harvard Yard. Here in a small meeting room they hammered out the details on the best way to bring down the regime in

Rangoon. Almost immediately Bo Mya dropped some news that shocked Gene and the Albert Einstein Institution team. He told them he wasn't willing to give up the military component of the struggle and insisted the nonviolent strategy was written into the order of battle alongside the military force which he would continue to command.

In a tense series of exchanges, Bob explained how political jujitsu would not work properly if violent force was still being used against the regime. He compared violence in a nonviolent struggle to getting water contamination in a gasoline engine. 'Mix a little water with petrol' he told them, 'and the engine will just about run, but performance would be compromised. Too much water and the engine will fail to function. Likewise mixing a little violence with a nonviolent movement might work, but the nonviolent movement would suffer. Too much violence would doom the nonviolent struggle.' In a guide for political defiance instructors he wrote:

'Violence is the most serious contaminant to the success of political defiance (nonviolent struggle) … violence by the political defiance organization may give the oppressor the public justification it needs to commit additional atrocities against the public … political defiance attempts to move the struggle away from the oppressor's strong points to areas where he is weak. We should never seek to fight on his terms.'

The general argued back that the regime was intent on genocide in the minority areas. There was no possibility that they could lay down their arms and risk total annihilation. Instead, he agreed to give up plans for bombings and assassinations in the cities and keep the military forces in a purely defensive posture to protect the ethnic minority areas from government attack. The military forces would hold on to the territory and buy time for the Political Defiance Committee to move enough trained nonviolent resistance operators into the cities to start the uprisings and overthrow the regime.

Gene disagreed with this accommodation. The experience of the Palestinians had shown that violence alongside nonviolent action greatly reduced the potential power of a movement. He eventually conceded, writing only, 'If one wanted the ordinary soldiers to mutiny and no longer support the dictatorship, it would not be wise to be attempting to kill them and their friends'. This was unusually pragmatic of Gene to continue to work alongside a military component when he knew it would undermine the struggle, but he defended the compromise.

When a young Burmese activist in the US asked how he could work with advocates of violence he told her, 'Because we both believe in fighting. We both believe in fighting militantly. We both believe in bringing down the dictatorship and we are exploring with them the potential of these other means. And they are willing and able to explore it. And they are now in the process of institutionally changing their policy. And if you don't work with people who are pro-violence, you have no way of changing their approach.'

To mitigate the damage, Bo Mya separated out both the people and the funding streams for the armed struggle and the nonviolent movement so that the Albert Einstein Institution would be protected against any accusation that they were assisting the military component of the campaign.

The plan agreed, Gene took the general took on a tour around Harvard Yard pointing out the notice board that had brought Gene and Bob together. They ate at one of the best restaurants in Boston and Bo Mya was presented with a modest parting gift. For months after his return to Burma the general was seen inspecting the defences of Manerplaw proudly wearing his combat fatigues with a bright blue Boston Red Sox baseball cap.

From Dictatorship to Democracy

At the end of June 1993, Bob received a tip off from his former colleagues in military intelligence that the Burmese regime was gathering their forces to overrun Manerplaw and deliver a knockout blow to the resistance. He wrote to Gene urgently, relaying the news. 'In what may be a race against the clock, a strategic political defiance capability must be generated before a major offensive is launched against Manerplaw and before there is a spontaneous uprising inside Burma precipitated by worsening economic conditions.'

Bob was frustrated at the lacklustre coverage of the military regime in Rangoon by the international papers and TV news networks. He knew that in order to communicate what was happening in the country to the Burmese people and to the outside world, they were going to have to do it themselves. He activated a plan with Tin Maung Win to launch a new magazine called 'Khit Pyiang' (New Era) to report on the regime activities and the political situation.

The publication would also carry training information in the form of editorials about political defiance and, if required, call for actions just like the Palestinian intifada leaflets had done. While the Burmese wrote most of the content of Khit Pyiang, the editorials were often ghost written by Bob or Gene. It was printed in Thailand, smuggled into Burma and delivered to the Burmese diaspora all over the world. Win was also its voice, reading and recording each issue onto cassette tapes which were also distributed widely.

There was one vital element that the trainees in Burma still lacked – a textbook for bringing down their dictatorship. Gene knew that his students needed some kind of guidebook to follow, but he still didn't know Burma well and he decided he couldn't pontificate on subjects about which he felt clueless. 'You should at least have the humility not to write about something you know nothing about, so I had to write generically. If there was a movement that wanted to bring a dictatorship to an end how could they do it?'

In the late summer of 1993, Gene set to work urgently on a new book, trying to answer that question. Tailoring a text specifically to Burma would have been time consuming and the draft was needed urgently. Instead, he developed a generic analysis of how to bring down a dictatorship, distilling the key elements of his 900 page *Politics of Nonviolent Action* into a smaller publication.

What could have been the book's weakness now turned into its major strength. By omitting any reference to particular countries, religions or cultures it would become applicable anywhere, by anyone in the world. With just 90 pages of simply written English it was also quick and easy to translate. He called it, *'From Dictatorship to Democracy'*.

For months Gene went quiet and wrote only occasionally to friends, apologising for a lack of contact. He told them he was 'hibernating' in East Boston writing a manuscript on 'how to disintegrate a dictatorship'. The book was finished by 10th October 1993 and serialised in Khit Pyiang before being published as a complete pamphlet in Burmese and English.

The books were first printed in Bangkok and smuggled into the free areas of Burma across the Moei river. They soon made their way with the students of the political defiance courses into all of the major cities of Burma. It wasn't long before some of the activists were arrested and found with the book, which was sent back urgently to the SLORC's intelligence agency in Rangoon.

The regime had long been aware of the foreigners training students in Manerplaw and across the border in Thailand, but the appearance of *From Dictatorship to Democracy* in several cities, far from the border areas, indicated a growing threat to their control. Activists carrying the book were jailed and the penalty for possessing a copy soon rose to 7 years' imprisonment.

A new way had to be found to reduce the likelihood of those carrying the book being caught. Bob came up with a plan to reduce its size into tiny smuggling editions. In addition to making them easier to hide, it meant more books could be distributed in smaller packages with less chance of discovery. A printer was found to produce a new batch of credit-card sized booklets with plain green and yellow covers. Fake book covers were also printed which disguised the full sized copies as children's stories and guides for playing chess. In all, more than 23,000 copies were printed, distributed and translated into Burmese and the minority languages of Karen, Mon, Chin and Jingh Paw.

As the PDC and the book smuggling operation were becoming more effective, Bob's nightmare of losing Manerplaw was slowly coming to fruition. Unbeknown to the inhabitants of the headquarters, the defences were being secretly undermined by an ingenious SLORC plan.

The majority Karen ethnic group at Manerplaw were mainly Christian, but there was also a significant number of Buddhists who called themselves the 'Democratic Karen Buddhist Organisation'. Many of the Buddhist fighters had been stationed on the defences of Manerplaw, but they were frequently badly equipped, poorly fed and felt discriminated against by General Bo Mya.

The Buddhists were led by a monk called U Thuanza and SLORC intelligence realised that if they offered him money and food to ensure safe refuge for the Buddhists, they could turn them against Bo Mya's Christian Karens. U Thuanza's strange ability to protect the Buddhists from attack was believed by the villagers to come from magical powers and they began to obey his commands without question.

In January 1995, SLORC gathered their troops, poised for what would be their final attack on Manerplaw. When the order to begin the attack was given, a coded signal was transmitted to U Thuanza who simply told the monks to abandon their defensive positions and melt into the jungle. Bo Mya, realising the inhabitants of Manerplaw had been betrayed, decided not to make a stand and instead fought delaying actions to allow a retreat across the river into Thailand.

Just minutes before the SLORC troops stormed into Manerplaw, a quick thinking staffer managed to set fire to all of the documents of the PDC, preventing the identification of the trainees who had been sent back into the cities to start the revolution. After Manerplaw had fallen, the state controlled national newspaper, 'The New Light of Myanmar', reported the activities of the PDC.

> 'They made contacts with underground elements within the country and distributed agitative pamphlets, set off bombs in townships to disturb peace and tranquillity and cause disturbances and resorted to other disruptive acts. Those who have provided training in political defiance (PD) activities were a former retired US Defense Attaché Robert Helvey and one Gene Sharp.'

The loss of their headquarters was a major blow to the Burmese resistance and the PDC, but while it made the military operations more difficult, it increased the importance of nonviolent action around the country. The PDC re-grouped with a new 'vision of tomorrow' and a concept for achieving that objective. They focused on building a capacity for massive civil disobedience and continued to include strategic nonviolent action as the primary means of waging their campaign against the regime.

> 'If we do not act soon we will have lost a window of opportunity opened by the courage and sacrifices of thousands in 1988', wrote Tin Maung Win. 'It is urgent that we design, adopt and execute a strategy quickly. Failure to do so will leave our nation in chains for another generation.'

Despite the setback of losing Manerplaw, the National Endowment for Democracy granted the Albert Einstein Institution an additional $45,000 to continue providing training in political defiance alongside consultation visits.

Mike Mitchell, a bright young project officer from the NED-funded IRI joined the mission to oversee the project. Bob quickly became fond of his young sidekick nicknaming him 'Hannibal' after he'd attempted to rent an elephant to reach an important meeting on the other side of a mountain. Part of Mike's job was to make trips into Rangoon to discretely meet PDC members, give them money and make sure that orders were being carried out in the capital. It gave him an opportunity to ensure, 'ground truth' and occasionally meet with Aung Sang Suu Kyi.

In his role as the IRI program officer Mike made three visits to Suu Kyi to make her aware of the progress of the PDC and also brief her on the latest news from the US Congress. Suu Kyi's house sat on a lake with a large thatched area for shade and a small stage for meetings in the garden. Weather-beaten and unpainted for years, the property was beginning to show signs of structural damage, but inside it was bright and airy.

At their first meeting, Mike told Suu Kyi about the training in non-violent action being carried out on the border. She was familiar with Gene's work, having read *From Dictatorship to Democracy,* and had heard his lectures on Voice of America. She told Mike that the heart and soul of the movement was nonviolence, perseverance and strength, not military means and he in turn reassured her that this was perfectly consistent with what the PDC was planning.

After his third visit, Burmese intelligence services realised what Mike was up to and linked him back to the work of Gene and Bob in Manerplaw. A press conference was announced and members of the international press and foreign diplomats were summoned to hear new allegations from the government.

Colonel Kyaw Thein, a high-ranking intelligence officer, took to a podium to accuse Suu Kyi of breaking Burmese law by meeting and colluding with revolutionary dissident groups. Foreign Minister, U Ohn Gyaw, then stepped up to some flow charts with a pointer documenting Suu Kyi's contacts with Mike Mitchell who was, 'working with Americans Bob Helvey, Gene Sharp and Bruce Jenkins'. Their aim, he said, was to bring down the Burmese government.

From her home on University Avenue, Suu Kyi was forced to issue a response. 'I have met Michael Mitchell,' she admitted, but insisted she had not broken any laws and asked, 'If they think he is involved in such activities, why did they let him into the country?'

In one of her 'Letters from Burma' she reported that Gene's work was causing the regime considerable alarm.

'There is an expression much bandied about these days which, in its Burmanized form, sounds very much like "jeans shirt." This has nothing to do with the denim mania that has come to Burma ...The expression actually refers to "Gene Sharp," the author of some works on "political defiance". These writings seem to be exercising the authorities in Burma considerably. Last month, 19 political prisoners were tried in Mandalay and they were all sentenced to seven years imprisonment, each on a charge of high treason. The possession of copies of books by Gene Sharp seemed to have been taken as part of the evidence against the defendants. (Not that "defendant" is an appropriate word to use in connection with political detainees in Burma as they have no real right of defense at all.)'

Gene respected Suu Kyi but was often frustrated by her inability to engage in any kind of strategic planning. He realised that her commitment to nonviolence was based on principle rather than a real understanding of its potential power, and she was showing no desire or ability to organise properly. 'For all her wonderful qualities and her heroism and inspiration for those who believe in democratic rights of the Burmese people [she] is not a strategist, she is a moral leader. That is not sufficient to plan a strategy.' To Gene, Suu Kyi epitomised the problem with the term 'non-violence', which indicated an absence of violence but not the presence of significant planned action to replace it. In fairness, she was under such close monitoring that any strategic planning she engaged in would soon have been gleaned by Burmese intelligence, so her involvement may have been a greater liability than a help.

At its peak, the PDC had 13 'cells' operating inside Burma. Teams were recruited and trained by the PDC organising staff and their primary mission was to establish and expand an underground presence, capable initially of conducting low risk activities until there was a call for them to initiate an action or help guide a spontaneous uprising that might erupt from an unknown quarter at any time. In the meantime, the little money available from the NED grant was given to the cell members for the daily costs of eating, housing, looking after their families and occasionally bribing policemen or local regime officials.

Mike Mitchell was still trying to squeeze more money out of the NED for the PDC. On 4th December 1996, he wrote to Bob making quite clear his ambitions for the project.

I am trying to get this funding locked away for the PDC. Yes, my dream of several sat phones could be realised. I do believe that it is time to kick this revolution in the ass and get it in gear.

Best, Hannibal

In late January, Bob flew to Thailand and met with the Chairman of the PDC, U Myint Zaw, to coordinate an advanced course which would be delivered in March 1997. But just as he arrived, the Burmese government launched a major offensive operation against the remainder of the resistance positions in the free areas and around 3000 civilians began to flee towards the Thai border. Bob was also passed intelligence from his friend, 'Major Paul', the US defence attaché in Thailand, indicating that the Burmese government planned to stop the New Era magazine by assassinating Tin Maung Win.

The Thai government, previously supportive of the resistance, had turned against them and now began to conspire in their destruction. Intelligence reports provided by the US Embassy in Bangkok suggested that Thai security forces had begun turning back Burmese refugees at the border the day after a high level meeting between a senior Burmese general and his Thai counterpart. Bob was concerned that the cover of some of the pro-democracy leaders had been blown and they would be rounded up and deported back to Rangoon. 'In my view it is unlikely they would survive the trip to Insein [prison]', he wrote.

In September 1997 the change in the Thai government position was confirmed by an article in the *Bangkok Phuchatkan* newspaper which reported that the Thai security service had ordered officials of all units to investigate foreigners who have been helping train minority ethnic groups to oppose the Burmese government. 'The security sources reveal that there is evidence indicating that at least three American nationals have provided political training for minority ethnic groups residing along the border.'

An unidentified official of the Thai National Security Council was quoted as saying 'Thailand now maintains a clear-cut policy of not interfering in the internal affairs of neighbouring countries, in particular Burma and that it will never allow anyone to use Thai soil as a base for the struggle against the Burmese government.'

As resistance leaders went into hiding, fearing the assassins who were now let loose in Thailand to track them down, final communications were sent to Gene in Boston. On 16th March 1998, Gene received a desperate letter from one of the members of the Political Defiance Committee.

'Three leaders of the KNU (Karen National Union) have become the main target of SLORC, Bo Mya, General Tamala Baw and I. SLORC have sent special soldiers to Thailand to kidnap and kill us. Now I stay mobile, the PDC is still trying to educate the people with political defiances methods and to organise them and prepare for a new uprising. In conclusion I want to mention again that we love, we respect, we remember and thank you forever.'

Tin Maung Win begged Bob to come back to Burma to shore up what was left of the political defiance campaign, but he regretfully declined. Their safety in Thailand could no longer be assured and he told Win they needed to avoid fuelling the rumours that Gene and the Albert Einstein Institution were in charge of the PDC and were passing instructions to Aung San Suu Kyi.

Despite the difficulties on the border, the PDC activists who had been slipped back into the cities, continued to operate. A leader codenamed 'K2' wrote to Bob on August 27th 1998 to report, 'Political Defiance activists inside Burma have been continuing to organise more hit and run guerilla demonstrations in more cities until the nationwide one comes up. The PDC is preparing at least 20 hand speakers, 50 flags and 10,000 stickers to provide them on their demand. We are also promoting the letters, phone, fax, high frequency radio transmission campaigns targeting at army and police forces'. But the revolution that these cells were preparing for would not come to fruition.

The loss of Thai support, exposure of Gene, Bob and Mike Mitchell by the Burmese government press and winding down of the IRI funding, saw the Albert Einstein Institution conclude their decade of involvement in Burma at the end of 1998.

On the 11th October the following year, Win relayed the news to Bob that Ye Kyaw Thu was in a coma at a hospital in Chiang Mai and would not recover. He died shortly afterwards. Less than six weeks later Tin Maung Win was moving out of his offices when he had a heart attack carrying a heavy computer down a flight of stairs. He passed away at midday on December 1st 1999.

Disease and hard living had succeeded in killing two of the Burmese regime's most wanted before their assassins had managed it. The end of the programme and the death of Ye Kyaw Thu and and Tin Maung Win was a blow to the continuation of political defiance in Burma, but over the course of ten years the team had distributed thousands of Gene Sharp's books and directly trained thousands of activists in strategic nonviolent action. Thousands more had listened to the broadcasts of the Democratic Voice of Burma and would learn second and third hand the methods of nonviolent action. Most importantly for Gene's work, the resistance in Burma had catalysed the creation of *From Dictatorship to Democracy* – a book born in the jungle, which would go on to shake the world.

Otpor

Marek Zelazkiewicz approached his agreed rendezvous point in a quiet corner of Belgrade for the third time in as many days. On his previous attempts he felt that he was being watched, but no-one had ever appeared to meet him. Now he scanned the faces of the occasional passers-by for signs they might be the secret police. To be caught would mean certain arrest and perhaps worse – but Marek was not a spy, he was a veteran of the Polish anti-communist Solidarity movement, and hidden in his duffle bag were photographs of Serbian army atrocities in Kosovo and a copy of *From Dictatorship to Democracy*. He told his friends, 'If you take out the ladies, it was nearly James Bond'.

On this occasion he was lucky – a young woman appeared from an alley and beckoned him to follow her. Marek set off in pursuit, winding his way through several paved courtyards and passages before finally climbing a set of stairs to an apartment door. The rooms inside had been converted into a headquarters, buzzing with photocopiers and computers with huddles of young people in meetings around little tables. As he entered, the occupants fell silent, staring at him suspiciously. 'This is Otpor', his guide told him. The name means "resistance" in Serbian. They're the best hope of bringing down President Slobodan Milosevic'.

As the Otpor activists gathered around Marek, he began to tell them his story. After the victory of the Solidarity movement against the communists in Poland he had become an academic at the University of California Berkeley. It was there he first discovered Gene Sharp's work. When he saw ethnic Albanians being persecuted by Serb forces in Kosovo he decided to fly there to teach them what he knew about nonviolent resistance, but the conflict had quickly become too dangerous. His last hope, he decided, was to head north into Serbia to see if he could change the country from within.

Marek talked about the potential of Gene's book for the movement against Milosevic and the importance of translating and distributing it. The students flicked through the pamphlet, but appeared unimpressed. 'We don't have the manpower for this, maybe in the future, but not now', one of the young men told him. Marek felt fobbed off, but left a loosely bound photocopy on a desk for them.

Undeterred, Marek kept trying new contacts, certain that he would soon meet a group which would realise the significance of the book. Eventually he was introduced to an organisation called 'Civic Initiatives', headed by a man called Miljenko Dereta. Marek handed him another slightly dog-eared photocopy of *From Dictatorship* and asked him if Civic Initiatives would be interested in publishing a Serbian edition. Dereta began to read through the shabby pages and to his delight, Marek noticed his eyes light up – it was immediately obvious to him that *From Dictatorship to Democracy* could be a useful tool for organising against Milosevic. Civic Initiatives translated the text into Serbian, but just as preparations were being made for a printing run, a NATO bombing campaign stopped everything.

At 7pm on the 24th March 1999, NATO began a military offensive against Serbia in an attempt to halt atrocities being committed by Serb forces in Kosovo. Over 1000 aircraft launched from Italy, Germany and aircraft carriers in the Adriatic, hitting targets across the country throughout April and May.

Serbia was under attack and its people rallied around their government, in some cases even camping on bridges to stop them being bombed. Any attempt to print literature hostile to the government could be treated far more severely during time of war, so the opposition groups like Civic Initiatives and Otpor went into hibernation.

By the beginning of June, a thousand soldiers were dead along with at least 480 civilians. Milosevic's air force was entirely destroyed and cities across the country were scarred by bombing. After diplomatic intervention from Russia, Milosevic agreed to withdraw his forces from Kosovo and the war was officially declared over on the 11th June. Serbia had suffered a military defeat, but to the embarrassment of NATO leaders, President Slobodan Milosevic remained in power.

Just like Civic Initiatives, the NATO bombing had disrupted Otpor's activities. Despite widespread animosity towards Milosevic in the country, the presence of an external threat had united the people around their leadership. It was clear to the democratic opposition that military action had only strengthened Milosevic and given him a chance to survive a little bit longer.

A few days after the NATO campaign ended, Dereta ordered the printers back into action to produce 2,500 copies of *From Dictatorship to Democracy* for Civic Initiatives. He followed up with a second batch of 2000 which were distributed free of charge to NGOs, activists, political parties and members of Otpor. Although he had quickly realised its value, Dereta was astonished by the interest. 'Every time people would see this book in someone else's hand, they would call us and ask for a copy. When there was a nonviolent action, people would say, 'It's by the book! This gave them courage and made them think about what they could do – the whole dictatorship was in a way demystified'.

Marek Zelazkiewicz's small action had planted the first seeds of Gene's work into Serbian civil society, and although Otpor had not paid much attention at first, they would soon embrace it as a vital tool in their battle against Milosevic.

Otpor had been founded in October 1998 at the Greenet Café in Stari Grad Street, Belgrade – a distinctly upmarket joint where waiters wore smart black uniforms and poured coffee from silver pots. At first they were just four close friends, then seven and finally eleven. Most were still students who had battled together through street protests against Milosevic in 1996/97 and they knew and trusted each other. These eleven would form the nucleus of the new movement.

Perhaps the most flamboyant of the group was Srdja Popovic, pronounced 'Surja' – a 27-year-old marine biology student from Belgrade whose mother had almost been killed by a NATO airstrike on the television station where she worked. He remembered the beginnings of Otpor as one of the most exciting times of his life.

'We understood that there was no way that political change was coming to Serbia through the existing political parties and that Serbia was slipping fast into dictatorship with new restrictive laws on media freedom and universities. We were in our 20s we felt like the world belonged to us and we had the experience of the struggle in 1996/97. We thought we could do it.'

There was a proud history of resistance movements in Serbia. One was called 'Skojevci' – an underground communist youth movement during World War Two. A popular TV series about them was screened while most of the members of Otpor had been growing up, so there was a glamour about following in the footsteps of their heroes.

Otpor wanted to introduce themselves as a cool 'brand' to the youth of Serbia, but they needed a symbol that was aggressive enough to demonstrate their power and yet still show their commitment to nonviolent action. 'We thought, if only those who were against Milosevic could recognise each other by saluting with a fist, then this big bubble of fear will just go. They would understand that we are the many and they are the few – and we will win.' Srdja explained. A clenched fist was chosen as a symbol that equally suited the political left and right. Nenad Petrović, known as 'Duda,' was a well known artist at the School of Graphic Design when the idea of the fist symbol was discussed. Two of the young women who'd been in the meeting knew that he was the perfect person to create their symbol.

'Dragana and Ana came to ask me to draw a stylisation of a fist suitable for stencil. I was madly in love with Dragana, so I did my best to impress her with what I am best at, drawing!' Duda remembered. Sadly he failed to impress Dragana, but after a little work, his design got the go-ahead and soon became the symbol of Otpor. Duda never did get together with Dragana, but he did eventually marry Ana.

Just like Gerald Holtom's peace symbol, Duda's fist immediately drew complaints – people who would call the office to say that the fist was intimidating and fascistic. One young mother complained to say she was terrified because there were posters with black hands everywhere.

Despite the criticism, Otpor felt that it struck the right balance between being edgy enough for the kids to get behind while still being appropriate for a nonviolent movement. It went on to be rendered millions of times on posters, stickers and t-shirts across Serbia and later by revolutionary and protest groups all over the world.

Otpor was convinced that the removal of Milosevic was possible in the presidential election of 2000 if they could convince the opposition to unite around a single candidate. In order to achieve this objective they developed a two part campaign. The first part used the Otpor fist and the 'Gotov Je' (He's Finished) slogan to highlight the crimes of Milosevic. The second was 'Get Out the Vote' – a positive, colourful campaign, which sought to involve as many civil society organisations as possible to get people to the polling stations.

On Serbian Orthodox New Year, January 13th 2000, Otpor arranged a street party for 30,000 people. After hours of music, a concert of drummers and a mock awards ceremony, the lights were suddenly turned off, plunging the square into darkness. On a big screen behind the stage, a film about the people who had died under Milosevic began to play. A foreboding voice told the people that it was time to go home because there was nothing for Serbia to celebrate in the year 2000. 'Go home and think about what is happening to you. This is the year that we make a change!' the voice told them. By quarter past midnight the square was empty – 30,000 people were on their way home. The next morning a co-ordinated, country-wide campaign had covered every corner of Serbia with posters exclaiming, 'This is the year'.

For a while Otpor had hidden away in the office that Marek had visited a few months previously, but as they became bolder so too did their premises. Slobo Dinovic was Otpor's tech geek and co-founder, but his wide frame, black leather jacket and occasionally menacing body language made him appear more like a Milosevic secret policeman than a democracy activist. His mother owned an office in the middle of the downtown shopping area of Belgrade and was willing to let the group use it. Everyone, including the secret police, would know where they were, but that could also play to their advantage.

Srdja wanted Otpor to live in the city centres where it could be seen, not hidden away like an insurgent group. 'The idea was to piss off the regime as much as we could, so an office in the centre of town meant that the flag with the prohibited symbol of the fist was waving over thousands of people who walked through the streets below every day.'

Another advantage was counter-surveillance. The office in Belgrade was bugged, nobody had any doubt about that, so meetings had to be held outside in small groups. Just across the street were gardens where walking meetings could be held. This made it far more difficult for the spies to monitor who was talking to whom and what they were saying. The secret police took up station in a building opposite, watching and noting who was coming and going from the building, but Otpor were determined to stay there until the end.

Huge efforts were spent making Otpor virtually indestructible, decentralising the organisation by setting up local branches in the regional towns and cities. Some campaigns had to be controlled at a national level and the regional offices were asked to undertake tasks from the centre, but it was seen as critical that if its top leaders were jailed, it could still function in the rest of the country.

The process wasn't always easy, some regional commands refused to comply with requests, but in general the system worked well. In one campaign, Otpor fly-posted 80,000 posters across the country in the space of an hour on the same day. The mass posting made it impossible for the police to arrest everybody involved.

The only aspect that was entirely centralised was the financing operation. Otpor had met with US and European diplomats soon after their formation and the money for photocopying, printing, computers and the internet soon started to flow. At first there was nervousness in the US State Department at giving money to a student organisation with a black clenched fist as their logo, but nerves soon calmed after close observation of the group. The total amount of money given by the US would reach a reported $25 million dollars, though Srdja maintains this was dwarfed by the amount of money which came from Serbs themselves.

The local Otpor branches would send proposals to Belgrade for financing particular actions and these were sent out in a master list to international donors. One of the US officials charged with liaison with Otpor was Scott Carpenter from the International Republican Institute, the same organisation that had financed the Albert Einstein Institution's work in Burma.

Otpor planned actions weeks in advance for what they called the 'neutral situation' and then had back up plans for every action the regime might take against them. The idea was to have some activity against the Milosevic regime going on every day of the week. This was the influence of US electoral 'campaign grids' applied to a revolutionary situation. The Americans were delighted with Otpor, but some within the IRI thought they needed some more formal training to increase their chances in the battle that would come.

Having recently wound up their relationship with the Albert Einstein Institution on the Burma project, Mike Mitchell from the IRI had been lobbying for a nonviolent training programme for the Serbs. Bob was at home at his cottage in West Virginia and about to have dinner when he received the email. Mike opened with his usual greeting.

'Moses,
You will probably be called by Julie Mashburn in our Central Europe Division [of IRI]. After much prodding they are finally looking at NVS [nonviolent struggle] as a tool for the student movement in Belgrade.'

Mike described how Otpor was experienced in protest, although none of it was yet strategic. They were bright and highly motivated, but felt that they had hit a wall in their development and could use at least a week long training course. IRI wanted someone to go to Belgrade to provide alternatives and talk with them about the problems they were encountering. Bob wrote back agreeing to do the training, but Otpor felt that it was far too risky to hold a workshop in Belgrade. Milosevic's spies were everywhere and identification of the Otpor leadership group could be disastrous.

Instead, the IRI flew 14 members of the group out of Serbia and put them up in a Hilton hotel in Budapest.

The workshop was held in a drab meeting room where Bob was waiting with some materials, including copies of *The Politics of Nonviolent Action*. He inspected each of the Otpor students in turn as they sat down, assessing the dynamics of the group. Bob noticed immediately that a sharp featured young man with floppy hair spoke the best English and asked him to translate the more difficult concepts he was teaching. This was Bob's first encounter with Srdja, who talked quickly and passionately, filled with nervous energy. Through the translation process the two men quickly built up a rapport. Bob called him 'Surjee' and resisted all attempts at correction. He would call him Surjee for the rest of their relationship.

A few hours into the first day Bob stopped suddenly, 'Well there's something missing here. We haven't talked about who's the leader of this organisation. Who is the leader?' The group looked around nervously at each other. After an awkward silence Srdja answered the question. 'We don't have a leader'.

Bob retained his gruff, no nonsense, military style with a deep commanding voice. It was a strange experience for a bunch of free thinking liberal student leaders who weren't used to answering to anyone, let alone a former colonel. 'Well wait a minute guys,' Bob exclaimed, leaning forward onto the table, looking at each of them in turn. 'I did not fall off a turnip truck coming over here! Somebody has to lead an organisation that's mobilised the entire Serbian society. There has to be a leader to that organisation! There has to be a leader who is coordinating all these demonstrations – there has to be a leadership that's getting these millions of dollars in funding!'

The Serbs began laughing. Despite the informality of the session they were nervous of an unknown foreigner learning their secrets. As they began to trust Bob, they explained it was a deliberate tactic to make sure the government never knew who was in charge.

Bob taught the Serbs about the pillars of support. Holding up a book with his fingers, just like he had done with Bo Mya in his hut in Manerplaw, he described how every dictatorship relied on key institutions without

which it would cease to function – the police, the army, the religious institutions. He folded his fingers one by one and let the book fall to the floor.
'Every dictatorship has weaknesses!' he told them, 'Your job is to find the
weaknesses, identify the pillars of support and don't break those pillars
but pull them onto the side of the democratic forces!'

Srdja was bowled over by the workshop. 'His presentation was something
that I had never seen in my life, I have seen maybe 200 trainings and
maybe performed 200 or 300. I'm really experienced, but he is a miracle!'

Bob was just as impressed by the Serbs. 'I knew the first day just
by looking at them I had a group of very bright, unique, committed,
courageous, activists. I just knew it. I could just watch their body language,
I could see how they were reacting to the comments I was making and
when that seminar was over I knew these guys were going some place.'

Over those few days, Bob became a mentor to Srdja and by the end
of it they were using Star Wars references to refer to each other. Bob
was Obi Wan and Srdja was Luke – Gene in his absence was christened
'Yoda'. 'My first impression of Srdja was just, "smart".' Bob remembered,
'Smart, brilliant and charismatic. Sort of nervous, you could almost see a
computer working in his mind'.

The Serbs seized on the idea of pillars of support as a model for
organising their strategy and left Budapest focused on undermining the
organisations which held up the Milosevic government. They first had to
build their human resources and most importantly train their training
teams. An Otpor training manual was compiled from the experiences
so far in the movement and a large component from Gene's *Politics of
Nonviolent Action,* which Bob had provided at the Budapest workshop.

This new training manual was distributed in its thousands across Serbia
and courses were given at weekly seminars. These training activities gave
strength and depth to Otpor and made it increasingly resilient to arrests.
Each of the Otpor regional offices knew the guiding plan, but could
innovate and operate independently if the head office in Belgrade was
eliminated by the Serb security forces.

Otpor had 30 to 40 spokespeople who would rotate so that there was
never just one face associated with the movement. This made arresting

them futile for the police and government forces. The mainstream press tried to get them to stick with one point of contact, but they resisted. 'We wanted to show that young people are the resistance. It's a living thing. It's not a job, it's something you either live or it doesn't exist', Srdja explained.

The Otpor leadership identified that the most significant pillars of support in Serbia were the police, media and judiciary. They set about trying to infiltrate these institutions through personal contacts and replicating the media pillar with their own alternative media to undermine the authority of the state TV.

During the protests in 1996 and 1997, the students had created noisy demonstrations during the TV news bulletins and now they reintroduced that action, asking people to go out onto their balconies and gardens to beat pots and pans at the exact time the state TV news went on air. When demonstrations were routed past the TV station, people would hold their nose as they walked past. While working to undermine the authority of the state media they created printed newsletters and email news updates to form an alternative news service for the country.

Srdja had identified the police as potentially the most important pillar of the Milosevic regime to counter. Otpor members across the country were tasked with writing letters to each police station in Serbia. The letters had two messages, the first was, 'beware of what you are doing because this regime will end so you must think about your life after that', and the second was, 'You are our friend. Your kids are in Otpor. If you hurt them your fellow citizens will avoid you'. They asked officers to post the letters on the police headquarters message boards.

Actions were staged in front of police stations where Otpor activists would talk to the police officers, telling them that the police and the people were on the same side. 'What we needed to tell them' said Srdja, 'is they wear blue uniforms and we wear blue jeans, but we are both victims and there should be no war between victims and victims.'

On 14th May 2000, the State Information Minister held a press conference to denounce Otpor as a terrorist organisation. 'Otpor is a neo-facist organisation in the tradition of the Red Brigades and this state will use the same means used by other states when presented with terrorism of such proportions,' he told the television cameras. This press conference was barely credible. Otpor was now present in so many towns and cities of Serbia that almost everyone knew someone working for them and that they weren't terrorists.

One of the most memorable lessons from Bob's Budapest workshop was on political jujitsu. A government carrying out senseless acts against unarmed civilians was bound to create a backlash and the more people who were touched by the oppression, the stronger the opposition would grow. Otpor designed situations that would force the police to make arrests for minor acts against the government which would rebound against them. They encouraged high school students of 16 and 17 to organise marches and demonstrations, and soon the teenagers were being arrested by the police. At a time when the government was trying to portray Otpor as terrorists, the arrest of 16-year-olds in small neighbourhoods where everyone knew everyone else, caused widespread consternation and anger.

Otpor soon began producing increasingly clever 'dilemma actions' like these to make the police look heavy handed or ridiculous. One example was a barrel positioned on a busy high street plastered all over with pictures of Milosevic's face. By dropping a small donation into the barrel people passing by could beat the picture of Milosevic with a baseball bat attached to the barrel which made a loud booming noise that could be heard all the way down the main street.

Otpor knew that it forced the police into a dilemma – they could arrest people who were beating the barrel for which there was no crime in law or they could arrest the barrel. The police arrested the barrel and Otpor photographers were there, ready to take photos of the comical moment that the officers had to try and squeeze the offending object into the back of their patrol car. Every day a new action like this was planned to make the regime look less intimidating or ridiculous and slowly erode the fear amongst the population.

Srdja had long been known to Serb intelligence as a main player in the resistance. He was driving from one group of students to another when a police jeep pulled out in front of his car and he was dragged from the driver's seat. 'I created a big drama, I swore like fuck and that's important because people need to see what's happening so your friends learn fast what has happened to you,' he told me. He was badly beaten for around an hour at the police station before a pistol was forced into his mouth in a mock execution. 'I was quite crazy at that point and not very polite, but somehow I knew that my friends would come and they would ask lawyers for help. I knew that I will be out in six hours. The beating hurts only when you are afraid and when you are not afraid, it doesn't hurt any more.'

The preparation campaign for the activists was uniquely difficult for the police to handle. To reduce fear of the security forces, Otpor trained people in exactly what to expect if they were arrested, where they would likely be taken, the questions they would be asked and what the inside of the cells would look and feel like. This was a method of training that could be traced back to the 1960s. The Reverend Jim Lawson, a friend of Gene's from university and an advisor on nonviolent action to Martin Luther King Jr., held trainings just like this for lunch counter sit-ins during the civil rights movement. The scenes were powerfully recreated in the 2013 film *The Butler* starring Forest Whitaker and Oprah Winfrey – as part of the training activists were screamed at, insulted, spat upon and slapped by their colleagues to prepare them mentally for what was to come.

When an Otpor activist was arrested, an alert system would be activated. Even if someone's cell phone was switched off for longer than three hours, a check would be made with friends and family to make sure nothing had happened to them. People would phone the local radio station to inform them of the arrest and the police knew that within an hour a crowd would form outside the police station demanding their release. A system of pro bono duty lawyers were always available to read the police the rule book.

Often the people who had been arrested could hear the crowd outside reassuring them that help was on its way. When the police attempted to arrest people protesting outside, the protest would only intensify. Teenage girls who had been arrested would look the police directly in the eyes during questioning and say, 'Yeah, I'm against Milosevic, aren't you?' and laugh. Once more, the arrests created a dilemma action for the police.

Every time they made an arrest they knew they would have to deal with a bigger problem.

Marches often started from the student square beside the Department of Philosophy at the University of Belgrade, one of the most active faculties in the movement. The square wasn't connected to any main road so assemblies couldn't be intercepted early by the police. Its small proportions meant that it could be filled with just over a thousand people which made it look like a much bigger protest than it really was.

Otpor became adept at making even minor protests look bigger by using clever camera angles or filling small spaces. They made the movement look successful by picking battles they could win, creating an action, retreating quickly and then claiming victory. They never occupied a public space for undefined period of time like the Chinese had in Tiananmen Square – they stayed agile and unpredictable.

To maintain nonviolent discipline on the marches, well trained marshals were employed all along the routes, directing the protest and isolating any violence. Instead of angry young men pushing to the front to confront the police, Otpor put the young women, the grandmas and the military veterans at the front to make it more difficult for the police to beat the protest back.

As the opposition threat grew, Milosevic ordered the shutdown of all the independent media in Belgrade. The move forced more people out onto the streets who had never previously engaged with the democracy movement. Protesters camped for two nights in the city centre before the police used tear gas and beatings to clear the streets. With the pressure rising, Milosevic triggered an early election to wrong-foot the opposition which he believed wouldn't be ready for a campaign. The date was set for 24th September 2000.

Eighteen opposition parties agreed to form a coalition, the Democratic Opposition of Serbia (DOS), to run a single candidate against Milosevic and maximise their chance of removing him from power. Their choice of candidate was the human rights lawyer and academic, Vojislav Koštunica.

When the election came, DOS and the international community used a sophisticated exit polling system that fed results back to a control room in Belgrade. By the early hours of the morning Koštunica announced that the exit poll clearly showed a DOS win. But, however convincing their data was, they knew that Milosevic would try to steal the election. As predicted, the ruling party announced that no party had won a clear majority and there would have to be a run-off.

DOS issued a counter-statement telling the country that a re-run was unnecessary and called the people to prepare for a general strike. The miners at the Kolubara mine, just south of Belgrade, were ahead of the game. They knew the mine was responsible for the generation of 70% of Serbia's electrical power and essential to the operation of the State. They called an early strike in order to encourage the rest of the country.

As the security forces converged on the mine to force the miners back to work, thousands of ordinary citizens surrounded the site to protect the workers. In other areas, taxis formed rolling go-slow blockades and soon the country ground to a halt.

On the morning of 5th October, the first convoys, which would carry thousands of people to Belgrade, set off from the regions across Serbia. The coordinated DOS/Otpor move on the capital was scheduled to reach its decisive climax outside the federal parliament building where the convoys would meet at 3pm and take control of the building.

Now Srdja gave his battle speech to a room in the Otpor office crowded with activists, crammed around desks and sitting on the floor. These would be the marshals sent out across the city to maintain nonviolent discipline on the final push. 'Now you will face the greatest task of your lives! You must lead the protests, you are trained to do this. You have networks at universities, this protest is yours! It is now up to you!'

Milosevic deployed his police around the main arterial routes into the capital, throwing articulated lorries across the roads to block the thousands of Serbs they knew were coming their way. The first to meet a roadblock was the convoy from the town of Cacak, led by the colourful mayor, Velimir Ilic. Ilic emerged from his car in a tracksuit and trainers and confronted the young police officers who nervously told him they had been ordered to block the road. The mayor explained that the motorway was packed with protesters in a traffic jam that now tailed all the way back to Cacak and they would push their way through if necessary. The officers soon stood aside helplessly and watched as the lorries they had moved into position were pushed off the road and down an embankment.

For months, Otpor and DOS had been cultivating contacts within the special police counter-terror units that they knew would be ordered to stop the revolution. Now as the convoys broke free along the highway with flags flying from their windows and doors, the mayor radioed one of these police units to give them information about their progress. As more convoys approached Belgrade it became clear that the police were following orders to build roadblocks, but would melt away as the convoys dismantled them.

The police and the army were infiltrated, intelligence personnel had been turned, the power companies were on side, the miners were on strike, the youth were on the streets, and trained and experienced marshals were enforcing nonviolent discipline. Every single piece of this revolution had been moved into position and now it was time to move to checkmate. The most advanced nonviolent campaign in history was reaching its climax.

The Cacak convoy entered the square outside the parliament building at 11am on 5th October and the protesters rushed up to the main entrance singing and chanting, 'Gotov Je! Gotov Je!' An early attempt to storm the parliament before all of the convoys had arrived was repulsed with tear gas, but when the police saw how many people were massing against them, they stood aside. Mayor Ilic climbed onto a makeshift stage encouraging the people to stay nonviolent and not throw things at the police. After a few hours, DOS members tasked with monitoring the radio traffic of the regime heard orders being given to the police and the army to clear the square, but the order was never carried out. Later it was reported that the commanders had refused to give the order to fire because they knew members of their own families were in the crowd.

A few protesters managed to reach the entrance of the parliament and thrust open the huge wooden doors for the crowd behind them. The people surged through the building and up the stairs and within minutes the Otpor flag was flying from a building. Boxes of fraudulent ballot papers pre-marked for Milosevic were found inside and tipped out of the windows, raining down on the people celebrating below.

As night fell on 5th October, the people of Belgrade celebrated in the streets with the soldiers still clinging to their armoured personnel carriers. But behind the euphoric scenes playing out on the international news networks, the disciplined nonviolent movement was losing control at the fringes of its influence. The parliament building was on fire and rumours were reaching Srdja of people breaking into Milosevic's Socialist Party Building, intending to burn it down. Srdja and some volunteers ran as fast as they could from the Otpor office and dragged the intruders out. To protect the building from more attacks they called in a music system and created a party out front with huge loudspeakers strapped to the top of a car.

The strange spectacle of Otpor protecting the headquarters of the regime which had oppressed Serbia for so many years looked bizarre, but it was essential. The government was gone, the police were dissolved and every single act of violence and destruction could have turned the revolution violent. Otpor knew it had to protect every piece of property and prevent an outbreak of violence to ensure a smooth and peaceful transition of power.

Srdja explained this as perhaps the most important lesson of Gene's teaching. Without maintaining nonviolent discipline until the transition, years of work could have been undone in an orgy of violence and destruction. 'Gene focuses on this situation of chaos and understands the importance of nonviolent struggle in preventing a coup. The moment where the government is gone and there appears to be chaos is dangerous because it's an excuse for the military to come out and grab the power. As a nonviolent strategist you want to prevent this at any cost'.

For Gene, the success of Otpor was the best evidence yet that a nonviolent campaign could work as he'd believed it could. It would serve as a model for many campaigns to come. In a letter to Gene just after the revolution Srdja wrote to thank him for his contribution to their struggle. It was, he wrote, 'an astoundingly effective blueprint for confronting a brutal regime while engaging the population into a pluralist, nonviolent struggle for self-liberation.'

That evening Bob was at home in West Virginia watching the revolution on CNN. In the crowd he thought he had just made out a couple of the students from the Budapest workshop. He settled back into his chair, poured a glass of scotch and raised it at the television. 'I felt proud that night, because I knew those brave kids… I knew em'.

Colour Revolutions

At 7:35 am on 11th September 2001, just a few minutes walk from 36 Cottage Street, Mohammed Atta and Abdulaziz al-Omari boarded American Airlines flight 11 at Boston Logan airport. Thirty nine minutes later, another airliner, United Airlines Flight 175 reported wheels up and made its slow arc across Boston Harbour on course for Los Angeles. Within an hour, these aircraft were being flown into Tower 1 and 2 of New York's World Trade Center.

The attacks set in train the War on Terror and the invasions of Iraq and Afghanistan – but 9/11 also became the most significant moment in US democracy promotion since Reagan's establishment of the National Endowment for Democracy.

As the US invaded Afghanistan to drive out the Taliban and hunt down Osama Bin Laden, the Bush administration began thinking about what 9/11 meant for the long term defence of US interests. Deputy Secretary of Defense, Paul Wolfowitz, commissioned the American Enterprise Institute think tank, to come up with ideas about how to combat the new threats associated with mass casualty terrorism originating from the Middle East. They convened a meeting codenamed 'Bletchley 2' which produced a report titled, 'The Delta of Terrorism'.

The assessment in that report is still classified, but enough has leaked out from the participants at the meeting that we know roughly what was concluded. The meeting agreed that 9/11 was not an isolated criminal incident, but part of a 20 year fight against radical Islam that could only be fully eradicated by a program of democratisation to free people across the Middle East. For countries like Iraq and Afghanistan which were weak enough to be changed by military force, that would be the means. For the rest of the region, where complicated relationships were in play, (Egypt, Saudi Arabia, The Emirates) there would be no destabilisation, but gentle pressure to change. For the most dangerous states where the military cost was too high (Iran and Syria), active regime change would be pursued.

Dictatorships were put on notice – freedom would prevail. So while the invasions of Afghanistan and Iraq were dominating the news throughout the early 2000s, behind the scenes the Bush White House began constructing an aggressive campaign of nonviolent influence to establish western leaning liberal democracy across the Middle East and the former Soviet states. It would become known as 'The Freedom Agenda'.

The birth of the Freedom Agenda and a renewed US focus on democracy promotion, threw greater focus on Otpor's successful campaign against Milosevic, and what could be achieved with assistance from US agencies. Gene Sharp's books had been central to Otpor trainings and now his theories, fused with Otpor's real world experience, would become a key weapon of the Freedom Agenda.

The first of the 'colour revolutions' took place in Georgia, a small former Soviet state, slightly smaller than South Carolina, sandwiched between Russia to the North and Turkey and Azerbaijan to its South. In 2003 it was led by a former Georgian Communist Party official, Eduard Shevardnadze, who was running the country like a Milosevic-style authoritarian state, plagued with poverty and endemic corruption.

With his popularity decreasing, democracy activists in the country believed Shevardnadze would attempt to steal the upcoming election due in November 2003 and they began lobbying international organisations for help. The Open Society Institute (OSI), a private democracy promotion foundation funded by billionaire George Soros, paid for a training team of Slobo Dinovic from Otpor, Marko Blagojevic from the Centre for Free Elections and Democracy and Sonja Licht from the Belgrade office of OSI to fly to Tiblisi to meet the activists and conduct an assessment. The problem was that in late 2002 there were very few activists to work with. Slobo was shocked at the level of apathy and reported back that the youth movement in the country was almost nonexistent.

This was very different from Bob's first workshop with Otpor, which was already an effective campaigning organisation by the time he met them. In Georgia, the Serbs would have to help grow the embryo movement from scratch. They found the seeds of the movement in an organisation called the 'Liberty Institute' run by two activists, Giga Bokeria and Levan Ramishvilli.

The OSI funded a trip for Giga, Levan and a handful of other promising activists to fly into Belgrade for some intensive coaching from the Serbs. There they met the leaders of Otpor, and were introduced to Gene's work. In their downtime they took the Otpor tour of Belgrade, with Slobo pointing out the cafe where it had all started, the university buildings and the square where they had staged the rock concert on New Years Eve 2000. This would be among the first of dozens of such tours with activists from all over the world.

Giga and Levan were stunned by the level of organisation that had gone into the Serbian movement. When they had watched the Serbian people swell into the parliament building on TV in October 2000 it looked like the whole thing had only taken a matter of days – people came onto the streets and Milosevic just fell. This was a common and dangerous mis-conception that Srdja was always keen to dispel early on. 'People only see what's on CNN that evening and they think a revolution is lots of people going to the streets and holding up banners and handing people flowers and then the government falls. But that's not the most important bit, that's just the last act. If you do that without putting the ground work in for months, and in our case years, you are destined to fail.'

The Georgians decided to adopt the Otpor model, but they didn't just implement its organisational structure and plans, they decided to mirror it exactly. They called themselves, 'Kmara' which means 'enough' in Georgian and copied Otpor's clenched fist logo, with the word 'Kmara' emblazoned below it in cyrillic script. Giorgi Kandelaki, one of the Kmara leaders, was proud to adopt their revolutionary cousin's visual identity. 'For us it was important to stress the connection, to say this was the same concept as Otpor, not least because we wanted to frighten the government'.

In April 2003, Kmara announced themselves to the country with an Otpor-style graffiti campaign across the capital, Tiblisi. Their Serb mentors had taught them that they must start with small acts of resistance to overcome what Gene described as the 'atomisation of the population', the stage at which the people are too scared to rebel.

Kmara launched its first campaign by night with a few members, an old car and a boot full of paint and brushes. By the morning there was barely a district of the city which didn't bear their mark. Even President Shevardnadze saw the painted Kmara slogans from his limousine as he was driven to work. The graffiti campaign was a force multiplier, an action which made it feel like Kmara was everywhere when they were still really small and, relatively, nowhere.

When Kmara analysed the pillars of support of the Shevardnadze government, it was clear that they already had some advantages over the Serbs. Milosevic had almost totally controlled the media in Serbia which was essentially just a propaganda wing of the state. Otpor had fought to create an underground media service to compete, but in Georgia there was still a strongly anti-government television station operating called Rustavi-2.

In nearly all revolutions there is an early battle for the communication system, and Georgia was no different. In October 2001, officials from the National Security Ministry launched a raid on the headquarters of Rustavi-2 on the pretext of tax irregularities. A rival TV station had been tipped off to film the event, but it had backfired spectacularly on the government. More than 7000 people rushed to the building to protest, many of them spontaneously, others mobilised by the Liberty Institute. They called for the resignation of the government, but Shevardnadze quickly defused the tension by firing the Minister for Security from his cabinet.

The attack on Rustavi-2 encouraged the resignation of Mikheil Saakashvili, the 33-year-old Minister of Justice who had been waging a lonely battle on corruption from inside the government. Saakashvili formed a new party, the 'United National Movement', to contest the election.

Now fiercely protected by Georgian citizens and bolstered by funding from a number of US democracy promotion agencies, Rustavi-2 continued to criticise the government. It began to screen mocking satirical cartoons of Shevardnadze and videos produced by Kmara which highlighted corruption. Possibly the most significant broadcast was *Bringing Down a Dictator*, a documentary about Otpor's experience in Serbia, made by the American director Steve York and funded by Peter Ackerman, Gene's co-founder of the Albert Einstein Institution. *Bringing down a Dictator* was a blow-by-blow account of the Otpor campaign against Milosevic, featuring Srdja and Bob explaining how it was done. As a means of effectively introducing the Georgian population to the principles of strategic nonviolent action, it was a powerful tool.

With Rustavi-2 broadcasting their message, supplemented by leaflets and newsletters, Kmara had achieved a substantial victory in their ability to communicate their message to the country. Now they moved to prepare for the parliamentary elections in November 2003, which they believed Shevardnadze would rig. There were two defences against this, the first was to mobilise the country behind a single candidate to maximise the chance of electoral success as the Serbs had done; and the second, to flood the country with election monitors to detect and deter corruption. Exit polling in any country is a major logistical and financial challenge but this was an area where Kmara, like Otpor, benefited from US and European funding.

The external funding and support was largely focused on the 'Get Out to Vote' campaign modelled on the one carried out in Serbia. Kmara collaborated with the International Society for Fair Elections and Democracy, a Georgian non-governmental organisation which carried out citizen monitoring of elections.

When it was time to grow the network of activists, Kmara arranged a summer camp in an abandoned Soviet mountainside retreat outside the capital Tbilisi. Hundreds of new members came to learn nonviolent resistance from the Serbs and their translated Otpor training manuals. Gene's work was transmitted through these training guides, but *From Dictatorship to Democracy* was only read by the core leadership, who considered it too academic to give in its raw form to the new recruits. The Serbs gave lessons on branding, secure communications, and organising marches. Journalists from Rustavi-2 were brought in to talk about communicating effectively with the national and international media.

The summer camp trainees returned to their towns and cities across Georgia forming a national network of local cells and swelling Kmara's numbers further. By October, the total stood at just over 3000 trained members.

When election day came on 2nd Novemebr 2003, the vote monitoring, paid for by the international community, was ready to detect any foul play. A parallel count and an exit poll both indicated that Saakashvili was in the lead, but when the government's Central Election Commission made its first announcement of the evening, it declared that Shevardnadze was likely to win a majority.

Kmara activists had spent months preparing for this eventuality and immediately fanned out across Tiblisi with leaflets and loudspeakers telling the people about the discrepancy in the reported vote count. A plan was activated to mobilise people for demonstrations at Freedom Square in the centre of the city and gradually they came, carrying the Georgian and Kmara clenched fist flags, yelling that the election was being stolen. A makeshift stage was constructed and a large screen appeared, broadcasting live coverage of the election result programme from Rustavi-2.

The vote counting was interminably long, but the final result was announced almost a week later, placing Shevardnadze in first place with Saakashvili trailing in third. Although Kmara had expected this, it still came as a shock that their victory was uncertain. Saakashvili travelled into the regions where the decentralised structure of Kmara activists was already at work mobilising support. Levan Ramishvili from the Liberty Institute decided that they should attempt to recreate the liberty convoys of the Serbs riding into Belgrade. Shortly afterwards Rustavi-2 broadcast pictures of Saakashvili being driven through the countryside in a red and white bus pursued by a convoy of vehicles.

When the convoy reached the outskirts of Tbilisi, they stopped for the night to discuss their next move and decided that the activists should storm the parliament building to stop Shevardnadze being sworn in the following day. As dawn broke, thousands of people began moving toward the parliament, methodically disassembling the barriers the police had thrown up overnight to block their entry into the city. The months of training in nonviolent resistance were paying off. As the protesters moved forward they avoided trading blows and handed the police food and roses which would soon give the 'Rose Revolution' its name.

Just before 4pm, as Shevardnadze was about to commence his speech, Saakashvili burst into the parliament chamber, shouting for the president to resign – a perfectly choreographed moment of political theatre which would ensure global media coverage. Saakashvili was wrestled out of the chamber, the bloom of his rose torn off in the tussle, but moments later he fought his way back in, pursued by his followers. President Shevardnadze was bundled ingloriously out of a back door by his bodyguards. For two days he continued issuing orders from the presidential palace to the security forces to break the uprising, but soon he realised, as Milosevic had, that his forces were not responding. His sources of power had been removed.

Hopeful young democracy campaigners all over the former Soviet bloc were watching the news from Georgia. Ukrainian activists led by Oleh Kryenko had been in the middle of their own training camp when they heard the news and abandoned their classes to gather round a small television to watch the live broadcast. 'It was inspiring' Oleh remembered, 'we hoped we would be next'.

Oleh had been involved in the Ukrainian opposition since the spring of 2001. As an intern for the Social Democrat Party in the Netherlands, he had taken part in organising the trainings for young activists from Croatia, Slovakia and his native Ukraine. It was there that he had first been introduced to Gene Sharp's work and the Serbs from Otpor.

At these training events, officials from US and European democracy promotion agencies had encouraged a number of Ukrainian opposition groups to set aside their differences and form a new unified opposition group. The way forward for Oleh was clear. 'I think there were ideas about taking the violent way but this was not considered as a serious option. We understood that the government had a much stronger position in terms of military force, they had the army, they had the police, so if we wanted to do the violent struggle we were doomed to lose. We had to be creative so the example of Otpor and Kmara from Georgia was very inspiring and so this was the only option.'

After the success of Georgia and increasing requests for their help, Srdja and Slobo had begun to realise that a permanent organisation might be required to deliver the Otpor training model around the world. Srdja had won a seat in parliament and Slobo had founded an internet company which was already on the way to making him his fortune, but they both decided that the demand for their knowledge was impossible to ignore. They founded a new organisation called 'CANVAS' – the Centre for Applied Nonviolent Strategies. Srdja left politics to run the new organisation and began to recruit a new training team. He wrote to Gene from Belgrade to tell him about their work.

'I wanted to take this opportunity to thank you again for providing Otpor with invaluable assistance in refining our strategy which successfully removed Slobodan Milosevic from power in 2000.... Otpor trainers transferred much of what we learned from The Albert Einstein Institution to the opposition movement in the Republic of Georgia that successfully brought democratic reform to that country. We also included it in training processes in Zimbabwe and Belarus where thanks to your teaching, pro-democracy movements were strengthened'.

Srdja set his sights on an ambitious goal. For years Serbia had been infamous for violence and brutality – now they would change all that. The students had become the teachers and they would make the knowledge of how to win freedom and democracy Serbia's greatest export.

The next mission for the Serbs of the newly minted CANVAS team was Ukraine. In the first days of 2000, Transparency International had rated Ukraine as one of the 15 most corrupt states in the world. Under president Leonid Kuchma, bribery and corruption were rife, university exam results and driving licenses could be bought and business elites appeared to have untamed political power. One of the few people brave enough to investigate these abuses was a 31-year-old journalist called Georgiy Gongadze who had founded a website called 'Ukrainian Truth'. In

November 2000, after complaining for months that he was being followed by the security services, his headless body was found in a shallow grave in woodland.

The blame for Georgiy's killing might have been passed off on a criminal gang he had exposed in another investigation were it not for a stunning revelation by the leader of the Ukrainian Socialist Party, Olexksandr Moroz. Moroz released a series of audio recordings made by, what he said, was one of Kuchma's bodyguards. The tapes appeared to record President Kuchma discussing the assassination of Georgiy Gongadze with his Minister for the Interior. Kuchma denied he had anything to do with the murder and insisted the tape had been doctored with sophisticated technology to make him appear to say things he hadn't said.

The constitution prevented Kuchma from standing for a third term in office, but he could promote his anointed successor, Viktor Yanukovych, a Russian-speaking eastern Ukrainian and favoured candidate of Russian president, Vladimir Putin.

The opposition candidate, friend of Washington and advocate of NATO membership was Viktor Yushchenko, a former Prime Minister of the country in the 90s. In a country split by a Russian-speaking and facing east and a Ukrainian-speaking west, the battle lines were drawn – a great game of superpowers wrestling for influence in the former Soviet state was ready to be played.

Before the grim discovery of murdered journalist, Georgiy Gongadze's headless corpse, his friend, Mykhailo Svystovych, had made a sombre pilgrimage around the country to publicise his disappearance. A veteran of past protest movements, Svystovych founded the 'Ukraine without Kuchma' campaign and took a small number of people to occupy one of the expensive shopping streets in Kiev. The small group shivered in bitter December temperatures, handing out leaflets while talking to people doing their Christmas shopping about the corruption in the country and the disappearance of Georgiy.

There was no Rustavi-2 equivalent in Ukraine – President Kuchma's business acquaintances owned and controlled most of the media outlets in the country, so the movement had to create an alternative media pillar.

In 2001 the internet was only just emerging as a major tool for organising a resistance movement. Svystovych was stunned when a website they set up with a message board began to be inundated by messages of support and leaked information from government employees, police and army personnel. He realised that the internet would become the best way to break what he called the 'information blockade'.

Despite their success on the web, the street occupation failed to grow and although they held out until March, it achieved little before being swept away in a police raid. In reaction to the attack on the camp, a major demonstration formed a week later and marched towards the government buildings. With improper planning and no training in nonviolent discipline or marshalling, the march quickly descended into violence, protesters throwing bottles and fighting with police. Hundreds were arrested and the nascent movement collapsed on its first contact with relatively mild repression. It was obvious the Ukrainians needed proper training in order to grow into a movement which could force real change.

The Ukrainians reached out to EU and US democracy foundations for help – a request they were only too happy to grant. Both the EU and NATO wanted to push their influence east into Ukraine, a policy British Foreign Secretary, Jack Straw, would later describe as a serious error.

Money began to flow for the trainings like the one in the Netherlands that Oleh had helped to organise. Immediately after that first event in 2001, Iryna Chemerys from an NGO called Institute Respublika, wrote to Gene in Boston to ask for materials. She told him they had been introduced to his work in the spring training session and requested permission for their organisation to translate *The Politics of Nonviolent Action* into Ukrainian.

The Politics was in three volumes – 900 pages in total and filled with technical terms which required precise translation, so this was no small undertaking. Gene wrote back to suggest the translation of the shorter, *From Dictatorship to Democracy*, but signed off his email with a stark warning. 'You must know that in some political situations mere possession of this literature is grounds for imprisonment'.

Copies of *From Dictatorship to Democracy* and some other pamphlets were despatched to Iryna by express mail, but for days they went missing in the post. When the box finally arrived at the correct address in Kiev it was clear the packaging had been tampered with. Who was watching? And why had they let the package continue on its way?

Aware that a potential trap could be sprung at any moment, the Ukrainians decided to accept the risk and begin the translation. Despite the obvious attention of the western democracy promotion agencies, correspondence with Gene shows that, at this stage, Ukrainian activists still had barely any money to perform these basic tasks. The Albert Einstein Institution didn't have any money to help them either and on 13th June 2003, Bob Helvey wrote to Gene's assistant Chris Miller, increasingly frustrated that they couldn't help the Ukrainians translate the book. 'Yet again the Albert Einstein Institution cannot fulfil its mission statement due to lack of funding and staff', he wrote. In desperation, Bob offered to defer payments of his own salary so that $6000 could be freed up to fund the translation and printing of the Ukrainian edition of *From Dictatorship to Democracy*.

Ukraine's version of Otpor would be born at a brainstorming session in Kiev. Oleh Kryenko had come up with the name 'Pora', which meant 'high time to change' and they chose a logo of a rising sun, symbolising it was time to act. They made the logo black and white because there was so little money to print in colour. Some initial funding came from the Westminster Foundation for Democracy (a British organisation which funded the same kind of projects as the US NED). This allowed Pora to travel and pay for printing and trainings from the Serbs. During 2003 they conducted more than 40 training events in every major town in Ukraine.

CANVAS advocated the early development of Otpor's hidden leadership model to reduce the likelihood of the arrests disrupting the movement. 'In order to be invincible you have to have several leaders or a leaderless structure', Srdja taught them. Pora established a board of 8 people who made the decisions and followed the Otpor model of constantly changing spokespeople. A sympathetic businessman provided their base in the form of an abandoned four room apartment in the Podil district of Kiev. It was an old building and rundown inside, but Kmara decorated the walls with graffiti and posters, adding a few electric heaters which fought to keep the rooms just above freezing. They managed to collect together five computers and a few printers for producing leaflets and the apartment was soon filled with people and a sense of mission.

A mass sticker campaign on the model of Otpor's poster campaign was launched. In almost every major city in the country, students and activists went out into the night to post thousands of black and white stickers with the image of a rising sun, a website address and the words 'Pora – It's Time' emblazoned across them. A few weeks later Pora launched another sticker campaign with a stopwatch reading fifteen minutes to midnight and a web link to their Manifesto. On the website they revealed their roots and aspiration, 'Serbia 2000, Georgia 2003, Ukraine 2004'.

One of the first challenges to hit Pora wasn't from the government or security services, it was a strange collision with another organisation. To Oleh's astonishment, he discovered one morning that there was no longer just one Pora, there were two. 'Where I had put up a black Pora sticker, the next day I saw that someone had put a yellow Pora sticker on top of my sticker.' While black Pora had started as an organic movement, bootstrapping their activities with small donations from ordinary Ukrainians, 'Yellow Pora' was a vehicle for big foreign investment coordinated by Western branding consultants and election specialists.

Some black Pora activists wanted to fight for their name which they felt had been stolen, but it was soon decided that this would cause pointless infighting which would only distract from their common cause. From this point on, the joint aims and methods of the two Poras meant that they were effectively seen as a single entity, even though they sometimes worked uneasily with each other.

In early August the seaside town of Yevpatoria on the Crimean Peninsula became home to a joint Pora training camp. Among the trainers were activists from a 1990 Ukrainian student movement, journalists who provided media training and the now ubiquitous foreign NGO representatives who had been involved in Serbia. In the sweltering summer heat, the Ukrainian translations of *From Dictatorship to Democracy* were handed out amongst nearly 300 trainees. In the evenings they discussed Gandhi, King and Gene Sharp, swam in the sea, drank vodka and read poetry around bonfires. It was an idyllic beginning and a stark contrast to the fight that would come in Maidan Square. It was here they decided that the demonstrators should adopt a symbolic colour which would highlight their unity and identify members on the streets.

The choice of orange was an easy one. Orange had been adopted by the fashion industry as their colour palette for fall of 2004. Shop windows were filling up with orange garments and so it was easy for people to buy an orange scarf or sweater right off the shelf. Most importantly, orange had no association with communism or Ukrainian nationalism and would stand out against the grey winter light of Kiev.

Opposition candidate Yushchenko was used to receiving death threats, but he decided to put his fate in the hands of God and dismissed the sort of armoured car protection that was a hallmark of the incumbent regime. However, in September 2004, he requested a meeting with the country's SBU intelligence service to discuss the death threats and how they could reduce the likelihood of violence on the streets in the upcoming election. The meeting was held in a luxury villa outside Kiev, where a small collection of intelligence officers and politicians dined on crayfish, traditional Ukrainian meat dishes and salads, washed down with beer, vodka and cognac. It was here, Yushchenko believed, that someone attempted to kill him with poison.

When he arrived home that night his wife noticed a metallic taste on his lips as she kissed him goodnight and asked him if he had taken some medicine. The next day Yushchenko fell ill, lesions appeared on his face and his condition deteriorated rapidly. His doctors couldn't explain his illness or offer any meaningful treatment. Days later he was flown urgently to the Rudolfinerhaus Clinic in Vienna where tests detected that he had received between 1000 and 6000 times the safe level of a chemical called Tetrachlorodibenzo-p-dioxin.

Weeks after the Vienna clinic had saved his life, Yushchenko reappeared defiantly in parliament, but in obvious pain – his grey, pockmarked face shocked the country and the international community. He warned gravely that the unless the country changed its government there would be more attacks on those seeking true democracy like the one that had nearly killed him.

Youth groups proliferated under the repression. The organization 'Znayu' (I know) was a get-out-the-vote campaign. It too was being funded by US and European money and staged Otpor-like stunts to encourage people to ask questions about voting. As Otpor's influence became more apparent, the trainers from CANVAS were put on watch lists to be arrested or denied entry to the country. Aleksander Maric, a former Otpor activist who had advised Znayu was identified as a threat to the security of the state, arrested at Kiev airport and deported back to Serbia.

In the background, Freedom House, the Canadian International Development Agency and the German Marshall Fund contributed around $130,000 to Pora, but a significant proportion of funds were coming from the Ukrainians themselves. The money was used for the stickers, posters and t-shirts, printing costs and preparing to feed and shelter people at street protests.

As the threat of Pora and the Orange movement increased, the government staged increasing numbers of raids where they would sometimes 'discover' explosives in the homes of Pora activists. The state media would then quickly celebrate the success of the police 'counter-terror operations'.

Pora organiser Mykhailo Svystovych was woken from a nap one afternoon by a police raid on his apartment. When the officer in charge demanded to know how Pora worked, Svystovych told him he had nothing to hide. He handed the officer a copy of From *Dictatorship to Democracy* and told him about Gene's books and the examples of Otpor and Kmara. One Pora leader, Volodymyr Viatrovych, estimated that by the end of 2004 a core group of around 10,000 people had been trained using *From Dictatorship to Democracy*. 'But the ideas were used by hundreds of thousands who never knew these ideas were from Gene Sharp,' he told me.

During the course of the election campaign Pora recorded 350 arrests of its people by the authorities, many of them subjected to assaults and terrifying simulated suffocations. Just like Otpor, they used text messages and the internet to organise flash mobs at police stations and prisons as soon as arrests were made.

The first round of the presidential election was held on 31st October 2004 and the results were very close – Viktor Yushchenko gaining 39.87% of the vote to Yanukovych's 39.3%. Victory for the Orange movement seemed close, but election rules dictated that a candidate reach 50% or more votes to win, meaning a run-off was scheduled for 21st November. Even in the first round of the election, international observers were reporting voting irregularities in the Eastern areas with strongest Yanukovych support.

Pora braced themselves for the run-off on 21st November, still expecting to win but when the result came, it was everything they had feared. Ukraine's electoral commission declared Yanukovych the winner with 49.42% of the vote. Yushchenko 's official vote count, they said, had reduced to 46.69%. The Orange movement reacted with fury. Observers for the Organization for Security and Cooperation in Europe (OSCE) protested that the run off, 'did not meet international standards' and the lead election monitor, US Senator Richard Lugar, reported that what he had seen amounted to a, 'concerted and forceful program of election day fraud'.

On December 3rd the Ukrainian Supreme Court ruled that there had been mass violations of the law in the second round of the election and moved to annul the results. Pora now put a plan into place to turn the country orange. People flowed into Maidan Square, the central square of Kiev, erecting tents, catering and sanitary facilities. Public benches and lampposts were removed to erect barriers around the camp and soon thousands of people, young and old began to arrive.

The opposition supporters in Kiev were soon out on the streets supporting the camp, producing thousands of meals a night and supplying doctors and nurses to treat colds and flu. Soon the snow began to fall and the camp was cast in hues of white and orange. Every night performers came to sing and people dressed in orange headbands jackets and shoes danced and chanted until they retreated home or back into their tents to see out the bitter nights. From all over Kiev, Maidan Square could be picked out on the skyline by its column of amber woodsmoke rising into the air.

Cracks in the state-run media were also starting to appear. Journalists went on strike at the three main channels, with one even announcing live on air that the election had been rigged. The obedience of the country's pillars of support were now on shaky ground.

The regime stepped up their propaganda effort against Pora whose support continued to grow. Yanukovych's wife Lyudmylla told a crowd of her husband's supporters in Donetsk that the demonstrators in Kiev had become zombified by drugged oranges being handed out in Maidan Square. Pora reacted to these accusations in the Otpor style, laughing at the accusations. The next day oranges with syringes sticking out of them were positioned around the camp, mocking the government propaganda.

A counter-revolutionary move was organised by the Yanukovych campaign, encouraging miners and industrial workers from the Russian leaning East of the country to come and protest against the Orange forces in Kiev, who they said were trying to steal the election.

The moment that counter-protests meet in a nonviolent campaign is a dangerous one – violence can very easily break out and tarnish the reputation of the democratic forces, but Pora had prepared for this. Instead of shouting them down or risking a confrontation, they sent their most disciplined people to bring them food and water, joke with them and explain what they wanted for the future of the country.

On several occasions the Orange movement was poised to make a move on the parliament building, just as the Serbs had done, but the leadership decided not to risk it and follow the legal process until all official mechanisms were exhausted.

Eventually, diplomatic efforts by the US and Russia resulted in a re-run of the election on 26th December. The result of the new poll produced a wildly different result, 52% to Yushchenko and 44% to Yanukovych.

Yanukovych conceded defeat on January 20th 2005 telling Ukrainians in his speech that, 'The right of force has won against the force of the law'. Almost a week later a crowd of a hundred thousand people gathered in Maidan Square amongst the remnants of the tent camp to watch Yushchenko become their new President.

The great hopes of the Orange revolution would not last for long. Yushenko's government soon became fractured with infighting and allegations of corruption. Less than two years later, the parliamentary elections of 2006 election saw Yanukovych gain enough seats to be installed as prime minister, setting up an uncomfortable battle with President Yushenko.

The techniques of nonviolent action were clearly no guarantee of post-revolution utopia. Gene was frequently asked in question and answer sessions why he hadn't done work on what happens after a revolution, wasn't this irresponsible? He told them that he had spent his life working out how to bring down dictatorships with very little money. Democracy building in contrast was a vast, well funded academic field. Nonviolent action made building a durable democratic society more likely by strengthening civil society, creating parallel government structures and reducing violence, but he couldn't possibly do everything. He normally ended his answer by telling the people in the room that it was their mission to take on now.

Survival

Gene lived a near monk like existence at 36 Cottage Street. His two room apartment was spartan at best – cold, dark wooden floors with a low bed, a small television in the corner and a galley-style kitchen with a four ring hob for heating up simple meals. The wallpaper was peeling and bleached in tones of brown. If he noticed this at all, it didn't bother him. In the evenings, often after working until past 10pm, he would sit alone reading, watching nature documentaries or perusing mail order catalogues of rare orchids.

Up the last flight of stairs on the fourth floor was his great passion, a dedicated hothouse filled with rare orchid blooms from all over the world – some of them illegally smuggled out of Burma. The room was flooded with light from large perspex domes and swathes of tree bark hung from the roof for different species to climb. The very few people who were invited into the orchid room were treated to the same warm, sweet smelling humidity familiar from the world's most famous botanic houses. The fourth floor became a sanctuary away from the pressures of work and he treated each of the little blooms almost like children.

Donations to the institution were beginning to dry up. Despite the success of the work in Serbia, nonviolent struggle did not fit the strictly delineated grants criteria for many organisations and even fewer of them wanted to be involved in work which might bring down a government.

That was at least part of the problem, but Bruce Jenkins had become increasingly frustrated with Gene's negative approach to applying for grants from big foundations. In 1997 they had successfully raised $160,000 by offering specific projects to be funded where donors could see a tangible output for their money. But Gene didn't like those kind of funds – what he wanted were big unrestricted grants with which he could do whatever he wanted. He would occasionally lament the short-sighted-ness of foundations in this regard in letters to the foundations themselves, which didn't help matters. This self-sabotage was frustrating for the staff to watch, especially when it undermined weeks of work and potentially put their jobs at risk.

This apparent complacency might have been exacerbated by the fact that Peter Ackerman had granted Gene an annuity which gave him a modest salary for life. This was intended so that he could concentrate fully on his work without financial stress, but it may have had the side effect that he wasn't quite as motivated or as diplomatic as he should have been when applying for money.

The 'founder's syndrome' was also felt in other areas. Gene had always been resistant to editing, even by Tom Schelling. If he didn't take kindly to one of the country's greatest minds critiquing his work, he was positively incredulous at substantive editing suggestions by his bright young team of assistants. This was despite Bruce and others frequently rescuing manuscripts which were verbose, repetitive and often unclear.

Gene was a genius, none of them doubted that, but as he became older they noticed his ability to structure his ideas in writing was becoming laboured and his tolerance of criticism increasingly dismissive. When Bob and Bruce tried gently to point this out, Gene simply replied, 'I am the one that studied totalitarianism and dictatorships all these years'.

Bruce Jenkins left the Albert Einstein Institution in 2000, at least in part due to these frustrations. He had helped shape some of the most exciting and challenging episodes in the institution's history – Tiananmen, the first intifada, the Baltics, and Burma among many others. Perhaps most importantly he had overseen the production and first translations of *From Dictatorship to Democracy*. He was a massive loss to Gene, the institution and the field in general, but it wasn't entirely clear that Gene registered this until it was too late.

For a young, newly-graduated Afghan American, the aftermath of 9/11 was the worst possible time to be looking for a job. Jamila Raqib's earliest memories were of being swaddled in blankets and rolled under a bed as Russian bombs fell around their village near Jalalabad. Her father, an Afghan army colonel had arranged the escape from the country of his wife and four daughters. Jamila was smuggled across the Afghan border into Pakistan in a sand truck with her mother, while her father and four sisters had each been taken by different routes. The family spent a short time living in a Pakistani refugee camp before moving to the rural north east coast of the US where the sisters quickly learned English and did well in school.

Jamila graduated from Simmons College in Boston at 21 years old, in the summer of 2001. The political climate after 9/11, even in liberal leaning Boston, was febrile, so she kept herself to herself, socialising with just a small group of trusted friends and her sisters, who sometimes toured the streets in the safe bubble of an old Jaguar with their pet parrot, Pepe. 'There was a sense in the US that you were either with us or against us and I didn't want to have to choose.'

For weeks, Jamila had been scanning a careers website for non-profit organisations, searching for work which might be meaningful when she saw the advert for a translations coordinator at the curiously named Albert Einstein Institution. It seemed intriguing so she applied.

In 2001, the institution was situated at the less glitzy end of Boston's Newbury Street, famous for its cocktail bars and boutique stores. In her interview with Gene, Jamila was honest – she hadn't read his books and neither was she convinced that violence could be replaced. She had even supported the Mujahadeen in their fight against the Russian occupation. 'I thought sometimes you really need to use violence. I thought that peace movements were naive.' Gene was advised to hire another graduate who was better qualified for the position, but he must have seen something in Jamila because he overruled the opinion of Bruce's replacement, Joshua Paulson, and insisted she be given first refusal.

Perhaps it was that she wasn't a pacifist, or that she had experienced war like none of the others had, but he described a raw intelligence that was obvious from her first interview. He may also have understood the difficulty of job hunting as an Afghan at the time. In any case, Jamila was told that the financial position of the institution was perilous, there was no long term security, but if she was willing to accept the risks then the job was hers. What Gene couldn't have realised from those first interviews was her loyalty and perseverance which would hold the institution together in its most dangerous days.

She joined a small staff which included Hardy Merriman, another graduate in his early 20s who had set about launching the first Albert Einstein Institution website. What could have been a dull collection of web pages was transformed by one very bright idea. Hardy asked Gene if they could post the existing translations of his most popular book, *From Dictatorship to Democracy* and some of the other small pamphlets on the website to download free. Gene didn't understand the full potential of the internet yet, but eventually Hardy got his way. The digitisation project of the existing work was massive. As the translations that Jamila was organising were completed they were posted online and the small number of visitors to the website began to grow.

The fourth edition of *From Dictatorship to Democracy* was put in the public domain, meaning that anyone could translate it without permission. With few funds at his disposal, Gene took his most popular work and made it nearly impossible to generate revenue from it, but the impact would be huge.

It was quite clear to Jamila that the Albert Einstein Institution was no ordinary first job. Within months of her arrival, Bob Helvey was preparing to leave Boston to meet a group of Zimbabweans at a hotel in South Africa, ahead of the 2002 Zimbabwe election. Once again, the project was paid for by the International Republican Institute which was assisting the democratic opposition to President Robert Mugabe whose rule had become increasingly authoritarian and brutal towards political opponents.

IRI officials had called Bob fearing that if the opposition party, the Movement for Democratic Change (MDC), won the election, but Mugabe refused to recognise the win, there could be a bloodbath on the streets. The Albert Einstein Institution team was asked to come up with a plan for preventing violence in the immediate 72 hours following a presidential election.

At their first meeting in Johannesburg the Zimbabweans told Bob that Mugabe might also concede defeat, but allow his militias to go to war against opposition. There were also worrying signs that police officers from the regions were being moved into the cities, where their own friends and relatives were unlikely to be in the crowds. The MDC estimated that they would have around 2 million supporters on the streets, whether they won or lost, risking serious clashes with Mugabe supporters.

On the 11th February the Albert Einstein Institution team met at one of the most expensive hotels in Johannesburg with the entire leadership team of the MDC including the man they hoped would become President, Morgan Tsvangirai. Bob introduced himself as a 'consultant from the Albert Einstein Institution with expertise in strategic nonviolent struggle'. Morgan Tsvangirai replied, 'I am Morgan Tsvangirai and I want to defeat Mugabe through strategic nonviolent struggle'. The room erupted in laughter.

Among other measures, the Albert Einstein Institution team suggested a combination of demonstrations and leaders of civil society condemning the election fraud. Lightning demonstrations could be used nationwide to avoid confrontation along with stay at home strikes.

There were also ongoing relationships with the Tibetan leadership in exile in Dharamsala, India. The team had made several trips already to try and improve the Tibetans strategy against Chinese oppression. As with many of the countries the Institution would become involved with, their location adjacent to Harvard, MIT, Boston University and a host of other good colleges meant that the world's best and brightest students would often appear in Cambridge, Massachusetts and be introduced to Gene during the course of their studies.

Among them was Lobsang Sangay who had grown up in near poverty in a family of political exiles, before being sent to school where his talents were discovered. Eventually he ended up at Harvard Law School, visiting Gene and studying his work. For years he facilitated the transmission of Gene's work back into Tibet to resist Chinese control. In 2012, Sangay was elected President of the Tibetan government in exile, taking over many of the Dalai Lama's executive functions. 'The major turning point in Tibetan movement was Gene Sharp's contribution.' He said, 'You can see Gene Sharp's fingerprints all over it.'

Despite these high profile consultations, the Institution was struggling to fund its operations. On 24th November 2003, Bob informed Peter Ackerman that the institution needed to embark on a major fundraising effort to fulfil the mission properly. Ackerman disagreed strongly – he felt he had donated enough to perform the basic tasks and didn't want any of Gene's time wasted on fundraising.

Bob and Gene talked at length about the objection, but decided to press ahead anyway, putting them on a crash course with their major donor. Ackerman was strongly opposed to the move and threatened to remove all of his funding. In the course of this difficult exchange, he reminded Gene that he had the rights to at least some of Gene's books, including *From Dictatorship to Democracy*.

Gene disputed that he had signed any agreement to this effect, but Ackerman must have felt justified in asserting his position. He had stopped Gene's exile from Harvard, given him millions of dollars to found the institution that was his dream, and provided him with an annuity that would provide a salary for the rest of his life.

Despite this, on the 14th January 2004, Gene typed out a letter addressed to Peter Ackerman, asking him not to assert the rights over the publications.

He wrote of his deep thanks for Ackerman's help and financial assistance over the years and the annuity which supported his basic living costs and allowed him to continue his writing. However, Gene had made it clear that he could not grant Ackerman a non-exclusive license to publish translations of his books. With perhaps an unfair sting in the tail, Gene wrote that his life's work was not up for barter. Although Ackerman would stand by Gene, visit occasionally and even help with medical costs in the coming years, the relationship would never be fully repaired. Gene signed off asking if he could possibly have misunderstood Ackerman's intention to stop the funding.

But he had not misunderstood. In a phone call, Ackerman repeated the ultimatum, to comply with his requests or he would cease further funding of the institution. This was much more than a professional cataclysm for Gene, it was a personal one – Peter had been like a son to him, but this was ending all of that. It was impossible for the staff in the office not to know what was going on. Gene was momentarily broken, shocked by the call.

Funding outside Ackerman's donations was not enough to keep them going. If he followed through with the threat, Gene knew the institution was finished. Bob intervened and pleaded with Gene not to contest the rights issue. 'What use were the damn rights without an institution? Peter made all that work possible, Gene was being crazy, why throw everything away?' Whether it was principle, stubbornness or both, Gene refused. Bob reported back to Peter that there was no way he was going to change his mind.

Bob called a crisis meeting. The money had been stopped and there was barely enough left to meet existing staff costs. Jamila and Hardy were told to start looking urgently for new jobs. Bob argued that the institution had to be wound up. 'I didn't want this thing to limp on looking weak and dragging down Gene's name. If we were going to do it we had to do it properly'. Gene remained almost entirely silent during the meeting. For years he had been convinced that fundraising was a waste of his time. In an emotional address to a conference in 1990, he told his audience, 'There has been more done by nonviolent struggle to liberate people from communist dictatorships and other kinds of dictatorships than anything the Pentagon has done with all of its billions and billions of dollars for 40 years, and yet we can't even get a five or ten million dollar budget to do some research in this field.'

He told me, 'I finally concluded, after many years, instead of spending my time trying to raise the money, which was usually fruitless, I would concentrate on the quality of my work and the amount of work I was able to produce in my lifetime, and if people could see that work was important, then they could also see that it was important that we receive funding.' Gene believed in his 'better mousetrap' theory – if he could produce the best analysis, then people would find their way to East Boston and they would bring funds to support the work with them. The trouble was, people *were* coming, and in increasing numbers, but they weren't coming with money.

In the middle of this crisis Gene sat down at his desk to record his six fears. The first was not being able to finish the three books he considered most important before he was 'finished'. These were a dictionary of nonviolent struggle, a guide to strategic planning and the *'Power and Practice of Nonviolent Struggle'*. His second fear was the inability to raise sufficient finances to retain good people, relating to the third, a lowering of the quality of the work. He also worried that impact of the work on popular movements would shrink or end and that the institution would be hijacked for another purpose or approach. Finally he worried that people might place more importance on him than the substance of the work itself and there would be a failure to produce a reservoir of competent people to continue the work after his passing.

As the stress in the office increased, the relationship between Gene and Bob broke down over how to handle the closing of the institution. Bob handed in his resignation a few weeks later. It was another painful professional and personal blow.

On the evening of Bob's resignation the rain was lashing down on the sidewalk as Gene walked out onto Newbury Street. Jamila followed him, just out of sight, a little way behind. Watching him bleary eyed, bowed and broken she struggled to fight back her own tears. 'I thought to myself, there is no way I'm going to let this institution die. If people are still coming here for help there's no way we can let it close.' That night she went home and tried to formulate a plan.

If they could just hold out a little longer, there might be a way out, a funder, some money from a will, something to keep them going. Jamila tapped furiously into a spreadsheet on her laptop. The office on Newbury Street was too expensive, there was no money for rent, bills or any staff. She narrowed down a list of core tasks and tried to work out how they could be maintained – responding to correspondence, curating the archive, enabling translations of the books and assisting Gene with further work. These things were not expensive. Answering emails just required a computer and a desk and they still had computers. Translations were mostly carried out by people donating time. Gene didn't require a lot of help, just a place to work and technical assistance.

Jamila had never been to Gene's house, but she knew it was big, needed a lot of work and that there was now a fantastic orchid garden growing under Perspex domes on the fourth floor. It was the only viable solution. The Albert Einstein Institution packed up and returned to Cottage Street for the first time since the 1980s with a very determined staff of two.

A couple of months later, Jamila was shopping for groceries at a store near her home and set her Albert Einstein Institution folder down on the counter in front of the cashier. She noticed the man's eyes light up as he read the writing on the paperwork. 'We're using the books in Eritrea', he whispered. The man was in touch with an Eritrean exile group that was studying the material on the institution website. They'd been working out how they could use it to fight corruption in the government. For Jamila, it was a small but significant sign that it had been right to fight for the institution. The work was still spreading and it hadn't nearly fulfilled its potential.

Those first weeks and months of the institution's new life, washed up, starved of funds and now on the ground floor of a poorly maintained old house might have been quite depressing, but the phones kept ringing and the email box was full of new enquiries every morning – the demand for help from people battling oppression was only growing stronger. As Spring arrived in East Boston, the Albert Einstein Institution's newsletter, written almost entirely by Jamila, dropped through the letterboxes of supporters all of the world. It glowed with the relief of survival. Jamila high fived Gene, 'We pulled off a coup!'

'Greetings friends and supporters! Since our last newsletter, we've moved to a new office located conveniently in East Boston, just a stone's throw away from Boston's Logan Airport. The new location has several advantages. Now, Senior Scholar Gene Sharp has a short walk to work, shaving two hours each day off his commute and our monthly operating costs are significantly reduced – enabling us to shift a big portion of our expenditures away from office rent to other, more important tasks.'

The institution had beaten attempts to close it down and that was all that mattered for now.

Peter Ackerman now turned his attention solely to his own organisation, the International Centre for Nonviolent Conflict (ICNC). He began a more active promotion of nonviolent resistance training, funding Bob Helvey and the Serbs from CANVAS to carry out consultations with democracy groups around the world. ICNC was innovative in a different way than Gene had been, producing documentaries and developing a video game to train activists which was sent to officials all over the State Department. They also commissioned new academic work and studies, but they still paid deference to Gene's writings. Ackerman told the Wall St Journal cryptically, 'My center is a bigger compliment to Gene than Gene is willing to make to himself.'

The activities of ICNC now meant that Gene's work was turning up in places that Gene and Jamila had had no direct contact with. When a training camp carried out by Bob Helvey for Venezuelan activists was discovered by the government, the first thing Gene and Jamila heard about it was Hugo Chávez personally denouncing Gene on Venezuelan national television. Chávez stood in front of a white board mapping out the connections between Gene, the US government and the opposition movement arrayed against him. 'Gene Sharp, George Bush, the ideologies and their "soft coup," ladies and gentlemen, here in Venezuela, this plan, forget it! The last thing that could happen is a revolutionary explosion'. It was a theme Chávez would revisit frequently in his statements. A book published in Venezuela accused Jamila of personally training paramilitaries on a farm in Colombia. 'I've never even held a gun!' she told me. Gene replied with an open letter to Chávez offering him his book, 'The Anti-Coup'. 'It can be sent to whatever address you designate, and is also available in electronic format on our website, www.aeinstein.org, he told him.

Cottage Street was soon being visited regularly by academics, journalists and activists from all over the world. Often they seemed mystified by the conditions they found Gene and Jamila working in. Most of the visitors were open about who they were and where they came from, but others gave almost no information away at all, sometimes not even their names. Jamila suspected a few of them had almost certainly been spies from foreign governments, but she believed that the transparency of their work and never telling people what to do, gave them some level of protection. If a dictatorship had sent intelligence officers to learn about the work, all the better, Gene was comfortable with that. When people questioned him on this, he would reply, 'Isn't it better that even the bad guys are fighting with nonviolent struggle than resorting to violence?'

The most damaging attacks were often not made by the dictatorships against whom the work was being used, but by conspiracy theorists and bloggers who were now using the power of the internet to push their theories. The most common attack was that Gene was an asset of the CIA assisting the US neo-liberal agenda in countries closed to trade.

This was a difficult charge to defend against, because although Gene personally avoided interactions with the CIA and discouraged activists from taking their money, he had certainly sought out and fostered links with the Department of Defense, the State Department and the agencies of the National Endowment for Democracy. His response was that he was an academic who made his work available to everyone – there was nothing secret about it and nowhere in any of his works did he suggest or commend neo-liberalism, or any other economic system for that matter. His work could be used by ordinary Tibetans or State Department planners, by citizens of dictatorships the United States supported as well as those it would like to see deposed.

Funds at the Albert Einstein Institution remained at a critical level and Jamila's clever rearguard action had only delayed the inevitable. The aftermath of the colour revolutions, increased scrutiny over the Bush administration's Freedom Agenda and direct attacks by President Chávez, had put the Albert Einstein Institution under the spotlight like never before. They could barely keep their minimal operations going let alone employ anyone to mount a public relations counterattack on the allegations that were proliferating across the internet. Instead, it was a collection of fellow academics who came to their aid.

Professor Stephen Zunes at the University of San Francisco drafted a letter of support from the academic community in support of Gene, rubbishing the allegations of his involvement with US imperialism and the CIA. It was signed by 138 academics, among them Noam Chomsky and Howard Zinn – neither famed for their love of US foreign policy.

'Rather than being a tool of imperialism, Dr. Sharp's research and writings have inspired generations of progressive peace, labor, feminist, human rights, environmental, and social justice activists in the United States and around the world.' 'Nonviolent struggle has historically been the weapon of the poor and disenfranchised through which they can gain an advantage over powerful and wealthy elites whose capacity to use violence against them is usually far superior. It is therefore ironic that some of those who view themselves as champions of oppressed peoples mis-characterize these popular nonviolent movements simply as tools of US imperialism and global capital. We therefore call upon people of conscience to reject the false allegations levelled against Gene Sharp, the Albert Einstein Institute and other groups promoting strategic nonviolent action; to continue to struggle against U.S. imperialism in all of its manifestations; and, to support popular democratic movements engaging in nonviolent action in the cause of human rights and social justice in the United States and throughout the world.'

Now in his late 70s, Gene did not feel strong for his age or look it. He had never been married or had children and his relationships with his remaining family were fond but distant. With few people checking in on him, Jamila often worried about his health and how well he was looking after himself. Occasionally she would make him meals and leave them for him in boxes, pretending they were leftovers that he might like. Years of sedentary writing and living alone had taken their toll, and in letters he was beginning to mention how much time he had left to live.

In 2005, he wrote to an old friend, Arthur Edelstein, listing the foundations that he had approached for money, all of which had replied with rejections. 'Obviously this is extremely stressful. Apart from other pressures, I am worried that all this delays completion of my major conceptual and technical dictionary for the field, with adjacent areas, a *must* do while I live'.

What the Albert Einstein needed now was a financial miracle, and through a curious connection they were about to get one. It was the 3rd March 2009 and the first buds of spring were breaking all over New York. At 595 Madison Avenue the sidewalk was six deep in press photographers and news cameraman yelling and jostling, hoisting their cameras aloft for a clean shot of an eccentric multi-millionaire. His name was James Lambert Otis.

Otis had been born to a rich family, a scion of the Listerine mouthwash dynasty on one side and the Otis lift empire on the other. During college he had become hooked on Gandhi and his work on nonviolence, under the tutelage of his college mentor Professor Lester Kurtz. After becoming a documentary maker in LA, he met and married, Lisa Henson, the daughter of Jim Henson, the creator of the Muppets.

One day he walked into a gallery in LA and saw the most beautiful work of art he had ever seen in his life, a 6 inch red line animation by Dr Seuss, creator of the classic children's books, *The Cat in the Hat* and *Green Eggs and Ham*. He bought the piece for $8000 and, within a week, had sold it for double. 'The internet auctions were just starting up and I just went apeshit. I bought every single original Dr Seuss in the country,' he told me. When he was done with Seuss, he went after the originals of Charles Shulz, the creator of Snoopy and then Maurice Sendak's *Where the Wild Things Are*. But it would be his next acquisition which would bring him to the streets of Madison Avenue that morning in March.

A fellow art collector who knew of his new wealth and interest in nonviolence told Otis that some of Gandhi's personal possessions were up for sale – but only if the buyer was extremely discreet.

After flying to India and navigating a series of middlemen, Otis was taken into a room to view the items. Presented in front of him were Gandhi's personal effects from the day of his assassination – the bowl in which Abha Gandhi had served him his last meal, the pocket watch which had heralded the appointment that would lead him to his death, his sandals and trademark spectacles. Otis agreed the sale immediately. The personal possessions of one of the 20th century's greatest figures were now in the hands of America's most prolific collector of Snoopy memorabilia.

The items were kept in a safe at Otis's Beverley Hills mansion and taken out on very special occasions until, in 2009, he decided to sell. The publicity of the sale at Antiquorum auction house in New York provoked an international outcry. The Indian government, who had known nothing of the items removal from the country, called Otis a 'terrorist' in the national media.

Death threats started to arrive and, panicked by the furore, Otis opened a dialogue with the Indian government stating that he would withdraw the items from sale if it committed to spending 5% of its GDP on the eradication of poverty. The request was dismissed out of hand as ludicrous.

The auction was due to begin at 3pm, but at 2.30pm, Otis's lawyer Ravi Batra stormed into the auction room to demand the sale be stopped due to the threats now being received for selling the items. The auction house told Batra in no uncertain terms that the agreement to sell was legally binding and had him escorted from the building by security.

Despite the drama, the sale began on schedule, the auctioneer intending to begin in increments of $10,000. Within seconds the bids had risen above $200,000 and continued rising in leaps of $100,000. Otis stood mesmerised as the lot hit $1 million dollars in two minutes, leaving just two bidders, the Kingfisher beer magnate Vijay Mallya, and former Indian cricketer, Dilip Doshi. With two of India's richest men locked in battle for the items, the value almost doubled again, until finally the gavel came down with Vijay Mallya at $1.8 million dollars.

The room erupted into applause and Otis emerged shellshocked out onto the sidewalk to a scrum of reporters. Aware that his primary concern was to prevent his own assassination at the hands of Indian nationalists, he told the reporters that the items were heading back to India and he would give away the money from the sale to causes that Gandhi would have approved of.

Jamila was sitting at her desk in Cottage St overlooking a small patio with the neighbour's washing flapping on the line. She hadn't yet noticed the article on the extraordinary sale of Gandhi's items on the BBC website. When the phone rang she could only just make out the voice through the sirens and traffic. 'My name is James Otis and I'd like to give Gene Sharp some money'. The funds from the sale of Gandhi's possessions couldn't have been a more appropriate saviour for the work. The institution received a substantial sum from the sale, and it was just enough to let them see the next revolution.

The Iran Programme

In May 2003, President George W. Bush announced the end of major combat operations in Iraq, from the deck of the aircraft carrier USS Abraham Lincoln. Afghanistan was now dominated, if not controlled, by the Americans and between the two countries lay what the US hawks now considered their worst nightmare – the possibility of a nuclear armed Iran.

Although the US and Iran had faced each other across the Persian Gulf for years, the Iranian nuclear programme was now seen as a critical issue by the Bush administration. The International Atomic Energy Authority predicted that they might be able to produce a deliverable nuclear weapon within a decade and the Israelis were spoiling for a pre-emptive strike.

However, with troops committed in both Iraq and Afghanistan and major US bases lying within range of Iran's latest ballistic missiles, the Americans were severely constrained by a series of potentially bad outcomes. Iran's military was professional and sophisticated, with modern equipment and few US officials were ready to consider military strikes to stop Iran getting the bomb. One of the few tools left in the armoury was a nonviolent political warfare campaign to influence the government.

Iran was a difficult military target, but it was also a fiendishly complex political system to undermine with a nonviolent strategy. Unlike many dictatorships like Slobodan Milosevic in Serbia, power did not reside with one individual. Nazila Fathi, who covered Iran for the *New York Times*, described it well when she said, 'You're talking about a regime that is like an octopus, it has so many different factions'.

There are three main centres of power in Iranian politics. According to Iranian law, the Supreme Leader Ayatollah Ali Khamenei is the nation's highest-ranking official and controls the military and the judiciary. The Supreme Leader also has a form of shadow cabinet whose members report directly to him and sit in almost every department of government – they are often seen in news reports sitting behind him dressed in black.

Secondly, there is a president who is elected by the population from a list approved by the Supreme Leader. The president largely controls the economy and other administrative functions, but can be dismissed by the Supreme Leader at any time.

The third centre of power is the Islamic Revolutionary Guards Corps or IRGC. The IRGC is an elite branch of the military founded to protect the country's Islamic political system – preventing foreign interference and coups by the rest of the military – it is the Supreme Leader's private military force, trusted to enforce his rule and given all sorts of perks to make sure he stays in power.

Some Iran analysts believe the head of the IRGC may even be more powerful that the Supreme Leader himself. This leaves any political warfare or nonviolent strategist with a difficult puzzle. Who exactly are you trying to influence or overthrow? If you only manage to undermine one of these centres of power, how do you stop one of the others taking its place?

The man charged with solving this problem was a former International Republican Institute staffer and State Department official, David Denehy. Denehy was working at the US headquarters in Iraq's 'Green Zone' in 2005 when he was recalled to Washington to lead the most controversial State Department brief in decades. His new boss was Liz Cheney, Senior Adviser to the Assistant Secretary for Near Eastern Affairs (and daughter of Vice President Dick Cheney), who led an organisation called the Iran and Syria Operations Group or 'ISOG'. ISOG was established to plot a more aggressive democracy promotion strategy for those two states of special concern to the US. Liz Cheney tasked Denehy with planning a campaign that would create 'citizen pressure' in Iran using a nonviolent strategy to 'modify its behaviour'.

After a hasty move back to Washington, Denehy's first task was to host a listening exercise at his office in the State Department, inviting as many experts as he could who were knowledgeable about various facets of Iranian politics, military and culture. Despite the fact that State Department had been involved in supporting the revolutions in Serbia and Ukraine, the turnover of successive Secretaries of State who appointed their own core staff and dismissed previous incumbents meant that there was little institutional knowledge of these campaigns left in the building. Most of the experienced people worked in the democracy promotion agencies of the National Endowment for Democracy and Freedom House.

Denehy met a procession of Iranian human rights professionals, lawyers, academics, media and US intelligence officials who had studied various elements of the Iranian regime in great depth and had strong views on how to tackle it.

Among them was the former Crown Prince of Iran, Reza Pahlavi – the man who would have become Shah, had his father not been deposed by the 1979 revolution. From his exile in Connecticut, Pahlavi had commissioned his own Persian translation of Gene's *From Dictatorship to Democracy* and distributed it throughout his networks in the country. Peter Ackerman paid a visit, and despite his recent disengagement from the Albert Einstein Institution, talked effusively about the potential application of Gene's theories in Iran.

Denehy released after many recommendations like these, that it was Gene Sharp's work that tied the strands together and provided a strategic framework for the new Iran programme. How could they best mobilise a diverse effort against the 'octopus' of Iran's political system? 'That's where we went to Gene Sharp who had thought through at the strategic level what it was, how organisations need to be structured and strategic planning of what they could do', Denehy told me. 'Did it affect our strategy or what we were attempting to invest in? Yeh sure it did … we took from those strategies, some certain core things …. activities where we looked to invest our money'.

Using Gene's writings, they identified the pillars of support of the Iranian government, including the judiciary, religious community, universities, army, police and IRGC. They then developed a funding and training plan to support media outlets, bloggers and student groups that could influence these structures.

On a tactical level, Denehy's team studied Bob Helvey's work and the experience of Otpor to learn about managing street protests and maintaining nonviolent discipline. Denehy also identified particular future trigger points which might be a focus for 'citizen pressure'. 'One of the strategies is that you have to like this tinderbox event right? There has to be a spark for some reason that moves people, sort of spontaneously, where they know that this is not in their best interest', Denehy told me. 'So we looked at a timeline of where there were different flashpoints and the development cycle that needed to occur.' He insisted they never set regime change as the goal, but many officials privately hoped for a 'Serbia-type effect'.

The contents of the strategy document that resulted from this study period are still classified, but we know they were finalised in late 2005. Condoleezza Rice reportedly took that document to the Bush ranch in Crawford, Texas where it was signed off by President Bush. According to Denehy, Gene's work had been formative in the writing of that strategy, even though the State Department had never reached out to him personally.

Before the full force of the programme could be put into action, Denehy ran into an unexpected diplomatic incident which threatened to derail the project before it had even begun.

Ramin Ahmadi was a respected doctor who had escaped Iran as a teenager and paid his way through Yale medical school by turning professional poker player. After his escape to the US he began researching ways of helping win freedom in the country he had left behind and discovered Gene Sharp's books. After arranging some Farsi translations he sent copies into Iran in any way he could, holding international workshops whenever his professional commitments would allow. Early in 2005, Ramin met a funder who agreed to pay for a series of training workshops for Iranians in Dubai. The money allowed him to hire the now highly experienced team of the Serbs and Bob Helvey for the training.

The workshops were advertised under a flimsy cover and were quickly detected by Iranian intelligence services, who sent a team of spies across the Gulf to attend. Bob noticed a group of men who didn't look like they fitted in with the others, their body language was suspicious and they looked more interested in their fellow trainees than the material being taught. Bob couldn't confirm his suspicions and the men were allowed to continue the training.

On returning to Tehran from Dubai the activists were monitored by the Iranian secret police to see who they met and then arrested. After days of interrogations they were paraded in front of Iranian TV audiences and told to describe how their workshop in Dubai had taught Gandhi and Gene Sharp. They were then forced into making false claims that the workshop had also taught them how to make explosives and blow up bridges. It was a disaster for Ramin, Helvey and Ackerman, but it also set off alarm bells at the highest levels in Washington.

News soon reached the White House that Americans had been accused of teaching Iranians how to build bombs in Dubai. A call quickly bounced down the chain of command from the White House to Liz Cheney at the State Department and then to Denehy demanding to know who was responsible. Denehy was pissed off – his finely crafted plan was being made to look amateurish by freelancers. 'Everyone assumed we funded those Dubai workshops and we didn't, but we caught the crap alright.'

Ramin had arrived back in the US and was about to start his morning rounds at the hospital in Danbury, Connecticut, when his secretary got a call. 'It's the State Department, they want to speak to you urgently,' she told him, startled by the request. He hurried down the hospital corridor, with his stethoscope bouncing around his neck, to be greeted on the phone by a terse sounding official demanding that he travel to Washington urgently.

Some days later, Ramin arrived at the State Department at Foggy Bottom and, after passing through several rounds of heavy security, was ushered into a room with a sombre group of officials who did not identify themselves. Denehy leaned forward gently in his seat, 'So Dr Ahmadi, can you tell us what exactly are you doing in Dubai?'

Ramin thought for a moment, 'I really can't tell you. It's confidential stuff. I made a promise to the activists that all of the workshops are confidential for their safety.'

'So what do you do in these workshops?' Denehy continued.

'I teach them about Gandhi and Martin Luther King and Gene Sharp'

'And when you teach them about that, what are they supposed to do?'

Ramin paused for a moment, weighing his answer. 'Well, they're supposed to overthrow their government through nonviolent means'.

Denehy threw himself backwards in his seat drawing a sharp intake of breath, 'Oh my God! Can you tone it down a bit?'

Denehy laid his cards on the table. 'The Iranian government believes that your workshops are supported by us. We've told them it's not true, but they don't believe us. They're putting pressure on the Emirati government to kick us out. Can you do us a favour and stay out of Dubai?' Ramin, appreciating the irony of the US government asking him to leave Dubai, began to joke with his inquisitors, 'I'm not leaving Dubai, you'll just move me on from the next place I go. You guys leave Dubai!'

The Americans looked angry and there was an awkward pause. Ramin shuffled uneasily in his seat. 'I'm sorry, I was joking. Of course we'll leave'.

'It was sensitive and we tried to be discreet', recalled Denehy, 'I think we were, but when you had activities like Ramin's, although well meaning, it made people nervous'. With Ramin kicked out of his sandbox Denehy was ready to continue his plans for Iran.

On 31st January 2006, President Bush announced in the State of the Union that the United States was releasing new funds to support Iranian civil society. Secretary of State, Condoleezza Rice, followed up two weeks later with the numbers. The budget for Iran democracy promotion activities would rise from $5million to $65million in a single financial year. The decision to publicise the funding was an unusual one. Historically this would have been a secret programme, but Denehy was among those who pushed for openness. 'We were sending a message to the Iranians to say … we're really serious about this. How does the US government show that it's really serious about something? It either bombs something or puts lots of money behind it'.

A call was put out by the State Department for invitations to tender for projects under the Iran program and on 15th March 2006, Gene wrote a letter to the board of the Albert Einstein Institution asking for opinions on whether they should make contact to investigate the projects. Curt Goering, an Albert Einstein Institution board member, whose day job was Chief Operating Officer of Amnesty International in the US, wrote back immediately to discourage any involvement, reasoning that working with the Bush administration could damage the institution's independence and credibility. It was quickly decided that the institution would not connect with the State Department. At this point no-one knew that Gene's work had already been instrumental in the Iran strategy just signed off by the President of the United States.

To make matters more complicated, as the Albert Einstein Institution's funds were dwindling again, a number of organisations began receiving thousands of dollars of State Department money to translate and distribute Gene's publications without his knowledge.

Liz Cheney's ISOG committee met regularly throughout 2006 to co-ordinate interagency activity directed at impacting the Iranian economy and supporting democratic forces that opposed the Iranian regime. Funding was signed off to train activists in organisational structures, leadership and secure communications technology to evade surveillance on the regime-controlled internet. They also attempted to make general strikes more likely by funding groups to provide a social security safety net for labour union members who went on strike. Food, clothes and occasionally cash would be dropped to the families of those in jail or whose income had been stopped.

The US officials at the programme were attempting to build to a critical point at which a change might happen. The exercise involved looking out to the future and identifying predictable trigger points for a revolution. Among these, the 2009 Presidential election was the major one. In many ways this operation only differed from the CIA operation during the Italian election in 1948 in the technology being used.

The working thesis was that if the newly-funded groups on the ground could train 100 people, 50 of those were going to understand what was taught, 20 were actually going to implement it in some way and, of that, 10 were going to be effective. The plan was to use this strategy to gradually build a cadre of people who would be significant enough in number and influence to become a centre of gravity in some way – to be ready to force a change.

Psychological strategies were also developed to create fractures among the ruling elite. By covertly supporting certain government figures or factions they hoped to foster jealousy and discord. Funds were also given to the Iran Human Rights Documentation Center in New Haven Connecticut whose job it was to document abuses and make sure the Iranian government knew that crimes against their people were being recorded.

The announcement of the US democracy programme put the Iranian internal security apparatus onto a war footing. Denehy's office at the State Department soon became deluged with reports of people being detained and arrested, NGOs getting raided and closed down.

The Iranian Basij militia was beefed up with extra equipment and training. The militia operated with a network of recruits in all towns and cities in Iran. Their job was to act as a kind of religious police and counter-protest force, informing on any revolutionary activity in their area, school or university. The Basij reported directly into the IRGC and gave the government an early warning of dissent.

The Iran programme had been made public, but the organisations receiving the money were still a secret. It meant that the Iranian government began to suspect every Iranian NGO was receiving US money. People who had just had chance meetings at cocktail parties with Denehy in Dubai and other capitals were rounded up. Many of them had absolutely nothing to do with the programme. Denehy privately admitted that this response had not been predicted. The accepted wisdom was that the Iranians would monitor communications to see who received the money, like cops do with the mob. 'When a bank gets robbed you watch who goes out and buys a Cadillac. That's the first person you look at right? he explained. 'So in this case which NGO all of a sudden has 4 or 5 new computers?' But the Iranians didn't operate like this. Whether their intelligence was poor or they just wanted to sow terror throughout the NGO community, the US funding was causing major problems for innocent Iranian civil society groups. Iranian Nobel Laureate Shirin Ebadi complained publicly about the policy to the US government. 'You're hurting a lot of people not involved in the program and that's not fair and not right', she told members of congress in Washington.

The strategy caused deep divisions within the State Department and the Iranian government started to complain loudly through diplomatic channels and the Swiss government that this was a violation of an agreement that the US would not involve itself in the domestic affairs of Iran. The US government sent back a communique that it disagreed with their assessment and the programme continued.

The Iranian secret police, now armed with the content of the Dubai workshops, which they still assumed to be part of the US program, began studying Gene's books. The propaganda wing of the service went to work on a public information campaign which included a cartoon TV commercial of Gene sitting with John McCain, George Soros and a CIA agent called Bill Smith, plotting the overthrow of the Iranian government from a room in the White House. As Gene appeared, the ominous voiceover introduced him as, 'Gene Sharp, the theoretician of civil disobedience and velvet revolutions, who has published treatises on this subject, he is one of the CIA agents in charge of America's infiltration into other countries.' The video was broadcast to millions of Iranians on state TV with an order that any suspicious activity be reported immediately to the spy agency.

When Jamila first saw the cartoon she was torn on whether it was a good or a bad thing for the Albert Einstein Institution, 'I was impressed that we were on the radar, and that they had Gene Sharp sitting at the White House. In a way I thought, I wish those in the White House would listen to us, I wish they would request a meeting with us, but they don't. We sit here. We operate out of our two room office. We have no connection with the White House.'

While it appeared comical to some, the Iranian's intelligence wasn't far wide of the mark. George Soros was chairman of the Open Society Institute, which had indeed funded many democracy groups; John McCain chaired the International Republican Institute which had funded activities in Burma and paid to introduce Gene's work to the Serbs and Otpor. The CIA officer, 'Bill Smith' was simply the embodiment of Denehy's role at the State Department and Gene was the academic mastermind. Although these people had never sat in a room together at The White House to discuss Iran, the cartoon was nevertheless an accurate illustration of the forces arrayed against the Iranian government and the program Denehy was conducting.

In late May 2007, the *Boston Globe* reported that the Iran Syria Operations Group had been shut down. Public and internal State Department criticism of the Iran programme had been growing to the point where continuing was proving impossible. State Department insiders said the group was terminated because of a 'widespread public perception that it was designed to enact regime change' – though officials continued to insist that the role of ISOG was never revolution, but behaviour modification.

In a written answer to a senator, Nicholas Burns, Under Secretary for Political Affairs at the State Department, confirmed the group had been disbanded in March 2007, in 'favor of a more standard process' of coordinating between the White House, the State Department, Defense Department, and intelligence agencies.

The final death knell for the US democracy promotion project in Iran came with the election of Barack Obama in November 2008. Bush's Freedom Agenda was thrown out for a grand bargain. The Obama administration was prepared to end support for what the Iranian's called 'regime change operations' in Iran so that they could make progress on a nuclear deal. For better or worse, it meant that after years of work and millions of dollars in funding, the US support for the Iranian democracy movement was largely removed, just ahead of the flashpoint 2009 presidential election that Denehy had been planning for.

Green Uprising

The beginning of the 2009 Iranian presidential election campaign looked every bit like the prelude to a new colour revolution. Supporters of the progressive candidate Mir-Hossein Mousavi adopted the colour green, donning green wrist bands, hats and scarves. Green was the brightest of the few drab colours acceptable to conservative clerics after the 1979 revolution – one commentator described it as 'like having an anti-war rally in the US and the demonstrators all painted in red white and blue'. It made it very difficult for the government to brand the democratic reformers as un-Islamic or supported by foreign enemies.

The Iranian people went to the polls on Friday 12th June 2009 in a huge turnout which required polling stations to stay open for an additional four hours. The Iranian people exercised their limited form of democracy, choosing a new president from a small group of candidates, pre-selected by a 12-member Council of Guardians and the Supreme Leader Khomeini. The two main presidential contenders were the incumbent, conservative Mahmoud Ahmadinejad and Mousavi, a former prime minister, considered a democratic reformer and friendly to the West.

By Saturday 13th June, the votes were counted and it was announced that Mahmoud Ahmadinejad had won 60% of the vote. Mousavi supporters complained of irregularities and urged people onto the streets to protest what they said was a fixed result. The following day, Mousavi's wife, Zahra, called for peaceful marches in Tehran and 19 other cities, followed by a national strike on Tuesday 16th June. Thousands of Mousavi activists formed a green chain down the entire 11 mile length of Tehran's Valiasr, the longest street in the Middle East. More than 120 academics at Sharif University resigned to protest outside their faculty buildings and hundreds of thousands of people marched in silence through central Tehran in a show of defiance – the largest demonstration in Iran since the revolution in 1979.

The government banned any further demonstrations, throttled the internet and switched off the country's text message system, but the following day saw another green march flow through Tehran from Revolution Square to the Azadi Tower, a monument which had formed the backdrop to the 1979 revolution. They marched in silence, throwing their green painted fingers into the air in victory signs. When anyone broke the silence and cried out they were quickly hushed by efficient marshals along the route. People came out into the streets in the cities of Isfahan, Ahwaz, Zahedan, Yazd and Mashhad shouting 'Allahu Akbar' in solidarity with the Tehran demonstrations.

The Iranian security forces reacted to the disciplined nonviolent campaign with subversive actions to make the green movement appear a chaotic force, hell bent on wrecking the country. Basij agents provocateurs went out in force, smashing shop fronts and the cars of ordinary people parked in the streets. The acts of vandalism quickly appeared on state television along with government ministers describing the latest deeds of the 'Mousavi supporting rioters'. The green movement struck back through its own media channels. In videos posted to YouTube, local people can be seen dismissing the suggestion that damage was the work of the green movement. One woman in Saadat Abat said she saw the security forces smashing the windows of resident's vehicles. Asked if she was sure it was the security forces, she asks the cameraman, 'Why would the kids break our cars?'

Although these were the largest protests that Iran had seen in decades, the movement was largely spontaneous and Mousavi's leadership on nonviolent strategy, limited. The actions were not growing beyond the symbolic street protests to the more powerful methods which might have been employed. Many ordinary Iranians started reaching out to the Albert Einstein Institution and Gene Sharp's work for guidance.

In East Boston, Jamila was dealing with the collapse of the Albert Einstein Institution website due to the thousands of extra visitors downloading the Farsi translation of *From Dictatorship to Democracy*. News was coming through that the PDF version had been reposted on a number of blog sites and message boards which were receiving even more hits. A video of Gene talking through some of his 'lessons' was translated by an unknown group into Farsi and also went viral. Jamila was analysing the website visitor data, which was surprising, 'Everyone says that revolutions are concentrated in educated middle class urban centres. That was true, the main demand was coming from Tehran, but our data was also showing the book being downloaded even in small villages in the middle of nowhere.'

On 17th June, eight members of the Iranian football team walked onto the pitch in Seoul for their World Cup qualifier against South Korea wearing green armbands in solidarity with the green movement. The match was being televised live to millions of people back in Iran and there was little the Iranian government could do to stop the broadcast. By the time the players came back onto the pitch, after half time, enough force had been exerted that most of the players had removed the armband – but by then the damage to the regime had already been done. The youth of the country had seen their heroes show their support for the people on the streets.

As the government repression increased, the activists were beginning to take casualties. Basij militia, often in plain clothes, were shooting into crowds and beating protesters mercilessly on the ground. One medical student working at a city hospital reported that the government had decreed that all riot-related injuries were to be sent to military medical centres. The bodies of those who lost their lives in civilian hospitals, mostly to gunshot wounds, were collected by government trucks before their families could locate them.

This was intended to frustrate the ability of the green movement to properly record evidence of the brutality being unleashed against the people, but the use of social media meant that the democracy movement had the advantage. As the repression increased, so did the strength of feeling against the government and the protesters numbers swelled. One protester tweeted, 'ppl are more angry now because of killed persons – they have more energy now to protest... Qeytarieh [an affluent neighbourhood in Northern Tehran] is so crowded like last two nights'

The power of political jujitsu that Gene wrote so much about was demonstrated with the killing of a 26-year-old student called Neda Agha-Soltan. Neda was studying philosophy at the Islamic Azad University – an aspiring musician she had clashed with conservative policies on dress and appearance in her university. From a young age she railed against the Islamic laws that prevented her from wearing the clothes she wanted or going to the beach uncovered. She joined the protest, despite her mother begging her not to go. A couple of Basij women had approached Neda in the street with her mother and told her to go home and not to come back. 'You are beautiful and the Basij men will kill beautiful girls if they see them', she was told.

At around half past six on the 20th June, Neda was driving her little Peugeot car back to the protest, accompanied by her music teacher, Hamid Panahi. It was a hot evening and the traffic on Kargar Avenue was backed up for over a mile due to the blocked roads ahead. The car's air conditioning was having little effect and Neda decided to get out and watch the protest.

A young doctor, Arash Hejazi, just a few metres away, noticed Neda as she stood shouting, 'Our leader is a dictator', and thought how brave she was. As he watched, he heard a crack of gunfire ring out. People ducked and began to run in fear and confusion. As Arash looked back he saw Neda standing with a look of astonishment as blood gushed from her chest. He ran to her as she collapsed to the ground, Hamid at her shoulder trying to staunch the blood from her wound. 'I'm burning, I'm burning', she told them.

As Arash and Hamid tried in vain to save her, Neda looked up for a brief moment directly into the lens of a camera phone filming her, before blood began to slip from her nose and mouth into her eyes. 'I know the footsteps of death' said Arash. 'When I realised I stood up and told her music teacher. She's dead'. Hamid didn't want to believe it – he kept yelling for her to stay with him, to stay alive. A passing car filled with young men stopped and dragged her lifeless body into the back seat with Hamid but there was nothing the hospital could do. Arash was left shocked looking at the pool of blood left on the tarmac where Neda had fallen. Behind him there was a commotion – a man being dragged through the crowd without a shirt. He shouted, 'I didn't want to kill her, by God I didn't want to kill her'. The crowd were beating him, some wanted to kill him, but others stopped them. 'We are not like them, we are nonviolent', someone shouted.

The protesters could hardly hand the man in to a police station so they removed his ID card as evidence and reluctantly let him go. The political jujitsu effect that Gene had described now super-charged the opposition. The brutality of the regime, encapsulated in the killing of Neda on video, drew thousands more people to the protest. Within hours, that desperate image of Neda looking into the camera in her final moments would be replayed millions of times. People marched with Neda posters and banners in more than 100 cities around the world.

The widespread brutality which the image of Neda now exposed began to create fractures in the security forces. This process was witnessed by a number of journalists still at large in the cities. British foreign corre-spondent Robert Fisk reported for ABC News that he had witnessed policemen smiling at the demonstrators and Iranian soldiers stopping an attack upon some Mousavi supporters by the Basij. He reported that one woman had approached the soldiers and asked if they would protect them from the Basij. The reply was, 'With God's help'. 'It was quite extraor-dinary', Fisk wrote, 'because it looked as if the military authorities in Tehran have either taken a decision not to go on supporting the very brutal militia – which is always associated with the presidency here – or individual soldiers have made up their own mind that they're tired of being associated with the kind of brutality that left seven dead yesterday'.

Roger Cohen from the *New York Times* also saw the security forces beginning to respond to the movement's nonviolent discipline, noting that women were bridging the gap between the men of the movement and the police. 'I've heard them [the women] whispering to the Basij and the police that "We are all Iranians", urging them to hold back'. Cohen wrote on the 15th June, 'I saw traffic police smiling at the crowd. Even the black-clad elite riot police were impassive'. On one march towards Enqelab Square in Tehran, the anti-riot police kept their distance and the protesters chanted, 'Police, police, thank you', in response, all along the route.

Had more strategic planning been done, it is possible that the green movement may have made greater progress in winning the support or at least weakening the effectiveness of these security forces. The Basij for instance were not the impenetrable force that they were thought to be. One Basij officer, Mohammed Hussein Torkaman, defected after witnessing the brutal oppression by the IRGC.

As the movement was pushed off the streets by the Basij and the IRGC there were some attempts to diversify from purely symbolic nonviolent actions. A campaign was launched to boycott advertisers on state TV and some viewers said they noticed the number of commercials running in the TV breaks fall. Another boycott of Nokia phones was successful after it was found that Nokia Siemens had installed monitoring software into the Iranian phone network which had been used to detect and imprison movement organisers. However, these more powerful economic actions were never deployed as part of a grand strategy and had limited impact. The workers' unions did not join forces with the green movement and the industrial sector was never convinced to move to a general strike.

In an effort to win the information war, the government was soon broadcasting rolling footage of pro-Ahmadinejad protests on state TV while attempting to clear the streets of both independent Iranian and international journalists. AP reported that reporters were banned from working on the streets and confined to their offices where they could only watch the censored state television news and receive phone reports from their contacts on the ground. Soon that was made even more difficult as the government shut down the mobile networks. Those foreign journalists who had been given permission to cover the election were refused visa extensions, rounded up and sent to the airport.

The journalists who were sent home may have been the lucky ones. For a few, whose activities were deemed serious enough, there was arrest and detention in some of Iran's most notorious prisons. One of those detained was Iason Athanasiadis, a Greek freelance photo-journalist whose experience was typical of those who were arrested. It also provided an insight into just how concerned Iranian intelligence was about Gene Sharp's influence in the country.

Iason knew Gene's work well. While studying as a Nieman journalism fellow at Harvard, he'd got interested in the work and visited Cottage Street on a number of occasions. He'd also been the first to report (under a pen name) on the disastrous training workshops in Dubai.

During the beginning of the green movement, Iason kept his head down, covering developments through a network of contacts cultivated over years of working in the country. But just as events were becoming interesting his visa was running out and he was forced to leave. After passing through security at Tehran Airport, he sat on the uncomfortable plastic seating at the gate, reading and sending out some last messages to those he hadn't had time to say goodbye to.

It was then that he became aware of being silently and efficiently surrounded by men in nondescript grey suits. He confirmed his name and was firmly gripped by the arms, his travel documents taken away. 'It looks like you won't be making your plane', they told him. 'I'd heard stories of people being arrested like this and how important it was to make sure people knew what had happened, to raise the alarm. So I started screaming and waving my arms and shouting my name at the people sitting around. 'Find a journalist and tell them Iason Athanasiadis has been taken', he yelled.

The eyes in the departure lounge around him looked, but not too hard. A few must have taken note of his cries and feigned disinterest, but one brave woman in the lounge wrote down the spelling of his name. The security service couldn't arrest the onlookers and almost a hundred of them would soon be landing in another country where they could raise the alarm. Within a few hours the news was out.

Rolled into the back of a car with a blanket forced down over his upper body, Iason was soon speeding away from the airport on the way to one of Iran's most notorious detention centres. Evin Prison sits on the northern edge of Tehran, backing onto the Alborz mountains which climb away from the execution yard along its back wall. It was notorious for its political prisoners wing which had held the inmates of Iran's previous political upheavals, including the 1979 revolution. The Iranian government had executed a total of 29 people there, by hanging, in the first six months of 2009 alone.

Numerous foreign journalists had been incarcerated at Evin on espionage charges, many languishing for months before their governments could strike deals to win their freedom. Iason knew more than he would like about where he was being taken and his prospects of release. When he arrived at interrogation center 4, the prison was noisy and crowded. The protests had filled the cells to capacity and the arresting officer bartered with the guards for space. Iason could not be kept with others, only in solitary confinement. 'In the background I could hear screaming and shouting, interrogations in process'. He was thrown roughly into a four by six foot cell, furnished with only a blanket and green plastic mat.

News of Iason's arrest reached The Albert Einstein Institution three days later. A friend charged with his contact book had begun rounding up support to begin a press campaign to release him. Few people knew why he had been arrested, but it crossed Jamila's mind that the security services could have read his articles about the disaster of the 2005 training workshop and realized he had been in contact with Gene. It was possible that the bad decisions made around the workshop could now have claimed Iason in addition to the Iranian participants. She sipped nervously from a take-out coffee and forwarded the appeal for information.

Back in Tehran, Iason was being hauled in front of a small wooden table and an angry looking Chief Prosecutor. 'There are very serious accusations against you', he told him, 'do you know what those accusations are?'

'I don't know', Iason shrugged

'Are you sure you really don't know?'

The prosecutor leaned in and whispered. 'Espionage!'.

A senior officer summoned a file on his computer and gestured towards the screen. 'This laptop contains Gene Sharp's guide to bringing down a government. It gives several easy ways by which people can bring down even a good government any kind of government. I've read this and so have my colleagues'.

Iason's arrest indicated that the Iranian government security apparatus was closely studying Gene's work. Even if many of the people on the streets had never heard his name, the regime believed that the organizing forces were using the book. The overt State Department Programme and the Dubai trainings had made real their fears of the US weaponising civil society groups that could be unleashed at the right time.

The arrival of a Farsi-speaking western journalist who had been in touch with Gene and was familiar with his work, was clearly going to raise some alarm, but, at no point during the interrogation was he asked about his connection to the institution or if he'd ever met Gene.

Iason was eventually released almost three weeks later, but several Iranian reporters were charged with 'sending pictures to enemy media'. By the end of July, 42 journalists were imprisoned in Iran, the highest total of any country in the world. Newsweek writer, Maziar Bahari was forced to confess that he had participated in promoting a 'colour revolution'.

The loss of so many Iranian and international journalists meant that the green movement began to rely increasingly on social media to spread its news. The Mousavi campaign team tweeted, 'We have no national press coverage in Iran, everyone should help spread Mousavi's message. One Person = One Broadcaster'. CNN reported that senior State Department officials were working with Twitter and other social media companies to maintain the Iranians ability to communicate with each other and get news of what was happening out to the world. Although by this point the green uprising was being branded the 'Twitter Revolution' in the western press, the number of Twitter accounts actually registered in Iran was extremely low, around 8654 in total. A larger number of users may have registered outside Iran using technology that disguised their location, but the impact of twitter was certainly inflated.

When asked about the role of social media in Iran's uprising Gene was ambivalent. 'What's important isn't the technology people are using to communicate with each other, it's what they are communicating' he told journalists, 'If they are planning wisely that's good, but if all of the activity is just symbolic then the technology doesn't really help you, beyond getting your message out'.

As increasing numbers of Iranian activists and demonstrators were arrested by the security forces, they were squeezed into overcrowded prisons like Evin and local jail cells all over Iran. The protesters had managed to stay on the streets for months, but without a clear strategy, a training programme, decentralised command structure and organisation, the resistance was too weak to weather the pressure of the government counter-revolutionary forces. When the prosecutors eventually decided the crimes the protesters would be tried for, Gene's work featured prominently in the charges. In at least one mass trial of protesters in Tehran, the indictment read:

'According to gathered evidence and the confessions of the accused, these events were planned in advance and took place according to the schedule of the Velvet Revolution. More than 100 of the 198 steps in the Gene Sharp manual of instructions for velvet revolutions have already been executed'.

The sight of movement leaders in light blue and green jump suits sitting in rows in court was a depressing closing chapter to the green uprising. The surviving leadership of the movement went back to their work and studies, perhaps to rise another day, but years later some of those sentenced for using Gene's work were still languishing in Evin Prison.

Bush staffers responsible for the Iran programme were still seething years later at Obama's team for dismantling their efforts just as they might have been able to help the Iranians on the streets. During a lecture at the Frontline Club in London three years later, Gene agreed that the change in administration had been detrimental to the green movement, but told the audience that the Iranian democracy groups should never have taken CIA or US money and direction in the first place. 'If it's directed from outside don't trust that … *rely on yourselves alone*. This was Gandhi's message too – don't depend on someone coming to save you, they may never get there.'

Shoots of Spring

On the 3rd June 2006, the US Ambassador to Cairo, Francis Ricciardone, sent a cable to his superiors in the State Department, giving his prognosis for democratic reform in Egypt. 'There will be no Orange Revolution on the Nile on Mubarak's watch, but we must aim to consolidate each modest democratic advance'. He continued, 'In all likelihood it will not be possible to make great progress on democratic reform as long as President Mubarak remains in office. Nonetheless, his firm rule offers space and time to prepare civil society and some institutions of the GOE [Government of Egypt] for the day of his departure. We do not have a silver bullet, but we can press reforms that will lead, inexorably, to the "death by 1000 cuts" of Egypt's authoritarian system'.

The Egyptian people were beginning to realise that Hosni Mubarak, president for almost 30 years, was lining up his son Gamal to succeed him. The prospect of a dynastic succession fuelled searches for materials and advice by Egyptian democracy activists at home and abroad. They saw Mubarak's retirement as the critical moment at which they might be able to win true democracy.

While Egyptian democracy activists were often critical of the US for propping up Mubarak, the picture on the ground was far more complex. The Egyptian offices of American democracy promotion agencies, like IRI and Freedom House were being provided with so much money by the US government in 2006 that they couldn't work out how to spend it. That year Freedom House received a grant of $900,000 for development of Egyptian civil society advocacy and reform, but spent less than half of the money – mainly due to restrictions the Egyptian government placed on funding of groups they deemed too threatening. Their Country Director reported to the State Department that the pot of cash for 2006 would last, at their existing rate of spending, until at least the end of 2008.

Ambassador Ricciardone reported in a cable, 'We believe we are funding very nearly every organisation in Egypt that wishes to work with us and meets our Grants criteria.'

In early 2005 a young Egyptian man arrived in East Boston for a meeting at the Albert Einstein Institution. A qualified engineer, he was committed, serious and had clearly studied Gene's work in depth. Over the course of an hour he discussed the problems in Egypt and the fractures in the movements currently fighting for improvements in human rights and democracy. The engineer was from a group that called itself 'Kefaya', which meant 'enough' in Arabic. Gene and Jamila wished him good luck like the others who came, sending him away with armsful of books, not knowing whether he would never be heard from again, or perhaps start something remarkable.

In Cairo a few months later another young Egyptian student, Dalia Ziada, began researching nonviolent action. At first inspired by the Martin Luther King story, she was searching for more literature about nonviolent strategy when she came across references to Gene Sharp.

'I couldn't understand how nonviolence would actually work in practice until I started to read Sharp,' she told me. '*From Dictatorship to Democracy* was a step by step guide – exactly what we needed to understand what really happens and what really affects the different forces. I was excited by the idea of pillars of support and how to pull every pillar away from the regime.' Dalia began to translate Gene's materials and immediately ran into the same translation problem with 'nonviolent action' as Mubarak Awad had done in Jerusalem 20 years earlier.

'I remember when I first translated the term "nonviolent action" into Arabic in late 2006, people at that time were asking what is this? What do you mean by "nonviolent", why don't you say peaceful. I remember one of them was even a sociologist, and even he didn't understand what it meant.'

In July 2007 Dalia travelled to Jordan for a workshop, organised by Peter Ackerman's ICNC, to train young people from all over the region in nonviolent strategy. The trainers came from the Serbs of CANVAS and were led by Slobo Dinović. They met in the inauspicious surroundings of the Amman Holiday Inn with a group of young trainers of a similar age to the students. Slobo taught Otpor's curriculum of nonviolent action and they played 'A Force More Powerful' – the strategy video game which had been developed by Peter Ackerman to help groups plan strategies. The following year Dalia travelled to the US to take part in the Fletcher Summer Institute, another Ackerman project, set up at Tufts University, which connected new activists and experienced campaigners and academics from all over the world.

As signs of a family succession in Egypt continued to grow, more individuals like Dalia and civil society organisations began looking for answers. It meant that multiple organisations discovered Gene Sharp at roughly the same time. Given the repressive conditions in the country and the risks of sharing information, several different Arabic translations of *From Dictatorship to Democracy* were produced independently and put into circulation. One of those organisations was the London-based 'Academy of Change' (AOC), founded by three Egyptians, Hisham Morsi, Wael Adel and Ahmed Abdel-Hakim, who came across a poor translation of Gene's *Politics of Nonviolent Action* in Arabic. Soon they were circulating Gene's work and using it in trainings in Cairo. AOC published their own book, *Nonviolent War: The Third Choice* which extracted some of Gene's writings and printed a series of pamphlets, and instruction manuals intended to be handed out on the streets. At the same time the Egyptian Muslim Brotherhood's (EMB) 'specialized translation unit' translated *From Dictatorship to Democracy* and posted it on their website where it received hundreds of downloads.

It was by these means that Gene's work became popular among the leadership groups and began to seep, often unsourced, into the indigenously produced revolutionary guides which would later be read by thousands of people. An effort to mask the author was understandable – these groups knew that they might soon be cast as foreign inspired traitors and puppets of US imperialism.

By October 2007, the US State Department had revamped its democracy strategy for Egypt and increased its financial clout. In fact, the sum for proposed spending on 'Democracy and Governance' in Egypt for financial year 2008–2009 was almost exactly the amount that had been given to David Denehy for the Iranian democracy programme. The total was $75 million – $50 million to be spent inside the country and $25 million for 'offshore programming', out of sight of the Egyptian government.

Freedom House was tasked with carrying out offshore human rights activities that included training for bloggers, assistance to human rights lawyers, coalition-building with civil society and civic education. In addition, the International Republican Institute was to conduct 'workshops, strategic planning and capacity building to assist in developing emerging leaders in all political parties ... in preparation for the 2010 parliamentary elections and the 2011 presidential election.' Just as they had done in Iran, the Americans had identified the upcoming election as a potential trigger point for revolution.

One of the up and coming student leaders was Ahmed Maher, a stocky young engineer with a shaved head and round spectacles who had been active for years within the Kefaya youth movement. Members of Kefaya had undertaken a serious period of study, researching Gandhi, Martin Luther King and Rosa Parks. Many of them were already familiar with Gene Sharp from the visit of one of their colleagues who had returned with copies of *From Dictatorship to Democracy*. Maher and his colleague Ahmed Rasheed also felt they needed a real world case study of nonviolent action that they could emulate. They were looking for a template with, what they called, the same 'four corners' as Egypt – a youth movement, a regime that didn't want to give up power, corruption in the country and a passive population. They found that model in Otpor. 'They really inspired us.' Ahmed Rasheed told me, 'We studied their organisational tactics, the way they marched, the organisation itself, how you should always commit to peaceful change no matter what happens, because that's better for the movement. We tried to understand from the tools and ideas that they used and adapt them to the Egyptian environment.'

By 2008, the labour movement in Egypt was becoming increasingly hostile to the government over low pay and poor conditions and the tech savvy young activists saw an opportunity to lend their skills in IT to these more traditional workers. Maher realised that labour strikes and civil disobedience for economic rights within the workers' movement could be united with a wider demand for political rights and democracy.

When workers at a textiles plant in the industrial city of Al-Mahalla scheduled a strike for 6th April, Maher and his colleagues decided to seize this opportunity to initiate a general strike across the country. They launched a Facebook page to support and spread the news of the industrial action and named it after the date of the protest – April 6th. A link to the page was sent to 300 activists and by the end of the day there were 3000 followers. After just a week they were astonished to see that grow to more than 70,000.

When the day of 6th April came, the Al-Mahalla workers abandoned their factories and posters glorifying Mubarak were torn down across the city. Two workers were killed as the police battled to break the strike and thousands more people joined Facebook groups supporting them. Kefaya's objective of a general strike failed to take hold across the country, but it would become a useful rehearsal for what was to come.

After Al-Mahalla, Maher realised that his home and those of his friends were under surveillance by the security services and he would soon be arrested. He decided to slip away from his watchers and spent almost a month in hiding, surfacing only occasionally to email guidance from different cyber cafés around the country. Life on the run could never last long and eventually the secret police managed to trace his movements and arrest him. He was tortured repeatedly, ordered to name the other organisers of the April 6th Facebook page and provide the login details. After his eventual release, the story of his treatment at the hands of his interrogators further galvanised support for the movement.

Over the course of the following year, April 6th stepped up their studying and international contacts, especially with the Serbs. In June 2009, Mohammed Adel, a founding member of April 6th, and 14 others traveled from Egypt to the CANVAS office in Belgrade to meet their mentors. The Egyptians wouldn't have looked out of place that summer, just another group of foreigners being guided around the capital's streets – but those who looked closely would have seen their tour guide was Srdja Popovic and they were learning how to start a revolution.

As they walked, Srdja led them through Republic Square, and told the stories of Duda's iconic black clenched fist, how small, low risk, actions could build the confidence of the people and how street theatre and satire created laughter which could be their greatest weapon. Outside the Communist Party headquarters he described the night in 2000 they had to stop their own side burning down the building, how the moment when a ruler falls can be the most dangerous and the revolution can be stolen by a military coup. By the end of the tour, at least some of the group were so inspired they began shouting in the city centre, 'Free Egypt, Down with Mubarak!' The police stopped by to ask if everything was alright. Srdja was amused, but there was serious work to do if they were ever to be able to express themselves like that on the streets of Cairo.

The Egyptians were driven to a hotel on the banks of Palic Lake, one of Serbia's most idyllic hideaways. Here they were given books and articles, photos of techniques in action and lessons in strategic planning. Srdja had modelled some of his teaching on Bob Helvey's first lecture to Otpor in Budapest and taught Gene's theories and the pillars of support.

At the end of the teaching, Mohammed Adel told Srdja that they had been impressed by the course, but a revolution like Serbia's could never happen in Egypt. It was a line that Srdja had heard many times before. Almost every group he taught would at some point tell the trainers that their country was different and, for unique reasons, this type of struggle was impossible there.

For Ahmed Rasheed, one of the most powerful elements of the teaching was the screening of the documentary, 'Bringing Down a Dictator' by Steve York. 'Personally I saw this movie dozens of times and every time I watched it I discovered something new,' Maher remembered, 'a new technique, a new message about what we can do. I was dreaming when I was watching that movie, can we be in a documentary about changing the face of Egypt one day?' When the members of April 6th returned to Egypt they would show the documentary to new recruits and as the credits rolled told them excitedly, 'This is what we are going to do here! Just believe in yourself, believe in your dreams and you will do it!'

In the meetings the members would sit around discussing Martin Luther King, Gandhi and Gene Sharp. How could these elements be brought together to make a difference in Egypt? 'We were looking to change the country by peaceful means and we got from Gene Sharp some examples of technique, how to organise yourself, we printed his books and gave it to our members,' Maher told me.

Rasheed was a marketing executive by profession and the Serbs' analogy of selling a revolution like an advertising campaign resonated with him. 'Our idea was to reach the maximum number of Egyptian people. So we are 85 million, but 40% are living under the poverty line, so can I send them message through Facebook? Of course not!' To reach the rest of the population the activists used graffiti and spray paint, flyers and even co-opted taxis to spread the message. Taxi drivers were notorious in Egypt for being unable to keep quiet or be discreet and so Ahmed would discuss plans for their demonstrations loudly on the phone in the back of a taxi, confident that the story would quickly spread around Cairo within days. He got into a cab one day and almost immediately the taxi driver started telling him the story he had intended to spread, 'Did you know there are some guys going downtown tomorrow to ask Mubarak to leave – they are crazy!'

Following Otpor's example, April 6th began recruiting and training activists across the country. This recruitment was quickly detected by the secret police who sent undercover agents to try and infiltrate the group. Rasheed implemented a technique of feeding potential new members false information to test their trustworthiness and watching carefully to see if the police acted on it.

'We knew we were becoming strong because of the actions of the police.' Rasheed remembered, 'When they came to arrest me and ask me for the passwords of the group, it told us how strong we were. We said, "we are dangerous to them guys, keep working!"' Other security procedures were more Monty Python than James Bond. Codewords were adopted when using mobile phones. Protests were referred to as 'parties' and their secret office as, 'the cave'.

The group then had to sell their vision of an Egypt without Mubarak to the people. This was their 'vision of tomorrow', a critical stage of the uprising. 'The initial strategy was to reach a maximum number of people, to speak to them about the idea, about our aim, how we were going to change the country – always making a link between people suffering problems and the change.' Ahmed Rasheed explained. 'If the poor asked, why should we join the protest?' April 6th explained that change meant they would have a salary, better life, better health care system. 'We had to explain the relationship between them and Mubarak. Mubarak is not the owner of the country. You had to tell them that they were giving Mubarak his salary from their pocket in taxes'.

It was a brutal killing, like Neda's in Iran, which primed the touchpaper of Egypt's uprising. Khaled Said was a 28-year-old from the coastal city of Alexandria who had grown up loving computers and studied programming in the US. On 6th June 2010 he was sitting in an internet café when, for reasons still unclear, two plain clothes police detectives entered the café to arrest him. As they cuffed his hands behind his back, he resisted and the police retaliated by smashing his head down hard onto a marble table top. The café owner pleaded with them to take the fight outside and they dragged him down the stairs into the doorway of a neighbouring building. Bystanders watched as the police slammed his head repeatedly against an iron door and the wall of the building. Two doctors who were passing by tried in vain to save him from the beating, but Khaled was dead in minutes – his skull fractured, jaw broken and his face bloodied and contorted beyond recognition.

Later that day, while his family stood weeping over his body in the morgue, his brother took a photo of Khaled's shattered face and shared it on the internet. Within hours, the photo had gone viral, shared on Twitter and some of the most high profile Facebook pages in the country.

Over a thousand miles away, Egyptian marketing executive, Wael Ghonim, who was working for Google in Dubai, was sitting at home when he saw the photo of Khaled for the first time and collapsed in tears at his desk. Determined to do something, he launched a new Facebook page called, 'We are all Khaled Said'. What distinguished this page from many others was his decision to write in the first person as if he *was* Khaled. After just 24 hours the page had 36,000 members.

Khaled Said was buried on 11th June with around 1000 people attending. In Cairo, Ahmed Maher and April 6th organised a march in his honour outside the interior ministry. The protesters carried placards with pictures of Khaled smiling before the attack alongside the picture of his distorted face taken after his death. The police were ready and surrounded them with what seemed like double their numbers. There were beatings and arrests, but the state media didn't run the story.

Wael's Facebook page became increasingly popular, distributing photos and videos of police abuse and news of new demonstrations that the state media wouldn't show. The growing number of followers turned the 'We are all Khaled Said' Facebook page into a significant alternative media outlet. Wael began co-ordinating with April 6th and Ahmed Maher on the ground in Cairo, but did so anonymously. April 6th had no idea who Wael Ghonim was, or that he wasn't even living in Egypt.

By September 2010, plans for the resistance against a Mubarak family succession were beginning to reach local journalists. Sarah El Deeb from the Associated Press, filed a story from Cairo describing her visit to a small apartment in a middle class area of the city where a team of instructors were teaching Gandhi, Martin Luther King and downloading books by Gene Sharp. The group were a handful of a reported 15,000 followers of Mohamed ElBaradei, the Nobel Peace Prize winner and former chief of the International Atomic Energy Authority, who was considering a Presidential bid. El Deeb wrote, 'Another 9,000 volunteers are to be trained or have applied to join the campaign of ElBaradei supporters. After operating mainly online, volunteers have started going door-to-door to gather signatures and reach out to people, following the ideas of Sharp.'

'Co-ordinators say they intend their new campaign, managed from the small office in Cairo's Mohandiseen neighbourhood, to one day be at the heart of a civil disobedience movement that will take on the Mubarak regime.'

The Egyptian Revolution

On the morning of 17th December 2010 Mohamed Bouazizi started his day in the central Tunisian city of Sidi Bouzid knowing he was $200 in debt from the fruit and vegetables he had bought to sell on his barrow – money that had to be made back at all costs unless he was to fall into a spiral of debt. Fate that day was not kind. He was confronted by a local government official who accused him of selling his goods without a permit and confiscated his barrow with all of his produce.

He ran to the local governors' office in desperation to complain, but when local government officials refused to see him he threatened to burn himself. Nobody paid any attention. Minutes later he returned with a can of fuel from a nearby gas station, poured petrol over his head and body and set himself alight in the middle of the road. Mohamed Bouazizi, or Basboosa as his friends knew him, was about to trigger a political storm which would change the course of history.

On the evening of Bouazizi's self-immolation, as he lay clinging to life in a local hospital, his fellow traders and the young people of the city staged a sit-in protest in front of the governor's office. In the following days the numbers grew and a co-ordination committee was formed through Facebook to call for protests in neighbouring towns.

With careful handling by the authorities the uprising might have been cooled, but instead it was met with severe beatings and on the 27th December the police shot dead a protester in the town of Menzel Bouzaiane. Bouazizi's injuries had been self inflicted, but this death was perpetrated by the government and swelled the numbers protesting across the country even further. Just over a week later Bouazizi died of his injuries. His martyrdom and funeral the following day became a new focus for the rage in the country. The street protests spread from the country's interior to the capital Tunis and the coastal towns.

On 14th January 2011, thousands of Tunisians gathered on Avenue Bourguiba for a march to the Presidential Palace demanding the resignation of President Ben Ali. It's unclear whether the President ever issued the order for the army to intervene, but as the protest surrounded the palace, a Facebook post went viral stating that the commanders had refused an order to fire on the protesters. The President had lost the support of his security forces and after 23 years in power he fled the country for Saudi Arabia.

When Ahmed Maher saw the news from Tunisia he knew instantly that what had happened made the fall of President Mubarak in Egypt a realistic possibility. 'We were waiting for the event that would ignite a spark – that would trigger a large movement of the people. We were waiting for it, and it turned out to be Tunisia. There has always been a rivalry between Egypt and Tunisia in football. So we asked ourselves, if we had started all this before Tunisia, why was Tunisia having its revolution before us?' The Egyptians were too proud to be beaten. They had planned endlessly for this – they were not as ready as they would like, but the time had chosen them.

The Egyptian people followed the Tunisians onto the streets, calling for Hosni Mubarak to step down. Dalia was living in the Shubra district of Cairo and had assumed a role in strategic planning, organising marches from her area to the city centre. She promoted the guidance materials for the protest online, across Facebook pages, Twitter and message groups and made sure the participants were following the strategy.

These activities were coordinated from secret operations rooms scattered around Cairo by members of civil society groups and political organisations sitting together working on laptops with dozens of mobile phones ringing constantly. Their role was to make sure that the people on the ground were connected, countering outbreaks of violence and moving in the planned way.

News of arrests, injuries and deaths were collated, reports, photos and videos were fed back out to activists, posted online and reported to the international media. At the same time, the planning teams were working on actions for the days and weeks ahead.

A clear strategy was announced in leaflets, by email and across social media and the Khaled Said page, with maps of where people should meet, how they should move there, advice on what to do if blocked by police and how to find a marshal or medical help in case of emergency. There was also a list of chants which had been agreed upon 'Bread .... Freedom ... Human Dignity', 'Raise your voice up high ... with injustice we will not comply', 'Let's make it happen, Egyptians wake your spirit ... The gates of liberty are open'. The demonstration would take place on Egyptian National Police Day – the 25th January.

Wael had compiled this information from April 6th and other groups into a single document which was uploaded to a Google Documents page and shared on Twitter and Facebook. In addition to outlining the reasons for the protest the document included a list of protest guidelines for nonviolent discipline.

'Please carry the Egyptian flag and refrain from carrying any signs of a political party, movement, group organization or religious sect. Jan 25 is for all Egyptians. We are all demanding equal rights and social justice and do not want to be divisive... If you are not an experienced protester leave the front lines for experienced protesters to lead the march in order to avoid conflicting decisions.'

'The chants are unified and agreed upon. Please refrain from all profanity and do not enter into quarrels with security force members. Central security is not your enemy. They are guards who have been forced to spend their compulsory military service in this capacity and if they disobeyed the orders they would be punished badly. Try as much as possible to target your anger at the real enemy. Do not come out alone. It is very important not to come out alone, because friends come in handy in situations like these. Please be with someone and talk someone into coming out together.'

'The protests are peaceful. We are peace advocates and not advocates of violence. We are demanding our rights and must uphold the rights of others. We will not respond to any provocation from security forces and lose control. This is what they want us to do. One of the main aims of the security forces is to portray the protesters as thugs who want to destroy our country... If you see someone behaving violently please circle around this person and take him out of the protest.'

Dalia recognised that a significant amount of this strategy came from Gene Sharp. He had not 'inspired' the revolution as some of the US media would soon claim, but his ideas were informing the strategy and improving its organisation. 'By 2011 many of the young people in Egypt knew about the work in *From Dictatorship to Democracy* in one way or another.' Dalia told me, 'If they didn't receive training or read the book they have been told about the principles by their colleagues and friends. I remember I was calling his book my bible. It was in my bag all the time.'

Early in the morning of 25th January, protesters began assembling in different neighbourhoods of Cairo, as the Serbs had taught them, with the objective of stretching the security forces too thinly to be able to contain the march. Wael Ghonim had flown into Cairo to take part and his group was initially cordoned in by the police before they broke out and made for Tahrir Square. On the way, they were intercepted by more police, who beat the men at the front of the procession. Eventually the police were ordered to stand aside by their commander and the people flowed into Tahrir where the other marches were meeting. Across Cairo, the police had used beatings and teargas to no avail, the weight of numbers had defeated them. Now massing in Tahrir Square, the protesters released fireworks announcing their arrival and the crowd chanted, 'The people want to topple the regime.'

The security forces responded by blocking Facebook and Twitter and launching a co-ordinated assault on the protesters using tear gas, water cannon and rubber bullets to clear the square. Nonviolent discipline broke down and the protesters hurled rocks and broke up the pavements to throw back at the police. This handed an immediate PR coup to the regime and the state media, which broadcast footage of the protesters attacking the security forces. Commentators blamed the disturbances on foreign interference, but the images of the majority of protesters standing up nonviolently to armoured police officers wielding batons, electrified the country and went viral across Egypt and around the world. No sooner were the protesters flushed out of Tahrir, there were new calls for an even bigger protest after Friday prayers on the 28th January. They would call it the 'Day of Rage'.

Mohammed El Baradei met with the Muslim Brotherhood and other community leaders ahead of the 'Day of Rage' to discuss the growing revolution. The Muslim Botherhood agreed to officially support the movement, although they would not advertise their presence to reduce the possibility of factionalism. The Egyptian secret police had begun targeted arrests of protest leaders, among them Wael Ghonim, who hadn't been in the country long before Egyptian intelligence discovered his link with the Khaled Said Facebook page.

The following day, January 28th, after Friday prayers, the demonstrations mobilised again in local neighbourhoods before heading off for Tahrir Square, where they were met again by tear gas and a hail of rubber bullets. The government imposed a curfew in response and tanks were ordered onto the streets. In the places where the protest remained nonviolent, the soldiers often stood aside and apologised for the crackdown. The protesters passed by chanting, 'The people and the army are one hand'. But in other areas where young angry youths began throwing rocks and attempting to set fire to police stations, the police retaliated remorselessly, firing live rounds and causing many deaths.

Aaron Pina, a US Foreign Service officer studying in Cairo, was one of those marching to Tahrir that day. Pina was a desk officer at the US Bureau of Intelligence and Research (INR), a longstanding, but little known part of the US intelligence community which punched above its weight in Washington. A forerunner to the CIA, the INR is composed of a small team of analysts who monitor and collate intelligence reports from all US intelligence agencies. Aaron was officially only in Egypt as a language student and was not supposed to gather information, but on this march he began to notice things he found unusual. Protesters manning information booths along the route, activists giving out bags with a mini Koran, a surgical mask and instructions on how to counter teargas. There was also a call for doctors, lawyers and organisers to report to the booths to join the organisation.

'You're telling me in four days you got all this together? This is Egypt, you can't do anything in four days.' he told his friends. 'Clearly people who do not normally get together were getting together, putting aside political interests and doing something more'.

There were uniform signs, pre-agreed chants and they were prepared for forceful repression by the security forces. When the protest reached Tahrir bridge, Aaron felt the situation was becoming dangerous. He left the march fearing he would be killed in a clash with police and ran back through the streets of Cairo to his house where he found the internet had been cut. As soon as the connection came back, he decided to break protocol and report what he had seen back to the INR. 'The regime is going to collapse, there is no doubt in my mind. The secular opposition is going to take over. They are going to do it.' he told them.

Cutting the internet had stopped most people accessing Facebook and Twitter, but the use of social media had pushed the regime into a dilemma action which began to backfire. Even at the height of the protests, most of the streets of Egypt's cities were quiet, with large concentrations of people in very limited areas. Most of the population were not involved in the protests nor could they see them, but an outage in the internet was a tangible impact which affected a large percentage of the population. It was a sign that the regime appeared to be losing control. Many of the people who had been content sitting at home following the marches on social media were deprived of news and went out onto the streets to find out what was happening first hand.

Ahmed Rasheed told a BBC reporter that day, 'We have broken this fear barrier. People are taking to the streets, young people, all walks of life, educated, non-educated, higher social classes, lower social classes.'

Aaron Pina began packing up his possessions within hours of returning home and a day later he was negotiating the tank checkpoints on the way to the airport to be evacuated with his wife. As they approached the airport their driver, Abdullah, asked aloud why the airport was so busy.

Aaron snapped, 'I'll tell you why. You're having a fucking revolution that's why!' Abdullah turned to him calmly. 'We know Aaron, but if we stop to think about it we'll lose our nerve. We just have to keep pushing.'

Aaron was back at INR headquarters in Washington 24 hours later telling everyone who would listen in the State Department that Mubarak was finished. His bosses were not convinced. 'There would be no Orange Revolution on the Nile', those had been the Ambassador's words five years earlier, and they still believed that was true. 'Basically nobody believed me. I was saying you better dust off your transition plans, you better start talking to the Muslim Brotherhood, get a Twitter feed, start talking to people under 20 because these are going to be the new centres of power – military, Islamist and youth.'

Now back at the nexus of US intelligence-gathering, Aaron was able to see the intelligence reports coming out of the embassy in Cairo. 'I can't talk about content, but I would say that it was ill informed, short sighted, uncreative, wishful thinking. The embassy didn't have the best contacts because they had ignored Islamists, they ignored youth, they ignored bloggers and they were in a bubble talking to the same people, the elites, they had always talked to and were not leaving the embassy because of security concerns. They really didn't have eyes-on at all. The reporting was not what you would like or expect to see during a revolutionary moment like this.'

Now Mubarak's men began a counter attack. Many of the police took off their uniforms and formed civilian counter-protest groups which went onto the streets to fight with the protesters. YouTube videos showed men in civilian clothes on top of buildings around Tahrir Square mixing with uniformed police, hurling boulders down onto the crowd below. Protesters began to report being shot at by unidentified men in civilian clothes. By doing this, the regime could inflict terror on the protest in the guise of civilian unrest rather than a government crackdown – and with the streets still filled with the international media, it could be done in plain sight.

One of the most effective counter-revolutionary attacks by the government unfolded on the 2nd February using one of the most recognisable symbols of Egypt. Mohammed Presht, a 27-year-old tour guide, was enlisted by government officials to charge into Tahrir riding his favourite camel to attack the protest. Flanked on either side by men on horseback, the riders carried pictures glorifying Mubarak and beat protesters with long sticks. In a frenzy of anger, the crowd retaliated against the camel and began slashing at his legs and underbelly with sticks and knives. Mohammed was thrown to the ground and escaped in the melee, but had to watch his faithful camel which had served his family for years, beaten to death by the people.

The camel charge was a brilliant counter-revolutionary dilemma action deployed against the protesters. The regime provoked them into attacking the camel, one of the national symbols of Egypt, in front of the television cameras. It played to the government narrative that the people in the square were disloyal to Egypt, violent and chaotic. It was also a missed opportunity. A camel in the square, injured by the regime and nursed back to health by the protesters would have been a major propaganda coup for the democratic opposition. It was a powerful lesson of the advantage being lost when nonviolent discipline breaks down.

Wael Ghonim's disappearance in the midst of Egypt's uprising, as an employee of Google, created enormous media attention and protests from the US State Department. The media campaign forced the government to order his release on the 7th February and he emerged to the cameras looking pale and gaunt. Keen to smooth over the arrest, government officials took Wael to meet Dr Hossam Badrawy, a ruling party moderate whom Mubarak had appointed Secretary General of the party a few days previously. Badrawy greeted Wael like an old friend and passed on his well wishes from his own daughter who had been inspired by the Khaled Said Facebook page to go to Tahrir Square. This small signal to Wael was critical. Just like Serbia, the admission that children of ruling party politicians were in the square meant that ordering a violent crackdown on the protest would have been fraught with danger for the regime's own people. At his first sit down interview after his release, Wael broke down in tears and wept throughout. He was not an ordinary Egyptian but he was emotional, relatable and the same age as the disconcerted youth of the country. His eloquent description of his treatment while in detention gave a new face to the abuses that the masses could not. The interview went viral in Egypt and around the world, drawing thousands more into the streets.

While the occupation of Tahrir was an impressive symbolic act, on its own it was no threat to the government. The real power of the regime began to erode on the 9th February when 20,000 factory workers refused to work, fuelling a nationwide labour union strike. The tourism industry, which provided 11% of the country's GDP and employed a significant workforce, was also being throttled by the uprising. Only the Red Sea beach resorts were operating close to their normal capacity.

The Supreme Council of the Armed Forces (SCAF) released its first statement the day after the strike, telling the protesters that the army was, 'in affirmation and support for the legitimate demands of the people', and was in, 'continuous session to consider what procedures and measures that may be taken to protect the nation'.

SCAF made clear that Mubarak was not present in its meeting, indicating that the army was now operating independently from its Commander in Chief. General Sami Hafez Anan, the Chief of Staff of the Egyptian military, was met with roars of applause when he was driven into Tahrir Square to tell the protesters that their demands would soon be met. The industrial base of the country was idle, the people were in the streets and now the army was not responding to government orders.

When Mubarak's speech came it was not what was expected. A hush fell over Tahrir as the protesters watched the big screens. Instead of the resignation they expected, Mubarak attempted a fudge where he would transfer authority to Vice President Omar Suleiman, but remain President. The crowds were enraged. Mohamed ElBaradei, issued an unequivocal message to the army on Twitter and through the international media. 'I ask the army to intervene immediately to save Egypt. The credibility of the army is being put to the test.'

After just two more days of pressure, on the 11th February, Vice President Suleiman made a live TV address to announce that Mubarak was waiving his presidential powers and handing over responsibility for the running of the state to the army.

'In the name of God the merciful, the compassionate, citizens, during these very difficult circumstances Egypt is going through, President Hosni Mubarak has decided to step down from the office of president of the republic and has charged the Supreme Council of the Armed Forces to administer the affairs of the country. May God help everybody.'

Protests in cities all over Egypt erupted into scenes of euphoria. In Tahrir Square, people mounted the tanks with the help of the soldiers and drove victory laps waving Egyptian flags under fireworks streaking overhead. As the announcement was being made, Mubarak was already on his way to exile at his beach resort home in Sharm El-Sheikh.

Ahmed Maher was walking back to Tahrir Square past a café with its TV blaring loudly when he realised Mubarak's resignation was being announced live on air. 'I went mad with joy when I heard the speech. I sat crying. At last! At last! The dream we've had for years, what we've endured for it.' He ran into the square shouting. Thousands of people were crying, screaming, dancing and singing. It was a historic moment – he stood, watching the people celebrate, in utter disbelief. 'Is this really possible?' he asked himself.

Maher's assessment of the role of April 6th in the revolution was modest. 'In any society there is a small group of people who will lead the charge and make the first push and try to make the rest of society follow. So the revolution was inevitable, it was going to happen one day. What April 6th did was act as a catalyst for political change by bringing in different tools, ideas and tactics.'

'What is it that made the army support us in the end? The army, at the end of the day, comes from the people. Those in the army are part of the people, and the army has an important national role. Perhaps the role of the police was more to do with rigging elections and protecting the corrupt. They were keen to protect themselves and ensure their survival'.

On 16th February 2011, the *New York Times* journalist, Sheryl Gay Stolberg, published a front page article under the headline, 'Shy U.S intellectual created Playbook Used in Revolution'. She described how Gene had been an inspiration for the Egyptian revolutionaries. Thousands of people Googled Gene Sharp and found the elderly Albert Einstein Institution website, now 10 years old, struggling to load under the weight of the hits it was receiving. The world's media, desperate to understand one of the biggest political events of the past decade, began descending on Cottage Street to try and understand Gene's role in the revolution. Jamila was working 18-hour days, with little time for food or sleep, just to keep up with the interview requests. For weeks, the only people she saw outside the office were the guys who manned the toll booth on the Callahan Tunnel from East Boston into the city.

In every interview Gene gave, he played down his influence and gave all the credit to the Egyptian people, but the interpretation of the *New York Times* piece was causing anger among Egyptians. Stolberg had written that he had 'inspired' the uprising, when really his work had only inspired the strategy and the nonviolent methods available to achieve it. It was a subtle but fundamental difference, lost on the internet.

One Egyptian blogger started a Twitter hashtag '#GeneSharpTaughtMe', to mock the idea of his influence. 'I was happy all my life under Mubarak, but suddenly #GeneSharpTaughtMe I must rebel', '#GeneSharpTaughtMe how to grow and eat garlic and breathe in my enemies faces so they will faint.' '#GeneSharpTaughtMe that the West always wants to be sure that white men get credit for all the great things that happen.'

A couple of months later, on Friday April 29th 2011, Ahmed Maher and Ahmed Rasheed from April 6th arrived from Egypt to speak at the Massachusetts Institute of Technology (MIT) Media Lab in Cambridge as part of a US speaking tour. Jamila and I sat in the front row watching as they spoke about the conditions in Egypt and the tactics they had used to overthrow Mubarak. When they finished, people lined up at microphones to take turns to ask questions. Just a few minutes into the Q&A, a middle aged academic with a white beard in a polo shirt took the microphone, 'Can you comment on whether you used the work of Gene Sharp during the revolution?' he asked Ahmed Maher. The room hummed with the approval of the question – everyone wanted to know if the rumours about their fellow Bostonian's influence was true.

'We used many authors. We did read Gene Sharp's books but when we contacted him he said he would not help us because it was against the interests of the US government' Maher replied.

Jamila looked aghast at the statement, 'What is he talking about?' The event broke up and the Egyptians were quickly besieged by members of the audience at the front of the hall. In the melee, Jamila spotted Ahmed Rasheed heading for a side door and intercepted him.

'I work with Gene Sharp and I need to talk to you about what Ahmed just said in there. Our work is a generic analysis... we don't say, "yes we'll help you, but not you", we help everyone – but our help isn't giving instructions, it's not to give advice, it's to provide things that you, apparently, did use. What you said could be very harmful to our work.'

Rasheed stood with his head hung low looking nervously at the floor with his arms wrapped around his body, as if being scolded by an elder sister.

'We translated his books and we printed them in Egypt. We learned from it many times, so there is no problem', he replied, barely raising his eyes to meet her.

'Well there is a problem if you're saying these things' she scolded him.

Rasheed began to complain bitterly about the articles which were now expounding the various democracy promotion efforts of the US in Egypt. 'It confuses the Egyptian people, they are thinking right now that the revolution in Egypt happened because of the support of America! No! We want them to stop saying these kinds of words because we need the people in Egypt to complete the revolution. We want to make it very clear that the Egyptian people did the revolution not somebody else.'

The dilemma of the Egyptians was obvious. The constant references to Gene were playing into the hands of former regime elements who wanted to paint the revolution as an un-Egyptian, US conspiracy. Where once Gene's work had been an asset to the revolution, now it was their Achilles heel, something to be denied, covered up and now actively discredited.

Jamila was frustrated. Among the hundreds of emails she fought to answer every week, one might just have been from these Egyptians. Had she dropped the ball, or was this deliberate misinformation to create distance between the revolution and US influence?

Gene was being attacked from all directions, Egyptian bloggers were mocking him on the internet and the activists who had actually used his work were now touring the US actively damaging him. Jamila feared for the future. If activists used the work but then denied it because it damaged their reputation, then future organisers would never learn about the writings. The Lithuanians, the Serbs and the Ukrainians had all given Gene's work some credit, but in the new revolutions was the work now a liability? The re-casting of the Egyptian revolution as unplanned and spontaneous could be disastrous for movements which followed.

Letter to a Sleepless Syrian

The first beat of the butterfly's wings that set Syria alight and sent millions of refugees on a desperate journey across Europe, came in the form of a small group of children writing anti-government graffiti in the town of Dera'a. 'It's your turn, Dr. Bashar al-Assad' they wrote. Atef Najib, the corrupt cousin of President Bashar Assad was the local Political Security Chief and gave orders to hunt down the children. Najib's men tortured them by electrocution and removed their nails with pliers.

Distressed parents rushed to the prison where they heard their children were being held, but the police just shouted insults, telling their mothers to go home and make new children to replace them. If their husbands didn't know how to do it the police would show them how. In a place where tribal respect was paramount, these insults sent the community into spontaneous, unplanned revolt.

Just like the death of Mohamed Bouazizi in Tunisia, Khaled Said in Egypt, and Hu Yaobang in China, the Syrian uprising was triggered by an event which could not have been predicted – yet there were a handful of Syrians who might have been able to control the revolution and avoid the descent into war which hollowed the country of its people. Years before the Arab Spring, just like Iran and Egypt, a small group of activists in Syria were already preparing for a nonviolent revolution.

In 2006, Ausama Monajed was a 26-year-old economics graduate who had lived in the UK for barely a year after fleeing the Syrian secret police, who were pursuing him for protest activities against the regime. In his spare time Ausama lobbied for international attention on Syrian government human rights abuses, putting forward his analysis to anyone who would listen that the country was a tinderbox ready to blow at any moment.

The timing worked in Ausama's favour. The Iran Syria Operations Group (ISOG) born out of the Bush administration's Freedom Agenda was just getting established and State Department officials were on the lookout for Syrian nationals who could assist them. Ausama was invited to Washington DC to meet Elliott Abrams, the man President Bush had just appointed Deputy National Security Adviser for Global Democracy Strategy. Abrams introduced Ausama to an organisation called the Middle East Partnership Initiative (MEPI) which had been created in 2002 to channel money into promoting democratic change in the Middle East.

MEPI was led by Scott Carpenter, the US official who had worked on Serbia with Otpor and the Iran program with David Denehy. MEPI would release a budget of more than $12m over the next ten years for a range of activities to help Syrian dissidents topple the Assad regime nonviolently. Ausama was encouraged to put forward ideas on how that cash could be spent.

With the possibility of some serious funding from the US government, Ausama returned to the UK to produce a plan of action and ordered all the books and films that might help in the struggle. The first of those was *From Dictatorship to Democracy*, recommended by one of his Washington contacts. After reading just a few pages on a train journey to London he was hooked. 'It was as if I was reading an exact description of Syria, as if this had been written for us', he told me. The hours passed faster on this journey than any other and his deep concentration was only broken by the guard informing him that the train had arrived some time ago. He looked up to find the carriage empty around him.

After reading *From Dictatorship to Democracy* and learning how the Serbs had been trained in Gene Sharp's work, he began to seek out and recruit a number of Syrians who would agree to the risky process of leaving Syria to be trained in nonviolent action. The funding for this programme came from MEPI, and was delivered through a cutout organisation called the Aspen Institute which would distance the US government from the activities. On 5th April 2007, an email arrived at Cottage Street from the Aspen Institute requesting Gene and Jamila give a training workshop on nonviolent struggle for a group of Syrians. The training was to take place over a number of days together with the Serbs from CANVAS and a group of media specialists.

Gene was immediately suspicious of the Aspen Institute. He sent back a request for more information and a long list of questions. He asked, 'Why is Aspen to introduce the strategy to US and EU officials and not others?' 'The group appears to be heavy with businessmen, what significance?' But what concerned him most was that the Serbs were being given more time to teach tactics than his fundamental lessons on formulating a grand strategy.

He insisted that without diligent reading of more than 700 pages of his work, the trainees would not be taking the task seriously. The tense exchange of emails over the next few months meant that the initial trainings were carried out without his input.

The first training course was considered so secret that it couldn't be carried out at a European hotel which might easily be monitored. Officials from the Aspen Institute arranged the use of Stauffenberg Castle, close to the German-Czech border. The castle was still in the ownership of the descendants of Claus Von Stauffenberg, the aristocrat, army colonel and secret leader of the German resistance who had attempted to assassinate Hitler with a briefcase bomb in 1944. The operation, codenamed 'Valkyrie', had failed to kill Hitler and Von Stauffenberg was soon discovered and sentenced to death by firing squad. Now his castle would be one of the first incubators of the Syrian revolution.

Seven potential leaders recruited by Ausama were taken out of Syria with a range of cover stories on their visas. They trained in identifying the pillars of support, creating an alternative media network and countering regime surveillance. In the evenings they relaxed in their palatial surroundings and dined on wild boar hunted from the Stauffeberg estate by men who rode horses and wore traditional green feathered hats.

Months later, in June 2008, a select few of those trainees along with Ausama were brought to meet Gene in East Boston for two days of talks on strategic planning. In his letters Gene describes the preparations for this meeting as the 'most serious undertaking the Albert Einstein has engaged in in recent years'. Jamila was left with no doubt by the group that the aim was not 'behaviour modification' of the Syrian regime as some diplomats would call it, but serious planning for the nonviolent overthrow of President Bashar al-Assad.

As Ausama became more prominent in the US-backed movement against the Syrian government, an invitation arrived from Elliott Abrams to meet President Bush and Secretary of State Condoleezza Rice at a 'dissidents' lunch' in New York. At the event on Governors Island, a former US army command centre, Bush told the small group of international activists, 'We believe there's an Almighty, and a gift of that Almighty to every man, woman and child is freedom. Here in America, we have an obligation to help others realise the blessings of liberty.'

Ausama, sat to the right of the president, began to count as Bush quoted the Bible no less than eight times during lunch. Even for a Syrian who wanted to rid his country of an oppressive government, the President's motivation for spreading democracy appeared uncomfortably close to a religious crusade.

US diplomatic cables released by Wikileaks reveal that in 2008/9 both the US Department for Human Rights and Labour (DRL) and MEPI were clearly targeting funds at the Syrian regime's pillars of support – a mirror image of the Iran program strategy that David Denehy had structured around Gene's work in Iran.

The DRL also funded a project by Freedom House to conduct workshops for a select group of Syrian activists on 'strategic non-violence and civic mobilization' – they paid for the American Bar Association to carry out legal education programmes in Damascus and for the American University in Damascus to research Syrian tribes and civil society. Sheikhs from six different tribes were taken to Beirut for interviews and training. The news agency Internews was commissioned to run media youth camps for university-age Syrians in Amman and Damascus. This was all underpinned by a financial assistance program to provide payments to the families of imprisoned activists and striking workers.

One of the biggest grant proposals championed by Ausama was to build an alternative media in Syria with a new TV channel at its heart, to counter the propaganda of the state TV. This request was quickly approved and granted an initial $2million. It launched in April 2009 as 'Barada TV' from a base in Vauxhall, South London.

Just as the Syria programme was ramping up, Barack Obama was sworn in as the 42nd President of the United States. Along with the Iran programme, the new team at the State Department under Secretary of State Hillary Clinton was discovering the true extent of the Syria democracy programme they had inherited. Bush's 'Freedom Agenda' directed from Washington had created considerable frustration in the US embassies around the world where the money was being spent. The task of the diplomats at US Embassies was to build relationships, but their meetings were increasingly derailed by protests from host governments about 'regime change funding'.

The Bush administration's solution to this problem had been to put distance between the embassies and Freedom Agenda projects by allowing local diplomats to credibly deny that they were responsible for the spending. In truth the embassies were still providing intelligence on where it was spent and oversight of grantees.

Some professional diplomats now exerted pressure on Clinton's new team at State to kill off the Freedom Agenda and its negative impact on their conventional diplomatic operations. On 28th April 2009, three months after Obama's inauguration, Wikileaks cables show the transition from Bush's aggressive programme of active democracy promotion to a more nuanced Obama/Clinton posture. Maura Connelly the chargé d'affaires at the US Embassy in Damascus issued a cable classified 'Secret' stating:

'Both MEPI and DRL fund projects on which Post [The US Embassy in Damascus] has varying degrees of visibility. Some programs may be perceived, were they made public, as an attempt to undermine the Assad regime...with the apparent collapse of the primary Syrian external opposition organization, one thing appears increasingly clear: U.S. policy may aim less at fostering "regime change" and more toward encouraging "behaviour reform".'

It's clear from documents released by Wikileaks, the Albert Einstein Institution archive and interviews with individuals involved, that a US-sponsored influence operation was certainly in action against the Syrian government from 2006 onwards. However, it is wrong to assume that all activities were directed by the US or that this effort could have been in any way successful without the willing collaboration of a significant part of the population. There were many democracy activists who discovered Gene's work on their own and were unaware of any western programme to bring democracy to their country.

It was just five days after President Hosni Mubarak's resignation when the group of schoolboys in Daraa sprayed the slogans on the wall by their school. The manhunt, or boyhunt as it turned out, was carried out with the same fervour as any counter-terror operation. The boys were rounded up, tortured until they gave up the names of more of their friends, who were rounded up too. The local authorities could have calmed the situation, but their brutality helped turn a daring school prank into a catastrophic uprising which would endure longer than the Second World War.

It's possible that this trigger incident could have happened almost anywhere in Syria. In late January 2011, a man had already set himself on fire in the town of Hasakeh, emulating Mohamed Bouazzizi in Tunisia. There were protests outside various embassies in support of the Arab uprisings and a number of local issues across the country, from unemployment to lack of education and availability of clean water, made the country febrile for change. On 15th March protesters assembled in Damascus demanding political reforms and the release of political prisoners. The police opened fire and at least six were detained. Five days later, protesters burned down a Baath party headquarters and other government buildings, a demonstration of the early spontaneous and undisciplined first steps of the uprising.

Unlike the Egyptians, the Syrians were not prepared for a nonviolent revolution. They lacked the experience of smaller campaigns like those run by Kefaya and April 6th. The majority of the people Ausama and the Serbs had trained at Stauffenberg Castle and in East Boston had failed to pass on their knowledge and instead became politicians and power brokers, squandering their training. The understanding of how nonviolent action really worked was still barely known among the population.

When the Egyptians went onto the streets demanding change and Mubarak fell two weeks later on 11th February, the Syrians could have been forgiven for thinking that the protests they saw on the TV news were all it took for success. This was the 'CNN effect' which Srdja so often warned his trainees about. Aspiring activists watching a revolution in another country on TV only saw the tip of the iceberg. It created the impression they could bring down a government in two weeks just by protesting, and meant they didn't believe they had to plan a strategy or prepare for a long term struggle. 'What people didn't realise was that the group of Egyptian revolutionaries given training by CANVAS in Belgrade had spent two years winning small victories, building coalitions and branding their movement before they undertook their Tahrir Square action', Srdja wrote later. 'Unfortunately the Syrians just dove right in'.

One of the influencers attempting to guide a revolution in Syria was Mohammed Alaa Ghanem, an academic from Damascus University who had won a Fulbright scholarship to study in the US. In 2010 he arrived at the Best Western hotel in Charlotte, North Carolina, threw his luggage in a corner and immediately opened his laptop to start his research on the Assad regime. He'd been looking forward to this moment for years. For the first time in his life he could research his own government without fear of regime spies monitoring his internet activity.

Mohammed studied conflict resolution and peace building and among the course materials were some of Gene's books. Just five months after arriving in the US, he watched the first reports on the Arab Spring from his basement apartment. Monitoring developments online he noticed the appearance of a new Facebook page calling all Syrians to take to the streets and demand reform. This would become the main page for organising the nonviolent movement throughout 2011, gaining over a million followers who logged on looking for news and guidance. Mohammed made contact with the administrators of the page and was quickly recruited as an associate editor and then strategy advisor. The strategy that Mohammed brought with him was taken directly from Gene Sharp's books.

'Brimming with ideas inspired by Gene Sharp and others we put pen to paper and before too long the page was rolling out a series of successive nationwide nonviolent campaigns to target the regime's main pillars of support', he wrote in a diary entry.

The first campaign was to undermine Assad's legitimacy to rule with a campaign called 'Bashar Al Assad is no longer my president and his government doesn't represent me'. 'We introduced the concept of representation. And it caught on *fire*. Like, to the extent that it almost backfired, because now Syrians are like, you don't speak for me, you don't represent me', Mohammed told me, 'Then we launched a campaign called the Syrian National Council represents me. So we're taking legitimacy away from the regime and granting it to someone else. The slogans that we picked were the main slogans on Fridays, when everyone took to the streets and you had banners made with the same slogans. We got Syrians to actually practice voting on what slogan and what campaign they want launched on what date.'

The next pillar was the military power of Assad. 'We called for the first time ever, for defections. And we were successful. We launched a campaign called, "I will not pay for the bullets that are killing me". The campaign resulted in a number of defections mostly from the lower ranks but among them were a few majors, colonels and generals. The highest ranking defector was Prime Minister Riyad Farid Hijab. The defections never penetrated the inner circle of the Assad regime, but they may have shaken Assad's confidence in the wider army because he began to rely on the Fourth Armoured Mechanised Division led by his brother, Maher al-Assad, considered the most loyal unit in the Syrian armed forces.

The next pillar to be targeted was the Syrian business community. The democratic opposition told business owners that if they cooperated with Assad's forces they were collaborating in the genocide of the people. They worked with businessmen in the Damascus old bazaar to list the executives, companies and brands that were believed to be financing the crackdown or had a deep alliance with regime. A campaign was then launched calling on Syrians to boycott those products. The action was so effective that some companies contacted the Facebook page administrators to plead to be taken off the list.

While initially the protesters only called for increased democratic freedoms, by the beginning of April the rising death toll of protesters had turned this into a demand for the resignation of Assad. On the April 8th there were demonstrations in ten cities and less than a month later that had doubled. The organisation of the revolution gradually began to catch up with the events. The first street protests helped seed the movement across the country. People were drawn in to the big cities like Damascus for demonstrations where they met other leaders and activists from towns across the country.

These new connections kickstarted the establishment of Local Coordination Committees or 'LCCs', as they would become known. The LCCs were groups of young, media literate activists, often English-speaking journalists, who knew how to organise demonstrations, use cameras and avoid internet censorship to get pictures out of the country and onto social media. The LCCs also managed to take on parallel government functions as the government withdrew services from areas taking part in the uprising, providing everything from field hospitals to traffic wardens. The LCCs became the conduit by which nonviolent actions were planned and executed, receiving ideas and tactics through the Facebook page that Mohammed was now administering.

Omar Edelbi was one of the founders of the LCCs. He told Al Akhbar news website, 'It was the first revolutionary body with a clear structure, organised action and field work. In addition to our media work, we were preparing slogans and banners and organising demonstrations and organising the requirements of the demonstrations, whether on the technical level of banners and slogans, in addition to our media work'. The organisational structure was formed into an executive office in charge of political activities, a media office to relay news, documents and video and a relief office which undertook humanitarian actions across the country.

Reports of human rights abuses were sent to a centralised Violations Documentation Centre. As the number of local committees expanded, a central membership office attempted to stop infiltration by the Syrian government, agents provocateurs or people who might advocate for violence.

The membership office 'has to verify this person's and this group's belief in peaceful revolution, non-violence, rejection of sectarianism and civil war,' Edelbi continued. 'We are very sensitive to these issues. These principles cannot be compromised.'

Western funds now paid for Srdja and his trainers from CANVAS to find a way of adapting their experiences to Syria, where a nonviolent movement had already begun. By now the Serbs were on the radar among the world's authoritarian regimes and any political activist with a Serbian entry stamp in their passport provided a slam dunk of guilt for security agents. Instead, they settled on a rough looking Mediterranean holiday resort with a hotel to accommodate 17 trainees. In a place where British holidaymakers were only interested in getting as drunk and sunburned as possible, it was an easy place to go unnoticed.

With Syria in a state of open revolt and the security services on high alert for leaders of the movement, a smuggler had to be employed to get the trainees out. Some had managed to get permits that allowed them to leave overland into Turkey and others were booked on flights with fake names and multiple stops in other countries to confuse anyone trying to track their movements. There should have been 20 participants, but three didn't make it – one was killed by the regime just a couple of days before leaving, another was arrested and the third became too scared after suspecting he was under surveillance.

When they were assembled Slobo came to the front of the class and compared fighting Assad with violence to playing David Beckham at football. 'You don't want to meet him on the soccer field. You want to play him at chess. That's where you can win.'

Soon, actions directly out of the Otpor playbook were being carried out on the streets. The fountains around Damascus were filled with red food colouring so that they flowed with what looked like blood. In another stunt, thousands of ping pong balls inscribed with slogans like 'enough' and 'freedom' rolled through the streets. The police were forced to respond immediately and chase the tiny balls around making them look ridiculous. Tiny battery-powered speakers which played revolutionary songs like 'Assad is a pig' were hidden in garbage bins, forcing the police to rifle through handfuls of foul smelling trash to find them. Flowers were put on the spots where fallen heroes fell, protesters were told how to march and clean the streets to demonstrate they could look after the people better than the regime.

For the political jujitsu to be effective, to encourage defections and win the support of the international community, the situation on the ground in Syria had to remain visible to the world. The vast quantity of mobile phone video and reports of government abuses were curated by the LCC media office, which produced a daily electronic newspaper. 'Syria Today' summarised events inside the country for Syrians and was translated into English for the international media and for posting to Facebook pages and international news websites.

US and EU government funding was paying to smuggle hundreds of digital cameras and satellite modems into the country. These were used by activists to film abuses by the regime along with the latest protests by the resistance. When footage of regime brutalities was obtained, it was uploaded to YouTube and often picked up by international networks like Al Jazeera. This became vital to show the regime that their atrocities would be seen by the world.

From their base in London, Barada TV began showing the YouTube videos of the protests across its satellite network. They were the first to air photographs of the tortured body of a 13-year-old boy from Daraa taken by his parents. The following day, news networks across the Middle East rebroadcast the story, highlighting Barada as an important source of news from the revolution. In many ways this was a revolution played out online, but broadcasting the online videos on traditional satellite tv meant the pictures were seen by Syrians even when their internet was cut.

Barada TV, steered by Ausama and others who had read Gene's books, explained the importance of nonviolent discipline and gave guidance on everything from evading internet censorship, to filming demonstrations safely. As the country became more dangerous and international journalists were pulled out, the burgeoning independent Syrian media became the best source of information. Ausama sat at the junction of information flowing in and out of Syria. He monitored the videos and sent important developments on to trusted journalists, often appearing on the international news networks himself to offer analysis.

At the height of the uprising, just a month after the start of the protests in 2011, Ausama offered to let me spend a day filming with him for my documentary on Gene's work. He arrived at my flat in south west London in a smart BMW wearing a neatly cut suit, dark Ray-ban sunglasses and a big smile. We wound our way up the six flights of stairs to my attic flat in a tall victorian house in Twickenham and he began to unpack his computers. After switching on the television in the corner of the living room and connecting to my internet, hundreds of emails began cascading into his inbox. He triaged them quickly, responding first to urgent requests from some of the news channels. We watched as the camera phone footage he had sent to CNN began to play out on the TV.

There was no doubt in Ausama's mind that Gene's work was having a fundamental impact on the strategy being used on the ground. 'Gene Sharp's tactics and theories are being practiced on the streets of Syria as we speak now.' He told me excitedly. 'The dynamics that the regime is facing in Syria is what Gene Sharp spoke about ... and that was what empowered people and made them believe more in nonviolent struggle – that this is going to work, and it *is* working!'

President Assad now found himself facing a largely nonviolent uprising which was managing to unite different communities around a common goal of toppling his government. The opposition was winning the media war, the international community was turning against him and his own soldiers, faced with the prospect of potentially shooting members of their own families, had started to defect. Meanwhile, the political jujitsu effect of committing atrocities against civilians in front of a generation of smart phone users only inflamed the uprising – but Assad didn't appear to care.

The Muslim Brotherhood had risen up against Hafez al-Assad, Bashar's father, in the town of Hama, in 1982 and the protesters had been shown no mercy. The town was besieged and almost completely destroyed by government bombardments. Some estimates on the numbers of dead ranged between 20,000 to 40,000. It was described as one of the single deadliest acts by any Arab government against its own people in the modern Middle East. The Muslim Brotherhood were driven out of Syria and never rose up again. Extreme force had won the Assad family another 30 years of unchallenged power and now Bashar al-Assad began to follow the example of his father.

Sunni army units were rotated out of Sunni areas and replaced with Alawite units closest to the regime who were more likely to fire upon civilians. Snipers were placed behind the regular soldiers with orders to shoot them if they didn't fire when ordered, or if they attempted to defect. An industrial scale of arrests to net protest leaders was employed to disrupt the organisation of the opposition. Arrested LCC members were tortured until they gave up passwords for social media accounts which could be used to round up their networks. The state media replayed the message time and again on TV and radio that the army wasn't killing protesters but fighting 'foreign inspired terrorists'.

Activists believed the regime was deliberately trying to turn the uprising into an armed insurrection which they could fight more easily with their military. Violent criminals were released from jails and tasked with creating splits in the democracy movement and spreading sectarian hatred. Many would join what became known as the dreaded 'Shabeeha', meaning 'ghosts', who drove around cities committing rape and murder upon Alawites, while posing as Sunnis, and then did the same in Sunni areas, leaving false clues that the murders had been carried out by Alawites. The use of the Shabeeha – men with no uniforms, attacking nonviolent protesters was a lesson learned by governments in Iran, Russia and throughout the Arab Spring. In an age where little could be done to stop videos of killings appearing on YouTube, the Shabeeha offered a mask of deniability to the state.

Horror tactics were used against the neighbourhoods involved in the protests. Extreme torture was inflicted upon both adults and children. Bodies were often returned to family and loved ones with horrific injuries. The homes of female protesters were raided and they were raped in front of their husbands and mothers. The effect was to seed utter hatred among the population – a hatred that many families of victims could only see being avenged with violent retribution.

The regime also made sure that symbolic centres of resistance like a Syrian version of Tahrir or Tiananmen Square, were immediately and violently swept away. When the people of Homs attempted to create their own camp in the centre of town, the response was swift and brutal. After the funerals of several protesters on 19th April, a peaceful march of thousands of mourners followed the dead through the city to the burial ground. As they passed through the city's Christian district, people sprinkled rice down on them from their apartments in solidarity.

After the burials, the chants began, 'to the clock! to the clock!' and the crowd began to wind its way to the clock square. For hours people filled the square, clambering on the pedestal of the clock itself to give rousing speeches and call for freedom and the resignation of Assad. The protesters threw up makeshift security barriers at the entrances to the square and checked the new arrivals for weapons or signs of infiltration by the security forces or Shabeeha. They chanted all evening for peace and unity until the sun began to fall and people began arriving with tents and food to sustain them through the night.

The security forces saw a mirror of Tahrir Square unfolding in Homs, but unlike the Egyptian government, they wouldn't let it stand. News reached the protesters that Shabeeha cars were driving towards the square and the army's 4th division, commanded by Assad's brother, was preparing to strike.

If the opposition leaders that day had understood the lessons of Tiananmen, that holding geographic territory was futile in the face of military force, they might have evaporated back into the night to reconvene again unharmed, outmanoeuvring the regime forces. But instead, a majority, mostly men, stood their ground and readied their medical supplies. The Shabeeha silently encircled the square and at just before 2am those who had returned to their homes heard the sounds of gunfire and smelled the cordite as it drifted across the city. Dozens were reported dead, but the numbers were too difficult to confirm. The security forces removed the bodies and washed the blood off the streets.

This extreme repression forced the opposition to innovate in lower risk nonviolent methods. They formed flash protests, where people filled a street for just long enough for photos to be taken and then disappeared just as quickly. People were filmed from behind, holding signs behind their heads to prevent identification. In one case an employee of a telecoms company managed to leak thousands of telephone numbers of Syrians which were used in a 'robocall' campaign. The familiar voice of a famous Syrian soccer player or actor would be recorded, calling for people to join the revolution and remain nonviolent. A computer system was set up to call numbers all over Syria playing the message. Similar actions were achieved using text messages. These were all ways the movement could still transmit the effect of large scale symbolic protest while reducing their exposure to live fire.

The internet offered a lifeline to Syrians engaged in the struggle and although the regime attempted at various times to shut it down, it was impossible to deny legitimate access to Syrians loyal to Assad. The provision of software and equipment to keep besieged areas of Syria online was still something that Clinton's State Department felt it could provide and most LCCs managed to obtain satellite phones and software for encrypting mobile devices and laptops. Software which disguised the location of internet users was in widespread use to prevent detection and monitoring. Inside the communication hubs of the regime there were those who leaked information or enabled communications to continue.

The number and diversity of opposition organisations carrying out activities in Syria meant the requirement for professional coordination had become urgent. Just like the Palestinian 'Command', an organisation was set up consisting of a representative from each of the active local and national groups inside and outside Syria to discuss issues and coordinate actions, normally via a Skype conference call. They called it 'Freedom Days'.

It was obvious that more could be achieved if actions were staged throughout the week, so an online calendar was produced with each group plotting their activity on a particular day. For security reasons the precise details of the activity planned was not revealed, only for instance that an action was to take place in a certain area of Damascus on a particular afternoon. This allowed the movement's media teams to look out for news and videos from that group and location to make sure it was properly covered. National actions and solutions to particular issues were also discussed and coordinated through Freedom Days.

In April 2011, Ausama flew into Boston for a progress meeting with Gene – their first meeting since the trainings in 2007. I sat in the back office with Jamila listening to the conversation as Ausama told Gene about the Syrian soldiers who were beginning to defect. He wanted to know what those defecting soldiers should do. Should they protect the nonviolent protesters with their weapons or lay down their arms? Gene argued against fighting back with weapons – the use of violent force to protect civilians would only put them in the crossfire and decrease their power as a nonviolent movement. The soldiers, he argued, should lock away their weapons.

As they wrapped up the afternoon, Ausama asked Gene if he any final messages for the revolution. 'Don't ask for outside help!' Gene replied immediately, punching a finger into the air. 'If the US or NATO offers to come and help you, say no thank you! Medical supplies you can welcome, communications only if what is being said is under your control.' Ausama hugged Gene goodbye and headed to Washington for meetings with the White House and the National Security Council.

Ausama and the Syrian nonviolent movement had achieved some level of influence from outside the country, but they were not in control of what was happening inside. As more regime soldiers began to defect they started to shoot back, intending to protect the people in rebel areas. People began chanting for the fighters to defend the protests, but the power this gave the few men with guns began to tear the nonviolent movement apart.

The defectors formed the 'Free Syrian Army' and assumed command of the demonstrations, giving orders to the protesters. They soon began to take control of whole neighbourhoods and soon the neighbourhoods were sheltering the fighters – the people had fallen directly into the regime's trap. The protesters appeared to be firing back, justifying the

Assad government's claims that they were 'terrorists'. As Syrian soldiers fell dead, the number of defections reduced.

Many soldiers, even from the Alawite sect of Bashar Al Assad, found the idea of killing unarmed civilians abhorrent, but as soon as they encountered armed fighters who were firing on their colleagues, those civilians increasingly became legitimate targets.

Ausama and Mohammed Ghanem were aware of each other's online pseudonyms but had never met and they were not coordinating their activities. A few weeks after Ausama's trip to meet Gene in Boston, Mohammed also wrote to Gene for the first time about the defection issues. Fearing that the Albert Einstein Institution was being monitored, Mohammed created a false identity specifically to communicate with Gene. Like Ausama he was concerned about the defecting soldiers turning the revolution from a success into a disaster and asked Gene to write something for the Syrian nonviolent movement. He signed off his email as, 'The Sleepless Syrian'.

Gene wrote back on June 2nd 2011. With the nonviolent campaign in the balance he replied with an essay containing a series of warnings which predicted accurately the road to ruin the country would later take. He called it, 'Letter to a Sleepless Syrian'.

'The present unease of the troops in obeying orders is clear. Otherwise the regime would have no need to order immediate killing of disobeying soldiers. That is strong evidence that the reliability of the army is very shaky and possibly on the verge of collapse. That means that wise resistance actions are crucial to take the army away from the regime... The regime clearly is desperate. They may intend for their brutalities to enrage protesters so much that they resort to violence. The protesters should not be tricked into that. Significant protest violence would guarantee the army's loyalty and the defeat of the revolution.'

Gene also warned of the army defectors who were coming to the protesters offering them protection with weapons.

'This supposed major help can dramatically change the conflict so that the regime's still overwhelming superior military capacity will shape the course of the continuing conflict. Then, without major external military intervention, the dictatorship is likely to triumph. Inevitable major casualties are likely to vastly exceed even exceptionally high casualties in a nonviolent struggle conflict. The nonviolent resisters are likely to become irrelevant to shaping the future of their country.'

This letter was unlikely to have had any direct effect on ordinary citizens who were increasingly supportive of the military resistance, but the Local Coordinating Committees of Syria did read it. Mohammed launched a new Facebook page campaign targeting Syrian army soldiers thinking about defection. 'If you want to join us, leave your weapon and join us' it said. With the nonviolent campaign slipping away, the Syrian nonviolent movement issued a joint statement on the 29th August 2011, appealing to the people to stick with nonviolent action. They did so paraphrasing the key arguments which Gene had used in his 'Letter to a Sleepless Syrian'.

'While we understand the motivation to take up arms or call for military intervention, we specifically reject this position as we find it unacceptable politically, nationally, and ethically. Militarizing the revolution would minimize popular support and participation in the revolution. Moreover, militarization would undermine the gravity of the humanitarian catastrophe involved in a confrontation with the regime. Militarization would put the revolution in an arena where the regime has a distinct advantage, and would erode the moral superiority that has characterized the Revolution since its beginning.

Our Palestinian brothers are experienced in leading by example. They gained the support of the entire Palestinian community, as well as world sympathy, during the first intifada. The second intifada, which was militarized, lost public sympathy and participation. It is important to note that the Syrian regime and Israeli enemy used identical measures in the face of the two uprisings.

The objective of Syria's revolution is not limited to overthrowing the regime. The revolution also seeks to build a democratic system and national infrastructure that safeguards the freedom and dignity of the Syrian people. Moreover, the revolution is intended to ensure independence and unity of Syria, its people, and its society. We believe that the overthrow of the regime is the initial goal of the Revolution, but it is not an end in itself. The end goal is freedom for Syria and all Syrians. The method by which the regime is overthrown is an indication of what Syria will be like post-regime.

If we maintain our peaceful demonstrations, which include our cities, towns, and villages; and our men, women, and children, the possibility of democracy in our country is much greater. If an armed confrontation or international military intervention becomes a reality, it will be virtually impossible to establish a legitimate foundation for a proud future Syria.'

The unfolding situation in Libya was not helping the argument for maintaining nonviolent discipline in Syria. Libya had started off like Tunisia and Egypt, as a nonviolent uprising against Colonel Muammar Gaddafi, but as his regime had become more brutal, shooting protesters and threatening to wipe out the citizens of Benghazi 'like rats', NATO stepped in. A bombing campaign and military assistance to the rebels saw Gaddafi flee from his palace, only to be tracked down and killed in the street. In that brief period between the fall of Libya's dictator and the descent of the country into a living hell of tribal conflict, the prospect of NATO assistance to an armed Syrian opposition suddenly seemed a possibility. The 'Libya Model' was promoted by figures in the Syrian opposition who could not have predicted the chaos that was about to be unleashed in Libya or that there would be no political will to provide similar military support in Syria.

Radical Islamist groups like the Al-Nusra Front began recruiting from the growing pool of angry young men who had seen their loved ones killed and tortured by the regime and the Shabeeha. Most of these recruits would never have joined an extremist group in peacetime, but the armed groups offered protection and an opportunity to fight back. In March 2013 the Free Syrian Army composed of defected regime soldiers and a loose coalition of moderate Islamic groups briefly won military control of the city of Raqqa only to be driven out themselves by a new darker and deadlier force. The new group called themselves the Islamic State of Iraq and the Levant or more commonly, 'ISIS'. Although the remnants of the Syrian nonviolent movement and the LCCs would continue to carry out nonviolent actions against the Syrian regime and ISIS in the areas they controlled, it was clear that by the Spring of 2012, Syria was embroiled in an increasingly violent civil war between armed groups.

Some academics and foreign policy professionals argue that the Syrian case clearly demonstrates a failure of nonviolent action – but in reality it only confirmed that armed struggle is even worse. Far greater numbers of people died and were forced to flee after the transition to violent resistance than during the nonviolent phase.

In the end, the move to violence put control in the hands of foreign states fighting a proxy war against each other with the lives of ordinary Syrians, just as Gene had warned. All sides of this conflict, the Saudis supporting the rebels and the Russians and Iranians supporting the Assad regime feared a similar popular uprising in their own countries – all of them had an interest in defeating not just the opposition, but the idea of successful nonviolent struggle itself.

These authoritarian governments could now point to a country which had been utterly destroyed by a struggle which began nonviolently. Without learning the right lessons from this disaster, the spectre of Syria handed dictatorships a powerful defence in deterring their own population from ever embarking on a similar struggle.

Russia's Counter-Revolution

Within the Russian government, one man worried about the danger of a nonviolent revolution perhaps more than any other. Vladislav Surkov was a veteran Soviet Army officer, former intelligence operative and one of President Putin's closest advisors. Surkov and the Russian intelligence services were well aware of Gene Sharp's books – his work had featured in almost every nonviolent engagement of the past 20 years, from the defence of the Baltics in 1991, to the defeat of the hardline Moscow coup and the colour revolutions. In 2011, the Syrian uprising was threatening the Russian's strategically important naval base at Tartus on the Mediterranean. To the Kremlin this was just the latest in a long line of US operations using political warfare to degrade Russia's strategic position.

The fear could hardly be described as paranoid. In 2005, just months after the Orange revolution in Ukraine, the Russian opposition group Oborona, led by Oleg Kozlovsky, translated Gene's work into Russian and adopted the Otpor fist logo, now synonymous with US backed democracy movements. Oborona's message to the Kremlin was unmistakably clear; Serbia, Georgia, Ukraine – Russia was next.

Oborona was joined by another group, 'Drugaya Rossiya' (The Other Russia), founded by former chess world champion, Garry Kasparov. Millions of people around the world had tuned in to watch Kasparov's ill tempered showdown match with IBM's Deep Blue supercomputer in 1997 – the first time a computer would defeat a grand master. The match made him one of the most famous chess players in history, but in 2005 he announced that he had no more ambitions in chess. He would turn his attention instead to the internal political problems in Russia.

Kasparov also recognised the importance of Gene's work on strategy and organised the second known translation of *From Dictatorship to Democracy* in Russian. In all – four independent translations of *From Dictatorship to Democracy* appeared in the country, published by different organisations. When news was received that a fifth translation had been completed, Jamila had all five evaluated to determine which was the most accurate and then posted it on the Albert Einstein Institution website for free download.

The Kremlin soon realised what was happening and found out where the books were going to press. The FSB (the successor to the KGB) raided the printing house and an officer demanded that the machines be stopped, 'This book is a bomb', he told the workers there. Just days later, the manuscript was smuggled to a private press outside Moscow and the printing was restarted.

There was no official banning of the book and no known pressure to prevent its sale, but on 14th June 2005, two shops which had been selling the most copies burned down. Bilingua a well-known bookstore and café, went up in flames, destroying all of its copies. The fire was blamed on an electrical short circuit. Just a week later in Falanster, another bookshop selling similar opposition literature caught fire after a grenade or Molotov cocktail was thrown through the shop window. All of the books on the shelves were destroyed. Despite these events, Oborona had managed to print and distribute some 1500 copies.

For the Russian leadership who now controlled the Kremlin, the signs of US backed youth groups, growing in number was a threat that had to be met. Pushing for action was Gleb Pavlovsky a self styled 'political technologist' who had been sent in to Ukraine during the Orange Revolution in 2004 to try and ensure victory for Putin's candidate, Viktor Yanukovich. Pavlovsky's hotel had been surrounded by the Orange camp, but instead of changing location, he revelled in the mischief of it, making his way through the crowds of opposition activists every day disguised in an orange hat and scarf. 'We felt the regiments were massing somewhere close. They would be taking to the streets of Moscow,' He told the BBC. 'Our youth needs to master the techniques of constitutional action, required for street fighting. In the case of an attempted coup they need to know how to stop it.'

According to some reports, Vladislav Surkov became an avid reader of Gene Sharp's books. He concluded that to combat the growing threat of a nonviolent movement using Gene's work, a counter-revolutionary force needed to be created.

In February 2005, shortly after the Orange revolution, Surkov arrived in St Petersburg to meet with a collection of young Kremlin loyalists. His message to them was stark. Russia needed a new weapon against American imperialist forces who intended to incite revolution and make the country a colony of the United States.

A former soldier, Vasily Yakemenko, was charged with building a counter-revolutionary force built on a similar model to Otpor and PORA, but to act in defence of Putin's Kremlin'. They would be called 'Nashi' which meant 'ours' or 'our guys'.

This new group was radicalised with patriotism for Russia's glorious past and anti-western and anti-fascist sentiment. The leaders were called 'commissars' and the Nashi website was placed on a retro Soviet Union domain, nashi.su, instead of the normal .ru Russian suffix. The young activists could not be recruited with the promise of overthrowing a tyrant or winning civil liberties, so instead they were indoctrinated with nationalism, fear of a western takeover and paranoid visions of spies and liberal turncoats. The lure instead, was joining a special cadre of people whose loyalty would win them connections and jobs in the highest offices and boardrooms of the country. One piece of recruitment literature read:

'YOU. Do you want to realize your own project? Do you want to change the world around you? Do you want to influence the future of your country? Do you want that the world would remember you? Do you search your place in your life? You have a chance to change your life, influence the world politics, to become a new intellectual elite Our people are already in the Public Chamber, political state organs and in the biggest Russian companies. Are you worth the higher education in our university with the best teachers of the country? Are you worth a traineeship in the company you want, in Russia, or abroad? Are you worth realizing your own project? Prove it! Fill the form! Come to our team.'

The Russian authorities created a semi-permissive environment in which opposition groups were harassed, boxed in and denounced in the state media, but allowed to vent their criticism sparingly in order to create the pretence of free speech. It was clear though that those who stepped too far out of line were in danger.

Activists, Eduard Limonov, Mikhael Kasyanov and Gary Kasparov implemented a campaign of street protests they called, 'the dissenters marches' to draw attention to Russia's descent into authoritarianism. Now a new game began. Kasparov and Limonov were going into battle with Surkov, and they were all using the same playbook.

If Nashi was conceived in the Kremlin it was born on the banks of Lake Seliger, a protected nature reserve surrounded by beautiful Pine forest, 350km North West of Moscow. It was here that Vasily Yakemenko organised the lavishly funded annual Nashi camp. 'The support of the Kremlin makes it possible to speak with any businessman and get financial support. To refuse to finance our project is a manifestation of an unpatriotic position', Yakememko boasted. Young men and women from all over Russia were brought to Seliger to train as leaders who would return back to every corner of the country. It was exactly the model Otpor had used in Serbia.

They adopted the Nashi flag, a white cross on a red background, with which they adorned their t-shirts and tents. In the mornings they woke to old Soviet anthems being played through loudspeakers across the campsite, they sang traditional songs and took part in paramilitary training.

In July 2005 Nashi held an exercise called 'Maidan in Seliger' where an Orange revolution 'war game' was role-played inside the camp. The opposition was played by hundreds of members of another pro-Kremlin youth group which set up camp, hoisted banners, lit fires and played loud music all night replicating the scenes of the Orange revolution in Kiev. This episode provided a glimpse of the understanding that the Kremlin had developed about how an uprising had to be handled.

At a meeting before the exercise, Yakemenko briefed the Nashi commissars that only nonviolent means could be used to disperse the

Orange camp. They had to deny the opposition their political jujitsu moment – their Bouazizi, Khaled Said or Neda. A nonviolent uprising was best countered, if possible, by a nonviolent response. However, this small exercise was a warning on how difficult it would be to control the forces they had created. In the early morning, instead of acting according to instructions, the Nashi activists stormed the camp in a swift and brutal attack, destroying everything in their path.

In July 2007, a record number of young pro-Kremlin activists attended Nashi's third annual camp at Lake Seliger where they were given lectures about the latest internal threats to the state. Master-classes were given by political strategists like Gleb Pavlovsky where the US was portrayed as their number one enemy. Putin was shown in a video sitting on a small wooden chair in the woods lecturing students about America's lack of respect for Russia.

Nashi was just one part of an imbricate defence against colour revolution which began in the run up to the 2008 Russian presidential elections. The government pressured local authorities to deny official permits for demonstrations and lean on meeting venues to deny access to opposition groups or cancel their bookings at the last minute, leaving them disorganised and out in the cold.

On the eve of a protest, police would launch pre-emptive roundups of organisers, impose last minute restrictions on assembling in public and occasionally, to stop bystanders from joining the march. Shops along the route would be closed for 'cleaning'. When permissions were given for demonstrations they were often in limited areas and corralled by security forces from marching anywhere symbolic or too visible.

For those who persisted there was an onslaught of elite OMON riot police who inflicted kettling tactics and intimidation, making it difficult to bring a cross section of people, including the elderly and children onto the streets. OMON were a feared force, but many of them were educated in Gene's work and understood the dynamics of political jujitsu. In one interview with an OMON officer, Russian journalist, Mikhail Mikhin, asked about a rumour that 90% of the police were ready to join the 'insurgent masses'. The officer told Mikhin, 'If you're familiar with Gene

Sharp's book on how revolution is spread, this is not surprising in this situation.' 'He has a whole chapter on how to work with law enforcement officers. This is obvious: for the success of the revolution it is necessary to attract police officers to your side'.

This small aside, buried in a much longer article, provides a clue on how well the leadership of the security forces were educating their security personnel against the threat of a Gene Sharp inspired strategy.

After removing the leaders and whittling the opposition numbers down, the Kremlin could simply use hundreds of Nashi activists to fill the public spaces the protesters intended to occupy. Photographs and state television news footage would then show the opposition outnumbered by fanatical Putin supporters. Sometimes Nashi would even orchestrate a mass blood donation to prove how much more devoted they were to their country than the 'foreign-inspired' Orange agitators.

It was obvious to Kasparov, Oborona and members of the other opposition groups that they were facing a very well prepared and intelligent defence against their movement. It was no stretch to portray this as a game of chess, the moves thought out and then countered in turn. The Kremlin banned unauthorised assemblies of more than one person, so the opposition instituted solo standing protests carrying placards outside the homes or offices of government officials. The Kremlin responded in turn by sending groups of Nashi members to stand beside the lone protester, instantly turning it into an illegal assembly. The sole protester would be arrested and the Nashi activists would walk free.

Used in this way, Nashi activists gave the Kremlin a far greater range of counter revolutionary tools than the security forces alone could provide. When speeches by opposition leaders were being made, Nashi would drive a van loaded with powerful speakers close by and drown out their voices with rock music – something the police would never be able to do. Most importantly the group was taught the geography of Moscow and how to use the city's night buses to ensure that, in an emergency, they could occupy Red Square within hours.

The humorous Otpor-style stunts were also turned back against the democratic opposition. In 2008, while Garry Kasparov was addressing a 700 strong group of anti-Putin activists, a pro-Kremlin youth group launched a radio-controlled flying penis towards him on the stage. The drone buzzed round his head for long enough to derail the event, and result in a viral YouTube video, before it was swatted out of the air by security. 'I think we have to be thankful for the opposition's demonstration of the level of discourse we need to anticipate', Kasparov retorted.

When two anti-Kremlin satirists, Arseny Bobrovsky and Katya Romanovskaya, began enjoying national press attention after being exposed as the duo behind a hugely popular Kremlin spoof Twitter account, the joke was replayed on them. They woke up one morning after returning from a foreign trip to find their BMW with a 200lb wooden penis strapped to its bonnet.

Despite these games of high wit between the two sides, elements within Nashi were also used as a blunt instrument. Opposition activists frequently reported street muggings and unprovoked attacks while walking home at night. Homes would be broken into, windows smashed and cars vandalised. It was difficult to tell whether these incidents were specifically directed or the spontaneous product of the hate indoctrinations at Camp Seliga and the state media denunciations of the liberal and fascist 'enemies of the state'.

An information war was waged portraying the opposition as traitors and agents of foreign imperialists. During the election campaign Putin angrily denounced them as those who 'lurk like jackals around foreign embassies'. Stop lists were issued to prevent television appearances by their leaders. TV presenter Aleksei Sushkov hammered the line that the protesters were agents of an American project to foment an Orange revolution.

Other commentators even compared the opposition to Al Qaeda. 'One must remember', said Surkov, 'that revolution is above all the squandering of the people, it is above all devastation, it is above all destruction.' To prevent this disaster the government was committed to 'make sure that there would be no revolution'.

The spectre of a Gene Sharp-inspired US assault on Russia made its way into the national conversation. During a Russian political talk show on the question of whether the Moscow street protests would lead to a rerun of the 1917 Russian Revolution [the overthrow of Tsar Nicholas II], one of the hosts, Sergei Kurginyan, summoned a huge looming image of Gene onto a screen in the studio to illustrate the item.

Assessments like these made nonviolent action and the groups who might use it a threat to the state and therefore a priority for the Ministry of Defence, not just a civil problem. Since the end of the Cold War, one of the greatest existential threats to Russia, its government and its sphere of influence was nonviolent uprising. In all of those threats, the work of Gene Sharp had laid the strategic framework for the opposition.

A study for the Russian Institute for Strategic Studies and Predictions stated, 'The works of Gene Sharp can actually be seen as laying the psychological ground for the eventual introduction of Unconventional Warfare in situations where a colour revolution does not succeed'. 'Gene Sharp's publications can be seen as Part 1 of the [United States] Hybrid War field manual.'

As the 2012 Russian election approached, President Medvedev announced that he would make way for Putin to run again for President – and this time on an extended term of 6 years. It was a blatant trick on the constitution which dictated that Putin should not have been able to serve more than his two terms.

The timing of the announcement was particularly bad in the wake of the Arab Spring which had shown democracy activists around the world what could be achieved. In December 2011, just months after Mubarak, Gadaffi and Ben Ali were deposed by their people, and with Syria now in the balance, Russia saw the biggest protests since the end of the Soviet Union.

Between 25,000 and 50,000 people gathered in Bolotnya Square with smaller rallies in 88 other towns and cities around the country. The people wore white ribbons as a symbol of discontent with the constitutional cheat and called for free and fair elections, the release of political prisoners and the sacking of Vladimir Churnov, the head of the electoral commission, who they claimed was corrupt.

For Putin and his highest Kremlin advisers, the protests were a worrying sign that the US had raised its ambitions from curtailing Russia's power in the former Soviet States and pushing NATO eastwards, to a fully fledged toppling of the Russian government. Putin communications advisor, Gleb Pavlovsky, told Newsweek, 'Putin believes that the West is constantly seeking to bring about his overthrow'. 'He was sure the protests of 2012 were orchestrated by the West, and this convinced him that it was time for a deeper reaction than anything that had gone before. Everything that we see today is based on this belief.'

Surkov spoke openly of the opposition's use of Gene Sharp's work in the country. 'There is absolutely no doubt that some people want to convert the protest into a colour revolution,' he wrote. 'They are acting literally according to Sharp's books and the latest revolutionary method guides so literally, that it's even boring.'

On the eve of Putin's 2012 inauguration and breach of the original two term limit, the protests in Moscow descended into violence. More than 400 opposition activists were arrested and 80 were injured. US Secretary of State, Hillary Clinton, took the unusual step of speaking out publicly in support of the Moscow protesters. She told the press, that the Russian people, 'deserve to have their voices heard and their votes counted, and that means they deserve fair, free transparent elections and leaders who are accountable to them.'

Putin was reportedly furious about Clinton's comments. He railed at the insult in a televised speech, 'She set the tone for some of the activists in our country, gave them a signal. They heard this signal and started active work with the US State department.' 'Pouring money into electoral processes is particularly unacceptable. We need to find ways to protect our sovereignty against interference from outside'. Some commentators suggested that Putin's fury at Hillary Clinton's interference in the 2012 Russian presidential election were the reason for his retaliatory strike upon the US political system in her 2016 run for US president.

Putin now tightened the noose on the US democracy promotion machine inside Russia. In November 2012, laws were passed requiring that any NGO receiving foreign money and engaged in political activity in the widest sense had to register with Russia's Ministry of Justice as a 'foreign agent' – a term intended to associate them with espionage and treason. Many of the groups designated as foreign agents chose to shut down rather than fight the legal action and state harassment. By the end of 2017 Putin boasted that their numbers had dropped from 165 to 89 in that year alone.

The 2012 protests also signalled the start of a new influence campaign over the domestic and international media. Where once the Kremlin only had to gain control of a handful of television news stations and newspapers to dominate the message, now social media was proving to be its new nemesis. Dominating the message on Facebook, Twitter, blogs and newspaper comment sections became fundamental to denying the opposition the 'information space'.

The Kremlin began pouring money into buildings filled with well-paid English-speaking bloggers and tweeters operating thousands of fake accounts in an effort to dominate the message online. On Savushkina Street, just outside St Petersburg, an anonymous four floor concrete building festooned with security cameras was getting particularly busy. This was the Internet Research Agency or what would become known in the West as the 'troll factory'.

In 2011, authoritarian regimes hadn't yet mastered the world of social media and the kids on the street still had the edge using the technology to organise and communicate. But those regimes, reeling from shock at what could be achieved with social tools began learning from the youth and regaining their advantage. Now social media and the big data they produced was being used by governments against the activists. In the run up to the 2012 presidential election the troll factory had been used to dominate the conversation online in favour of Putin and drown out the democracy movement pushing for change within the country.

The digital space was now a new field of nonviolent warfare in which most of Gene's methods could be applied in cyberspace. Haunting public officials (Twitter trolling), blockade (denial of service attacks), humorous skits and pranks (YouTube videos), revealing names of secret agents (disclosures to Wikileaks). Emboldened by the use of these new tools in the domestic political sphere and angered by Clinton's attacks on Russia's electoral system, Putin was about to turn this new form of political warfare force back on the United States.

There was good reason for Russia to favour one candidate for the US Presidency over the other. While Trump talked openly about his relaxed attitude to lifting sanctions on Russia over their invasion of Crimea, Clinton maintained a hard line. While Trump talked in admiring tones about Putin's leadership, Clinton actively denigrated him. Gathering information about the likely new president of a country and their attitudes to opposition interests was fair game for international espionage, but actively using that information to change the course of an election was a high risk strategy. It appears that in 2016, Putin chose to take that risk.

In the report, 'Assessing Russian Activities and Intentions in Recent US Elections' published by the Office of the Director of National Intelligence, the US intelligence community stated with 'high confidence' that, 'Russian President Vladimir Putin ordered an influence campaign in 2016 aimed at the US presidential election which aimed to undermine public faith in the US democratic process, denigrate Clinton and harm her electability and potential presidency.'

Russian intelligence contracted criminal gangs to hack into a number of US state and electoral boards and accessed the personal email accounts of democratic party officials including John Podesta, Colin Powell and Hillary Clinton, pulling gigabytes of data back onto Russian servers. Compromising information found in the course of these attacks was then introduced back into the US 'information space' through an online personality calling themselves 'Guccifer 2.0' (allegedly an independent Romanian hacker). Dumps of data were also released to DCLeaks and Wikileaks, a trusted source to many in the US and Europe.

There were incursions into the real world too, which demonstrated that Russian agents could even generate street protests inside an opposition country. Facebook groups were created to gather large numbers of followers with positive rhetoric about Trump and derogatory information about Clinton, using stolen identities of US citizens. When these Facebook pages reached sizeable numbers of followers, the fake US citizens began calling for organised protests which attracted hundreds of people onto the streets of New York.

In the last days of the campaign when most commentators were predicting a clear win for Clinton, the Russian effort began focussing on eroding her legitimacy as President elect. The troll farm prepared a Twitter campaign with the hashtag #DemocracyRIP and Russian diplomats described the US electoral system as corrupt and untrustworthy. When Trump finally won the election on 9th November 2016, the United States, and by many accounts Trump himself, was taken by surprise. Clinton was incandescent – she felt the leaked emails had been enough to tip the balance in Trump's favour – and that was before the full extent of Russian meddling was exposed.

Speaking about the Russian influence campaign in a speech at Oxford University, the former Director of the CIA and NSA General Michael Hayden told his audience, 'This is the most successful covert influence campaign in the history of covert influence campaigns, that's what this is and I will not embarrass you or me by claiming other countries have not conducted covert influence campaigns.' From a man who had led two of the world's most well funded intelligence agencies what Hayden was staying was a stunning admission. After years of US political manipulation in the former Soviet states, the Russians had played the US at their own game.

The Orchid Keeper

'Do you think we might be able to film in the orchid house', I asked, nervously. Jamila raised an eyebrow. 'No-one is ever allowed up there, not even me. You can ask but don't be disappointed.' I slipped quietly back into Gene's office where he was reading some papers by lamp light. 'Gene, I have to ask about the orchids. I really need to show a bit of the rest of your life, not just sitting at your desk talking about the work.' He looked up, barely containing his horror at the prospect. 'What's wrong with just talking at my desk?'

I left Jamila to talk to him about it and the next morning I rang the bell at Cottage Street, anxious to hear his decision. Jamila swung open the door again and took a deep breath, 'Ok, he says you can go'. Gene led the way, silently. He didn't want to take us there but he did it in good grace because Jamila had asked him to – had pleaded with him probably. We slow marched up the rough wooden stairs, one by one, behind him. I felt my chest tighten with embarrassment at the intrusion, tempered only by the fear of leaving East Boston knowing that no good film could be made without it.

As we turned the corner on the last landing, we emerged from the gloomy stairwell. As the door opened, the warm sweet smell of flowers filled the air and sunlight streamed down through perspex domes in the roof. Wooden masks from Burma and Thailand greeted us from above. Gene paused for a moment in front of us with his hand still on the handle, enjoying it alone for a moment.

And then he moved more quickly than I had seen him move in four days – checking the temperature and humidity, inspecting the orchid spikes close to bloom. A radio crackled into life. Everything downstairs was brown and old and dusty, but here it was bright, fresh, and alive with new growth. At one end of the orchid house were some large plants which had burst into flower with big crimson and white petals. Gene walked me down the row to a small unremarkable green spike which didn't look like it was in flower. 'This is my favourite' he told me, running a finger gently down the stem, 'They take quite a bit of work but they became very important because it was something I could treat as they needed to be treated. If you don't treat orchids right or anything else in life, then they're not going to thrive.'

Jamila shook out her hair, picked up a small pink orchid flower which had fallen to the floor and twisted it between her fingers before tucking it behind her right ear.

She stood with Gene looking up at a rare tree orchid which he had provided with a long piece of tree bark suspended from the roof by wires. It had become clear over this first week I had spent with them that Jamila wasn't just his Executive Director or assistant, they had formed a father and daughter like bond. This unlikely duo had survived here to do some of the most unique and important work that could be done.

On the 18th September 2011, *How to Start a Revolution*, the documentary about Gene I'd been working on for more than two years, finally premiered at Boston International Film Festival. Friends and colleagues assembled from all over America. Bob flew in from West Virginia, the first time he had seen Gene since he left the Institution in 2005. The 400 seat theatre filled slowly at first, but as we approached curtains up, people began to flow through the doors until there was standing room only and the organisers hurriedly added extra seats. I sat in the back, nervously watching the reactions of the audience, every uncomfortable shuffle, until the last shots of the film showed Gene and Jamila walking away from the camera towards Cottage Street, autumn leaves tumbling around them.

As the credits rolled I introduced Gene to the stage. Slowly, he took Jamila's arm and they walked towards the front of the cinema together. People rose to their feet as they saw them, some wiped away tears. Jamila composed herself and beamed back as the audience stood and the roar of clapping intensified all the way to the back of the theatre. At a small gathering at the end of the festival it was announced that we'd won Best Documentary. It was a modest prize, but a sign of good things to come.

The day before our premiere on the 17th September, the Occupy Wall Street protests had begun in Zucotti Park, New York. As the camps spread across America and then the world, Occupy screened *How to Start a Revolution* in tents, projected it against the sides of financial buildings and even in an occupied former bank in the City of London. It was shown in the streets of Brazil and Spain, on the Burma/Thailand border and on board anti-whaling ships patrolling the Southern Antarctic Ocean. As television channels began to buy and translate it for broadcast, the YouTube rip offs were going viral in Arabic, Spanish and Portuguese.

Gene hadn't felt strong enough to travel for a few years, but the success of *How to Start a Revolution* and the potential for using it as a vehicle to talk about his work re-energised him. We travelled to London where we were invited to show the film in a grand committee room at the Palace of Westminster. At the end of the screening the veteran MP, Tony Benn, a lifelong anti-war campaigner stood up and began to applaud. The rest of the room, packed to the gunnels, followed him and the ovation lasted for minutes. After the audience began filing out, Benn waited for Gene and held his hand. 'I met Mr Gandhi a number of times and I know he would have been very proud of you', he told him. Gene was deeply moved and, for a moment, was too choked to speak.

We headed on to a screening at Canterbury Cathedral and met a class of newly appointed bishops of the Church of England before returning to London for more interviews. On the BBC World Service 'Hardtalk' programme Gene was introduced by the presenter as, 'a political thinker now spoken of in the same breath as Mahatma Gandhi and Martin Luther King'.

After another packed screening at a cinema in Soho, we flew on to Oslo where the major national newspapers were all running features about Gene's visit and the likelihood of him winning the Nobel Peace Prize. It was a second homecoming for Gene – he delighted everyone he met by breaking into Norwegian and telling the audiences about the inspiration he gained by researching the Norwegian teachers' nonviolent campaign against Hitler's occupation. Perhaps most importantly, he met the Norwegian foreign minster to discuss the work and the financial support it needed to continue.

When the film tour was complete I was given a desk in the office of the Program on Negotiation at Harvard Law School, thanks to Susan Hackley, the director of the Program and a long term supporter of Gene's work. As a visiting researcher I would have a quiet place to work and access to the libraries to complete the initial research for this book.

On the morning of 3rd October 2012, I walked across Harvard Yard from my little cube office at the back of the law school with a bounce in my step. The falling leaves had burst into a riot of New England colours, lit up against an icy blue sky and the internet was buzzing with speculation that Gene was about to win the Nobel Peace Prize. People I met along the way had heard the news and asked me to pass on their good wishes. As I sat on the blue metro line to Maverick Square, I could hardly believe that after three years following this story, desperate financial difficulties, the brief dangers of Tahrir Square and thousands of miles in the air, I might be about to see Gene Sharp win the Nobel.

As articles on Gene being the most likely winner of the prize began to be published, national newspapers were booking their journalists on flights to Boston. The interest was so intense that we decided we would have to make plans for a press conference and a prepared statement, if the news was good. A local music charity, Zumix, which had converted East Boston's beautiful old fire station offered up their space for a press conference and Gene reluctantly gave a few words to be used – just in case.

The office at Cottage Street, which had lain almost untouched since the move in 2004, was reorganised. Boxes of books and old papers were filed, carpets were beaten and some thrown away. Sally, Gene's Labrador, was given a new bed and we pushed desks that had been in the middle of the office to the sides of the room. The curtains were beaten out and dusty blinds were drawn so that the sun poured back into the room. For the first time in years the office was clean, open and light.

With every call and email wishing Gene luck we grew more excited, before dragging ourselves back again and refusing to believe it. Could it happen? Could the story really end like this? We were exhausted, covered in dust and wrought with tension. In a few hours the world's media would either be descending on this little house in East Boston or there would be nothing but desperate disappointment.

At 3am, Eastern Time we checked the news. One of the biggest online bookmakers had made Gene the 6-4 favourite to win and a Norwegian news site had already called it for him. At 11am Norway time, the tall wooden doors in the Nobel Institute opened and Torben Jagland, the chair of the Nobel Committee, walked calmly to a podium to address a tightly packed scrum of journalists. 'The Norwegian Nobel committee has decided that the Nobel Peace Prize for 2012 is to be awarded to … the European Union.'

Jamila and I sat with our head in our hands, the rest of the press conference faded into background noise. The loss of the Nobel was a bigger blow to us than to Gene who had refused to believe the speculation all along and was still sleeping soundly upstairs. In the morning he shrugged his shoulders at the news and went back to work as if nothing had happened.

The loss of the Nobel left many in Norway and around the world perplexed but, shortly afterwards, Gene received a letter informing him that he had been awarded the Right Livelihood Award or 'Alternative Nobel'. The award had been set up by a group in Sweden to honour worthy Nobel nominees who fell through the net and was held annually in the Swedish Parliament.

We arrived into Stockholm just a few hours before a blizzard had blanketed the city in almost three feet of snow and closed the airport. Even for a country used to arctic conditions the snow paralysed the city for almost a day. The snowploughs which fought to clear the roads piled up four foot berms of snow onto the pavements, burying parked cars entirely and blocking the entrances to government buildings where we had a number of official meeting scheduled. As an unofficial assistant, I had to steal a shovel from the Ministry of Foreign Affairs to dig through the snow berm to the front door of the Ministry of Defence. It took almost 20 minutes to cut a hole through which we could get Gene into the building.

I sat, soaked with sweat, in the office of the Minister for Defence as she listened to Gene talk about civilian based defence and the importance of educating the population in nonviolent resistance as a deterrent to invasion. Jamila and I looked at each other nervously. Civilian based defence hadn't been discussed in Sweden since the 80s and early 90s when events in the Baltics meant the threat of invasion from Russia had been a possibility. It was clear the minister was more interested in the application of nonviolent action for groups in the Middle East.

Just a few years later, the rhetoric of a new cold war is ringing in Europe. Putin has increasingly expeditionary rhetoric and the invasion of Crimea has seen people dig out the books on civilian based defence – Gene had correctly anticipated that the knowledge would be needed again one day.

That evening we ate at a vast polished table with members of the Swedish parliament before being ushered into the candlelit debating chamber. The organisers wore suits with scarlet sashes and the sound of choirs filled the auditorium. Gene slept in a small bedroom adjacent to the chamber until, at ten minutes to the hour, Jamila woke him, helped straighten his suit and hair and escorted him to his seat at the front by the stage.

When the award was called Gene took Jamila's arm again and they walked carefully to the podium. She stood at the side of the stage in the shadow of a curtain watching the speech, until it was time to collect the award. This wasn't quite the Nobel Peace Prize but it crowned a year of recognition that might never have come.

The Arab Spring and the *How to Start a Revolution* tour gave new exposure to Gene's work and the Albert Einstein Institution, and the funding soon followed. Book sales spiked sharply and contributions of all sizes came in from people who had seen the film and TV and newspaper coverage. By the end of 2012 the Institution had accrued enough money to move into a new suite of offices in South Boston and hire two new members of staff.

Jamila decided that it was time to go back to Afghanistan for the first time since her family's escape from the country in 1984. Gene had encouraged her to go and dismissed her concerns about leaving him for an extended trip. During her return to her village in the South East of the country the Taliban attacked a police compound neighbouring her family home. Explosions and gunfire rang out across the neighbourhood and soon the air was filled with the sound of NATO helicopters and drones high above the village. As she prepared to return to the US, news came through that Gene had been taken ill and was in hospital. The flight back to Boston was a nervous one, but she was relieved upon her return to find Gene alive and improving in hospital.

During the months of his recovery at a rehabilitation unit not far from Harvard I would often visit him after a day in the library to ask for advice or memories of particular events for this book. Although he was still weak, he loved hearing about the characters from his past who I'd found, still alive, or the discovery of a foreign group using his work in a new and exciting way.

By the fall of 2013, my studying visa was due to expire. I had left it as long as possible, but it was time to go home. I drove with Jamila to say goodbye to Gene, who was beginning to feel much better. We talked about his transfer home to Cottage Street and he grabbed my hands and Jamila's and held them together with his. It was a moment that said everything that needed to be said about our time with each other.

For the next few years as a BBC news producer, I witnessed first hand the fallout from the Arab Spring, reporting everywhere from the great migration across Europe to the US aircraft carriers in the Persian Gulf carrying out strike operations against ISIS. There was much to be depressed about and yet I'd glimpse Gene's influence in the most surprising places. Despite the carnage and displacement from Syria, people still carried out nonviolent actions against Assad and even ISIS.

In Angola, a Gene Sharp book group was raided by police and thirteen readers arrested. In Malaysia, the government set up a special unit to counter his influence among young activists. When Mexicans and Venezuelans feared their election had been stolen, they turned back to distributing *From Dictatorship to Democracy*. In universities across South America they weren't following Che Guevara, they were tweeting about Gene Sharp. Gene had changed the very idea of what a revolution should look like.

In 2018, I got the call that I'd been dreading. Jamila told me that Gene's health had declined and that I should come back urgently to say goodbye. When I arrived back in Cottage Street, he was living downstairs in Jamila's old office. I couldn't help but notice that above his bed was a slightly lighter patch on the wall where the Otpor sign used to be stuck – 'Gotov Je', 'he's finished'.

'They tell me I've only got a few days', he told me, smiling, 'But I don't think it's true'. He held my hand and I read him some of the draft passages from this book. Sometimes visitors would sit around listening. One of his oldest friends, Nelia Sargent, a veteran campaigner whose father's company had published *The Politics of Nonviolent Action* sat with her hands clasped on the top of her white stick, like a guardian angel watching over him. After a couple of days we hugged goodbye, he kissed my cheek and told me he was pleased to have known me. I could barely reply. I had spent almost a decade covering his work and in that time I knew more about his life than my own grandparents.

Gene Sharp passed away three days after his 90th birthday, his major works completed, his legacy enormous and yet somehow still in the balance. Jamila organised his cremation and returned his ashes to Cottage Street, placing them on the desk where she had left him every evening for years, toiling into the night. In 2017 Gene and Jamila had been nominated together for the Nobel Peace Prize. Even at his weakest he had insisted that his passport was in date – it was the only indication he gave that he hadn't given up hope of getting the ultimate prize from Norway.

Academics and commentators will argue for years to come over the extent to which Gene Sharp's work shaped the democracy movements of the late 20th and early 21st century. That question is impossible to answer definitively, but before the ink is dry on these pages, new groups will be planning actions based upon his work, and dictators will be organising to counter them. The events in this book show that nonviolent movements can be made substantially more powerful with improved planning and strategy, while reducing the likelihood of violence, but dictatorships will constantly adapt and the techniques of resistance must too.

Gene's work is continued by a handful of committed academics, researchers and activists, but the field of nonviolent resistance desperately needs more people to carry on the legacy he has left us. Soon our freedoms will be challenged by new advances in technology, surveillance and artificial intelligence. Resistance campaigns must be waged to protect our environment, curb the control of multi-national companies and defend against a new generation of authoritarian systems.

This is a battle of ideas which can scarcely be more important to win. The life and work of Gene Sharp is dedicated to this one appeal to reason. Study and refine the technique of nonviolent action, not because it is good or morally superior, but because it has the potential to be far more powerful in the pursuit of liberty than violence and war.

198 Methods of Nonviolent Action

Practitioners of nonviolent struggle have an entire arsenal of 'nonviolent weapons' at their disposal. Listed below are 198 of them, classified into three broad categories: nonviolent protest and persuasion, noncooperation (social, economic, and political), and nonviolent intervention. A description and historical examples of each can be found in volume two of *The Politics of Nonviolent Action*, by Gene Sharp.

THE METHODS OF NONVIOLENT PROTEST AND PERSUASION

Formal Statements

1. Public Speeches
2. Letters of opposition or support
3. Declarations by organizations and institutions
4. Signed public statements
5. Declarations of indictment and intention
6. Group or mass petitions

Communications with a Wider Audience

7. Slogans, caricatures, and symbols
8. Banners, posters, and displayed communications
9. Leaflets, pamphlets, and books
10. Newspapers and journals
11. Records, radio, and television
12. Skywriting and earthwriting

Group Representations

13. Deputations
14. Mock awards
15. Group lobbying
16. Picketing
17. Mock elections

Symbolic Public Acts

18. Displays of flags and symbolic colors
19. Wearing of symbols
20. Prayer and worship
21. Delivering symbolic objects
22. Protest disrobings
23. Destruction of own property
24. Symbolic lights
25. Displays of portraits
26. Paint as protest
27. New signs and names
28. Symbolic sounds
29. Symbolic reclamations
30. Rude gestures

Pressures on Individuals

31. 'Haunting' officials
32. Taunting officials
33. Fraternization
34. Vigils

Drama and Music

35. Humorous skits and pranks
36. Performances of plays and music
37. Singing

Processions

38. Marches
39. Parades
40. Religious processions
41. Pilgrimages
42. Motorcades

Honoring the Dead

43. Political mourning
44. Mock funerals
45. Demonstrative funerals

46. Homage at burial places

Public Assemblies

47. Assemblies of protest or support
48. Protest meetings
49. Camouflaged meetings of protest
50. Teach-ins

Withdrawal and Renunciation

51. Walk-outs
52. Silence
53. Renouncing honors
54. Turning one's back

THE METHODS OF SOCIAL NONCOOPERATION

Ostracism of Persons

55. Social boycott
56. Selective social boycott
57. Lysistratic nonaction
58. Excommunication
59. Interdict

Noncooperation with Social Events, Customs, and Institutions

60. Suspension of social and sports activities
61. Boycott of social affairs
62. Student strike
63. Social disobedience
64. Withdrawal from social institutions

Withdrawal from the Social System

65. Stay-at-home
66. Total personal noncooperation
67. 'Flight' of workers
68. Sanctuary
69. Collective disappearance
70. Protest emigration (hijrat)

THE METHODS OF ECONOMIC NONCOOPERATION: ECONOMIC BOYCOTTS

Actions by Consumers

71. Consumers' boycott
72. Nonconsumption of boycotted goods
73. Policy of austerity
74. Rent withholding
75. Refusal to rent
76. National consumers' boycott
77. International consumers' boycott

Action by Workers and Producers

78. Workmen's boycott
79. Producers' boycott

Action by Middlemen

80. Suppliers' and handlers' boycott

Action by Owners and Management

81. Traders' boycott
82. Refusal to let or sell property
83. Lockout
84. Refusal of industrial assistance
85. Merchants' 'general strike'

Action by Holders of Financial Resources

86. Withdrawal of bank deposits
87. Refusal to pay fees, dues, and assessments
88. Refusal to pay debts or interest
89. Severance of funds and credit
90. Revenue refusal
91. Refusal of a government's money

Action by Governments

92. Domestic embargo
93. Blacklisting of traders

94. International sellers' embargo
95. International buyers' embargo
96. International trade embargo

THE METHODS OF ECONOMIC NONCOOPERATION: THE STRIKE

Symbolic Strikes

97. Protest strike
98. Quickie walkout (lightning strike)

Agricultural Strikes

99. Peasant strike
100. Farm Workers' strike

Strikes by Special Groups

101. Refusal of impressed labor
102. Prisoners' strike
103. Craft strike
104. Professional strike

Ordinary Industrial Strikes

105. Establishment strike
106. Industry strike
107. Sympathetic strike

Restricted Strikes

108. Detailed strike
109. Bumper strike
110. Slowdown strike
111. Working-to-rule strike
112. Reporting 'sick' (sick-in)
113. Strike by resignation
114. Limited strike
115. Selective strike

Multi-Industry Strikes

116. Generalized strike

117. General strike

Combination of Strikes and Economic Closures

118. Hartal
119. Economic shutdown

THE METHODS OF POLITICAL NONCOOPERATION

Rejection of Authority

120. Withholding or withdrawal of allegiance
121. Refusal of public support
122. Literature and speeches advocating resistance

Citizens' Noncooperation with Government

123. Boycott of legislative bodies
124. Boycott of elections
125. Boycott of government employment and positions
126. Boycott of government depts., agencies, and other bodies
127. Withdrawal from government educational institutions
128. Boycott of government-supported organizations
129. Refusal of assistance to enforcement agents
130. Removal of own signs and placemarks
131. Refusal to accept appointed officials
132. Refusal to dissolve existing institutions

Citizens' Alternatives to Obedience

133. Reluctant and slow compliance
134. Nonobedience in absence of direct supervision
135. Popular nonobedience
136. Disguised disobedience
137. Refusal of an assemblage or meeting to disperse
138. Sitdown
139. Noncooperation with conscription and deportation
140. Hiding, escape, and false identities
141. Civil disobedience of 'illegitimate' laws

Action by Government Personnel

142. Selective refusal of assistance by government aides
143. Blocking of lines of command and information
144. Stalling and obstruction
145. General administrative noncooperation
146. Judicial noncooperation
147. Deliberate inefficiency and selective noncooperation by enforcement agents
148. Mutiny

Domestic Governmental Action

149. Quasi-legal evasions and delays
150. Noncooperation by constituent governmental units

International Governmental Action

151. Changes in diplomatic and other representations
152. Delay and cancellation of diplomatic events
153. Withholding of diplomatic recognition
154. Severance of diplomatic relations
155. Withdrawal from international organizations
156. Refusal of membership in international bodies
157. Expulsion from international organizations

THE METHODS OF NONVIOLENT INTERVENTION

Psychological Intervention

158. Self-exposure to the elements
159. The fast
   a) Fast of moral pressure
   b) Hunger strike
   c) Satyagrahic fast
160. Reverse trial
161. Nonviolent harassment

Physical Intervention

162. Sit-in

163. Stand-in
164. Ride-in
165. Wade-in
166. Mill-in
167. Pray-in
168. Nonviolent raids
169. Nonviolent air raids
170. Nonviolent invasion
171. Nonviolent interjection
172. Nonviolent obstruction
173. Nonviolent occupation

Social Intervention

174. Establishing new social patterns
175. Overloading of facilities
176. Stall-in
177. Speak-in
178. Guerrilla theater
179. Alternative social institutions
180. Alternative communication system

Economic Intervention

181. Reverse strike
182. Stay-in strike
183. Nonviolent land seizure
184. Defiance of blockades
185. Politically motivated counterfeiting
186. Preclusive purchasing
187. Seizure of assets
188. Dumping
189. Selective patronage
190. Alternative markets
191. Alternative transportation systems
192. Alternative economic institutions

Political Intervention

193. Overloading of administrative systems
194. Disclosing identities of secret agents
195. Seeking imprisonment
196. Civil disobedience of 'neutral' laws
197. Work-on without collaboration
198. Dual sovereignty and parallel government

Without doubt, a large number of additional methods have already been used but have not been classified, and a multitude of additional methods will be invented in the future that have the characteristics of the three classes of methods: nonviolent protest and persuasion, noncooperation and nonviolent intervention.

It must be clearly understood that the greatest effectiveness is possible when individual methods to be used are selected to implement the previously adopted strategy. It is necessary to know what kind of pressures are to be used before one chooses the precise forms of action that will best apply those pressures.

Notes

FOREWORD

1. **freedom of the press and the rule of law were at their worst level for decades:** *Freedom in the World 2019 Freedom House* https://freedomhouse.org/report/freedom-world/freedom-world-2020 (accessed 16/10/20)
2. **with only 37 reporting gains:** Ibid
3. **14th year of consecutive decline in global freedom:** Ibid

THE SQUARE

1. **Shy US Intellectual Created Playbook Used in Revolution:** *The New York Times*, 16 February 2011
2. **Peter Mandaville was called in:** Author interview with Peter Mandaville, 20 February 2013

EASTIE

1. President Hugo Chávez, 'Alo Presidente' https://www.youtube.com/watch?v=Emv1bpH8_Is
2. Iranian Intelligence Service cartoon https://www.youtube.com/watch?v=v2MuYWupPIc
3. **I recognize that films can convey ideas powerfully Gene Sharp:** email to author, 7 January 2009
4. **Most people are pretty shocked when they arrive:** Author interview with Jamila Raqib, 28 May 2009
5. **I've never been very good at raising money:** Author interview with Gene Sharp, 25 May 2009
6. **Build a better mousetrap:** Ibid

LETTERS FROM EINSTEIN

1. Scenes from Gandhi's assassination from Fischer. L *The Life of Mahatma Gandhi*, p11
2. **might in some way continue Gandhi's work:** Author interview with Gene Sharp, 25 May 2009

3. **Lonely ritual:** Gene Sharp, an autobiographical essay, Ohio State University (personal file, undated)
4. **Dolls head:** Ibid
5. **When the public sees the gentle person's courage and fortitude:** Gregg, R., *The Power of Nonviolence*, (1934) p54
6. **try to learn from military men:** Ibid
7. **attempts to consciously improve my personality:** an autobiographical essay, Ohio State University (personal file, undated)
8. **I can no longer cooperate with the machinery of military conscription:** Gene Sharp, Letters to the Draft Board (personal file, undated)
9. **We must become integrated loving individuals:** Gene Sharp, introduction in *Gandhi Wields the Weapon of Moral Power* (1960)
10. **people did not believe in nonviolence as an ethic!** interview with Gene Sharp 25 May 2009
11. **become the destroyers of their own dreams:** Gene Sharp, introduction in *Gandhi Wields the Weapon of Moral Power (1960)*
12. **What is it I have done for which I may be sentenced up to five years:** Gene Sharp. Note to self (personal file, undated)
13. **An important part of my conviction:** Gene Sharp letter to Paul Sharp (personal file, undated)
14. Gene Sharp letter to Einstein, 30 March 1953, Albert Einstein Institution Archive
15. Albert Einstein Letter to Gene Sharp 2 April 1953, Albert Einstein Institution Archive
16. Gene Sharp letter to Albert Einstein 12 April 1953, Albert Einstein Institution Archive
17. **I found it to be the most difficult situation I ever was in:** Letter from Eva Sharp
18. **I thought you conducted yourself magnificently:** Letter from John Clellan Holmes
19. **We will be remembering you daily and hourly:** Letter from Paul Sharp to Gene Sharp
20. **last wishes before his sentence:** Letter from Eva Sharp to Einstein
21. **I thank you for your kind and interesting letters:** Letter from Einstein to Eva Sharp

PRISON

1. **As you know I was sentenced to two years:** Gene Sharp, Letter to Einstein, 14 June 1953

2. **The men are lonely men, frantic men:** Gene Sharp prison diary (undated)
3. **Take away his escapes, his freedom:** Ibid
4. **What should intellectuals do against this evil:** Einstein letter to William Frauenglass, 12 June 1953
5. Commentator letters to the Washington Post et al, taken from Isaacson. W. *Einstein: His life and Universe* (2007) p528
6. **It was almost as if he [Einstein] was adopting him**: Author interview with Professor Gerald Holton, 10 July 2017
7. **I shall have difficulty in getting my things published:** Letter from Gene Sharp to Eva Sharp 5 September 1953
8. **I know this has been especially hard on you:** Letter from gene Sharp to Paul Sharp 5 September 1953
9. **Yesterday I took 77 X-rays:** Letter from Gene Sharp to parents, 26 August 1953
10. **stultifying effect on the mind:** Gene Sharp prison diary (personal file, undated)
11. **I felt it gave me self confidence and clarity:** Ibid
12. **Even the eating of a single pecan:** Ibid
13. **parted telling each other they would look each other up:** Gene Sharp Interview 26 May 2009
14. **Remington Dies In Prison:** *The New York Times* 25 November 1954
15. **treated psychiatrically:** *The Personal Life of Bayard Rustin*, Interview with Bayard's partner Ralph Naegle, www.out.com, 18 January 2016
16. **They talked about Gene's frustrations:** Interview with Gene Sharp 26 May 2009

ON THE MARCH

1. **It's more than an ocean I cross tonight:** Author interview with Gene Sharp, 26 May 2009
2. Voyage of the *Italia*, found via ancestry
3. **If you believe in freedom, justice and Peace:** from photographs at the Peace News Archive, Bradford Peace Museum, UK
4. **He was a very good lecturer:** Author interview with April Carter, 24 June 2013
5. **giving a rousing rendition of one of the traditional union songs:** Author interview with Michael Randle, 6 May 2014
6. **So you're the one who's been causing all the trouble are you:** Ibid
7. **More than 1000 military personnel:** A good history of the British test can be found in Arnold. L. *Britain and the H-bomb*

8. **The power behind the throne:** Interview with Michael Randle, 6th May 2014

9. **Shurrup, or I'll smash yer face:** Ibid

10. **We have to make sure this kind of thing doesn't happen again:** Author interview with Gene Sharp 27 May 2009

11. **immediately withdraw, leave an empty space and sit down. Isolate the violence:** From Aldermaston March, information leaflet authored by Gene Sharp, March, 1958

12. **If you believe in the objectives:** Ibid

13. List of instructions for Aldermaston March from information leaflet authored by Gene Sharp, March, 1958. This can be found in the Bradford Peace museum or in the instagram feed for this book @GeneSharpBook

14. **I was in despair. Deep despair. I drew myself:** Holtom letter to Hugh Brock, 1973

15. **So, Gerry, let's see what you have:** Ian Jack, He gave his unforgettable work for nothing. Shouldn't the designer of the peace symbol be commemorated? *The Guardian*, 28 November 2015

16. **We have decided to provide our own posters:** letter from Barbara Webb to *Peace News* 1958

17. **What on earth were you thinking:** Author interview with Gene Sharp 25 May 2009

18. **Later regretted the image of despair:** Kathyryn Westcott, World's best-known protest symbol turns 50, BBC News Website, 20 March 2008

19. **We are nonviolent because injury to one is injury to all:** Bayard Rustin Speech 4 April 1958, The footage of the speech can be found on Youtube by searching 'Bayard Rustin at Anti-Nuclear Rally in Trafalgar Square'

20. March to Aldermaston, documentary narrated by Richard Burton, 1959, from the archives of the BFI

21. **This is a nonviolent demonstration:** Author interview with Pat Arrowsmith, 22 February 2015

22. **Aldermaston March Ends in Riot:** *Evening Standard*, 7 April 1958

23. **Macwhirters admitted to the BBC:** Author interview with Pat Arrowsmith, 22 February 2015

24. **I couldn't understand his position:** Ibid

25. **a plan to enter Wethersfield airfield:** Author interview with Michael Randle, 6th May 2014

26. Transcripts of the trial of the Committee of 100 available from the National Archive Kew

27. **I would like you to ask yourselves a question:** Ibid

28. **Well you've got 18 fucking months to get over it:** taken from Randle & Pottle, *The Blake Escape: How we freed George Blake and Why*, p19

29. **I do not call myself a pacifist:** Gene Sharp note to himself (personal file, undated)

30. Michael Randle went on to orchestrate the escape from prison of the notorious MI6 traitor George Blake, smuggling him in a specially constructed secret compartment in his camper van to the east German border. The full story can be found in, Randle & Pottle, *The Blake Escape: How we freed George Blake and Why*

NORWAY

1. **Inside the box of matches contained the plan:** Gene Sharp, *Tyranny Could not Quell Them*, *The International Pacifist Weekly*, 1958

2. **Between 8000 and 10,000 teachers:** Ibid

3. **When the demonstration succeeded:** Ibid

4. **You must not think you will be martyrs:** Ibid

5. **You teachers have destroyed everything for me:** Ibid

6. **I was amazed at the intense interest:** Interview with Gene Sharp 25 May 2009

7. **In Algeria we tried nonviolence:** Ibid

8. **When they went over to guerrilla warfare:** Ibid

9. **more than 10% of their population dead:** Ibid

10. **There is this romantic belief:** Lecture to Norwegian Q&A session, Oslo, 7 February 2012

11. **To Galtung, Gene wasn't a social scientist:** Author interview with George Lakey, 20 September 2012

12. **The deterrent effect of a nation prepared for nonviolent resistance:** Gene Sharp, *Tyranny Could not Quell Them*, *The International Pacifist Weekly*, 1958

EUREKA

1. **Pushed the cheap furniture to the sides:** interview with Gene Sharp May 27 2009

2. **Jews protesting the raising of idolatrous images in Jerusalem:** Ibid

3. Lysistrata is an ancient Greek comedy by Aristophanes, originally performed in classical Athens in 411 BC. It is a comic account of a woman's extraordinary mission to end the Peloponnesian War between Greek city states by denying all the men of the land any sex

4. On modern sex strikes see: Elisabeth Braw, *Nobel Peace Prize Laureate Leymah Gbowee: 'Sex Strikes Help Good Men, The Huffington Post*, 6 January 2012

5. **thoughtful and patient:** interview with Gene Sharp May 2009

6. **Why in the world do people agree to be looted:** Etienne La Boetie, *On Voluntary Servitude* (1577)

7. **Who has the public as a whole for his enemy:** Machiavelli, *The Prince*, 1532

8. **nasty brutish and short:** Hobbes, *Leviathan*, 1651

9. **If they wanted to withdraw that obedience:** Interview with Gene Sharp 25 May 2009

10. **he would tie all these fragments together:** Ibid

11. **relied on the support of the people they ruled for their maintenance of power:** Ibid

12. **you know what the dictatorship depends on for its existence:** Ibid

13 Sources of power list taken from Sharp, *The Politics of Nonviolent Action*, 1973

14. The term 'Pillars of Support' was coined later by Colonel Robert Helvey in Burma

15. **Since all those sources of power are dependent upon the good will:** Author interview with Gene Sharp, 25 May 2009

15. **I just didn't know anyone who was interested in that kind of thing:** Ibid

16. **I wasn't doing well always, I was sometimes overwhelmed:** Ibid

17. **Gene's instincts were so good:** Author interview with Hugh Brody, 26 March 2017

18. The 198 methods of nonviolent action are listed in the back of this book

19. **could quite easily have rounded up to 200:** Author interview with Gene Sharp 28 May 2009

20. **We are simply at the bow and arrow stage:** Author interview with George Lakey 20 September 2012

21. For a biography of Liddell Hart see: Danchev. A. *Alchemist of War: The Life of Sir Basil Liddell Hart* (1998)

22. **No expert on military affairs:** Book review by Senator John F. Kennedy of *Deterrent or Defense*, in the *Saturday Review of Literature*, 3 September 1960

23. **I wonder if you could suggest two or three of the best sources:** Sharp letter to Liddell Hart, June 1958, Albert Einstein Institution Archive

24. **On the question of the best books on the subject:** Liddell Hart letter to Sharp 1 July 1958, Albert Einstein Institution Archive

25. **I was very interested to see in the Sunday Telegraph:** letter from Liddell Hart to Sharp 31 March 1964, Albert Einstein Institution Archive

26. Elements of 'The Indirect Approach' from *Alchemist of War: The Life of Sir Basil Liddell Hart* (1998)
27. **The technique of nonviolent action:** Gene Sharp, *The Politics of Nonviolent Action (1973)* p495
28. **He hated the terms 'non-violence and 'passive resistance:** Gene Sharp interview 25 May 2009
29. **mushy:** Ibid
30. **thought-barrier:** Foreword to *Defence in the Nuclear Age*, Stephen King-Hall
31. *The Strategy of Civilian Defence,* Edited by Adam Roberts, (1967)

COLD WAR

1. **the US government's umpire:** Author interview with Thomas Schelling 14 October 2015
2. **provided much of the nightmarish reality:** Ibid
3. **Two things impressed me:** Ibid
4. **whether there might be a place at Harvard:** Author interview with Gene Sharp 25 May 2009
5. **I couldn't believe that you could fill a whole book:** Author interview with Thomas Schelling 14 October 2015
6. **this award which I receive on behalf of that movement:** Martin Luther King Speech at the Nobel Peace Prize Ceremony, Oslo, 10 December, 1964
7. **he did nothing but work:** Interview with Thomas Schelling 14 October 2015
8. **ARPA money:** See Project Agile and Project Camelot
9. **would you rather the money be used for waging war:** Author interview with Gene Sharp 26 May 2009
10. **I would much prefer to stay around here:** Gene Sharp letter to Thomas Schelling 1 November 1969
11. **There were questions as to whether he had been there too long:** Author interview with Joe Nye, 18 October 2013
12. **this volume … reminds one of (Adam Smith's) The Wealth of Nations:** Coretta Scott King introduction to *The Politics of Nonviolent Action*, (1973)
13. **not even a working toilet:** Interview with Gene Sharp 28 May 2009
14. **Clausewitz of Nonviolent Warfare:** Thomas Weber review of *The Politics of Nonviolent Action*, (1973)
15. **Machiavelli of nonviolence:** Professor William B Watson, Massachusetts Institute of Technology, review of *The Politics of Nonviolent Action* (1973)
16. **required reading at military schools:** Major General Edward B. Atkeson review of *The Politics of Nonviolent Action*, (1973)

17. **Could dominate the Western Mediterranean:** Consequence of communist accession to power in Italy by legal means, Central Intelligence Agency assessment, ORE-648, 5 March 1948

18. 'the brink of catastrophe' *Time Magazine*, June, 1947

19. **Soviets were spending between $8-10 million a month:** Cold War Episode 3: Marshall Plan. Interview with F. Mark Wyatt, former CIA operative in Italy during the election. CNN

20. **the main element of any United States policy toward the Soviet Union:** https://history.state.gov/departmenthistory/short-history/kennan

21. **National Security Council Directive NSC 4-A:** https://history.state.gov/ historicaldocuments/frus1945-50Intel/d256

22. **The directive was considered so secret that only three copies were produced:** Ibid

23. **the employment of all the means at a nation's command:** Kennan, G. *The Inauguration of Organized Political Warfare*, 30 April 1948

24. **intervened in 117 elections around the world from 1946 to 2000:** Levin, D. *When the Great Power Gets a Vote: The Effects of Great Power Electoral Interventions on Election Results, International Studies Quarterly*, Volume 60, Issue 2, June 2016

25. **CIA spent nearly four million dollars:** https://nsarchive2.gwu.edu/ news/20040925/index.htm

26. An account of CIA operations against Allende: Seymour M. Hersh C.I.A. Chief Tells House Of $8-Million Campaign Against Allende in 70–73, *The New York Times*, 8 September, 1974

27. **I thought CIA might be interested in this work:** memorandum from Andrew Marshall to Ed Proctor, Deputy Director CIA, 22 April 1975

28. **bad dealings:** interview with Gene Sharp 25 May 2009

29. **sponsored, subsidised or produced by the intelligence agency:** David Price, The CIA Book Publishing Operationsm, *Counterpunch*, 13 September 2020

30. **A little rebellion now and then is a very good thing:** Reagan speech to House of Commons London, 8 June 1982

31. **we used to do some of this covertly:** David Ignatius, *Innocence Abroad: The New World or Spyless Coups, Washington Post*, 22 September 1991

32. **pretext to discredit the entire project:** Franklin. B. Project democracy takes Wing, *The New York Times*, 29 May 1984

33. **Senator Proxmire:** Ibid

34. **On behalf of the intelligence community:** Franklin, B. *Project Democracy takes Wing, The New York Times*, 29 May 1984

35. **legislation to provide initial funding of $31.3 million for NED:** Lowe, D. *Idea to Reality: A Brief History of the National Endowment for Democracy* www.ned.org

35. **I have agreed with senator Proxmire:** Franklin, B. *Project Democracy takes Wing, The New York Times,* 29 May 1984

36. **If you're interested in that subject:** lecture by Peter Ackerman, *Why Skills Can Make Civil Resistance a Force More Powerful,* Fletcher School, 2013

37. **350 pages is only a quarter of the way done:** Peter Ackerman tribute at Gene Sharp memorial service, Boston, 1 October 2018

38. **second longest phD the Fletcher School had ever received:** lecture by Peter Ackerman, Why Skills Can Make Civil Resistance a Force More Powerful, Fletcher School, 2013

39. **When I first met Samuel Huntington:** Author interview with Bob Irwin, 29 September 2013

40. **He had a kind of contempt for pacifists:** Author interview with Thomas Schelling 14 October 2015

41. **This book is mostly about ...civilian based defence:** Gene Sharp foreword to *Making Europe Unconquerable* (1985)

42. **the view in this book deserves consideration:** George Kennan introduction to *Making Europe Unconquerable, 2ⁿᵈ edition,* (1985)

INTIFADA

1. **Palestinian Gandhi:** Jeff Stein, *The Palestinian Gandhi who still thinks non-violence is the answer, Newsweek,* 8 December 2014

2. **fallen to a sniper's bullet:** Author interview with Mubarak Awad 30 October 2013

3. **She told us never to seek revenge:** Ibid

4. **I think you will find these useful:** Ibid

5. **quite unpleasant:** Ibid

6. **You can't do that when you don't understand the full concepts:** Ibid

7. **between 4000 and 7000 copies of this new book:** Author interview with Mubarak Awad 30th October 2013

8. **Once I was on a bus from Jerusalem to Ramallah:** Ibid

9. **Awad and Sharp's works:** Mary *King. A Quiet Revolution: The First Palestinian Intifada and a Strategy for Non-violent Resistance* (2007)

10. **You see this skinny person:** Author interview with Mubarak Awad 30 October 2013

11. **Shirabi very quickly raised $30,000:** Ibid

12. **what can we tell people like these:** Author interview with Mubarak Awad 30 October 2013
13. **I had to indicate this is not pacifism:** Ibid
14. **We were in the home one time, with Mubarak:** Gene Sharp trip notes, Albert Einstein Institution Archive
15. **frontier Gandhi:** for a profile of Abdul Ghaffar Khan see, *'Islam' Means Peace: Understanding the Muslim Principle of Nonviolence Today* (2011)
16. 100,000 strong trained and uniformed nonviolent army: Ibid p100
17. **I am going to give you such a weapon:** Halverson, J. *Searching for a King: Muslim Nonviolence and the Future of Islam* (2012)
18. **Abu Jihad was the one that told some of the Fatah groups to leave me alone:** Author interview with Mubarak Awad, 30 October 2013
19. **reported to have begun reading The Politics of Nonviolent Action:** Ibid
20. **unless he renounced violence publicly:** Ibid
21. **Abu Jihad was the one that told some of the Fatah groups to leave me alone:** Ibid
22. **Began in the Jabalia refugee camp in Gaza:** Mary King. *A Quiet Revolution: The First Palestinian Intifada and a Strategy for Non-violent Resistance* (2007) p203
23 **Analysis of the first 18 months:** Ibid
24. **Sari would fax the leaflets to an intermediary:** Author interview with Sari Nusseibeh, 24 August 2015
25. **Gene assessed that between 80% and 95% of the Intifada was nonviolent:** Gene Sharp trip notes, Albert Einstein Institution Archive
26. **I have found it extremely difficult to find a Palestinian justification for this:** Ibid
27. **in their poetry they idolized these people:** Ibid
28. **ultimately the Palestinians had to find a way to share the land:** Author interview with Sari Nusseibeh 24 August 2015
29. **Mary King met Abu Jihad a number of times:** Interview with Mary King 4 September 2015
30. **He had become a much greater threat to Israel:** transcript of conversation between Mary King and Mubarak Awad in the Albert Einstein Institution Archives (undated)
31. For an account of Abu Jihad's assassination see - *24 years later, Israel acknowledges top-secret operation that killed Fatah terror chief, The Times of Israel* 1 November 2012
32. **admitted to him that the Palestinian struggle could not succeed militarily:** Interview with Gene Sharp 26 May 2009

33. **When I raised this with one Israeli, they thought I was trying to make Abu Jihad into a saint:** Interview with Sari Nusseibeh 24 August 2015
34. **His assassination is because of the nonviolent activities:** interview with Mubarak Awad 30th October 2013
35. **You need more Awads not fewer:** *Mary King. A Quiet Revolution: The First Palestinian Intifada and a Strategy for Non-violent Resistance* (2007) p160
36. **the main brains of the intifada:** Ibid p158
37. **his [Mubark's] ideas began to find actual expression in the leaflets that were issued by the command of the uprising**: Witness statement from 'Yossi' Transcript from Israeli High Court 282/88, 5 June 1988 http://www.hamoked.org/files/2010/1430_eng.pdf
38. **If your opponent is afraid of this:** Author interview with Gene Sharp 25 May 2009
39. **The power in Palestine is with Arafat:** Author interview with Mubarak Awad 30 October 2013
40. **How would you help me deal with this:** interview with Bruce Jenkins 9 January 2014
41. **The office was pretty cool:** Ibid
42. **during the oil embargo of 1973:** Interview with Gene Sharp 27 May 2009
43. Six strategic objectives from 'Basic Presentation to Palestinian Leaders' by Gene Sharp, March 1989 , Albert Einstein Institution Archive
44. **There is much skepticism it appears in the PLO ranks:** Bruce Jenkins trip notes, Albert Einstein Institution Archive
45. **you'll never change these people:** Author interview with Mubarak Awad 30 October 2013
46. **You're asking people to go through a lot:** Author interview with Sari Nusseibeh 24 August 2015
47. **This second phase of resistance, introduced by an extended fast:** Gene Sharp trip notes, Albert Einstein Institution

TIANANMEN

1. **weeks before the unrest hit the international tv networks:** Author interview with Huang Jing, 23 August 2015
2. **More than 300 towns and cities:** Lily Kuo, *China's other Tiananmens: 30 years on, The Guardian*, 2 June 2019
3. **Agreed on a mission:** Author interview with Gene Sharp, 25 May 2009
4. **A visiting Canadian diplomat:** Sharp & Jenkins, *Nonviolent Struggle in China. An Eyewitness* Account, Nonviolent Sanctions: News from the Albert Einstein Institution Vol.1 No.2 Fall 1989

5. **Asked him to join the team:** Author interview with Huang Jing 23 August 2015

6. **Braced themselves for the Chinese security agents:** Author interview with Bruce Jenkins 9 January 2014

7. **Offer them food and a bed:** Ibid

8. **Protests had begun spontaneously:** Tiananmen interview transcripts, 28 May -4 June 1989, Albert Einstein Institution Archive

9. For a biography of Hu: Khoon Choy Lee, *Pioneers of Modern China: Understanding the Inscrutable Chinese* (2005)

10. **nobody had researched how a hunger strike actually worked:** Interview with Gene Sharp 26 May 2009

11. **I wanted to get married:** Tiananmen interview transcripts, 28 May–4 June 1989, Albert Einstein Institution Archive

12. **A vast street fair:** Author interview with Gene Sharp 26 May 2009

13. **Dead pigs are never afraid of hot water:** Tiananmen interview transcripts, 28 May -4 June 1989, Albert Einstein Institution Archive

14. **Please tell the World why we are here:** Author interview with Gene Sharp 26 May 2009

15. 'We were aware of improper ideas' Tiananmen interview transcripts, Albert Einstein Institution, 28 May–4 June 1989

16. **peppered with leading questions:** Ibid

17. **Spread support to as many parts of society as possible:** Ibid

18. **If they arrest people** Ibid

19. **But the government want this:** Ibid

20. **Not let even one escape:** Author interview with Gene Sharp 26 May 2009

21. **We will mobilise the people around the world:** Transcript, *The Gate of Heavenly Peace,* 1995

22. **the square is our only stronghold:** Ibid

23. **Long Live the People's Liberation Army:** Ibid

24. **whose army are you:** Ibid

25. **Huang grabbed a metal fence:** Author interview with Huang Jing 23 August 2015

26. **You can't do that! That's not why we're here:** Interview with Gene Sharp 26 May 2009

27. **animals, animals:** Transcript, *The Gate of Heavenly Peace,* 1995

28 **We know you're not afraid of dying:** Ibid

29. **What we actually are hoping for is bloodshed:** Ibid

30. **Woke from a few hours of fitful sleep:** Author interview with Gene Sharp 26 May 2009

31. **Borrowed a bicycle:** Author interview with Bruce Jenkins 9 January 2014

32. **Led Zeppelin albums:** Ibid
33. For an account of Operation Yellow Bird: Liu, Melinda, *Still On The Wing; inside Operation Yellowbird, the daring plot to help dissidents escape, Newsweek* 1 April 1996
34. **5 key points in the movement:** Gene Sharp trip notes from China, Albert Einstein Institution Archive, June 1989
35. **They were not planned they were not prepared:** Interview with Gene Sharp 26 May 2009
36. **It is well past time for a major expansion of our knowledge:** Gene Sharp trip notes from China, Albert Einstein Institution Archive, June 1989

THE BARRICADES

1. **Gene's books already sat in the KGB library:** Author interview with Audrius Butkevicius 20 October 2013
2. **The need for a coordinating centre:** Miniotate, G. *Nonviolent Resistance in Lithuania,* Albert Einstein Institution monograph (2002)
3. **stuffed her suitcase with as much reading material as it would carry:** Author Interview with Gene Sharp 26 May 2009
4. **Can we really be the bombers of Gorbachev:** Author interview with Audrius Butkevicius 20 October 2013
5. **described Gene Sharp as a CIA officer:** Ibid
6. **Audrius, we have something for you:** Ibid
7. **I thought to myself, there is a system to this:** Ibid
8. **cutting off 90% of their oil and gas supplies:** Miniotate, G. *Nonviolent Resistance in Lithuania,* Albert Einstein Institution monograph (2002)
9. **We told them that it is not 'us' against Russia:** Interview with Audrius Butkevicius 20 October 2013
10. **threatened some of these pro-Moscow activists with death:** Ibid
11. **every angle of the confrontation had been filmed:** Miniotate, G. *Nonviolent Resistance in Lithuania,* Albert Einstein Institution monograph (2002)
12. **'there was too much meat at the parliament'** Author interview with Audrius Butkevicius, 20 October 2013
13. **The plan was destroyed by the courage of the people:** Ibid
14. **I would rather have Dr Sharp's book than the nuclear bomb:** Author interview with Audrius Butkevicius, 20 October 2013
15. **writing one of the first ever 'blogs':** Emails from Igor, 1991, Albert Einstein Institution Archive
16. **I hope this is not my last message:** Ibid
17. **keep praying for us and we will keep praying for you:** Ibid

18. **Operation Thunder:** 'Novaya Gazeta' No. 51 of 23 July 2001 Archived 15 February 2012 at the Wayback Machine – via Wikipedia
19. **raindrop in the ocean:** Emails from Igor, 1991, Albert Einstein Institution Archive
20. **distributed between 1500 and 2000 copies.** Ibid
21. **Without the support of the people:** Ibid
22. **Audrius Butkevicius still keeps a memento:** Interview with Audrius Butke-vicius, 20 October 2013

COLONEL BOB

1. **everyone wanted to fight alongside Helvey:** email correspondence with a soldier of Helvey's platoon
2. **stumbled into an ambush:** For a history of this period see Krohn. C. *The Lost Battalion of Tet* (2008)
3. **ran into the open to direct artillery:** Helvey, R. Citation for the Distin-guished Service Cross
4. **a God on the battlefield:** email correspondence with a soldier of Helvey's platoon
5. **returned to the US with one stand out conclusion:** Author interview with Bob Helvey 23 October 2010
6. **The Cold War remained a top priority**: Ibid
7. **Tin Maung Win hated the Burmese military regime:** Ibid
8. **sat for hours drinking whiskey:** Ibid
9. **I thought I'd just go up there and see who these peaceniks were:** Ibid
10. **seize political power and deny it to others:** Ibid
11. **I say nonviolent struggle is armed struggle:** Gene Sharp, The Power and Potential of Nonviolent Struggle lecture component given between 1983 onwards. Available on YouTube
12. **Moses and Coach:** Interviews with Srdja Popovic and Ausama Monajed respectively
13. **Vietnam convinced me we need to have an alternative to killing people:** Author interview with Bob Helvey 23 October 2010
14. **dispatched a team of assassins to hunt them down:** Correspondence from Tin Maung Win, Albert Einstein Institution Archive
15. **ordering 240 copies for the trainee defence attachés:** Correspondence from Colonel Robert Helvey, Albert Einstein Institution Archive
16. **Four student leaders were reported so far as being arrested:** Email from Ye Kyaw Thu to Gene Sharp

17. **Lakey agreed to do the trip:** Author interview with George Lakey, 20 September 2012
18. **Given the magnitude of the physical threat:** fax from Helvey at the Defence Intelligence School to Gene Sharp, 23 April 1990
19. **Gene asked him frankly whether he had ever worked for the CIA:** Notes of this conversation from the Albert Einstein Institution Archive.

JUNGLE FORTRESS

1. **Beheaded at least seven men for betraying him:** Author interview with Bob Helvey 23 October 2010
2. **the most active Burmese democracy campaigners:** Interview with Charmaine Craig, Louisa Benson Craig's daughter, 24 April 2014. Louisa Benson Craig passed away in 2010 and her husband Glen Craig was suffering from dementia by the time the initial research for this book was being conducted. Charmaine Craig published a fictionalised biography of her mother, *Miss Burma* published by Grove Press, 2017
3. **Glen still believed that if he could channel enough arms:** Interview with Bob Helvey 23 October 2010. Bob Helvey rebuffed Glen's requests to become involved in the military component of the struggle on a number of occasions. The argument over whether nonviolent discipline was the best option for Burma became a serious issue in Louisa and Glen's marriage
4. **He never said a fucking word:** Author interview with Bob Helvey 23rd October 2010
5. **don't ever use the term nonviolent again:** Ibid
6. **Where in the hell has this information been:** Ibid
7. **Dr Sharp I presume:** Ibid
8. **Dr Sharp I have read all of your books:** Ibid
9. **obviously cowards:** Ibid
10. **Gene beckoned the young man into his arms and began to cry:** Author interview with Michael Beer 5 June 2015
11. **dreaming about bombs falling on the camp:** Interview with Gene Sharp 26 May 2009
12. **PDC planned three phases of action:** taken from Burma consultation notes, Albert Einstein Institution Archive
13. **Mix a little water with petrol:** Author Interview with Bob Helvey 23 October 2010.
14. **violence is the most serious contaminant:** unpublished guide by Bob Helvey, Albert Einstein Institution Archive

15. **If one wanted the ordinary soldiers to mutiny:** Gene Sharp personal notes on this meeting, Albert Einstein Institution Archive

16. **Because we both believe in fighting:** Interview with Gene Sharp 26 May 2009

FROM DICTATORSHIP TO DEMOCRACY

1. **tip off from his former colleagues:** Emails from Major Paul Fegolino, US Embassy, Bangkok, Albert Einstein Institution Archive

2. **In what may be a race against the clock:** Email from Bob Helvey to Gene Sharp, June 1993, Albert Einstein Institution Archive

3. **often ghost written:** Author interview with Bob Helvey 23 October 2010

4. **You should at least have the humility:** author interview with Gene Sharp 26 May 2009

5. **7 years imprisonment:** Ibid

6. **more than 23,000 copies were printed:** Interview with Bob Helvey 23 October 2010

7. **a quick thinking staffer:** Ibid

8. **They made contacts with underground elements:** New Light of Myanmar, SLORC denunciations file, Albert Einstein Institution Archive

9. **'If we do not act soon:** Tin Maung Win email to Gene Sharp, Albert Einstein Institution Archive

10. **National Endowment for Democracy granted the Albert Einstein Institution an additional $45,000:** financial documents, Albert Einstein Institution Archive

11. **nicknaming him Hannibal:** Author interview with Mike Mitchell 22 July 2014

12. **ground truth.** Ibid

13. **told Suu Kyi about the training in nonviolent action:** Ibid

14. **working with Americans Bob Helvey, Gene Sharp and Bruce Jenkins:** SLORC press conference

15. **Why did they let him into the country:** *Burmese activist denies allegations The pro-democracy leader calls conspiracy charges against her 'bogus'*, Associated Press, 3 September 1996

16. **expression actually refers to Gene Sharp:** Suu Kyi, *Letters from Burma*

17. **For all her wonderful qualities:** Peter Popham, *The Lady and the Peacock*, p394

18. **At its peak, the PDC had 13 cells:** correspondence from Ye Kyaw Thu Albert Einstein Institution Archive

19. **In my view it is unlikely they would survive the trip:** Email from Bob Helvey to Gene Sharp
20. **at least three American nationals have provided political training:** Bangkok Phuchatkan
21. **Thailand now maintains a clear-cut policy:** National Security Council
22. **Three leaders of the KNU (Karen National Union) have become the main target:** Email from 'K2', Albert Einstein Institution Archive
23. **Tin Maung Win begged Bob to come back:** Author interview with Bob Helvey, 23 October 2010

OTPOR

1. **Marek Zelazkiewicz approached his agreed rendezvous point:** Author interview with Marek Zelazkiewicz, 5 August 2015
2. **If you take out the ladies, it was nearly James Bond:** Ibid, but retold from Philip Shishkin, American Revolutionary, Wall St Journal, 13 August 2008
3. **'This is Otpor', his guide told him:** Ibid
4. **Dereta ordered the printers back into action:** Ibid
5. **When there was a nonviolent action, people would say, It's by the book**: Philip Shishkin, American Revolutionary, *Wall St Journal*, 13 August 2008
6. **they were just four close friends, then seven and finally eleven:** Author interview with Srdja Popovic 14 November 2010
7. **We were in our 20s we felt like the world belonged to us:** Ibid
8. **Go home and think about what is happening to you:** Author interview with Srdja Popovic 14 November 2010
9. **The idea was to piss off the regime:** Ibid
10. **Otpor fly-posted 80,000 posters:** Ibid
11. **nervousness in the US State Department:** Ibid
12. **this was dwarfed by the amount of money which came from Serbs:** Ibid
13. **You will probably be called by Julie Mashburn:** Email to Bob Helvey from Mike Mitchell, Albert Einstein Institution Archive
14. **Well there's something missing here:** Author interview with Bob Helvey 24 October 2010
15. **Every dictatorship has weaknesses:** Ibid
16. **he is a miracle:** Author interview with Srdja Popovic 14 November 2010
17. **I knew these guys were going some place:** Author interview with Bob Helvey 24 October 2010
18. **An Otpor training manual was compiled:** Author interview with Srdja Popovic 14 November 2010
19. **We wanted to show that young people are the resistance:** Ibid

20. **beware of what you are doing because this regime will end:** Ibid
21. **they wear blue uniforms:** Ibid
22. **I was quite crazy at that point and not very polite:** Ibid
23. **Jim Lawson lunch counter trainings:** from the film, *The Butler*, (2013)
24. **Even if someone's cell phone was switched off for longer than three hours:** Author interview with Srdja Popovic 14 November 2010
25. **Yeah, I'm against Milosevic, aren't you:** Ibid
26. **young women, the grandmas and the military veterans at the front:** Ibid
27. **Now Srdja gave his battle speech:** *Bringing Down a Dictator documentary*, York Zimmerman Productions, (2002)
28. **Now you will face the greatest task of your lives:** Ibid
29. **rushed up to the main entrance singing and chanting Gotov Je! Gotov Je:** Ibid
30. **fraudulent ballot papers pre-marked for Milosevic:** Author interview with Srdja Popovic 14 November 2010
31. **Gene focuses on this situation of chaos:** Ibid
32. **an astoundingly effective blueprint for confronting a brutal regime:** Letter from Srdja Popovic to Gene Sharp, 2000. Albert Einstein Institution Archive.

COLOUR REVOLUTIONS

1. **convened a meeting codenamed 'Bletchley 2':** See Oz Hassan, *Constructing America's Freedom Agenda for the Middle East:Democracy Or Domination*
2. **Corruption in Georgia:** see, Collin. *The Time of the Rebels* p64
3. **The OSI funded a trip:** see, Collin. *The Time of the Rebels* p64
4. **youth movement in the country was almost non existent:** Ibid p67
5. **For us it was important to stress the connection:** Ibid p69
6. **announced themselves to the country with an Otpor-style graffiti campaign:** Author interview with Giorgi Kandelaki 3 July 2017
7. **atomisation of the population:** Interview with Gene Sharp 25 May 2009
8. **Possibly the most significant broadcast was Bringing Down a Dictator:** Author interview with Giorgi Kandelaki 3 July 2017
9. **From Dictatorship to Democracy was only read by the core leadership:** Ibid
10. **just over 3000 trained members:** Ibid
11. **It was inspiring:** Author interview with Oleh Kryenko, 7 December 2017
12. **I think there were ideas about taking the violent way:** Ibid
13. **thank you again for providing Otpor with invaluable assistance:** Srdja Popovic email to Gene Sharp, Albert Einstein Institution Archive

14. **freedom and democracy Serbia's greatest export:** Author interview with Srdja Popovic 15 November 2010
15. **wrote to Gene in Boston to ask for materials:** Email from Chemerys to Gene Sharp, 2001, Albert Einstein Institution Archive
16. **possession of this literature is grounds for imprisonment:** Sharp email to Chemerys 2001, Albert Einstein Institution Archive
17. **Yet again the Albert Einstein Institution cannot fulfil its mission:** Bob Helvey email to Chris Miller, Albert Einstein Institution Archive
18. **Bob offered to defer payments of his own salary:** Author interview with Bob Helvey 24 October 2010
19. **Oleh Kryenko had come up with the name 'Pora':** Interview with Oleh Kryenko 7 December 2017
20. **Some initial funding came from the Westminster Foundation for Democracy:** Interview with Oleh Kryenko 7 December 2017
21. **In order to be invincible:** Author interview with Srdja Popovic 15 November 2010
22. **where I had put up a black Pora sticker:** Author interview with Oleh Kryenko, 7 December 2017
23. **From Dictatorship to Democracy were handed out amongst nearly 300 trainees:** Ibid
24. **contributed around $130,000 to Pora:** Roberts & Garton Ash, *Civil Resistance and Power Politics: The Experience of Non-violent Action from Gandhi to the Present* (2009)
25. **When the officer in charge demanded to know how Pora worked:** Collin. *The Time of the Rebels* p128
26. **But the ideas were used by hundreds of thousands:** Author interview with Volodymyr Viatrovych, 19 April 2011

SURVIVAL

1. **I am the one that studied totalitarianism:** internal communications, Albert Einstein Institution Archive
2. **swaddled in blankets and rolled under a bed:** Author interview with Jamila Raqib 28 May 2009
3. **There was a sense in the US that you were either with us or against us:** from documentary short, *Coffee with Jamila* (2002)
4. **I thought that peace movements were naive:** Interview with Jamila Raqib 28th May 2009
5. **Hardy asked Gene if they could post the existing translations of his most popular book:** Author Interview with Hardy Merrimen, 16 October 2013

6. **'I am Morgan Tsvangirai and I want to defeat Mugabe':** Johannesburg trip notes, Albert Einstein Institution Archive
7. **'You can see Gene Sharp's fingerprints':** Author interview with Lobsang Sangay, 27 June 2019
8. **reminded Gene that he had the rights to at least some of Gene's books:** Interview with Gene Sharp 27 May 2009
9. **deep thanks for his help:** Letter from Gene Sharp to Peter and Joanne Ackerman, 14 January 2004
10. **What use were the damn rights without an institution?:** Interview with Bob Helvey 24 October 2010
11. **I didn't want this thing to limp on looking weak:** Ibid
12. **we can't even get a five or ten million dollar budget:** The Power and Potential of Nonviolent Struggle, lecture by Gene Sharp, 11 February 1990
13. **I finally concluded, after many years:** Interview with Gene Sharp 27 May 2009
14. **sat down at his desk to record his six fears:** Gene Sharp note to self, Albert Einstein Institution Archive
15. **there is no way I'm going to let this institution die:** Interview with Jamila Raqib 28 May 2009
16. **We're using the books in Eritrea:** Ibid
17. **we've moved to a new office located conveniently in East Boston:** Albert Einstein Institution Newsletter, Spring 2004
18. **'My center is a bigger compliment to Gene'** Philip Shishkin, American Revolutionary, *Wall St Journal*, 13 August 2008
19. **Gene Sharp, George Bush, the ideologies and their 'soft coup':** President Hugo Chávez, 'Aló Presidente' https://www.youtube.com/watch?v=Emv1bpH8_Is&t=2s
20. **I've never even held a gun!:** Author interview with Jamila Raqib 28 May 2009
21. **Isn't it better that even the bad guys are fighting with nonviolent struggle:** Ibid
22. **Open Letter in Support of Gene Sharp and Strategic Nonviolent Action:** edited by Stephen Zunes, http://stephenzunes.org/wp-content/uploads/2010/12/Open-Letter_Academics_Zunes.pdf
23. **Obviously this is extremely stressful:** letter from Gene Sharp to Arthur Edelstein, Albert Einstein Institution Archive
24. **Otis had been born to a rich family:** Interview with James Otis 19 September 2013
25. **I just went apeshit:** Ibid

26. **the gavel came down with Vijay Mallya at $1.8 million dollars:** *Vijay Mal- lya buys Gandhi's items for $1.8m*, The Times of India, 6 March 2009
27. **The institution received a substantial sum from the sale:** Author interview with Jamila Raqib 28 May 2009

THE IRAN PROGRAMME

1. **nuclear weapon within 10 years:** *Iran Is Judged 10 Years From Nuclear Bomb*, *Washington Post*, 2 August 2005
2. **modify its behaviour:** Author interview with David Denehy, 4 March 2013
3. **talked effusively about the potential application of Gene's theories:** Ibid
4. **That's where we went to Gene Sharp:** Ibid
5. **reportedly took that document to the Bush ranch:** State Department Offi- cial off record
6. **met a funder:** Interview with Ramin Ahmadi 23 October 2013
7. **Bob noticed a group of men who didn't look like they fitted in:** Author interview with Bob Helvey 24 October 2010
8. **After days of interrogations they were paraded in front of Iranian TV:** Interview with journalist Iason Athanasiadis 27 November 2010
9. **It's the State Department, they want to speak to you:** Interview with Ramin Ahmadi 23 October 2013
10. **I really can't tell you. It's confidential stuff:** Ibid
11. **It was sensitive and we tried to be discreet:** Author interview with David Denehy, 4 March 2013
12. **President Bush announced in the State of the Union:** Dinmore, G. *Bush calling for Iran regime change*, *The Financial Times*, 1 February 2006
13. **Secretary of State, Condoleeza Rice, followed up two weeks later with the numbers:** Rice Asks for $75 Million to Increase Pressure on Iran, *Washing- ton Post*, 16 February 2016
14. **We were sending a message to the Iranians:** Author interview with David Denehy, 4 March 2013
15. **the institution would not connect with the State Department:** Board cor- respondence with Gene Sharp, 15 March 2006, Albert Einstein Institution Archive
16. **Pahlavi commissioned his own Persian translation of From Dictatorship to Democracy:** Author interview with Reza Pahlavi, 13 January 2014
17. **ISOG committee met regularly throughout 2006:** State Department offi- cial, off record
18. **provide a social security safety net:** State Department official, off record

19. **When a bank gets robbed you watch who goes out and buys a Cadillac:** Interview with David Denehy, 4 March 2013
20. **You're hurting a lot of people not involved:** Shirin Abadi, Evidence to US Congress
21. **The US government sent back a communique that it disagreed:** Author Interview with David Denehy, 4 March 2013
22. **Gene Sharp, the theoretician of civil disobedience and velvet revolutions:** Iranian Propaganda Video featuring John McCain, George Soros & Gene Sharp, YouTube (2005)
23. **I wish those in the White House would listen to us:** Author interview with Jamila Raqib 28 May 2009
24. **Iran Syria Operations Group had been shut down:** Farah Stockman, *US unit created to pressure Iran, Syria disbanded, The Boston Globe*, 26 May 2007
25. **thrown out for a grand bargain:** Author interview with David Denehy, 4 March 2013

GREEN UPRISING

1. **won 60% of the vote:** Ahmadinejad wins surprise Iran landslide victory, *The Guardian*, 12 April 2009
2. **Jamila was dealing with the collapse of the Albert Einstein Institution website:** Author interview with Jamila Raqib, 28 May 2009
3. **A video of Gene talking through some of his 'lessons':** A Conversation with Gene Sharp https://www.youtube.com/watch?v=54oUnvDPWFA YouTube uploaded by Bikhoshoonat.net
3. **being downloaded even in small villages in the middle of nowhere:** Interview with Jamila Raqib 28 May 2009
4. **Iranian football team:** Iranian football team wears green armbands to support Mousavi at Seoul World Cup qualifier. *The Daily Telegraph*, 17 June 2009
5. 'ppl are more angry now because of killed persons'
6. For an account of Neda's death see: M. Fletcher, Doctor tells how Neda Soltan was shot dead by Ahmadinejad's basij, *The Times*, 26 June 2009
7. **Robert Fisk reported:** Robert Fisk, *Extraordinary scenes: Robert Fisk in Iran*, 17 June 2009
8. **saw the security forces beginning to respond:** Roger Cohen, *Iran on a Razor's Edge, The New York Times*, 15 June 2009
9. Mohammed Hussein Torkaman, defected: *Iran's Revolutionary Guards point to fresh dissent within oppressive regime. The Guardian*, 11 June 2010

10. **Nokia Siemens had installed monitoring software:** *Nokia, Siemens Help Iran Spy on Internet Users, Wired Magazine,* 22 June 2009
11. **The workers' unions did not join forces:** *Missed Opportunity? Was Iran's Green Movement an Unconventional Warfare Option?* US Army Command and General Staff College, (2015)
12. **shut down the mobile networks:** *Social Networks Spread Defiance Online, The New York Times,* 15 June 2009
13. **Iason knew Gene's work well:** Author interview with Iason Athanasiadis, 27 November 2010
14. **executed a total of 29 people there:** Interview with Iranian Human Rights monitoring officer, 22 May 2013
15. **it crossed Jamila's mind:** Interview with Jamila Raqib 28th May 2009
16. **This laptop contains Gene Sharp's guide:** Author interview with Iason Athanasiadis, 27 November 2010
17. **By the end of July, 42 journalists were imprisoned:** With 47 journalists in jail, Iran sets notorious records, Committee to Protect Journalists, February 3 2010
18. According to Sysmos, the number of Twitter accounts registered in Iran in May 2009 was 8654 and that rose to 19,235 by June 2009. www.iranhumanrights.org/2017/02/briefing-twitter-third-wave-in-iran/
19. **What's important isn't the technology people are using:** Author Interview with Gene Sharp 27 May 2009
20. **Gene's work featured prominently in the charges:** *Iran protesters: the Harvard professor behind their tactics, Christian Science Monitor,* 29 December 2009
23. Also see: Crist, D. *The Twilight War, The Secret History of America's Thirty-Year Conflict with Iran.* (2013)
24. **Bush staffers responsible for the Iran programme were still seething:** State Department Official off record
25. **If it's directed from outside don't trust that:** Gene Sharp Q&A, The Frontline Club, London, 30 January 2012

SHOOTS OF SPRING

1. **There will be no Orange Revolution on the Nile on Mubarak's watch:** Next Steps for Advancing Democracy in Egypt, US Diplomatic cable from Ambassador Ricciardone, 6 March 2006
2. **death by 1000 cuts:** Ibid

3. **funding very nearly every organisation:** Egypt's FY 2009 ESF: Proposed Budget for D&G Egypt's, US Diplomatic cable from Ricciardone, 12 May 2017

4. **In early 2005 a young Egyptian man arrived:** Author interview with Jamila Raqib 28 May 2009

5. **Dalia Ziada, began researching nonviolent action:** Author interview with Dalia Ziada, 24 February 2013

6. **I couldn't understand how nonviolence would actually work in practice:** Ibid

7. **travelled to Jordan for a workshop:** Ibid

8. **came across a poor translation of Gene's Politics of Nonviolent Action:** Author Interview with AOC leader, 12 February 2013

9. **workshops, strategic planning and capacity building:** Ambassador James K. Glassman and Secretary Dan Glickman, *Strategic Public Diplomacy: The Case of Egypt, National Security Project* (2011)

10. **They were looking for a template:** Author interview with Ahmed Rasheed, 3 May 2011

11. **They really inspired us:** Ibid

12. **under surveillance by the security services and he would soon be arrested:** Author interview with Ahmed Maher 3 May 2011

13. **14 others traveled from Egypt to the CANVAS office in Belgrade:** Popovic & Miller, Blueprint for Revolution, p16

14. **Free Egypt, Down with Mubarak!** Ibid

15. **could never happen in Egypt:** Ibid

16. **Personally I saw this movie dozens of times:** Author interview with Ahmed Maher, 3 May 2011

17. **can I send them message through Facebook?** Author with Ahmed Rasheed, 3 May 2011

18. **Did you know there are some guys going downtown:** Ibid

19. For an account of Khaled Said's death see: Ross & Cole, *Egypt: The Face That Launched A Revolution, ABC News,* 25 January 2011.

20. **Wael's Facebook page became increasingly popular**: See Ghonim, *Revolution 2.0,* (2012)

21. **gather signatures and reach out to people, following the ideas of Sharp:** El Deeb, Egypt's youth build new opposition movement, Associated Press, 16 September 16 (2010)

22. **Co-ordinators say they intend their new campaign:** Ibid

THE EGYPTIAN REVOLUTION

1. For an account of Bouazizi's death see: Abouzeid, *Bouazizi: The Man Who Set Himself and Tunisia on Fire, Time Magazine*, 21 January 2011
2. A General history of the buildup to the Tunisian Revolution by Jamila Raqib in *Sharp's Dictionary of Power and Struggle*, (2011)
3. **We were waiting for the event that would ignite a spark:** Author interview with Ahmed Maher 3 May 2011
4. **Dalia was living in the Shubra district of Cairo:** Author interview with Dalia Ziada, 24 February 2013
5. **Wael had compiled this information from April 6th:** See Ghonim, *Revolution 2.0*
6. **By 2011 many of the young people in Egypt knew about the work:** Author interview with Dalia Ziada, 24 February 2013
7. **Wael Ghonim had flown into Cairo:** See Ghonim, Revolution 2.0
8. **Aaron Pina, a US Foreign Service officer:** Author interview with Aaron Pina, 26 June 2013
9. **You're telling me in four days you got all this together:** Ibid
10. **You're having a fucking revolution:** Ibid
11. **The camel charge:** *Egypt speaker 'plotted battle of the camel'*, Al Jazeera, 14 July 2011
12. **Badrawy greeted Wael like an old friend:** Ghonim, *Revolution 2.0*
13. **I ask the army to intervene immediately to save Egypt:** Mubarak Refuses to Step Down, Stoking Revolt's Fury and Resolve, *New York Times*, 10 February 2011
14. **In the name of God the merciful, the compassionate:** Text of Omar Suleiman's Address, New York Times, 11 February 2011
15. **I went mad with joy:** Author Interview with Ahmed Maher, 3 May 2011
16. **In any society there is a small group:** Ibid
17. **#GeneSharpTaughtMe:** Gene Sharp Taught Us How To Revolt! https://www.newmediarights.org/node/31848
18 **I work with Gene Sharp and I need to talk to you:** Author present during exchange, 3 May 2011
19. See also Roberts, Willis, McCarthy & Garton Ash. Civil Resistance in the Arab Spring. Oxford University Press, New York, (2016)

LETTER TO A SLEEPLESS SYRIAN

1. **It's your turn, Dr. Bashar al-Assad:** *For many Syrians, the story of the war began with graffiti in Dara'a*, CNN, 15 March 2018

2. **Ausama Monajed was a 26-year-old economics graduate:** Author interview with Ausama Monajed, 22 April 2011

3. **The Iraq Syria Operations Group:** Stockman, F. *US unit works quietly to counter Iran's sway*, *The Boston Globe*, 2 January 2007

4. **The Iraq Syria Operations Group:** Rosner & Benn, *Everything but the War*, Haaretz, 24 January 2007

5. **Ausama was invited to Washington DC:** Author interview with Ausama Monajed 22 April 2011

6. **as if this had been written for us:** Ibid

7. **email arrived at Cottage Street from the Aspen Institute:** Albert Einstein Institution Archive papers, 5 April 2007

8. **Why is Aspen to introduce the strategy to US and EU officials:** Internal memo from Gene Sharp, Albert Einstein Institution Archive

9. **diligent reading of more than 700 pages of his work:** Ibid

10. **Seven potential leaders recruited by Ausama were taken out of Syria:** Author interview with Ausama Monajed, 22 April 2011

11. **most serious undertaking:** Internal memo from Gene Sharp, Albert Einstein Institution Archives

12. **Jamila was left with no doubt:** Author interview with Jamila Raqib, 28 May 2009

13. **we have an obligation to help others realise the blessings of liberty:** Author interview with Ausama Monajed 22 April 2011

14. **Both MEPI and DRL fund projects:** Behaviour reform: Next steps for a human rights strategy, US diplomatic cable from Maura Connelly, 28 April 2009

15. **failed to pass on their knowledge:** Author interview with Ausama Monajed, 22 April 2011

16. **Unfortunately the Syrians just dove right in:** Popovic & Miller, *Blueprint for Revolution*, (2015)

17. **quickly recruited as an associate editor and then strategy advisor:** Author interview with Mohammed Alaa Ghanem, 7 December 2019

18. **Brimming with ideas inspired by Gene Sharp:** Diary entry supplied by Mohammed Alaa Ghanem to the author, 7 December 2019

19. **We introduced the concept of representation:** Author interview with Mohammed Alaa Ghanem, 7 December 2019

20. **establishment of Local Coordination Committees:** See the excellent book *Burning Country: Syrians in Revolution and War*, by Leila Al-Shami, Robin Yassin-Kassab, which offers a brilliant overview of the LCCs and nonviolent movement in Syria.

21. **It was the first revolutionary body:** Alakhbar news

22. **settled on a rough looking Mediterranean holiday resort**: Popovic & Miller, Blueprint for Revolution, (2015)
23. **smuggler had to be employed to get the trainees out:** Ibid
24. **There should have been 20 participants:** Ibid
25. **You don't want to meet him on the soccer field:** Ibid
26. **Otpor playbook were being carried out on the streets.** Author interview with Ausama Monajed, 22 April 2011
27. **paying to smuggle hundreds of digital cameras**: Author interview with Ibrahim Al-Assil, 24 May 2018
28. For an account of the attack on Hama: 1982: Syria's President Hafez al-Assad crushes rebellion in Hama, *The Guardian*, from the archives, 1 August 2011
29. **Arrested LCC members were tortured:** Author interview with Ibrahim Al-Assil, 24 May 2018
30. **deliberately trying to turn the uprising into an armed insurrection:** Author interview with Ausama Monajed, 22 April 2011
31. **For an account of Homs:** Leila Al-Shami, Robin Yassin-Kassab, *Burning Country: Syrians in Revolution and War* (2016)
32. **LCCs managed to obtain satellite phones and software:** Author interview with Ausama Monajed, 22 April 2011
33. **Don't ask for outside help! Gene replied**: Witnessed by the author
34. **People began chanting for the fighters to defend the protests:** Author interview with Mohammed Alaa Ghanem, 7 December 2019
35. **signed off his email as, 'The Sleepless Syrian'** Ibid
36. **The present unease of the troops in obeying orders is clear:** Letter to a Sleepless Syria, from Gene Sharp 2 June 2011. Albert Einstein Institution Archive
37. **If you want to join us, leave your weapon and join us:** Author interview with Mohammed Alaa Ghanem, 7 December 2019
38. **While we understand the motivation to take up arms:** Syrian Nonviolent Movement, statement issued to the Facebook page 29 August 2011

RUSSIA'S COUNTER-REVOLUTION

1. **Oleg Kozlovsky, translated Gene's work:** 'Kozlovsky Conversation' Albert Einstein Institution Archive
2. **Kasparov also recognised the importance of Gene's work on strategy:** Author interview with Garry Kasparov, 20 October 2014
3. **This book is a bomb:** Interview with Gene Sharp 25 May 2009 – the original source was an Oborona activist who cannot be identified at the time of writing.

4. **two shops which had been selling the most copies burned down:** Interview with Gene Sharp 25 May 2009

5. **Surkov became an avid reader of Gene Sharp's books:** Mark Bennetts, *Nemtsov's Friends Fear Kremlin's Brutal Crackdown*, Newsweek, 3 November 2015

6. **'YOU. Do you want to realize your own project?** Taken from the Nashi website, wayback machine (accessed 15 May 2009)

7. **The support of the Kremlin makes it possible:** Opposition will face a united pro-Kremlin youth front, www.gzt.ru, 2 October 2005

8. **Maidan in Seliger:** Horvath, R. *Putin's Preventive Counter-Revolution: Post-Soviet Authoritarianism and the Spectre of Velvet Revolution* (2013) p197

9. **only nonviolent means could be used:** Ibid

10. **one interview with an OMON officer:** Mikhail Mikhin, https://echo.msk. ru/blog/onepamop/856565-echo/

11. **flying penis:** Grandmaster Flashed: Kasparov Attacked by Flying Penis-Copter. Wired Magazine, 20 May 2008

12. **revolution is above all the squandering of the people:** Horvath, R. *Putin's Preventive Counter-Revolution: Post-Soviet Authoritarianism and the Spectre of Velvet Revolution* (2013) p187

13. **Part 1 of the [United States] Hybrid War field manual:** Korybko, A, Hybrid Wars: The Indirect Approach to Regime Change, p68, Moscow Peoples' Friendship University of Russia, (2013)

14. **Between 25,000 and 50,000 people gathered in Bolotnya Square:** Horvath, R. *Putin's Preventive Counter-Revolution: Post-Soviet Authoritarianism* and the *Spectre of Velvet Revolution* (2013) p187

15. **Putin believes that the West is constantly seeking to bring about his overthrow:** Mark Bennetts, Nemtsov's Friends Fear Kremlin's Brutal Crackdown, Newsweek, 3 November 2015

16. **They are acting literally according to Sharp's books:** Some Russian protesters want revolution: Kremlin aide, Reuters, 23 December 2011

17. **deserve to have their voices heard and their votes counted:** Clinton cites 'serious concerns' about Russian election, CNN, 6 December 2011

18. **She set the tone for some of the activists:** Weaver, C. *Putin Blames Moscow protests on US, Financial Times*, December 8 2011

19. **dropped from 165 to 89 in that year alone:** Putin says foreign agents' number among NGOs significantly drops, Tass News agency, 30 October 2017

20. See also Van Herpen, *Putin's Wars, The Rise of Russia's New Imperialism*, (2015)

21. ***Assessing Russian Activities and Intentions in Recent US Elections***, *Office of the Director of National Intelligence,* 6 January 2017
22. ***The troll factory:*** Neil MacFarquhar, *Inside the Russian Troll Factory: Zombies and a Breakneck Pace, The New York Times,* 18 February 2018
23. Troll factory poses as news sites: Wang, S. *How the Kremlin Tried to Pose as American News Sites on Twitter,* Bloomberg, 5 December 2017
24. **most successful covert influence campaign in the history of covert influence:** Michael Hayden, Oxford Union, Full Q&A https://www.youtube.com/watch?v=exw9HpK_ytI

THE ORCHID KEEPER

1. **This is my favourite:** Author interview with Gene Sharp 28 May 2009
2. **a political thinker now spoken of in the same breath as Mahatma Gandhi:** Tim Franks presenting BBC Hardtalk, 1 February 2012
3. **nonviolent actions against Assad and even ISIS:** Taleb, J. From Assad to ISIS, a tale of Syrian resistance, Waging Nonviolence, 22 August 2014
4. **In Angola, a Gene Sharp book group:** Angola court orders conditional release of jailed activist, *The Guardian,* 29 June 2016
5. **When Mexicans and Venezuelans feared their election had been stolen:** Review of The Dictator's Learning Curve: Inside the Global Battle for Democracy in the Financial Times, 25 June 2012
6. **Gene the 6-4 favourite for Nobel Peace Prize:** Keating, J. *Handicapping the Nobel Peace Prize,* Foreign Policy, 10 October 2012

Bibliography

ARCHIVES

Bradford Peace Archive, Bradford, United Kingdom
Gene Sharp Archive, Swarthmore College, Swarthmore, Pennsylvania, USA
Gene Sharp personal papers archive, East Boston, MA, USA
Liddel Hart Archive, Kings College London, United Kingdom
National Archives, Kew, United Kingdom
Norway Resistance Museum, Oslo, Norway
Widener Library, Harvard University, Cambridge, MA, USA

PUBLISHED SOURCES

Ackerman and Duvall. *A Force more Powerful*, Palgrave Press, New York, 2000
Bakhtavar, S. Iran, *The Green Movement, Parsa Irving TX*, 2009
Barker, E. Ed. *Social Contract. Locke, Hume, Rousseau.* Oxford University Press, 1960
Chenoweth & Stephan. *Why Civil Resistance Works. The Strategic Logic of Nonviolent Conflict.* Columbia University Press, New York, 2011
Clark, H. Ed. *People Power, Unarmed Resistance and Global Solidarity.* Pluto Press, London, 2009
Collin, M. *The Time of the Rebels.* Serpents Tail, London, 2007
Crist, D. *The Twilight War, The Secret History of America's Thirty-Year Conflict with Iran.* Penguin Books, New York, 2013
Danchev, A. Alchemist of War, *The Life of Basil Liddell Hart.* Weidenfeld & Nicolson, London 1998
De La Boétie, E. *Discourse of Voluntary Servitude*, Black Rose Books, 2007
Dobson, W. J. *The Dictator's Learning Curve.* Vintage Books, London, 2013
Engler & Engler. *This is an Uprising.* Nation Books, New York, 2016
Ebadi, S. *Until We Are Free. My Fight for Human Rights in Iran.* Rider Books, London, 2016
Fischer, L. *The Life of Mahatma Gandhi*, Vintage Books, London, 1950
Finlay, C. *Terrorism and the Right to Resist. A theory of Just Revolutionary War. Cambridge University Press*, 2017
Freedman, L. *Strategy, A History.* Oxford University Press, 2015

Bibliography

Ghonim, W. *Revolution 2.0.* HarperCollins, London, 2012

Glantz, D. *Soviet Military Operational Art, In Pursuit of Deep Battle.* Frank Cass, New York 2005

Greene, S. *Moscow in Movement. Power and Opposition in Putin's Russia.* Stanford University Press, Stanford, 2014

Grossman, D. *On Killing.* Back Bay Books, New York, 2009

Guevara, G. *Guerilla Warfare.* Souvenir Press, London, 2003

Harding, L. *Collusion, How Russia Helped Trump Win the White House.* Guardian Faber, London, 2017

Hassan, O. *Constructing America's Freedom Agenda for the Middle East.* Routledge, London, 2014

Helvey, R. *On Strategic Nonviolent Conflict: Thinking About the Fundamentals.* Albert Einstein Institution, Cambridge MA, 2007

Hodgson, G. *Martin Luther King.* Quercus, London 2010

Horvath, R. *Putin's Preventative Counter-Revolution.* Routledge, New York, 2013

Isaacson, W. *Einstein, His Life and Universe.* Simon & Schuster, London, 2007

King, M. L. K. Jr. *The Autobiography of Martin Luther King Jr.* Warner Books, New York, 2000

King, M. E. *The Quiet Revolution, The First Palestinian Intifada and Nonviolent Resistance.* Nation Books, New York, 2007

Krushelnycky, A. *An Orange Revolution.* Harvill Secker, London, 2006

Lampe, D. *Hitler's Savage Canary. A History of the Danish Resistance in World War Two.* Frontline Books, London, 2010

Lijphart, A. *Patterns of Democracy. Government Forms and Performance in Thirty-Six Countries*, 2nd Ed. Yale University Press, New York, 1999

McFaul, M. *From Cold War to Hot Peace.* Penguin Books London, 2018

Nathan & Norden. *Einstein on Peace.* Avenel Books, New York, 1981

Nye, J. *Soft Power.* Perseus Books, Cambridge MA, 2004

Pacepa and Rychlak. *Disinformation.* WND Books, Washington DC, 2013

Popham, P. *The Lady and the Peacock. The Life of Aung San Suu Kyi.* Rider Books, London, 2012

Popham, P. *The Lady and the Generals. Aung San Suu Kyi and Burma's Struggle for Freedom.* Rider Books, London, 2016

Popovic et al. *A Guide to Effective Nonviolent Struggle*: Canvas, Belgrade, 2007

Popovic & Miller. *Blueprint for Revolution.* Scribe Publications, London, 2015

Randle & Pottle. *The Blake Escape.* Harrap Books, London, 1989

Riste and Nökleby. Norway 1940–45 The Resistance Movement, Tanum-Norli, Oslo, 1978

Roberts, Willis, McCarthy & Garton Ash. *Civil Resistance in the Arab Spring.* Oxford University Press, New York, 2016

Russell, B. *An Autobiography of Bertrand Russell.* Allen and Unwin, London, 1969

Sanger, D. *Confront and Conceal, Obama's Secret Wars and Surprising Use of American Power.* Random House, New York, 2012

Schock, K. *Unarmed Insurrections. People Power Movements in Nondemocracies.* University of Minnesota Press, London, 2005

Sharp, G. *The Politics of Nonviolent Action.* Porter Sargent Books, Boston, 1973

Sharp, G. *Gandhi Wields the Weapon of Moral Power.* Navajivan Trust, Ahmedabad, 1960

Sharp, G. *Sharp's Dictionary of Power and Struggle.* Oxford University Press, 2012

Sharp, G. *There are Realistic Alternatives.* Albert Einstein Institution, Boston, 2003

Sharp, G. *From Dictatorship to Democracy.* Albert Einstein Institution, Cambridge MA, 1994

Sharp, G & Raqib J. *Self-Liberation.* Albert Einstein Institution, Cambridge MA, 2010

Van Herpen, M. *Putin's Wars.* Rowman & Littlefield, London, 2015

Yassin-Kassab and Al-Shami. *Burning Country, Syrians in Revolution and War.* Pluto Press London, 2016

Yavlinsky, G. *The Putin System, An Opposing View.* Columbia University Press, New York, 2015

Zunes, Kurtz & Asher Ed. *Nonviolent Social Movements, A Geographical Perspective.* Blackwell, London 2007

Acknowledgements

This book was only made possible with the assistance of Gene Sharp, Jamila Raqib and the participants of many of the revolutions described in these pages. Jamila first arranged a few days filming with Gene in May 2009, but I doubt she expected how much of her time I would use up in the course of the next decade. This book is just a placeholder for hers, which I hope we will not have to wait too long for.

I am enormously grateful to Susan Hackley, Director of the Program on Negotiation at Harvard Law School who gave me an academic home to complete the initial research for this book. Susan was a huge supporter of Gene's work and I'm not sure I would have been able to start the project if it hadn't been for her kindness.

Rick Shaw drove through the production of the *How to Start a Revolution* documentary with energy, fun and endless generosity and in doing so he made telling this story possible. My team on the How to Start a Revolution documentary are just as big a part of this book. I could not have chosen a better companion to sit with me in a tiny edit suite trying to tell the story than editor, Mike Crozier, who made real my slightly erratic vision. Cailean Watt, Ke Cai, Tracie Dudley Craig and the team at Lion Television with Harriet Armston-Clarke, Jessica Bennetts, Leila Monks and the terrific crew at TVF International – thank you all, it was a pleasure to share the journey with you. To James Lambert Otis, our Executive Producer, who left $20,000 in a freezer for us to pick up in San Francisco, thank you for the stories, I will never forget them. Thanks too to everyone who gave so generously for the Kickstarter project which got us across the line. It would not have been possible without you.

I am incredibly lucky to have a family that supported me through an adventure which has had such incredible highs and a few inevitable lows. My mother in particular has been my rock and chief cheerleader throughout. To Kate, Martin, Pete and Dave, thank you for the encouragement, the fun, and the restorative weekends away from London. It could not have been done without your faith, understanding and humour when the challenges seemed a bit too daunting. My grandmother, Mary, read the first three chapters, but sadly didn't get to see it complete. I know she would have had something funny to say about how long it's taken.

This project came out of an initial discussion with Rukhsana Yasmin at Profile Books who took a punt on publishing *From Dictatorship to Democracy* in the UK for the first time. She has continued to offer invaluable help and advice ever since. Julia Mills, Pat McGauley, Jessica Drawe, Stef Macbeth and Richard Simmonds read, copy-read, proofed and offered vital guidance on the manuscript. Rose Taylor probably read more drafts than anyone should ever have to, and all while completing her own book and PhD in a fraction of the time it's taken me to complete this project. I could not be more grateful. Any mistakes and omissions that remain are, of course, my own responsibility.

Finally, thank you to all of those brave individuals all over the world past and present who have stood up to oppression and sacrificed their lives and liberty to make this world a better place.

About the Author

Ruaridh Arrow is a journalist and film-maker based in London and the Highlands of Scotland. After training at Sky News, he produced documentaries for Channel 4's Dispatches programme and National Geographic before becoming a Senior Producer on BBC Newsnight and Executive Producer at NBC News. His documentary, *How to Start a Revolution*, about the work of Gene Sharp, won multiple inter-national awards including Best Documentary at Raindance and a BAFTA for New Talent. In 2012–2013 he was a Research Affiliate at the Program on Negotiation at Harvard Law School.

@Arrowonthehill / howtostartarevolution.org

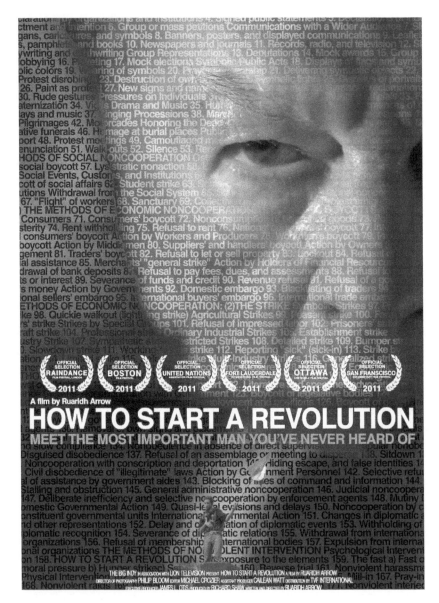

Watch the award-winning documentary *How to Start a Revolution* on video on demand at www.howtostartarevolution.org 25% off with code GeneSharpBook

Index

AEI refers to Albert Einstein Institution; GS to Gene Sharp; IRI to International Republican Institute

Lightning Source UK Ltd.
Milton Keynes UK
UKHW012139290321
381201UK00001B/32